TRANSFORMING PLACES

Transforming Places
Lessons from Appalachia

EDITED BY
STEPHEN L. FISHER
AND BARBARA ELLEN SMITH

UNIVERSITY OF ILLINOIS PRESS
URBANA, CHICAGO, AND SPRINGFIELD

© 2012 by the Board of Trustees
of the University of Illinois
All rights reserved
Manufactured in the United States of America
C 5 4 3 2 1
∞ This book is printed on acid-free paper.

Library of Congress Cataloging-in-Publication Data
Transforming places : lessons from Appalachia /
edited by Stephen L. Fisher and Barbara Ellen Smith.
p.   cm.
Includes bibliographical references and index.
ISBN 978-0-252-03666-8 (hbk. : alk. paper) —
ISBN 978-0-252-07838-5 (pbk. : alk. paper) —
ISBN 978-0-252-09376-0 (e-book)
1. Community organization—Appalachian Region.
2. Social action—Appalachian Region.
3. Political participation—Appalachian Region.
4. Appalachian Region—Social conditions.
I. Fisher, Stephen L., 1944– II. Smith, Barbara Ellen, 1951–
HN79.A127T73   2012
330.974—dc23   2011027791

CONTENTS

PREFACE

It has been some twenty long years since the publication of Stephen L. Fisher's *Fighting Back in Appalachia: Traditions of Resistance and Change* (Temple, 1993). The book documented an outburst of grassroots organizing across Appalachia that led to significant victories on a number of fronts. The ensuing decades, however, brought the collapse of key Appalachian organizations and the growth of new groups and strategies. "Globalization," barely in our vocabulary in that earlier political moment, now names the age and preoccupies those activists who seek leverage, relationships, and representation across the boundaries of nation-states. On the domestic front, a neoliberal fetish for markets and individualism predominates, with literally sickening consequences in a region where poverty is endemic and organized labor has historically been the most important bulwark against ruthless exploitation. Today, the exuberant solidarity of the Pittston coal strike (1989–1990), which drew people from all over the world to rural southwest Virginia, has given way to bitter divisions between coalfield residents who vocally oppose the mining practice of mountaintop removal and those who view such activists as threats to their jobs and way of life. *Transforming Places: Lessons from Appalachia* seeks to capture this complicated and difficult political context and the social justice organizing that intends to change it.

This book also originates from a more personal context: the ongoing conversation between us, extending across many years, about movement-building in Appalachia. As scholar-activists with long histories of teaching, writing, and acting politically for social justice in Appalachia and the South, we both recognized the importance of place as a source of personal identity and motivating force in local and regional resistance struggles. But we each brought our own questions, commitments, and ambivalence to our discussions. Steve, who initially rejected his lower-working–class West Virginia roots and later taught so many first-generation Appalachian students during his thirty-five years at a small liberal arts college in southwest Virginia, had personally experienced and witnessed the transformative power of claiming Appalachia and a sense of place. His political work in the region made him wary of the limits of place-based organizing but also reinforced his convictions about the importance of it. Barbara Ellen, the offspring of out-migrants from Appalachian Virginia and West Virginia, came to identify with the region and her family's mountain homeplace at a young age, but also deplored the popular, exclusionary definition of Appalachian identity as "insiders" (vs. outsiders). The stories of certain aunts and female cousins, combined with political work involving working-class women of various races in Appalachia and the deeper South, taught her that some people's romanticized views of "home" and "place" can conceal others' experiences of misery and violence. Barbara Ellen was often skeptical about Steve's arguments for the value of Appalachian identity, but in the end, from different experiences, we both agreed on the personal and political significance of place. This exchange illustrates the fully collaborative nature of our work together on this project; the only exception is the conclusion, on which Barbara Ellen took the lead.

The unifying theme of place also grew organically out of the diverse political strategies, experiences, and lessons documented by the authors of each chapter. To be sure, they offer no single definition of or strategy for place-based organizing; rather, it is their wide spectrum of political approaches to place that we believe makes this book valuable. We selected these chapters (from an overwhelming collection of more than fifty excellent proposals) with an intentional commitment to capture as much as possible of the array of social justice organizing taking place on the ground in Appalachia; nonetheless, we were regrettably unable to cover many important organizations, issues, constituencies, and strategies.

A detailed bibliography of dissent in Appalachia prior to 1990 appears in *Fighting Back in Appalachia*. We take heart from the impressive number of new books, articles, and dissertations written about resistance efforts in the region over the past two decades, and regret not being able to offer a bibliography of these works here because of space considerations. Fortunately, Jo. B. Brown has compiled a comprehensive "Annual Bibliography" for the *Journal of Appalachian Studies* since 1995. In addition, he has posted an online file at the West Virginia University Libraries' Web site (http://www.libraries.wvu.edu/appalachian/bibliography.htm) that cumulates the "Annual Bibliography" sections for the years 1994–2010. We recommend these resources to those wanting additional information about the Appalachian region.

The Appalachian Community Fund, an activist-controlled foundation committed to supporting progressive social change in central Appalachia, will receive the royalties from sales of *Transforming Places*.

This book owes its existence and is dedicated to the countless individuals who are transforming the many places of Appalachia and thereby inventing new possibilities, social relationships, and reasons for hope.

ACKNOWLEDGMENTS

Many people helped make this book a reality. First and foremost, we want to thank the contributors for their cooperation, patience, belief in the importance of the project, and quality of their work. A number of authors played a key role in helping us identify and acquire photos for the chapters. Some offered helpful comments on the introduction and conclusion, and we are especially indebted to Fran Ansley for her insightful critique.

The book's cover is a patch from the mural "The True Cost of Coal," created by the Beehive Design Collective, whose work is discussed briefly in chapter 15. We are inspired by the Bees' work and are honored and delighted to share a small piece of it on the cover. More than two years in the making, the mural is an elaborate narrative illustration that explores the complex story of mountaintop removal coal mining and the broader impacts of coal in Appalachia and beyond. The image is the culmination of an intensive and collaborative research process, which involved interviewing hundreds of community members throughout the Appalachia region. We encourage readers to learn more about the Bees at www.beehivecollective.org.

Pat Beaver read and commented on both the initial prospectus and the entire manuscript, offering much-appreciated encouragement and guidance. Larry Richman provided invaluable editing advice at every stage of the process, including reading the entire manuscript in page proofs. Richard Couto offered an important critique of the full draft, and Jamie Winders sent helpful comments on the introduction and conclusion. The interdisciplinary "Spaces of Identity" research group at Virginia Tech (Gena Chandler, Laura Gillman, Minjeong Kim, Katy Powell, and Emily Satterwhite) reviewed the conclusion and their suggestions significantly improved its quality. Brittaney Brown, Melissa Burgess, Maria Elisa Christie, Diane Gilliam, and Ashley Tomisek provided assistance during various stages of the process, and Kathy Shearer helped with technical issues related to several of the photographs. Tena Willemsma was the driving force behind identifying and securing permission for use of the photograph in chapter 10. Laurie Matheson of the University of Illinois Press understood and believed in this project from the beginning, and Tad Ringo offered support and direction throughout the editing process. We would be remiss if we did not mention our debt to the bourbon distillers of Kentucky. Finally, we most gratefully acknowledge the love, support, and good company of family and friends, especially Nancy Garretson for her companionship, generosity, and unyielding support of our work.

INVOCATION/INVOCACIÓN

by/por Marta Maria Miranda

On this night, at this moment, with this breath
En esta noche, este momento, con este respiro
We evoke the communal spirit of justice
Evocamos el espíritu comunal de justicia
We break bread with our neighbors, we extend our hand to
    our enemies, and we pray for global justice
Partimos pan con nuestros vecinos, extendemos la mano a
    nuestros enemigos y oramos por la justicia universal
We feed our souls with the courage of those who have dared
    to break the silence of oppression
Alimentamos nuestras almas con la valentía de aquellos que se
    atrevieron a romper el silencio de la opresión
We honor the holy places of protests, the streets, the marches,
    the public halls, the seat on the segregated bus, the brown
    hand who refused to pick the grape, the power to love in
    spite of hatred and shame, and we are strengthened by the
    conviction of those who dared to spit in the master's soup.
Honramos los lugares sagrados de protesta, las calles y los
    desfiles, los espacios políticos, el asiento en el autobús
    segregado, la mano morena que se negó a recoger la uva,
    el poder de amar a pesar del odio y la vergüenza, y nos
    fortalece la convicción de aquellos que escupieron en la sopa
    del patrón.

Placing Appalachia

Stephen L. Fisher and Barbara Ellen Smith

We live in a world of many Appalachias. These are places of extravagant natural wealth and enduring poverty, places where the raw consequences of unsustainable economic practices predicated on human and environmental exploitation are unusually stark. These places include the oilfields of the Niger Delta, the Himalayan forests of India, the coalfields of Colombia. Far from the great urban centers of global power, these are nonetheless sites of critical economic activity because they contain the arable land, abundant water, fossil fuel deposits, and other resources on which the global economy depends. These places also represent some of the weakest links in the far-flung supply chains of global capitalism because they are often home to indigenous movements contesting the apparent imperatives of gross economic inequality, environmental degradation, and the antidemocratic power of elites.

In diverse struggles across the world, "place" and its many meanings push back against the valorization of placelessness and "virtuality" associated with globalization. Place in these varied contexts is at once a symbolic landscape of cultural tradition and human connection (the place of home) and the tangible ground that is a source of livelihood and focus of contestation (forests, watersheds, farms). Defined by capital and its boosters in terms of exploitable resources—"coalfields," "timberlands," "water reserves," "scenic views"—these places are also given meaning by the human relationships, histories, and desires arising there, different from the commercial ones though by no means uniform. Who will control the future of such places, and to what ends?

Struggles over coal-containing mountains, scenic farmlands, and suburban backyards, as well as more desolate sites abandoned by capital but not by human residents, have become the hallmark of twenty-first-century activism in the Appalachian region of the eastern United States. *Transforming Places* consists of seventeen original essays, plus a conclusion by the editors, that chronicle and analyze these diverse struggles. Appalachia—like other resource-rich yet marginalized regions across the globe—is often construed as a place of cultural backwardness and economic isolation. The region's intractable poverty, joblessness, low wages, and other economic woes are often attributed to its failure to attract the "modernizing" influences of global capital. By contrast, we argue that such features of Appalachia's political economy attest to the stark *impacts* of globalization in both its contemporary manifestations and historical legacies. They also render the region an unusually instructive political battleground for all engaged in movements for social justice. In frequently localized battles, issues of global scale and implication—from corporate privatization of public goods to climate change and the future of fossil fuels, from militarization and the expansion of the U.S. empire to the production of local foods and sustainable economies—are being contested. This book assembles lessons from Appalachia in the hope that they may be of use to others engaged in similar place-based struggles within this region, the nation, and across the globe.

The Appalachian Context

Struggles over definitions of Appalachia—its geographic boundaries, cultural legacies, historiography, relationship to the rest of the United States, and the (frequently insulting) depictions of its residents—are rife throughout literature on the region, making it impossible to provide a finite, accurate summary of regional characteristics. Framed within the cultural politics of American nationhood, Appalachia is an internal "Other," a repository of either backwardness and ignorance or, alternatively, the homespun relics of the frontier; in both cases, it is a place behind the times, against which national progress, enlightenment, and modernization might be measured.[1] Despite such a role in the American imaginary, the region contains great internal diversity and contrast. Whether limited to the central coalfields of West Virginia, eastern Kentucky, and southwest Virginia, or expanded southward to the mountains of north Georgia, western North Carolina, and east Tennessee, Appalachia encompasses significant racial/ethnic, sexual, and class diversity. Appalachian people live in small and relatively remote towns like Clinchco, Virginia, and in urban centers like Knoxville, Tennessee, and Charleston, West Virginia. Some enjoy opulent wealth, while a far larger number live on even less than the modest means available to many U.S. households in the early decades of the twenty-first century.[2]

Of greatest relevance to this book is the region's long tradition of individual and collective resistance to severe political, economic, and cultural oppression.[3] The heroic narrative of militant coal miners, striking for union recognition, black lung benefits, and adequate medical care, is most familiar, but hundreds of grassroots community groups are organizing across Appalachia around a variety of issues.[4] The majority of these groups arise in response to a single issue and on occasion win important victories, but their singular focus typically means that they are short-lived, disappearing once the issue is resolved. In contrast are thriving and influential multi-issue, membership-driven organizations such as SOCM (for many years, Save Our Cumberland Mountains, now Statewide Organizing for Community eMpowerment) in Tennessee, Kentuckians For The Commonwealth (KFTC), and Virginia Organizing (formerly the Virginia Organizing Project), which are building for the long haul within state-based boundaries that often spill beyond Appalachia.[5] In addition, a number of explicitly regional institutions—such as the community-based cultural, educational, and media arts organization Appalshop, the Appalachian Community Fund (which offers financial support to grassroots groups), and the Appalachian Women's Alliance (see chapter 7)—have offered vital forums for the elaboration of regional identities and modes of resistance.[6]

Some of this activism and lessons learned from it were examined in the early 1990s in Stephen L. Fisher's collection, *Fighting Back in Appalachia: Traditions of Resistance and Change.* This book appeared after almost three decades of particularly vibrant organizing across the region. From the mid-1960s until the early 1990s, union democracy, black lung compensation, welfare rights, the preservation of family farms, and many other issues spawned new organizations and became the focus of distinct, sometimes overlapping, social movements. Although never successfully framed within an overarching "Appalachian movement" per se, these and other constituencies came together as loose regional networks for occasional campaigns. Two examples stand out. Between 1978 and 1980, the Appalachian Land Ownership Task Force, a participatory research effort involving community groups, scholars, and organizers, documented landownership and taxation patterns and their consequences for the quality of life in eighty counties in six Appalachian states. The task force produced a seven-volume, 1,500-page study that was used throughout the region to launch challenges to outside corporate ownership of mineral resources and inequitable tax structures that externalized the costs of corporate practices onto citizens. KFTC, originally named the Kentucky Fair Tax Coalition, was one of the organizing efforts that originated in part from this massive participatory research project.[7]

A decade later during the 1989–1990 strike by the United Mine Workers of America (UMWA) against the Pittston Coal Company, the union, understanding that it could not win the fight alone, defined the issues at stake in collective, ethical terms—for example, retirees' rights to previously promised health-care benefits—and called on supporters across the coalfields and beyond to rally behind the strikers and their families. Individuals and groups from across Appalachia and, ultimately, the world provided tactical and financial support, participated in weekly rallies and mass civil disobedience, and played crucial roles in enabling the union to win a settlement more favorable than anyone believed possible when the strike began.[8] Although the Pittston strike remains an illuminating example of the victories that become possible when labor unions enter meaningful partnerships with community-based groups and other allies, it occurred at a time of drastic decline in the size and bargaining leverage of the UMWA and the U.S. labor movement more generally. Since well before the victory against Pittston, nonunion coal mines began spreading across the former stronghold of militant unionism in the central Appalachian coalfields, and the size of the coal mine labor force (union and nonunion) shrank below 100,000, to levels not seen since the nineteenth century and the inception of coal mining in the United States.[9]

Today, the political climate and infrastructure for organizing in Appalachia contrast dramatically with twenty years ago. Although the labor militancy for which Appalachia is known has not disappeared entirely, the locus of workplace organizing has shifted to new constituencies and industries, particularly Latino immigrants in low-wage work such as poultry processing. Meanwhile, the UMWA and its dwindling rank and file have united with their former adversaries, the coal operators, to challenge with bitter rhetoric and mass demonstrations the environmental activists who seek an end to mountaintop removal and other destructive mining practices. Astonishingly, at least to those who witnessed then-UMWA vice president Cecil Roberts's declarations of "class war" during the Pittston strike, the coal industry has successfully positioned itself alongside its workers and the union as an embattled "insider" forced to fight for economic survival against extremist "tree-huggers" and other presumed "foreigners" to the region.[10]

Moreover, even as processes of globalization have generated, been shaped by, and seem to require new transnational understandings and alliances (such as cross-border linkages between labor unions), organizing effectively at the regional level, much less at larger scales, has in many ways become more difficult. Indeed, since 2006, two of the more valuable regional institutions, the Southern Empowerment Project (see chapter 8) and the Commission on Religion in Appalachia (see chapter 10), have shut their doors, and some efforts to link Appalachian organizing to similar national or global struggles have faltered.[11] As a result, many have observed that poor and working-class Appalachians remain more isolated from similar populations elsewhere than from the corporate and political forces that oppress them daily.

Such constraints on the reach and capacity of progressive organizations are neither unique to Appalachia nor produced primarily by forces internal to the region. Corporate-driven globalization, characterized in part by the relocation and insulation of economic decision making to multinational corporations and supranational organizations like the International Monetary Fund, has diluted the capacity of community organizations and labor unions to influence economic policies and corporate behavior. Although international NGOs (nongovernmental organizations) and transnational, anticorporate, civil society linkages are growing, multinational corporations and their allied supranational entities enjoy capacity, authority, and representation at a global scale that the ensemble of oppositional organizing termed "globalization from below" has not yet begun to approach.[12] Moreover, the dominance of neoliberalism in the

United States and many other nation-states, which promotes market forces as the optimal determinant of social relations and individualism as the supreme ethos of human beings, has legitimated a frenzied attack on "big government" and the unraveling of social welfare supports for vulnerable populations. As some critics point out, this "roll back" of the welfare state has been accompanied by the "roll out" of repressive aspects of state power: intensified militarization, dilution of civil liberties, increased "homeland security" measures, and the social containment and disproportionate incarceration of certain populations, especially those of color (for example, poor and working-class African Americans, undocumented immigrants).[13]

Although the financial crisis of 2008 stimulated some skepticism about and critiques of neoliberalism, it remains the prevailing philosophy of governance in the United States and much of the world. The combination of corporate-driven globalization and state-sponsored neoliberalism has worked to unravel organizational solidarities, visionary alternatives to injustice, and progressive social policies. In this climate of fear and insecurity, when commitment to collective well-being is derided as evidence of "creeping socialism" and/or potential dependence, it is no wonder that the capacity and reach of progressive organizations are compromised. The widely lamented decline of "associational life" and "civil society"—though often delinked from critical political analysis and blamed on "social capital deficits" in ways that exemplify more than explain the problem—is related to the ascendance of neoliberalism.[14] When rural schools are consolidated to plug holes in county budgets and local unions shut down because of job losses, a decline in "associational life" is to be expected.

Although the tangible impacts of deregulation, the shrunken welfare state, and other neoliberal initiatives are easily documented—crumbling infrastructure such as bridges and highways, environmental degradation, financial crises, declining public schools and libraries—other implications are more subtle. What counts as a "social problem" and what remedies exist to treat it have shifted in ways that render collective political action more elusive. Within Appalachia, the examples of public health and entitlement to medical care illuminate this change vividly. The conviction that hard physical labor, particularly in the mines, both produces disease and collectively entitles workers at the very least to adequate health care has inspired numerous activist campaigns, including in part the Pittston strike and the black lung movement. In the present moment, however, when the organizational strength of trade unions (especially the UMWA) and the employment base of mining and manufacturing are on the wane, community after community in central Appalachia faces additional, more isolating, diseases related to despair and hopelessness, such as OxyContin and other substance abuse (see chapters 6 and 13). Such health problems are no less socially produced and in that sense political—though far more difficult to organize around—than black lung. The contrast between a collective sensibility of disease as the product of class exploitation and emblem of entitlement to redress, as was the case with black lung, and the highly individualistic, victim-blaming discourse associated with drug addiction, vividly exemplifies the self-fulfilling logic of neoliberalism: What is individually borne is no more or less than the fault of the individual and therefore should not be collectively redressed.

To be sure, the declining viability of many communities in Appalachia has also been a spur to action. The defense and reinvention of "place" are central to many of the organizing initiatives documented in this volume. However, organizing in defense of place can also be exclusionary, and the political content of such efforts, as we analyze further in the conclusion, can be ambiguous if not downright reactionary. Appalachia, particularly the predominantly white and rural areas of the region, has been a receptive ground for the culture wars. Right-wing politicians have successfully channeled class resentments and anxieties (which are often intensified by their policies, for example, opposition to an increase in the federal minimum wage) into cultural condemnations of immigrants, the poor, peoples of color, feminists, homosexuals—in short, any group that apparently does not meet narrow standards of national belonging. Defense of "place" and "community," in short, can have multiple, contradictory political trajectories.[15]

Situated in the vortex of these complex political crosscurrents, Appalachia is a site of intense and instructive resistance. As the essays in this volume demonstrate, new forms of progressive organizing are emerging alongside and in complex relationship to reactionary political impulses. A wide range of intellectual, cultural, and political work is reaching toward innovative conceptual models and organizing strategies that more accurately explain the region and its relationship to the nation and world. These foster a progressive oppositional consciousness rooted in people's daily lives and lead to specific policy demands that are often linked to struggles beyond Appalachia. From popular mobilizations against mountaintop removal to localized contests over land development, from locally integrated food economies that bridge rural farmers and low-income urbanites to transnational peace organizing that brings together Buddhists, Christians, secular youth, and other constituencies, the region is teeming with new forms of activism.

This ferment raises crucial questions about building coalitions and movements with sufficient traction to challenge the dominance of neoliberalism and corporate-driven globalization.[16] How can activists most effectively counter the market abandonment of entire places and peoples—including their needs for living-wage jobs, quality health care, and sustainable communities—in the face of global economic upheaval and migration? How, amid cries of "energy independence," can those in areas dependent on fossil fuels best struggle for just labor practices, educate the nation about the true costs of fossil fuel, and envision a future beyond our collective dependence on harmful sources of energy? How, in this post-9/11 security state where defense of the embattled nation sometimes takes form as white Christian xenophobia, can we build sturdy coalitions and movements that bridge across race, place, religion, gender, class, national origin, and sexual identity?

The contributors to *Transforming Places* offer hard-learned, illuminating, and widely relevant answers to these and related political questions. They share a deep commitment to social change, a willingness to be accessible and self-critical in their analyses, and a desire to draw concrete lessons from their research and experiences. They come from diverse backgrounds, speak in a wide variety of voices, and tell their stories in differing formats. Many were or are directly involved in the organizing they describe. Indeed, we view the multiple voices and styles, combined with the personal and ground-level experiences of so many of the authors, as one of the major strengths of this volume.

Transforming Places

This collection is divided into three sections. The chapters in section I, "Go Tell It on the Mountains: Place, Identity, and Culture," take on some of the most common and significant dynamics associated with contemporary globalization—the economic destabilization and popular reinvention of place-based communities— thereby offering lessons of wide-ranging application. Treating "place" not only as tangible landscape but also as continually re-imagined social relations and possibilities, these essays examine the cultural politics of place and offer different models for the mobilization of place-based identities.

To counter the widespread notion that organizing in Appalachia is either localistic or occurs primarily in the coalfields, we intentionally begin this first section of the book with two case studies that underscore the diversity of resistance in the region and its frequent connection to national and global issues. Chapter 1 explores long-term, place-based organizing around the massive environmental, political, economic, and other harmful effects of militarism in the company town of Oak Ridge, Tennessee, home of the federal government's leading research and production facility for nuclear weapons. Ralph Hutchison, coordinator of the Oak Ridge Environmental Peace Alliance, describes the organization's efforts since 1988 to mobilize local, national, and global constituencies and allies, address the impacts of nuclear production in Oak Ridge, and contribute in significant ways to the worldwide nuclear disarmament movement.

In chapter 2, Rees Shearer recounts the successful battle waged by RAIL Solution to defeat a proposal by Star Solutions, a subsidiary of the corporate giant Halliburton, to redesign and rebuild Interstate 81 in Virginia, a 325-mile-long highway that is western Virginia's single most valuable public asset. Seen by its proponents as a launching pad for a nationwide system of tolled, truck-only lanes, the proposal was a key transportation wedge-point in the neoliberal crusade to privatize the public domain. As the founder and chair, Shearer offers an intimate view of how RAIL Solution, relying heavily upon e-mail technology and the positive vision of a safer, greener, less costly twenty-first-century rail infrastructure and service, constructed a "virtual" community with phrases like "I-81, it's our Main Street." Hutchison and Shearer's analyses of the ways broad public alliances can confront others' control of local places offer instructive antidotes to the cynical and apathetic responses common among those facing seemingly unbeatable governmental and corporate agendas.

Nina Gregg and Doug Gamble explore in chapter 3 how community history, rapid population growth, the scenic beauty of the Great Smoky Mountains National Park, and belief in a "grow or die" philosophy interact and collide in public discourse and policy over land development issues in Blount County, Tennessee. They examine the different histories, strategies, successes, and failures of several single-issue local organizations and mission-focused groups, each identified with some aspect of the land development economy. Compared with Shearer's tale of successful organizing growing out of an invented common place, these authors offer a more cautionary story of the difficulties of using "place" to create unity, alliances, and alternative visions in a bounded location, a county, where local government and a significant segment of the population are conservative, resistant to new ideas, and committed to unfettered growth as the only route to prosperity. The authors' analysis highlights the importance of understanding the basis of power in local, place-based organizing and shatters the widely held assumption that "community" implies shared interests.[17]

The last three chapters in section I offer examples of efforts that have intentionally and successfully lifted up notions of place-based identity as the central component of their organizing strategies, albeit with different constituencies and goals. Chapter 4 demonstrates how place can "move," carried by migrants living outside the boundaries of Appalachia who have developed a stronger regional identity than the majority of those who live within the region. As millions of Appalachians headed to large urban centers in search of work during the last half of the twentieth century, they and their descendants faced negative stereotypes and discrimination that influenced urban Appalachian organizers' political strategies and aims: they organized around not only the fundamentals of economic security, such as access to decent housing and jobs, but also the psychological security of knowing who you are—of embracing a positive identity as Appalachians. Phillip J. Obermiller, M. Kathryn Brown, Donna Jones, Michael E. Maloney, and Thomas E. Wagner describe identity-based organizing among urban Appalachians in Cincinnati, Ohio, in the context of strategies involving race, class, and gender. In so doing, the authors, each of whom has been an active participant in at least one of the case studies, demonstrate how a sense of Appalachian identity has been a crucial element in building lasting Appalachian-controlled institutions; negotiating coalitions with other groups, especially African Americans; crossing class boundaries to further Appalachian interests; and standing up for health-related needs in Appalachian neighborhoods.

There are similarities between the urban Appalachian struggle for identity and others' efforts to help young people in low-wealth, central Appalachian communities confront messages and experiences that denigrate their culture and encourage them to leave their mountain homes. The Appalachia Media Institute (AMI), founded in 1988 as part of Appalshop, has been a leader in developing strategies and programs designed to foster positive identity development and a new generation of leaders among youth. Using concrete examples from AMI's history and interviews with current participants and alumni, Katie Richards-Schuster and Rebecca O'Doherty examine in chapter 5 how AMI has helped Appalachian youth re-envision their own communities and represent their ideas through the production of videos, frequently addressing controversial topics, and subsequent public dialogues about the content. These activities enable participants to challenge stereotypes, propose new solutions to persistent regional problems, make concerted efforts to involve fellow youth in their communities, and connect the struggles, beliefs, and stories of their Appalachian communities to marginalized communities in the United States and internationally.

In chapter 6, Maureen Mullinax reflects on the coalition-building efforts of a community-based arts project in Harlan County, Kentucky, that is deliberately using the arts and participatory research to build community capacity for democratic practice; in the process, participants engage in a subtle form of resistance to social and economic decline in their rural communities. The overarching goal is to reflect creatively on and re-present the hard realities and unique resources of Harlan County in the hope of building awareness of commonalities among area residents across deeply entrenched divisions of class, race, religion, and geography. The project raises important questions about the role of culture in social justice organizing, the significance of place-based pedagogy to transformative efforts, and the ability of civic organizations to be inclusive.

Section II, "Where No One Stands Alone: Bridging Divides," gathers essays that foreground the contentious and challenging work of building alliances and coalitions across divergent identities and institutions. Insofar as the mobilization and collision of social identities persist as central features of contemporary politics, not just in the United States but across the globe, these essays offer hard-won and far-reaching insights about organizing across deep social divides to find strength, rather than debilitating factionalism, in diversity.

In chapter 7, Meredith Dean, in collaboration with Edna Gulley and Linda McKinney, reflects from the inside out on the twenty-year history of the Appalachian Women's Alliance's attempts to organize in a more intentional, efficient, and explicitly "women's" way. Using strategies and tactics ranging from regionwide caravans to end violence against women, to Dismantling Racism workshops, to creative uses of the arts to enable women to speak in their own voices, the Alliance has created manifold leadership opportunities and touched thousands of women's lives. But the Alliance's journey to articulate an inclusive, Appalachian, feminist agenda, while creating and practicing nonhierarchal models of power, has been difficult and, using class as a lens, the authors offer a frank and self-critical discussion of the obstacles and conflicts that often undermine such efforts.

The Southern Empowerment Project (SEP) was a unique community-organizing school created by five southern and Appalachian community-based groups. Its governance structure, curriculum, and regional emphasis, along with its incorporation of the analysis of race, class, gender, and heterosexism as part of community organizing, made it stand out among training programs. Drawing from their insights as former directors, June Rostan and Walter Davis in chapter 8 offer important lessons about social justice organizing from SEP's twenty-year history; they critically examine what made the school different, its strengths as well as its weaknesses and limitations, the turning points in its development, and the factors and circumstances that led to its closure in 2007.

Chapter 9 offers a model for organizing different from that of SEP. Craig White, Paul Castelloe, Molly Hemstreet, Yaira Andrea Arias Soto, and Jeannette Butterworth, all current or former staff at the Center for Participatory Change (CPC), describe and critique their Grassroots Support Organizing (GSO) model. Rather than training organizers in formal settings or concentrating on a single issue or policy agenda, CPC operates within a broad and inclusive values framework: a commitment to racial and economic justice. This is rooted in the conviction that, while specific issues and policies will come and go, the key to sustainable regional social justice movements is creating a diverse and flexible grassroots infrastructure of skilled and experienced leaders, groups, and networks. The authors discuss the long-term nature of CPC's work, the necessity of developing an anti-oppression framework, the challenge of making effective alliances across lines of difference, and other big-picture questions. They also reflect on the fact that the strength of GSO—building a regional, diverse, decentralized infrastructure of people and groups working for justice—can also be seen as its primary weakness: What holds this infrastructure together, and is it really building a movement?

The United Mine Workers of America during their strike against the Pittston Coal Company in the late 1980s attracted the support of a broad range of social justice and religious organizations. The last two chapters of this section offer examples of similar alliances that raise important questions about how sympathetic community- and faith-based groups, accountable to different constituencies and goals, can ally with labor in sustained and effective ways. In chapter 10, Jill Kriesky and Daniel Swan describe the Justice at Peabody campaign launched by the UMWA between 2005 and 2007 and the strike by United American Nurses at Appalachian Regional Hospitals in West Virginia and Kentucky in 2007, in which an array of churches supported the workers and their unions in achieving their goals. The authors conclude that unions and their faith-based supporters need to collaborate both in public policy reform at a larger scale, nationally and internationally, and build stronger community relationships at a smaller, local scale to counter effectively the opponents of workers' rights. They ask if local clergy, particularly those associated with independent churches, have either the power or inclination to sign on to this broader struggle, and, if not, how might other local clergy, particularly those in mainline Protestant denominations that can easily be discredited as "outside agitators," identify appropriate and effective roles for themselves in future Appalachian labor struggles.

In chapter 11, Fran Ansley describes efforts by the Knoxville-based Jobs with Justice of East Tennessee to support a union-organizing drive at a chicken processing facility in Morristown, Tennessee, where the workforce had become virtually 100 percent Latino. She examines the elements that contributed most to the success of this campaign and the many challenges that remain for workers and the union after their initial victory. Ansley argues that there is legitimate ground in Appalachia—both material and ideological—for class solidarity across borders of race and nation, even though class will always be in some state of tension and coproduction with other forms of identity, and even though the relative power of these intersecting differences to motivate people and structure possibilities will often be in question. She insists that class solidarity cannot be productively framed or socially achieved without taking account of the asymmetries and dissimilarities among workers that characterize our domestic and global economies and that have now thoroughly penetrated the region's workplaces through recent immigration.

The final section, "Climbing Jacob's Ladder: Scaling Up," addresses the challenges, which have emerged so potently in this era of supranational institutions and their economic decision making, of marshalling sufficient leverage to be politically successful at different scales. The authors explore divergent organizational settings and offer a rich array of lessons about building relationships that are informed by local particularities but nonetheless reach toward wider visions, linkages, and political influence.

Because many problems cannot be contained or solved locally and there exist no meaningful, formal levers of political power at the regional level, place-based organizing requires astute political strategies. In chapter 12, Joe Szakos, executive director of Virginia Organizing, and board member Ladelle McWhorter argue that Appalachians must be part of statewide organizing efforts to achieve substantive change locally or regionally. Drawing from Virginia Organizing's experience, they look at obstacles to effective statewide organizing and how these are best overcome by shifting away from issue campaigns, adopting new organizing models that have a truly statewide, multi-issue, multi-constituency focus, and building long-term "strategic capacity" for borrowing and sharing power.

Sue Ella Kobak in chapter 13 describes how a small group of citizens in Lee County, Virginia, helped educate their communities about the spread of Oxy-Contin abuse and the resulting addictive problems. The author, an active participant in this battle, critically reflects on the various strategies used to address the OxyContin issue and raises challenging questions about regionwide organizing in Appalachia. Why were many in the Appalachian Studies academic community and most statewide and regional grassroots organizations unable or unwilling to coalesce into a movement to confront the OxyContin problem that was destroying so many lives and communities throughout Appalachia? What exactly is required to transform a specific problem into a regional or even a national issue? Kobak's questions challenge commonly held assumptions about how and why certain issues become defined as "political" and worthy of attention while others do not.

The Community Farm Alliance's (CFA) political work and its model of locally integrated food economies helped Kentucky become the first state to attempt a systematic and comprehensive food system. In chapter 14, Jenrose Fitzgerald, Lisa Markowitz, and Dwight B. Billings reflect on CFA's remarkable accomplishments. They pay particular attention to how CFA linked production and consumption, scaled up geographically (rural to urban) and socially (predominantly white farmers connected to African American residents of low-income neighborhoods and middle class "foodies"), and engaged with issues beyond farm survival to embrace food justice, health disparities, and antihunger activism. Their analysis underscores Szakos and McWhorter's argument for the importance of a statewide policy focus and the need for organizing strategies that envision imaginative alternatives to what is customary and taken for granted. Though their study examines local food systems, the authors' findings are relevant to broader movements for sustainable development in Appalachia and beyond.

For older, more established activists and organizations, scaling up often involves bulking up the organization: increasing staff, financial resources, membership, and the scope of their work, and on occasion joining alliances with other groups. A younger generation of activists throughout the world is pursuing a different model less grounded in a particular place; they are committed to decentralized, nonhierarchical decision making, rely heavily on the Internet and related technology for sharing information and planning activities, and seek out national and transnational connections. The best example of this model in the central Appalachian region is Mountain Justice (MJ), a loosely organized network of environmental and community activists and groups that has used a variety of tactics, including civil disobedience, to fight mountaintop removal (MTR) mining. In chapter 15, MJ members Cassie Robinson Pfleger, Randal Pfleger, Ryan Wishart, and Dave Cooper discuss MJ's origins, philosophy, goals, strategies, tactics, successes, and failures. In addition to positioning MJ within the political landscape of other regional social justice organizations working on MTR in Appalachia, they describe MJ's connections to anarcho-environmentalism and other environmental, climate, and global justice movements around the world. The authors conclude by describing how MJ, well aware that an end to mountaintop removal does not necessarily mean prosperity, justice, and liberation in Appalachia, has begun to play a role in envisioning and promoting alternative possibilities for economic development in the coalfields.

Knowledge is a fundamental component of power: Whose knowledge is considered legitimate? What knowledge is widely circulated? Thus, scaling up involves not only issues of organizational development and linkages, but also the creation of new spaces where people with critical perspectives, experiences, and knowledge can articulate their ideas in forms that are widely accessible at local, regional, national, and international scales. Such spaces provide a means of validating knowledge derived from participatory research, experiential learning, and community-based education. In chapter 16, Anita Puckett, Elizabeth Fine, Mary Hufford, Ann Kingsolver, and Betsy Taylor, drawing on their MTR activism and research, use both real time-and-place encounters and electronic means of accessing knowledge as examples of how to involve civic professionals, academics, local activists, and others in reconfiguring communication paths. In developing a "knowledge commons," they advocate for building a movement with transnational applications to confront neoliberal facades of concern for the environment that actually construe the "coalfields" as a market rather than as places for the exercise of democratic participation and eco-cultural sustainability.

Success in building such movements often involves learning from and building relationships with those fighting similar struggles in other parts of the world. In this context, Aviva Chomsky and Chad Montrie in chapter 17 compare the trajectory of popular organizing in Appalachia and Colombia and investigate how different peoples affected by coal mining have defined local and particular identities and interests. They look at moments when groups have deepened their political analysis to intersect with each other on both local and global scales. Chomsky and Montrie also draw on contemporary examples of solidarity, including a growing relationship between Kentuckians For The Commonwealth and unions and communities in the Colombian coal region. The authors conclude that, despite disappointments working with U.S. unions and environmental organizations, some members of Appalachian coal communities are at the epicenter of a growing global solidarity network that ties economic to environmental rights and seeks to create a global challenge to corporate power.

In his conclusion to *Fighting Back in Appalachia,* Fisher cited the need for a critical discourse and practice that could strengthen and link existing organizations while creating new models for political organizing and social transformation. The essays in *Transforming Places* respond to that need by examining the cultural and political models, strategies, innovations, and challenges that have emerged over the past two decades. In our conclusion, we draw out and reflect upon the many important lessons about place-based movement building present in these essays, commenting on the ways that they suggest both continuity with past traditions and new approaches to the challenges that currently face the region and the world.

Notes

1. Anthony Harkins, *Hillbilly: A Cultural History of an American Icon* (New York: Oxford University Press, 2004); Allen W. Batteau, *The Invention of Appalachia* (Tucson: University of Arizona Press, 1990); Nina Silber, *The Romance of Reunion: Northerners and the South, 1865–1900* (Chapel Hill: University of North Carolina Press, 1993); Dwight B. Billings, Gurney Norman, and Katherine Ledford, eds., *Back Talk from Appalachia: Confronting Stereotypes* (Lexington: University Press of Kentucky, 1999); Mark T. Banker, *Appalachians All: East Tennesseans and the Elusive History of an American Region* (Knoxville: University of Tennessee Press, 2010); David E. Whisnant, *Modernizing the Mountaineer: People, Power, and Planning,* rev. ed. (Knoxville: University of Tennessee Press, 1994); David E. Whisnant, *All That Is Native and Fine: The Politics of Culture in an Appalachian Region* (Chapel Hill: University of North Carolina Press, 1983).

2. For example, in 2008 in West Virginia, the only state that lies entirely within Appalachia, half of all households had incomes below $37,870, compared with a median household income of $52,175 for the United States as a whole. U.S. Census Bureau, American Community Survey 2006–2008, available at http://factfinder.census.gov.

3. Stephen L. Fisher, ed., *Fighting Back in Appalachia: Traditions of Resistance and Change* (Philadelphia: Temple University Press, 1993).

4. Richard A. Couto with Catherine S. Guthrie, *Making Democracy Work Better: Mediating Structures, Social Capital, and the Democratic Prospect* (Chapel Hill: University of North Carolina Press, 1999); see also the list of groups supported by the Appalachian Community Fund, www.appalachiancommunityfund.org.

5. www.socm.org; www.kftc.org; www.virginia-organizing.org and chapter 12 in this volume; Fisher, *Fighting Back in Appalachia.*

6. www. Appalshop.org and chapter 5 in this volume; www.appalachiancommunityfund .org; www.appalachianwomen.org and chapter 7 in this volume.

7. Appalachian Land Ownership Task Force, *Who Owns Appalachia? Landownership and Its Impact* (Lexington: University Press of Kentucky, 1983); Shaunna Scott, "The Appalachian Land Ownership Study Revisited," *Appalachian Journal* 35 (Spring 2008): 236–52.

8. Richard A. Brisbin Jr., *A Strike like No Other Strike: Law and Resistance during the Pittston Coal Strike of 1989–1990* (Baltimore: John Hopkins University Press, 2002); Jim Sessions and Fran Ansley, "Singing across Dark Spaces: The Union/Community Takeover of Pittston's Moss 3 Plant," in *Fighting Back in Appalachia,* ed. Fisher, 195–223; chapter 10 in this volume.

9. U.S. Census Bureau, 2007 Economic Census, "Sector 21: ECO 7211: Mining Industry Series: Detailed Statistics by Industry for the United States: 2007," and the National Mining Association, "Trends in U.S. Coal Mining 1923–2010." See www.nam.org.

10. Cecil Roberts is now, as of 2011, the president of the United Mine Workers of America.

11. Eve S. Weinbaum, *To Move a Mountain: Fighting the Global Economy in Appalachia* (New York: The New Press, 2004).

12. Nancy Fraser, "Reframing Justice in a Globalizing World," *New Left Review* 36 (November–December 2005): 69–88.

13. Jamie Peck and Adam Tickell, "Neoliberalizing Space," *Antipode* 34 (July 2002): 380–404; David Harvey, *A Brief History of Neoliberalism* (New York: Oxford University Press, 2005).

14. Robert D. Putnam, *Making Democracy Work: Civic Traditions in Modern Italy* (Princeton, N.J.: Princeton University Press, 1993); Couto, *Making Democracy Work Better*; Harvey, *A Brief History of Neoliberalism*; Herbert Reid and Betsy Taylor, *Recovering the Commons: Democracy, Place, and Global Justice* (Urbana: University of Illinois Press, 2010).

15. James DeFilippis, Robert Fisher, and Eric Shragge, *Contesting Community: The Limits and Potential of Local Organizing* (Piscataway, N.J.: Rutgers University Press, 2010).

16. Ronald D. Eller, *Uneven Ground: Appalachia since 1945* (Lexington: University Press of Kentucky, 2008).

17. James DeFilippis, Robert Fisher, and Eric Shragge, "Neither Romance nor Regulation: Re-evaluating Community," *International Journal of Urban and Regional Research* 30 (September 2006): 684.

PART I

Go Tell It on the Mountains

Place, Identity, and Culture

CHAPTER 1

Stop the Bombs
Local Organizing with Global Reach

Ralph Hutchison

It could be a classic Appalachian organizing story: outsiders with a plan take over the land and its rich resources, locals line up for jobs in the company town. Local power is constrained by economic dependence on the absentee employer—big decisions that impact the lives of everyone in the valley are made hundreds of miles away by wealthy members of the ownership class. This is a company town: the company controls information in the local press, health care through the local medical center, and air and water because its size insulates it from meaningful oversight by state officials. Discouraging words are seldom heard—the wrong word uttered in the wrong place may cost you your job.

Here is the twist: this town's public schools are among the best funded—through self-imposed tax increases—in the state.[1] The per capita Ph.D. ratio approaches that of the Research Triangle in North Carolina. Median income for those working for the company is well above the regional average and many jobs are in cutting-edge high tech. And though the population is below thirty thousand, there is a full-size chain bookstore, multiplex cinema, and science museum. The civic center hosts an indoor, Olympic-size public swimming pool. When it came time to clean up hundreds of thousands of pounds of mercury in local waterways, the community argued, successfully, to modify the Environmental Protection Agency's (EPA's) recommended standards to allow the toxin to remain in floodplains and streams.[2]

This is Oak Ridge, Tennessee, a city born in secrecy as part of the Manhattan Project in 1941. It has intentionally operated "under the radar" ever since, quietly going about its business—building thermonuclear bombs, encouraging nuclear power, and doing basic energy, scientific, and supercomputing research. In the process, the Oak Ridge Nuclear Reservation has contaminated soil, air, and water—in 1989, the nine-hundred-square-mile reservation was placed on EPA's Superfund List—and it has inhaled hundreds of billions of our tax dollars. In 1995, according to *Newsweek* magazine, Oak Ridge and Anderson County ranked in the top five U.S. congressional districts in federal largesse.[3]

Since 1988, the Oak Ridge Environmental Peace Alliance (OREPA) has been the most prominent and often the lone public voice addressing the federal government's activities in Oak Ridge. This is a story of how a local grassroots group is meeting a challenge that is both local and global in scope.

History: Theirs

The history of Oak Ridge starts in 1941 when the U.S. Army seized hundreds of acres of land, and citizens of several small communities were summarily removed from their property. That land became home to the Manhattan Project and three huge industrial sites producing radioactive material that would ultimately be fuel for the world's first atomic bomb. They were successful. The Y12 Plant in Oak Ridge produced the highly enriched uranium that fueled *Little Boy,* which destroyed Hiroshima; the graphite reactor at the X10 Plant, the world's first full-scale operating nuclear reactor, produced plutonium and served as a model for the larger reactors in Richland, Washington, which made plutonium for *Fat Man,* the bomb that destroyed Nagasaki.

The army's General Leslie Groves selected the valleys in east Tennessee for the abundant, clean water in the Clinch River, the isolated terrain ideal for a secret program, a workforce that needed jobs, and, thanks to the Tennessee Valley Authority's (TVA's) dam building in the 1930s, abundant electrical power.

In the years that followed, X10 became the Oak Ridge National Laboratory, the country's leading research facility for nuclear power, which built and operated thirteen nuclear reactors; one still operates. Y12's mission shifted from enriching uranium to producing the thermonuclear "secondary" for nuclear warheads; Y12 still builds bombs today. Across town, the K25 site enriched uranium through massive gaseous diffusion operations. Now the site is a waste processing facility and the giant buildings are being demolished.

Oak Ridge Operations provides jobs for more than fifteen thousand people, making it the largest single employer in Tennessee except for the state itself. Many jobs are white collar—researchers working on today's projects and scientists cleaning up yesterday's messes—but even machine operators make good wages.

It comes at a price. From the earliest days, secrecy was the watchword in Oak Ridge and dissent led to quick dismissal. The federal government operated with impunity, shielded from all oversight by the Atomic Energy Act of 1949. Standard workplace safety requirements are not enforced in Oak Ridge; the Occupational Safety and Health Administration (OSHA) has no regulatory authority. For more than forty years, state regulators were barred from the nuclear reservation. The EPA was formed in 1970, but it would take congressional hearings and a citizen-led lawsuit thirteen years later before the agency was granted access to the site. The price of lax oversight can also be measured in community and worker health. After fifty years of denying that workers at its nuclear weapons plants had been subjected to health risks, the federal government admitted that tens of thousands of workers were ill and their illnesses could be traced to workplace exposures. A program to provide compensation has been set up. Workers complain the process is slow and cumbersome, designed to discourage applicants, and payouts are insufficient to meet medical needs.[4]

History: Ours

OREPA arrived on the scene in 1988 when a small cadre of local residents formed a coalition to sponsor a demonstration against nuclear weapons on Hiroshima Day, August 6. The initial group included Quakers and other religious denominations, peace groups from North Carolina and Kentucky, antinuclear activists, the local anarchist chapter, and students from the University of Tennessee. The core organizers, who ultimately formed OREPA after the successful demonstration, were Steve Smith, veterinary student at the University of Tennessee; Stephen Clements, nuclear engineer with the TVA; and Judith Hallock, a nurse from western North Carolina. The August 6, 1988, Hiroshima Day peace demonstration included the first-ever civil disobedience in Oak Ridge; five activists crossed the "blue line" painted on the highway to demarcate the bomb plant's perimeter. During the next year, OREPA did extensive research and published *A Citizens' Guide to Oak Ridge,* and in 1990 disclosed extensive contamination of the Watts Bar Reservoir, a large recreational lake in east Tennessee. The disclosure generated national media coverage and established OREPA as a force the Department of Energy (DOE) could not ignore.

In 1992, the DOE announced (misleadingly, it turned out) that it was no longer producing nuclear weapons in Oak Ridge—the local headline trumpeted "Final Bomb Part Made at Y-12."[5] OREPA's focus shifted almost exclusively to environmental, safety, and health concerns. We served on federal advisory boards, published newsletters, attended hearings, schooled ourselves in cleanup technologies and regulatory requirements, and worked to assure that cleanup funding would materialize. The technical nature of environmental work was daunting. Though dozens of people supported OREPA financially, only a handful of core activists trudged through detailed technical documents, wrote comments on cleanup proposals, and spoke at public hearings.

By 1997, two things had changed. OREPA's advocacy of a "Site Specific Advisory Board" for Oak Ridge was successful, and a federal advisory committee was appointed that, for the first time, brought the local public into decision making in a meaningful role. And the *Knoxville News-Sentinel* disclosed that the Y12 Plant in Oak Ridge was, in fact, still making bomb components—not for new bombs, but to refurbish old bombs through the Life Extension Program.[6] In response, OREPA reached out to individuals and organizations that had engaged nuclear issues in the past and launched the Stop the Bombs campaign in 1998. The campaign's goals included educating, organizing, and mobilizing the public to oppose continued nuclear weapons production at Y12.

A Global Issue and Local Challenge

Nuclear weapons are a global issue. Many of the crucial decisions, which have a direct impact on activities in Oak Ridge, are made by arms control negotiators as they craft international treaties. Policy decisions by the president of the United States drive funding decisions by the U.S. Congress that determine, finally, what projects get done. Some of the work is profoundly important—the development of new insulators, creation of new radioactive materials for medical purposes, cutting-edge supercomputing, energy research to combat global climate change, and manufacture of thermonuclear components for weapons of mass destruction. In positive and negative ways, the work in Oak Ridge impacts the entire planet.

Organizing grassroots opposition to the production of thermonuclear weapons of mass destruction is complicated by the distance—geographical, political, and psychological—between the work on the ground and the decisions that drive it. In meetings with workers and plant officials, questions about responsibility for producing weapons of mass destruction are deferred. "We don't set policy; we just carry it out," is a typical mantra used by workers to avoid moral reflection, deflect criticism, and absolve themselves of responsibility.

Even those who feel their health has been compromised by operations at the federal facilities have a powerful social incentive to suppress questions. The long-held prohibition against public discussion of activities at the plant, stemming from the days of World War II, has been reinforced across the decades by a public campaign to maintain tight security. Billboards on site and throughout the county carry security warnings. When whistleblowers call attention to questionable activities, the company's chilling response serves notice that rocking the boat will result in unfortunate consequences. The economic dependence of the community on the federal facilities for jobs requires that everyone be a "team player." Whether one works directly for DOE or one of its contractors, having and maintaining security clearance is essential for high-paying jobs. The Oak Ridge Nuclear Reservation is responsible for pumping at least $2 billion into the local economy each year. That is a lot of money anywhere, but the depth of need in southern Appalachia exaggerates the impact of federal dollars. The money not only provides jobs with higher than average wages, it buys consent, or at least silence, from the community.

Add to this enormous vested economic interest the inertia behind a government program that has existed for almost seventy years and you have Goliath, a seemingly unassailable giant that threatens peace and security. The challenge of confronting Goliath is daunting, but not impossible. It requires an adjustment of perspective. As Sister Mary Dennis Lentsch put it: "I just feel like David, who when he went out and saw Goliath, must have thought, 'He's so big. How can I possibly miss?'"[7]

Organizing an Opposition

In Oak Ridge, the prevailing mythology is that weapons production is the reason the community exists. To speak out publicly against bomb production, most people believe, is to advocate community suicide.

Organizing an effective opposition, then, requires a structure, strategy, and program that are unconventional, at least in terms of traditional community organizing in Appalachia. And even this is problematic, because most funders committed to organizing in Appalachia do not recognize OREPA as doing community-based organizing.

In the earliest days, OREPA operated as a collective. The first—and only—objective of the nascent alliance was to stage a large peace demonstration in Oak Ridge that included nonviolent direct action. The collective was self-selecting and open to all who came to participate; the only funding available was what participants contributed from their own pockets; decisions were made by consensus; there was no hierarchy or power derived from seniority because everyone was, by definition, a newcomer. Following the first successful action in 1988, three leaders emerged and committed to focused organizing for the purpose of staging a larger peace demonstration the following August. Members of the collective traveled throughout the Southeast to tell people about Oak Ridge and encourage them to attend the August gathering. In the process, OREPA connected with groups and individuals who would form the enduring core of the organization's constituency—people of faith who, even as the nuclear freeze movement waned, remained committed to a world free of nuclear weapons, and members of the broader social justice community who recognized that nuclear weapons reflect a fundamental problem: inequities of power, racism, and inappropriate distribution of our common treasury that sacrifice true security (education, housing, health care) for a false sense of invulnerability .

The highly technical and time-intensive work during OREPA's "environmental years" limited the organization's ability to involve members. Monthly meetings of the Decision-Making Council (DMC) were open to anyone and advertised in local alternative papers, but attending one, for the uninitiated, was like being dropped midstream into whitewater, with a cascade of technical terms like "in-situ vitrification" substituting for water and dozens of acronyms bubbling up unannounced to swamp the raft. OREPA evolved into a small organization with a core of deeply committed volunteers surrounding staff. The organization enjoyed power somewhat disproportionate to its size because of the quality of its research, an unyielding commitment to accuracy, and the capacity to turn out people for public hearings.

Adequate during OREPA's environmental heyday, this structure changed when OREPA began to refocus on bomb production at Y12. Weapons production had broader appeal and was more accessible. As our movement grew, we restructured to create a more formal organization that could sustain the work in a more coherent way. Until 1999, OREPA existed as a project of the Foundation for Global Sustainability; in 2000 we established a separate charter with the state of Tennessee, adopted bylaws, formed a board of directors, and set up committees. This structure continues to serve us well today: a board of eight to twelve people; an executive committee to oversee financial and staff issues, and three other working committees: Action & Events; Organizing & Outreach; and Fundraising. Staffing has ebbed and flowed with funding, supplemented by interns or full-time volunteers, but as of 2011 we have one staff person whose title is coordinator. The majority of our funding (about 90 percent of an $80,000 budget) comes from members' contributions, special fund-raising events, and support from religious communities.

The Campaign to Stop the Bombs

When OREPA learned in 1996 that Y12 was still producing thermonuclear weapons, we gathered allies for a two-day consultation that led OREPA's DMC to establish several key strategic goals and launch the Stop the Bombs campaign. It was clear that nuclear weapons would not go away quickly and that organizing would be long-term. Our organizing principle became "educate, organize, and mobilize." We identified three key constituencies: faith communities, most of which have long-standing principled positions opposing nuclear weapons; students and young people (the future we want to build is, after all, their future); and traditional social change allies who focus on other issues but support an end to nuclear weapons production.

Though OREPA's earliest meetings took place at the Quaker meetinghouse, many participants were not typical "people of faith." But faith communities have formed the foundation of opposition to nuclear weapons as long as there has been resistance, so they were an obvious constituency. Efforts in 1989 to reach religious communities built bridges that, ten years later, were still standing. OREPA hosted interreligious services, engaged local clergy and religious leaders in press conferences, and in 1995 held a two-day convocation involving Buddhist, Hindu, Christian, Jewish, Muslim, Unitarian, and earth-centered religious representatives. Through the Office of Justice-Peace-Integrity of Creation of the Knoxville Catholic diocese, we made connections with religious communities and orders throughout Appalachia and, because of the connectional nature of the church, far beyond.

Three faith communities are most prominent: Christian, Buddhist, and earth-centered. The leadership of Pax Christi, USA, the Roman Catholic peace movement, participated in a local civil disobedience and put Oak Ridge on the reading tables in thousands of Catholic homes. We have traveled as far as South Dakota to address gatherings of Catholic women religious (nuns). Several local churches that have members actively involved in our work support OREPA financially and provide space for meetings and trainings. The Buddhist community is a strong presence through the Nipponzan Myohoji order, which sponsors peace walks around the world, including annual walks from Atlanta to Oak Ridge. Leaders of the order constructed a temple in Cocke County, Tennessee, and launched a project to build a peace pagoda there; OREPA members have been active in building the temple. Cooperation with Nipponzan Myohoji has connected us with international peace walkers on several continents, where OREPA has developed relations with antinuclear weapons campaigners. These connections have enabled OREPA's participation in briefings of delegates and NGOs at the United Nations.

Essential to OREPA's success in organizing among faith communities is an attitude of appreciation for diverse spiritual experiences and faith expressions. OREPA's board developed a statement on religious participation that welcomes authentic expressions of spirituality from each person and encourages mutual respect for all. Our attitude of appreciation is intended to be at least a step beyond mere tolerance.

Most of OREPA's organizing with young people has involved the children of adult members or students on college campuses. Our outreach has identified key campus communities, most within an easy drive of Oak Ridge, where OREPA staff or members make presentations and encourage student engagement. The results vary and often seem to reflect timing. Young people present moving targets for organizing; they are most easily found on campuses, but are likely gone three or four years later. OREPA made a strategic decision to move its major annual peace demonstration from August to April primarily because we can talk to students in February and March and encourage them to participate; in June and July they are at summer jobs, traveling, and are hard to reach. In years past, we offered internships that attracted high-quality students; we have also had students on our board of directors, waiving our "two-year term" requirement to accommodate education plans. The effort to encourage young people to develop their own "youth movement" is just beginning.

One particular challenge for OREPA is making use of communication tools popular among young people today (though electronic organizing is not limited to young people). Organizations like MoveOn.org, which rely almost exclusively on electronic organizing, have demonstrated that the age of electronic social networking is no longer on the horizon, it is here. For an organization with limited capacity and resources, setting up and maintaining Web sites, Facebook pages, and MySpace accounts, and using YouTube and other social networking tools and media require a sustained commitment to the keyboard that is difficult to add to an overflowing plate of activities.

OREPA's outreach to allies has included efforts to engage labor unions, traditional social change warriors, but we have met with mixed success. In the early 1990s, we invested considerable energy in studying Oak Ridge's economic future and engaged labor unions in meetings. Partly as a result of that effort, OREPA and the Oil, Chemical and Atomic Workers (OCAW) joined forces to support workforce transition legislation.[8] OCAW and OREPA were joined by Save Our Cumberland Mountains in working on environmental issues. But OCAW's star was on the wane. K25 was shutting down, and the Atomic Trades and Labor Council, the prevailing labor power at Y12, consistently expressed hostility to OREPA's agenda. We continue to seek avenues for cooperative work; recently Knoxville's Jobs with Justice (the local chapter of a national organization dedicated to community support for workplace justice) has joined with OREPA in sponsoring the Martin Luther King Jr. symposium and in other efforts to promote nonviolence.

Reaching out to other social change allies has been easier because OREPA members are not single-issue people. Most groups working on social change in east Tennessee have OREPA members active in their organizations, if not on the board of directors. Those organizations, of course, are overwhelmed with the challenges inherent in their issues, and shifting their focus to nuclear weapons is as hard for them as it would be for us to take on, for instance, health-care reform. Still, we have been enriched by the participation of other groups in many of our events. These traditional social change allies include groups in our community working on justice and peace issues—in Central America, the Mideast, Iraq, and Afghanistan—as well as those working for other progressive goals: a just tax structure in Tennessee, immigrants rights, labor, anti–death penalty, anti-racism and oppression, health-care reform, and civil liberties, among others. We do not have a "plan" for engaging other allies, but we do try to follow several rules to build bridges and connect our issues:

- Being an ally is a two-way street. We expect to be asked to divert some of our attention, energy, and resources to other causes. We can usually turn out bodies for a rally, speakers for a cause, or phone calls for a campaign.
- Share. Limited resources—not just money, but people, time, and the spotlight—erect barriers between groups and threaten to make competitors of colleagues. If we refuse to compete, but insist on sharing, we enter a win/win situation—the pool of resources grows bigger and, instead of getting a smaller slice of the pie, there is more pie to go around. When OREPA purchased a portable, battery-operated public address system, we adopted a policy of free use; dozens of local groups have used the speaker for rallies and demonstrations.
- Advertise. Five years ago, if you went to a death penalty rally, or a fair taxation demonstration, or an antiwar protest, you might find fifteen to fifty people, maybe more. A third of them, at least, would be OREPA members. They looked like everyone else who shared an interest in the cause. Realizing this,

OREPA asked its members to wear an OREPA T-shirt or carry a sign identifying the organization. This simple step has raised our profile in the social change community.

- Get serious about racism and oppression. The nuclear disarmament movement is pretty white, but the issues it deals with are not "whites only." OREPA's first formal experience of anti-racism work was a workshop sponsored by the Military Production Network. Becoming sensitized to the power of racism and oppression in our culture is a first step. Taking action requires thoughtful reflection and some daring; it is also essential to being part of the larger community working for social change. OREPA's action began with study—every member of the board attended an anti-racism workshop—and a statement. Action began several years ago when OREPA sponsored a public symposium during the Martin Luther King Jr. birthday celebration in Knoxville and created giant street theater puppets to carry in the King holiday parade. Both events initiated relationships through which we will work to dismantle racism and overcome oppression.
- Make connections. In 2008, OREPA sought to recognize 2009 as a Year for the Celebration of Nonviolence in Knoxville and the surrounding region. By the time the year was launched, twenty-three local groups, organizations, and institutions had joined the call; more joined later. OREPA's goal was not to realize a direct benefit for itself, but to elevate nonviolence in the community and encourage allies to recognize our common ground—so a domestic violence shelter, an environmental group, Jobs with Justice, peace groups, church groups, and others linked their issues and thereby opened possibilities for future collaboration.

Every Tool in the Toolbox

While our guiding principle is "educate, organize, mobilize," our program reflects OREPA's early commitment to use "every tool in the toolbox." Public hearings, fund-raising appeal letters, mass demonstrations and peace rallies, lobbying trips to Washington, D.C., with the Alliance for Nuclear Accountability (successor to the Military Production Network), civil disobedience campaigns—all are organizing opportunities. We took a page from the successful organizing of mass demonstrations at the School of the Americas in Columbus, Georgia, and developed a twenty-four-minute video, narrated by Martin Sheen and Paloma Galindo, to be used as an organizing tool by others. We travel to events in other communities to set up tables with information about OREPA events.

In the first year of the Stop the Bombs campaign a series of actions, beginning in August 1998 and concluding in August 1999, raised voices from across our community: first the Mother's Action, then an Artist's Action on Human Rights Day, a People of Faith Action, a Women's Disarmament Day Action, and a Father's Day Action, all sandwiched between two Hiroshima Day Actions. At least one-quarter of the planning committee for each event was new to OREPA. For each action we also created a list of people who might consider an act of conscience—civil disobedience—at the bomb plant. By the end of the year scores of people had been arrested in Oak Ridge. Each action was preceded by a day-long nonviolence training session that offered workshops on communication and consensus decision making, reflections on the history of nonviolence, role-plays and, usually, descriptions of the arrest scenario planned for the next day.

The civil disobedience component of the Stop the Bombs campaign serves three purposes. First, it increases media attention, forcing coverage of events that, because they are often held on weekends at a relatively remote and isolated weapons plant, could otherwise be ignored. We have learned the only way to get our message out clearly is to make certain it is the only thing we say to reporters. We stay on point, working our way quickly around to our message, regardless of questions put to us.

Second, civil disobedience encourages deeper commitment from members and others new to the organization. Being arrested, even for a Class C misdemeanor, is not a common occurrence for most middle-class people in this country. Even witnessing the arrest of others is a powerfully moving event that has lasting impact. Participants regularly report their arrest has unforeseen consequences. One woman recounted going to her office uncertainly the day after her arrest was reported in the paper. One of her colleagues was an Oak Ridge resident whose views on nuclear weapons were unknown to her. The encounter turned out to be good: the woman from Oak Ridge said, "Thank you for your action," and provided an entry point for broader discussion. Others note that just being asked to consider civil disobedience has a significant impact. Six months after being asked to consider taking such action, a woman said, "You probably think I just forgot about your question since you didn't hear back. The truth is, I have thought of little else since you asked."

Third, civil disobedience works in unforeseeable ways to generate, in the words of Martin Luther King Jr., a "creative tension" in the community that compels response. So far in our case, most of the response has come from the judicial system. From judges releasing protestors with reduced fines or sentences of community service to protesters originally given two months in federal prison, we have experienced the full range of justice. Gordon Maham, sentenced to five days in jail and forty-eight hours of community service for blocking the road leading to the bomb plant, told his tale at the weekly peace vigil: "On Monday I was in jail because I was a danger to society, and on Wednesday I was sitting at a desk at Briceville Elementary School playing checkers with first graders as part of my community service—still wearing my jail ID bracelet." After one group of women performed community service at a local arts cooperative, mixing glazes and cleaning the building, the director of the cooperative wrote a letter to the local paper thanking the women for their service and praising them for their action.

The letter led to a tirade from the judge and the end of community service as a sentencing option.

Art and Social Change

Over the past five years, OREPA has added a delightful new component to its toolbox—the creative arts. The inspiration came from puppet workshops held in Georgia in preparation for annual School of the Americas protests that always include a mass street theater event. After participating in these programs, OREPA members embarked on their own efforts. The Riverside Nonviolent Community now hosts a week-long puppet workshop before each major demonstration in Oak Ridge. Participants create giant puppets and a twenty-minute skit from scratch in the course of a week, and the drama unfolds onstage at the concert that precedes the demonstration.

What began as street theater has expanded into other parts of OREPA's work. A "road show" has been developed, incorporating participatory games and skits in infotainment, delivering a substantive educational piece along with fun, laughter, and occasionally moving drama. The road show team has traveled to North Carolina, Virginia, Tennessee, Georgia, and even Detroit.

Puppetistas create a many-headed hydra (the nuclear industry) for peace demonstration, Oak Ridge, Tennessee, August 2005. (Photo by Ralph Hutchison)

Public hearings in Oak Ridge have also provided a venue for drama. Robin Hood and Scrooge have appeared, along with giant cardboard cockroaches and the Grim Reaper, interrupting the smooth flow of dry public comments with thoughtful and creative presentations of the dangers and costs of nuclear weapons. At one hearing, the professional facilitator welcomed OREPA members with a twinkle, saying, "I just had to come back to Oak Ridge to make sure everyone was still 'on script.'" He was assured that he would not be disappointed, and we were assured he would not invoke the five-minute rule on the skit.

Social change artists have also had an impact on the broader community. For the last three years giant street puppets of Martin Luther King Jr., Sojourner Truth, Gandhi, and Myles Horton (cofounder and longtime director of the Highlander Center) have cavorted in the street during the annual MLK parade, to the delight of spectators.

Art is also often the focus of OREPA's weekly peace vigils, held each Sunday afternoon since November 1999 at the Y12 weapons complex. One Sunday, the leader asked everyone to imagine waking on Monday morning to a world exactly the same, with one exception: all wars had ended, militaries were disbanded, and weapons were destroyed. "What would you do?" asked the leader. After a moment's reflection we went around the circle. "I would sit down at the piano and play," said one. "I'd go down the street to the coop and throw clay," said another. "I'd paint a picture," said a third, "a watercolor." After the circle was completed we realized what peace looks like. It is not just the opposite of war; it is the creative act—each in the circle had described doing something creative on the first day in a world without war.

Art and creativity have become significant vehicles for OREPA's work. They have provided alternative forms of involvement for those uncomfortable with the confrontational nature of direct action/civil disobedience, and they follow the injunction of Gandhi that "we must be the peace we seek."

Measuring Success

Organizing around a global issue is an exercise in delayed gratification. Funders want to know how we measure success, but so do grassroots workers who invest in OREPA's mission. To date we are unable to say, "Well, all the bombs are gone, aren't they?" Fundamental change in our society and culture is a long-term project. We take encouragement from knowing Gandhi's movement for independence took decades, as did movements for woman suffrage and civil rights in this country. In this context, simply persisting in a hopeful spirit could be counted as success.

On a more practical level: twenty years ago weapons activity at the Y12 plant in Oak Ridge was simply not talked about in east Tennessee. OREPA's work has raised awareness of U.S. weapons production and placed DOE's activities in Oak Ridge in the context of U.S. obligations under the Nonproliferation Treaty. In 1991, then again in 2008, DOE attempted to rebuild the nuclear weapons complex, but grassroots opposition was instrumental in thwarting both efforts. Citizen pressure has forced state and federal regulators to address environmental contamination from weapons production. So, though we cannot celebrate final victory, we can look back and recognize that our work has been instrumental in, as Steve Earle sings, "things not gettin' worse," and in some cases things getting better.

More recently, OREPA's board adopted as its strategic goal raising awareness about the Life Extension Program that is refurbishing old nuclear warheads to maintain an enduring stockpile. Our first "target" constituency was our allies, many of whom are tightly focused on their own sites and activities. In September 2007, the Alliance for Nuclear Accountability made stopping the Life Extension Program a priority strategic goal; we mark that as one more successful step in our long journey.

This kind of success is nurtured by the experience of community—a gathering of 1,500 people for a peace demonstration; the testimony of a ten-year-old girl in front of hundreds at a public hearing on the new bomb plant; a dozen people shivering in subfreezing temperatures on Sunday afternoon as they celebrate nine years of uninterrupted weekly peace vigils—these are markers on the way to success and, in and of themselves, a form of success. It is the experience of community that sustains us as we persist toward a goal that remains unfulfilled.

Notes

1. www.bestplaces.net/city/oak_ridge-tennessee.aspx.

2. Environmental Management Program Overview, 1995: www.ornl.gov/sci/env_rpt/aser95/ch-3.htm.

3. Jon Meacham, "Mr. Wamp Goes to Washington," *Newsweek,* April 17, 1995.

4. Laura Frank, "Deadly Denial: Government Fails to Help Sick Nuclear Workers," *Rocky Mountain News,* July 20, 2008.

5. Paul Sloca, "Final Bomb Part Made at Y-12," *The Oak Ridger,* October 6, 1992.

6. Frank Munger, "Oak Ridge Plant Still Building Bombs," *Knoxville News-Sentinel,* August 21, 1996.

7. *One World: Stop the Bombs,* video produced by RadioActive Films and Oak Ridge Environmental Peace Alliance, 2000.

8. Frank Munger, "K-25 Union Joins Hands with Activists for Nuclear Transition," *Knoxville News-Sentinel,* July 22, 1992.

CHAPTER 2

RAIL Solution

Taking on Halliburton on the Home Front

Rees Shearer

Grading the path of an ancient bison trail, highway builders constructed Interstate 81 along Virginia's mountainous spine in the 1960s. I-81 was one link in realizing President Eisenhower's dream for safe travel on a seamless national asphalt web, free from tolls and traffic lights. Its route along the Blue Ridge and through the Appalachian Mountains literally links small valley communities and their destinies together and to the world, just as it did for centuries.

Settlers variously called the time-worn thoroughfare Warrior's Path, the Great Road, and Valley Pike. Indian, settler, and Civil War soldier fought in turn alongside the road. In 2002, a different sort of conflict broke out on this critical artery. This time, the battle would be waged for control of the road itself. The struggle matched aspirations for privatization and profit against the futures of communities. On one hand, a mysterious corporate consortium bid to seize control of I-81, doubling its size and charging tolls for "safety improvements." On the other, people in adjoining localities organized to retain title to I-81, their call to arms: "Take back our Main Street."[1]

Over the years, I-81 truck traffic doubled and in some locations nearly tripled because of subtle shifts in national shipping and distribution patterns.[2] Truckers and shipping dispatchers turned to I-81 to bypass I-95 and the congested eastern seaboard. Other trucks, with freight generated by the North American Free Trade Agreement, also hammered down I-81. By 2003, big rigs averaged 28 percent of total traffic—exceeding 40 percent at certain times and places—on an interstate designed for 15 percent trucks.[3] The I-81 corridor south from Harrisburg, Pennsylvania, to east Tennessee became the densest truck freight corridor in the nation.[4] Travelers saw horrific accidents and worried about their own safety.

Don Young had a solution to dangerous truck congestion on the nation's highways. The bold and powerful U.S. representative from Alaska, Young in 2003 chaired the House Transportation and Infrastructure Committee. He championed a revolutionary new system of truck-only interstate lanes—the pilot project earmarked for Virginia, "Where the rest of my Congressional friends can see it, and once they see it, then they [truck-only lanes] will be mandated across the country."[5]

Sixteen months earlier, STAR Solutions, an enigmatic construction consortium, was proposing to redesign and rebuild I-81 in Virginia. The 325-mile-long highway is western Virginia's single most valuable public asset. A critical economic and transportation link, I-81 crosses some of the nation's most beautiful and historic landscapes. STAR Solutions pitched reconstructing I-81 into an enormous eight- to twelve-lane leviathan, with four center lanes exclusively for heavy truck traffic. For the first time in the United States, a free public interstate would be converted into a mega-truck toll road.

The STAR proposal emerged as a wedge-point in the transportation arena for the political crusade to privatize the public domain. Committing Virginia to build his truckway would launch Representative Young's play for a nationwide system of privatized, tolled, truck-only lanes. If the STAR partners won in Virginia, privatization of I-81 would be secured from Tennessee to Pennsylvania. Appended at the north and south ends of the corridor, the other I-81 states would be left no alternative but to build their own truck-only lanes. Such a massive highway scheme would checkmate an environmentally benign and cheaper rail freight alternative.

The Reason Foundation,[6] a Los Angeles–based libertarian think tank, is a mastermind behind privatization of the American commons. The foundation promotes privatization of everything from airports and state lotteries to prisons and highways. Reason forged an enviable relationship with Chairman Young, lobbying for construction of truck-only lanes nationwide, particularly along I-81, and strongly opposing any public support for rail transportation.[7]

But well before Chairman Young was openly promoting his pet truck lane project, agitation was stirring in the valleys of Virginia. Appalled at the prospect of a monster truckway bisecting rural Virginia, I organized what came to be called RAIL Solution, a citizens' group promoting a rail-based freight and passenger alternative to the STAR Solutions concept.

STAR Solutions rolled out its project before a Virginia General Assembly starved for transportation revenues but besieged by demands for improvements. The consortium confidently claimed that its influence in Congress would leverage $1.6 billion in federal subsidies. The General Assembly heartily embraced STAR Solutions, exempting the project from competitive bidding under the state's Public Private Transportation Act of 1995 (PPTA).

Harrowing stories of close calls with trucks on I-81 had become common conversation for residents of western Virginia. So, the driving public was primed for relief when the Virginia Department of Transportation (VDOT) reported STAR Solutions would improve I-81 safety and reduce congestion by separating cars and trucks. This concept seemed the answer to a prayer.

However, as citizens began to visualize the reality of STAR's plan, they recoiled from the prospect: Did we need a New Jersey Turnpike slithering down Virginia's valleys? The burden of diesel emissions and greenhouse gases from the projected four to seven million additional trucks per year by 2035 would be enormous.[8] Asphalt would entomb acres of agricultural land and forests and displace local businesses. STAR proposed truck tolls up to $129 for one pass through Virginia, tolls that would sour regional business and economic prospects. Businesses located along I-81 and captive to it for procurement and distribution may not be competitive with industries able to access untolled routes. Our places of employment could be forced to move or shut down.

As an elementary school counselor, I was frequently reminded that air quality in southwest Virginia is already poor.[9] Many students suffer from asthma. Air frequently stagnates in our valleys between the ridges. The prospect of all these trucks accelerating through our towns, belching diesel smoke, was, in a word, breathtaking. As details emerged, I was unable to find any citizen supporting the STAR scheme, but virtually no one was willing to fight it either. "It's a done deal," I heard over and over those first nine months.

In March 2002, I wrote a lengthy letter about the situation to the editor of the *Roanoke Times,* the principal newspaper along Virginia's I-81 corridor. Close to three months later, in June, it was published, not as a letter, but as a guest op-ed. I noted that "Star Solutions has succeeded in ramming through legislation that eliminates any roadblocks for its scheme. . . . What will happen to our respiratory disease rates . . . ? It is clear that Star Solutions' overbuilding plan is only a 'solution' for gigantic construction companies that want to make big bucks on the backs of interstate users."[10] I received one response. Roanoker Ann Rogers, a seasoned highway fighter, tracked me down at school. The founder of Virginians for Appropriate Roads, Ann introduced me to a number of highway opponents, several of whom came to take up the cause against massive I-81 expansion.

One opponent was longtime rail advocate Michael Testerman, president of the Virginia Association of Rail Patrons. Michael, along with state senator John Edwards of Roanoke, explained that through-state truck freight was the real cause of congestion on I-81. That freight, they asserted, could be carried on a new, faster, modernized intermodal version of the existing Norfolk Southern railroad, already paralleling I-81, between terminals near Knoxville, Tennessee, and Harrisburg, Pennsylvania. Intermodal freight employs two or more transportation modes for shipment. Typically a truck picks up the load, hauling it to a nearby terminal to be shipped the long distance on rail. Then it is off-loaded to another truck for final delivery to the customer. Michael introduced me to former federal railway administrator Gil Carmichael's vision for Interstate II: "The concept is not radical. . . . Once the rail line is adequately upgraded . . . the I-81 Corridor rail line could handle all long-distance freight shipments and offer auto and plane-competitive passenger service . . ."[11]

Dave Foster, a retired Norfolk Southern economist, soon joined our team. Dave envisioned a truck ferry operation, carrying not just trailers but whole trucks. Independent drivers could maintain their loads, eat, sleep, and update their log-books in "sleeper" cars while their trucks rode the rails toward their destinations. Shipping whole trucks and trailers by rail is vastly greener, cleaner, and safer than trucking individual loads and would boost the local economy, offering a cheaper, but time-competitive, shipping alternative. Rail is less impacted by fuel costs or availability. And restoring passenger service would be warmly welcomed in a region without it since the 1960s. The "rail solution" or steel interstate, as we came to call it, became our positive alternative concept.

Our vision was taking shape, but a huge obstacle remained. I recognized it from 1983 when, as director of the Coalition of American Electric Consumers (CAEC), I worked alongside the Brumley Gap (Virginia) Concerned Citizens in their successful six-year battle to defend their valley. American Electric Power (AEP), the nation's largest investor-owned utility, contrived to seize their valley and build the world's largest pumped storage dam. But dam opponents defeated the mammoth utility by drawing upon a deep well of solidarity knit tight by generations sharing the same space within their valley. Moreover, community was cultivated by mutual pledges of support—fund-raising activities such as turkey shoots and cake walks, and the display of plywood signs with Bible verses articulating its mission in the shared religious vernacular.

A less successful part of the CAEC's broad struggle for people's land involved fighting a proposed web of AEP extra-high voltage transmission lines. These power lines would be suspended above homes and farms from Wythe County toward Danville, Virginia. Organizing against these lines was tough. The lines' inherent linear quality would similarly affect people dozens or even hundreds of miles away from each other, while the neighboring farm family over the hill might feel no real impact. We lost the power line battle for lack of proximity, failing to achieve a sense of community along the transmission right-of-way. By the time we began the struggle against STAR, however, a new tool would help us overcome this obstacle.

In the intervening twenty years, wide distribution of personal computers and Internet access offered a bridge, enabling people to come together across distances. E-mail, cheap and largely accessible, radically altered the dynamic for linear organizing by creating "virtual" community. In 2002, few felt over-whelmed by spam and listservs. People were open to entering into virtual con-versation with strangers.

A Virginia Tech graduate student volunteer set up the RAIL Solution listserv. The listserv became our glue, our town crier, an electronic community—quicker and cheaper than telephone or a newsletter and far less labor-intensive. Supporters could be involved in daily, ongoing, strategic discussions by e-mail or elect to receive only special messages or alerts.

Throughout 2002, stunned by what we were learning, I contacted state and national environmental groups, still fantasizing that some national organization would champion the fight against STAR Solutions. Come December, I heard no cavalry hoof-beats. With no money or resources, we needed a low-cost strategy to build opposition and bring quick success. I wrote a boilerplate resolution supporting improved rail capacity over highway expansion. My goal was to find people to submit ten to twelve resolutions to county supervisors and city and town councils along the I-81 corridor. Ann Rogers teased, "If you start this, you'll work full-time fighting this road for years." I laughed at her hyperbole. But by 2012, I have already logged ten years and counting.

Over succeeding months, like kernels of resentment in hot oil, rail support resolutions popped up from Winchester to Knoxville. Sometimes a few people, frequently only one, offered a resolution, convincing their supervisors or council to adopt it. Doggedly calling on friends of friends, I begged for e-mail addresses of electronic acquaintances. An organizer develops immunity to rejection. Almost none of this organizing involved any contact so human as a voice or a face. Bitterness against STAR's plan was spreading like the flu, so as I broadcast word of a strategy to fight the disease, people emerged from the electronic ether. These good citizens ultimately won forty-eight pro-rail local government resolutions! Persistence. As our successes grew, we paraded the results on our new Web site (www.railsolution.org). Only one county ultimately rejected our resolution. All those resolutions compelled the media, officials in Richmond, and some citizens who were initially too dispirited to fight, to pay attention. Our resolution campaign won national notice for our efforts. As part of their "Road to Ruin" project, Friends of the Earth and Taxpayers for Common Sense named the STAR I-81 proposal the second most wasteful highway scheme in the nation.[12]

Though "virtual" organizing was producing results, supporters needed to meet face-to-face to take ownership and create democratic organization. Early in 2003, my e-mail entreaties to urge highway opponents to meet got no response. Ellen Shepard of Virginia Conservation Network asked, "Why haven't you called a meeting?" I said, "I tried, but no one responded." "Let me try," she said. She then telephoned people. At times, only direct human contact works.

"Choose an initial fight you can win" is a basic tenet of community organizing. When Ellen Shepard first called these e-mail collaborators together in April, we were not only excited to see the faces behind the e-mails, we were already winning. Several resolutions had passed and more were clearly in the works. Local voters are the best advocates before local boards and councils, and our early strategy required every participant to become an activist in their own community. "I can't do this for you; if you don't, who will?" We structured RAIL Solution to quickly absorb newcomers. Our steering committee, not our executive board, serves as our principal governing and strategizing body. We wrote bylaws to provide that if you attend two consecutive meetings, you participate as a voting steering committee member.

Because Republicans predominate in the I-81 corridor, we needed to uncouple the ideological from the partisan. We did that in 2005 by nurturing a sense of public ownership in an effort to counter the drive for privatization, a libertarian, conservative, and capitalist mantra. With leadership from the Rockbridge Area Conservation Council, an allied environmental group, and member donations, we produced and distributed a fanciful "local newspaper" as an educational tool. The *Shenandoah & Southwest Citizen* editorialized, "Speak up—Take back our 'Main Street.'" It called citizens to "Stand up for your family and your community. . . . Your neighbors volunteered to write and paid for printing this paper, to help people make up their own minds and to restore public control over this momentous transportation decision. . . . The Interstate is our 'Main Street.' Let's keep it ours—and free."[13]

We appealed to Virginians to claim ownership and fight Representative Young's expropriation even as our leaders, from the governor on down, forsook this public trust. "No toll-taxation by Alaskan representation!"[14] *Citizen* articles further examined the STAR project's sordid political-corporate genesis, safety issues, proposed tolls and their impact on the regional economy, and how our intermodal rail vision would work. The *Citizen* also included a map showing forty-one community resolutions supporting rail and pictures and contact information for state and federal officials.

Early in our struggle, we used the Internet to try to unmask STAR Solutions. We knew it was a corporate conglomerate, including Halliburton, a huge energy and engineering company where Dick Cheney worked prior to becoming vice president. But not until we requested their proposal to VDOT did we begin to adequately size up our adversaries. We learned that Halliburton Corporation's then-subsidiary KBR (formerly known as Kellogg Brown and Root) was the lead contractor of forty STAR Solutions collaborators. A giant international engineering firm, KBR was also the notorious war-profiteering, no-bid contractor for military supplies in Iraq and Afghanistan and for cells at Guantanamo Bay detention camp. The company had been reprimanded by the Securities and Exchange Commission for its bookkeeping and had come under multiple investigations for overbilling the Pentagon and provisioning supplies deadly to the troops. In our *Shenandoah & Southwest Citizen*, we criticized VDOT for entering contract talks with a corporation with such a reprehensible history. "Contractors for any VDOT job should meet reasonable standards . . . be stable financially, have a reliable history of ethical behavior. . . . KBR . . . fails to meet these standards. Yet VDOT is now negotiating a contract with STAR Solutions to 'improve' I-81. Who is selling this snake oil?"[15]

Our struggle took place in a climate of inappropriately cozy relationships at high levels of business and government. In 2003, Congressman Young was under four separate federal criminal corruption investigations.[16] Yet, during the truck lane battle, Young was at the height of his power, the czar of federal transportation funding, and able to insert earmarks at will. He named the 2005 omnibus transportation bill SAFETEA-LU in honor of his wife, because he could.[17]

STAR Solutions–related contributions of $150,000 to Young's 2004 congressional campaign were discovered by RAIL Solution volunteer John Hutchison on the Federal Election Commission Web site. These contributions from executives of STAR's partner corporations greased earmarked pork toward Virginia's pot. Virginia officers and employees of the STAR consortium alone donated at least $64,000—for a race run and won in Alaska.[18] In another 2003 example, STAR Solutions partner Vanasse Hangen Brustlin, Inc. (VHB) left the STAR Solutions consortium for the purpose of bidding on the contract to perform the Environmental Impact Statement (EIS) study for the I-81 project. Despite the conspicuous conflict of interest, VDOT accepted VHB's bid.[19]

Crucial to waging a war on the home front are a handful of citizens possessed by passion and commitment. You have to believe, as Ann Rogers and I and our RAIL Solution prophets do, that it does not matter that you have no chance of winning. It does not matter that no foundation will fund you. You fight viscerally because it is right to oppose something so awful. It is like this: The week of the Iraq invasion, a third grader asked me, "Was that you, yesterday, holding up a sign, protesting against the war?" "Yes," I said, pleased to be recognized. "Well, you lost!" he retorted. "Son," I responded, "sometimes you take a stand, even when you know you're going to lose."

Only people who have had positive experience with citizens' groups grasp their power. They "get it" that in working together you risk time and energy in exchange for hope. It is actually fun for them, or at least invigorating. If an issue resonates, almost mystically a core of dedicated supporters emerges, each with his or her own passion and reasons. You cannot manufacture passion, only offer yours up and hope it is contagious. Usually only a few respond with deep commitment, but often that is enough. For this chapter, I polled key participants in RAIL Solution, asking what motivated them to become involved and stick with our long struggle. I left the question open-ended. Remarkably, "making the political system work" outstripped concern for environmental sustainability issues or affection for passenger railroad service in volunteers' self-analysis of what was their motivating rationale.

They embrace democratic process in statements like: "David v. Goliath: it is inspiring to see grassroots democracy." "Working against the tide of 'business as usual.'" "The upbeat feeling of being on the right side, of joining with Robin Hood to battle the bullies (KBR, et al.), of helping to expose bluster and greed." "I discovered that 90% were opposed to a 'pilot project' by a congressman from Alaska of all places. Who the hell did he think he was?" "I recognized a call for ordinary people to help create a better path into the future. . . . We ARE the government, here in the U.S. We foot the tax bills and should have a hand in determining how they pay for transportation and how they rearrange our landscapes and lives. This is our 'place' in the big picture." Dave Foster summed it up, "We are in this for the long term. . . . We live here."[20]

Here is how I, for one, juggled this democratic responsibility. I would get home from work, make some small contributions to keep home and family intact, and then get to my second job—organizing. My tapping away on the bedroom computer in the wee hours was exasperating for my usually forgiving wife, but, nevertheless, I was able to carve out time early mornings, nights, weekends, holidays, and summers to hold down the equivalent of two full-time jobs—a day job at a public school, and a volunteer job for RAIL Solution. Why was I driven? Partly it was rage at corporate greed and government complicity. Partly it was the fun of playing Lilliputian.

Using e-mail was freeing. Conventional organizing is time-bound. It is socially unacceptable to phone someone at 1:39 A.M. or to come by for a quick visit before work at 7:00 A.M. Electronic jiggering of time and space afforded me and others the opportunity to subsidize RAIL Solution "full-time" or part-time as

Area residents rally for a rail alternative at the old Abingdon, Virginia, freight depot, February 2, 2005. (Photo by Kathy Shearer)

our obsessions compelled us. STAR Solutions and VDOT are stuck inside a rigid eight-hour-day-five-days-a-week-and-holidays corporate construct.

Leadership and support are hard to maintain when addressing a multiyear, perhaps multidecade, problem. Corporations and bureaucracy grind forward slowly as suits their purposes. While, as at Brumley Gap, project delay can work to the people's advantage, it is also wearing. Life goes on—key supporters move, become disgruntled, or flat wear out. A few die.

Tabling at local events, RAIL Solution volunteers attracted new supporters by asking people to sign a petition, then harvested their contact information. After four years, our supporter list remained steady at about 1,300. Most were inactive, but many would respond to special alerts. The most devoted volunteers were already committed rail fans, environmentalists, or community activists.

We held steering committee meetings every two or three months on Saturdays. Working through lunch, we typically met for over five hours. It was trial-by-ordeal. We wore out potential committee members with this approach. However, some participants drove two to four hours, one way, to attend a meeting, so planning more frequent, shorter meetings was not realistic. As the elected chair, I favored sufficient time to illuminate background for newcomers and allow for open and full airing of issues and strategic decisions. Meeting via e-mail was much easier.

In the Brumley Gap struggle, we not only took a positive stance, offering cheaper and environmentally benign alternatives for meeting AEP's electrical demand projections, but we attacked AEP as greedy and cold-hearted. We hammered home that AEP already had excess capacity but wanted to generate even more power for the lucrative wholesale market—proof that AEP's specious claim to need more generating capacity was actually bullying the people of Brumley Gap at great cost to all electric ratepayers. Early on, I sought to carry this experience over to RAIL Solution, but the steering committee meeting burst into heated debate. Many advocated for an exclusively positive approach and decried the negativity of my determination to drive a stake into STAR so that our positive vision could be clearly heard. RAIL Solution ultimately adopted a forked strategy: *advocate*, explaining and supporting our positive rail vision, but also *attack*, vilifying STAR Solutions and federal earmark purveyor Don Young as carpetbaggers, wasting our tax funds, recklessly sacrificing our air and land, the public's health and safety, our local economies, and our children's future on an altar of greed. Along with fierce fighters, RAIL Solution is blessed with visionaries. Michael Testerman and Dave Foster applied modern rail technology to our corridor to develop a freight rail service concept unique in the United States.

RAIL Solution operated on volunteer labor for four years before we were able to hire a part-time director. The organizing described in this chapter occurred without staff assistance. Volunteers donated uncounted hours. They lobbied the General Assembly; updated the Web site, supporter, and listserv lists; performed research; wrote op-eds; composed formal responses to VDOT; tabled at local events; presented the RAIL Solution story to local civic clubs and organizations; created and distributed the *Citizen*; and submitted resolutions to local governments. Hundreds commented at VDOT public hearings and attended the governor's transportation town meetings.

In all of 2003, we raised only $350 from outside our membership. By 2005, we needed $20,000 to print and distribute the *Citizen*. Congress was debating the final details of the SAFETEA-LU bill, including the STAR Solutions' federal earmark in a House-Senate joint committee. VDOT would soon schedule public hearings on its draft EIS, which completely excluded our rail concept. Yet, all but two organizations committed to funding change in Appalachia or the South, promoting citizen involvement in public policy or environmental protection, locked us out. Several funding agencies initially appeared to be an ideal fit. Yet, these grantors rejected our applications because they maintain applicant screens converging on demographic organizing and group process rather than outcomes. This bias discriminates in practice in favor of more established multi-issue organizations over emerging single-issue groups. In the view of these foundations and churches, fighting an environmental and economic crisis was not enough; it appeared to matter more who was doing the fighting.

Lacking outside financial resources to print and distribute the *Citizen*, we turned to our own members. Stopping all other activities, we trained volunteers to ask other members or potential supporters to contribute at least $100. In six months, we raised almost $20,000 for the *Citizen*. We distributed one-quarter million copies as an insert in regional and local newspapers throughout the I-81 corridor. It is good internal organizing to meet our own financial needs, but I recall feeling angry, frustrated, and isolated seeing so little institutional funding for our efforts.

The risks we took investing our energy in RAIL Solution began to pay off. Chairman Young introduced a nearly $900 million I-81 truck lane earmark in the 2004 federal transportation bill, but the bill failed to pass. Undeterred, Young came back in 2005, inserting some $600 million for the "demonstration project" in the transportation bill. The House bill passed with a $500 million earmark in it for exclusive truck lanes for I-81 in Virginia, a big step down from the $800 million STAR had promised to leverage from Congress. Using the prerogative of his chairmanship, Rep. Young slipped the earmark in just hours before the vote by the House. There was no opportunity to debate the project. The Senate version did not include any similar earmark.

Senator John Warner (R-Va.) sat on the House-Senate joint committee charged with marking up a compromise version of the separate House and Senate versions of the transportation reauthorization bill. RAIL Solution, its regional and national partner organizations,[21] and state and national trucking interests, opposed to high truck tolls, lobbied Senator Warner all year. Governor Mark Warner (D), Representative Bob Goodlatte (R-Va. 6th), and House of Delegates majority leader Morgan Griffith (R-Salem) lobbied in support of the earmark.

Senator Warner stayed neutral on the earmark controversy until the committee neared the end of its dealing. Then he announced he had supported the earmark. But Warner damned it with faint praise because the committee reported a series of three I-81 earmarks for Virginia, totaling "only" $142 million. Just $100 million of this amount was designated explicitly for I-81 truck-only lanes in the final SAFETEA-LU Act. There would be no $1.6 billion federal truck lane subsidy, as STAR had promised. Citizen organizing and lobbying had rolled back over 90 percent of the Young-STAR Solutions boondoggle. Presidential pressure to reduce transportation spending also played a role. The highly vaunted federal subsidy that had driven state support for the STAR proposal came down to an expensive but hollow gesture to campaign contributors. This was the beginning of the end for STAR Solutions.

RAIL Solution acted primarily as an environmental organization, but much of the public perceived and welcomed it simply as pro-rail. The citizens' group found fast friends and tenacious enemies in each political party. To maintain a political diversity of supporters, the group remained strictly nonpartisan. That tactic allowed openness left, right, and center. Organizing along the length of the interstate corridor also enhanced the group's legislative strategy. The I-81 corridor is divided among many delegate and senatorial districts, creating a substantial "I-81 caucus." In 2006, RAIL Solution authored a bill to reverse VDOT policy excluding a multistate rail alternative to massive highway construction in its EIS. Under the savvy leadership of conservative Republican delegate Ben Cline, RAIL Solution's bill mandating state study of that multistate rail option passed the Senate and House of Delegates unanimously. All other transportation legislation remained bottled up in a tug-of-war between an evenly divided Senate, a Republican-controlled House, and a Democratic governor.

In April 2006, one thousand citizens attended VDOT public meetings to comment on the I-81 draft EIS. The draft supported massive widening of I-81, but rejected truck-only lanes as excessive for projected demand, expensive, inflexible, even dangerous.[22] Ninety percent of the citizens opposed VDOT and STAR Solution's border-to-border widening plans; most endorsed a rail alternative. Truckers and shipping companies strongly opposed STAR Solutions' $129 per trip truck tolls. That opposition, along with the organizing by RAIL Solution, most certainly doomed the STAR project.[23]

Finally, in December 2007, its aspirations diminished from a $13 billion project to a $142 million truck hill-climbing lane, KBR quietly withdrew from STAR Solutions. VDOT responded in January 2008 by suspending all Public Private Transportation Act contract talks with STAR Solutions, ending a six-year engagement.

Despite the collapse of STAR Solutions in 2009, VDOT still planned for a mostly eight-lane I-81. Road building is VDOT's culture. Virginia Secretary of Transportation Pierce Homer, a key player in the PPTA process, became our principal adversary. He refused to meet with us even after Governor Tim Kaine directed him to do so during a 2006 meeting with RAIL Solution and the governor's transportation team.

Taking a cue from STAR, in 2009 RAIL Solution initiated a campaign to request federal financing to jumpstart construction of the steel interstate. Returning to our local resolution strategy, we urged governments to petition Congress to make I-81 a pilot project for a national steel interstate system. We had failed to build constructive bridges to the trucking industry, and so, in the absence of the STAR Solutions bogeyman, local officials with a background in trucking-related services succeeded in blocking several resolutions. In their eyes, the railroad potentially competes with trucks. Nevertheless, fifty-one resolutions were adopted in just six months.

Yet, Secretary Homer blocked initial efforts by Ninth District Virginia Congressman Rick Boucher (D) to place into the reauthorization of SAFETEA-LU a study for the Knoxville to Harrisburg segment as a pilot project for a national steel interstate system. This system would offer nationwide advantages for meeting goals articulated by the Obama administration, including vastly increased energy efficiency, fuel conservation, and public infrastructure as fiscal stimulus. The electric-powered national steel interstate system we described would also enhance safety and national security while reducing costs and environmental and public health damage related to highway widening. The Millennium Institute, in modeling options for the United States to contend with an oil-constrained future, found that "[t]he most positive result by every significant metric (GDP, greenhouse gas emissions, oil used) came from the combination of the two most environmentally positive policies: a massive push for electrified rail transportation . . . coupled with a massive push for renewable energy, to be completed by 2030."[24]

Many obstacles to making public investments in a private railroad remained. Still, RAIL Solution, in contrast to STAR Solutions, worked to leverage real public benefit from the private sector. It pressed Norfolk Southern to offer freight and passenger services that were not in the railroad's business plan. At this writing the I-81 steel interstate was still a distant dream.

In sum, RAIL Solution modeled civic involvement that reconceived and reinterpreted development schemes in human terms and at a scale suited to human understanding. The language the group used clearly illustrated each citizen's stake in preserving public ownership and control of I-81 as a local and regional asset. Though it didn't hesitate to attack its adversaries, RAIL Solution embraced a positive, realistic vision of how to handle the freight problem rather than adopting a preservationist or not-in-my-backyard stance. RAIL Solution employed computer technology to stretch conventional concepts of place and time. It constructed community out of the e-mail ether. Organizers must be alert, though, to employ personal contact where appropriate.

RAIL Solution devised a locally based strategy to attack a regional problem—building one small success upon another, it constructed power out of weakness.

The group urged local citizens across the corridor to propose a resolution before their city or county. This strategy strengthened the organization by being achievable and by creating the RAIL Solution supporter-base.

RAIL Solution consciously provided background at its meetings to make them welcoming to newcomers and offered almost immediate access to its listserv and to democratic decision making and policy generation. However, the group encountered some class conflict. Its few attempts to reach out to truckers and the trucking industry failed. These efforts would have benefited from greater priority, more skilled volunteers leading the effort, courage, and better timing. This failure prevented RAIL Solution from pressing state and federal officials more effectively.

Because both grantor and recipient benefit from their longstanding relationships, funding agencies make a leap of faith if they put aside preference for multi-issue groups. Multi-issue groups have broader perspective, more resources, greater stability, and a longer view. They can more flexibly address questions of class, race, and gender or other process issues at the center of a foundation's mission than groups with a tightly focused goal. These organizations frequently can point to proven track records and clearly established fiscal procedures. In contrast, single-issue groups may be here today and gone tomorrow—suffering from a failure of leadership or division, tactical or administrative blunders, or insufficient resources and funding. Yet, single-issue groups have the power of focus and clarity that generates popular energy.

Single-issue organizing is an often spontaneous, organic, energetic response of the people to perceived injustice. These organizing struggles take on issues that might otherwise be submerged in a multi-issue agenda. RAIL Solution undertook a task that multi-issue groups and conventional wisdom dismissed as unwinnable. Many communities will benefit if funding agencies take on more risk, ferreting out, welcoming, and supporting the work of worthy single-issue citizens' groups.

Every citizens' battle is potentially winnable, despite the entrenched power of corporate interests and their political allies. Winning requires that citizens fashion creative strategies and easily accessible democratic processes. Strategizing is not easy and requires some luck as well as creative thinking. Democratic process, on the other hand, is a learned skill and is achievable with persistence. Two RAIL Solution volunteers, summing up how group action afforded them meaning and efficacy, said of their experience, "From the beginning I thought of RAIL Solution as a very fine example of citizen organization and advocacy. Seeing that example in action is the greatest benefit I derived from my participation in the struggle." "We are changing the world. We are having more of an impact than I could have dreamed. Most of these are only battles which you might win today only to get stomped tomorrow. But if we build a railroad, we will have won the war, not just a skirmish. What more can we ever ask for but to make a real improvement in the world?"

Notes

1. RAIL Solution, *Shenandoah & Southwest Citizen,* "Speak up—Take Back Our 'Main Street,'" 2.

2. Virginia Department of Transportation, *I-81 Corridor Improvement Study: Tier 1 Draft Environmental Impact Statement,* 2005, 2–2.

3. Ibid.

4. Phillip Longman, "Back on Tracks: A Nineteenth-Century Technology Could Be the Solution to Our Twenty-First-Century Problems," *Washington Monthly,* January/February 2009, 24.

5. Morton Kondracke, ed., interview, "Driving Forward: Young Steers Transportation Reauthorization through Congress," *Roll Call,* May 5, 2003, 3.

6. Reason Foundation Web site, reason.org, lists scores of research reports on privatization. The foundation issues an annual "Privatization Report." It has issued reports titled: "Privatization Opportunities for States," "Mining the Government Balance Sheet: What Cities and States Have to Sell," "Virginia Spending and Budget Reform," and "How to Navigate the Politics of Privatization."

7. Robert Poole, "Report Identifies Best Toll Truckways Pilot Projects," *Surface Transportation Innovations,* no. 14 (February 2004) at http://reason.org/news/show/surface -transportation-innovat-13#feature1. In the report Poole brags:

> In June 2002, two Reason colleagues and I accomplished the seemingly impossible. We persuaded both the American Trucking Associations and the National Safety Council . . . to endorse . . . that these highly productive trucks (long doubles and triples) be allowed to operate . . . where they are currently banned by federal law, provided that they operate on new, barrier-separated truck-only lanes. . . . House Transportation & Infrastructure Committee Chairman Don Young (R, AK) liked the idea so much that he arranged a room for our news conference in the Rayburn building, and personally expressed his interest in the idea.
>
> Fast forward 20 months. The pending House reauthorization bill, TEA-LU, contains a provision for truck-only lanes, but thus far no specifics. To help Chairman Young and the Committee fill in the details, Reason is today releasing a new study which identifies . . . the 10 best routes. . . . And the winners [include] . . . I-81 from Knoxville, TN to Harrisburg, PA. . . .

8. Virginia Department of Transportation, 2–11.

9. "The Smokestack Effect: Toxic Air & America's Schools," *USA Today,* December 7, 2008. See http://content.usatoday.com/news/nation/environment/smokestack/index.

10. Rees Shearer, "For I-81 Overcrowding, Rail Is a Better Answer: Cheaper, Cleaner, Safer, and More Convenient," *Roanoke Times,* June 2, 2002.

11. Michael Testerman, "For the I-81 Corridor, a 'Steel Interstate' Is Better Than More Asphalt," *Roanoke Times,* September 22, 2002.

12. Friends of the Earth & Taxpayers for Common Sense, "Road to Ruin: The 27 Most Wasteful Road Projects in America." Now available at *Common Dreams* ("Elimination of the Most Wasteful, Environmentally Harmful Highway Projects Would Save Billions, according to New Report," June 2, 2004), http://www.commondreams.org/news2004/0603 -05.htm.

13. RAIL Solution, 2.

14. Ibid.

15. Ibid. Snake oil, indeed! At the time, lobbyist Randolph DeLay, another STAR Solutions partner, was CEO of the Texas firm Public/Private Strategies Consult. Randy is the brother of then-U.S. House majority leader and former House Speaker Tom "The Hammer" DeLay. At the state level, STAR Solutions partner McGuire Woods had helped conceive Virginia's Public Private Transportation Act of 1995. The firm's unabashed slogan *"Relationships that drive results"* plays on their access to power.

16. Citizens for Responsibility and Ethics in Washington, "CREW's Most Corrupt Members of Congress—Rep. Don Young, *(R-AK)*," http://www.crewsmostcorrupt.org/mostcorrupt/entry/most-corrupt-2008.

17. Kondracke, "Driving Forward," 3. In 2003, *Roll Call* reported that Young was able to flex his political brawn in a way few in Congress ever have:

ROLL CALL: Should we switch off to TEA-21 [federal transportation bill] . . . ?

YOUNG: It's "Tea-Lu." I'm serious about that. Transportation Equity Act, logistics unlimited or lanes unlimited or something like that, but it's going to be "Lu." And I don't care whether they want to make fun of that, I'm the chairman, that's what's going to happen.

ROLL CALL: And the "Lu" is what again?

YOUNG: That's my wife's name. [laughs]

18. RAIL Solution, 2.

19. Vanasse Hangen Brustlin, Inc., http://www.vhb.com/template_genco.asp?pagename =About_VHB; VHB's motto includes its commitment toward "maintaining clients for life."

20. RAIL Solution release: "Interstate 81 Public Private Transportation Act (PPTA) Advisory Panel," February 13, 2004.

21. On the national level, "Road to Ruin" partners—Friends of the Earth and Taxpayers for Common Sense—lobbied against wasteful, environmentally damaging federal spending; regional partners—Southern Environmental Law Center, Virginia Organizing, Rockbridge Area Conservation Council, Virginia Chapter Sierra Club, and the Piedmont Environmental Council projects (Coalition for Smarter Growth and Shenandoah Valley Network)—offered organizing and special project assistance along with links to the Shenandoah Valley Battlefields Foundation and the National Trust for Historic Places.

22. Virginia Department of Transportation, 3–29.

23. The Virginia Department of Transportation continues to study truck tolls ranging from $65 to $114. http://www.fhwa.dot.gov/programadmin/032003.cfm.

24. A. Drake, A. M. Bassi, E. L. Tennyson, and H. R. Herren, "Evaluating the Creation of a Parallel Non-Oil Transportation System in an Oil Constrained Future," The Millennium Institute, Arlington, Virginia, 2009, 1. www.millenniuminstitute.net/resources/ . . . /Transportation_MI09.pdf.

CHAPTER 3

This Land Is Your Land
Local Organizing and the Hegemony of Growth

Nina Gregg and Doug Gamble

The Hegemony of Growth

On a Sunday afternoon in February 2006, about fifty middle-aged white people listened to Matt Murray, chair of the Blount County Economic Development Board (EDB), address the annual meeting of The Raven Society (TRS) at the Blount County Public Library in Maryville, Tennessee. EDB's purpose is "to bring new industry to the area."[1] The goals of TRS, a local community organization, include promoting sustainable development and preserving the rural character of the county. As the meeting ended, someone asked if there was a limit to the growth the county could accommodate and retain its attractiveness as a place to live. Murray replied that the EDB did not consider that issue; its work was to encourage economic development. Asked when the county would have enough industrial growth, Murray replied, "I don't know the answer to that."[2]

The governments that finance the EDB (Blount County and the cities of Maryville and Alcoa) employ growth as their dominant economic development strategy. Underlying this strategy is an assumption that growth is necessary to fuel property and sales tax revenues, which are the primary financial resources for public services.[3] The resulting development efforts have catalyzed the formation of several community-based organizations.

In this chapter we consider three organizations that attempted to influence local governments' single-minded commitment to growth. We examine the histories, strategies, and successes of these groups, explore the extent to which a connection to place informed their activities, and speculate whether and how these endeavors could become part of a movement for sustainable communities. Our personal experiences[4] with these organizations inflect our analysis, and we remain involved in efforts to address these issues—which are not unique to Blount County or Appalachia. What we call the hegemony of growth—widespread popular consent to the dominant belief in unfettered growth as the only way to assure prosperity—and hostility toward attempts to guide, manage, or choose whether, how, and where a community grows—are the twin guardians of the status quo against which all three efforts contended.

Blount County, a gateway to the Great Smoky Mountains National Park (GSMNP) in east Tennessee, lies between Knoxville and North Carolina. Public land accounts for 33 percent of the county, agricultural and open space for 56 percent, and the remaining 11 percent is in residential, commercial, industrial, and other nonresidential uses.[5] Throughout the nineteenth and early twentieth centuries the county was primarily small-scale agricultural. In 1910, the Aluminum Company of America (ALCOA) began building seven hydroelectric dams and several large aluminum smelting and production facilities in the county. The corporation built the city of Alcoa as a company town, and industrialization began. By the mid-1950s, ALCOA was the largest employer in the county,[6] but the area remained primarily rural and the population stable. No serious economic development strategy existed.

Few thought that the county's unhurried and unplanned growth posed any serious problems until the 1970s, when the population increased significantly from 57,525 to 77,710. By 2005 the population reached 115,535,[7] and projections for 2020 range from 139,000 to 148,000.[8] Of the 2000 population, 70 percent (74,969 people) resided outside the city limits of Maryville and Alcoa.[9] The county is 94.7 percent white.[10]

Beginning in the 1970s, the overwhelming majority of the county's population increase resulted from net in-migration of new residents, a dramatic reversal from the 1950s, when more than seven thousand people left.[11] Strong linkages to metropolitan Knoxville and the county's internal characteristics drove this growth. Developable lowlands, recreation afforded by easy access to mountains and Tennessee Valley Authority (TVA) lakes, a tourist gateway to GSMNP, relatively good public schools, cooperation between county and city governments for economic development, low property taxes, attractive small towns, and rural character drew developers, families, and retirees. At the time of Murray's presentation to TRS, there was tenuous agreement about the need to guide the location of residential development and commercial enterprises.[12] Even though schools were overcrowded,[13] local roads carried far more vehicles than designed capacity, and the cost of providing community services surpassed revenue from property taxes,[14] few considered that growth itself should be restricted. Yet, simmering discontent about loss of "the small town and rural character of the county" was evident in public discourse.

A few months after TRS's annual meeting, a local newspaper, reporting the outcome of the primary election for Blount County mayor, quoted a prominent politician: "Tonight was a vote for pro-growth. Put that in your paper."[15] The winner was elected county mayor in August 2006 and, like the city managers of Maryville and Alcoa, consistently promoted growth as necessary and desirable.[16]

The Blount County planning director had conducted numerous public meetings over several years seeking input to the nonbinding "Policies Plan" that had as its first guiding policy "Preserve the County's rural, small town, and natural character."[17] Political and business leaders often proclaimed support for the plan, but considerable evidence supported public skepticism about their sincerity. The county mayor's appointments to the planning commission supported an environmentally destructive residential project on Chilhowee Mountain, a largely undeveloped area bordering the GSMNP.[18] These commissioners also proposed major zoning changes to accommodate a large private sports complex and commercial development in a rural area including a large wetland.[19] The proposed changes would have increased the allowed density of residential development in rural zones.[20] Later that year, the County Planning Commission removed restrictions on residential development in areas with overcrowded schools,[21] and public officials continued to advocate for a new interstate highway through a rural, agricultural, and undeveloped area.[22]

In counterpoint to these official actions was growing awareness of the consequences of the hegemony of growth. The assistant county mayor made presentations about the inadequacy of residential property tax to generate sufficient revenue to educate children from the new subdivisions.[23] A rezoning request mobilized opposition from realtors, who were beginning to understand that their ability to sell a desirable quality of life was threatened by inconsistent enforcement of zoning regulations.

In a context of little history of community-based organizing, any formal resistance is noteworthy, even when the number of people mobilized is small. The activists discussed in this chapter were responding to perceived threats to the larger community, a valued way of life, and their own livelihoods. Many were new to activism, and their concerns and relationships to the land were diverse. Their organizations differed in their analyses of the perceived threats and their strategies for intervening in governments' decision making. These differences reflected the context of each precipitating event as well as each organization's understanding of the issues and its own power. These differences also inform our reflections on whether and how a larger movement could strengthen local organizing.

Alternatives for Blount County

The sudden announcement in 1977 of plans for Smoky World, a huge theme park and condominium development, drew the county's first organized resistance to growth. Developers acquired 2,300 acres around Townsend and planned a thirteen-story Ferris wheel, two twenty-one-story apartment towers, and a two thousand–person convention center close to the GSMNP entrance and next to the Little River, source of Blount County's drinking water.[24] Townsend, population fewer than five hundred, lies at the westernmost Tennessee entrance to the GSMNP and is known as "the peaceful side of the Smokies," in intentional contrast with the entertainment and shopping orientation of nearby Pigeon Forge.[25] The Townsend Chamber of Commerce supported the project.[26]

Opposition built quickly, but without zoning, the County Planning Commission was powerless to stop the project. Keith Megginson, from the planning commission staff, said, "The people don't want zoning. Yet they're jealous of their rural community. It's the longtime residents who are objecting. They don't want such commercial development."[27]

Some longtime residents formed a nonprofit organization, Alternatives for Blount County (ABC), to "provide a citizen's forum which will investigate and publically [sic] present responsible directions" for development of the county.[28] ABC held its first public meeting in January 1978; citing potential pollution of the Little River by sewage disposal as well as traffic congestion and audio and visual pollution, ABC challenged the county's "do-nothing" policy regarding rapid development.[29]

A hurdle for Smoky World developers was the Tennessee Division of Water Quality Control's opposition to a wastewater treatment plant on the Upper Little River because of its threat to drinking water downstream and aquatic life and water contact recreation.[30] Encouraged by the state's position, ABC asked the U.S. Environmental Protection Agency (EPA) to conduct an environmental impact study. Before the study was completed, Smoky World faded from view, perhaps because developers had difficulties with financing or because they knew EPA was unlikely to sanction the treatment plant.

ABC's leaders focused on educating politicians and residents about the importance of land use planning. With volunteer labor and a small membership primarily of middle-class professionals, ABC adopted the phrase "Know Growth, Not No Growth," organized a forum on farmland preservation,[31] and distributed a newsletter about national and local land use issues. In 1981, the local newspaper editorialized in favor of countywide zoning,[32] but no politician dared raise the subject. ABC hoped to create changes in public policy through education, but the political climate was unreceptive.[33] Another twenty years would pass before the county adopted zoning.

One of ABC's founders, Gail Harris, a local farmer whose husband's family had deep roots in the county, turned to a different strategy for farmland preservation. She helped establish the Foothills Land Conservancy (FLC), "a Trust designed to protect agricultural land and other lands considered unique in the Foothills area of the Great Smoky Mountains."[34] The FLC relied on "purchase and resale as its primary means of preserving farmland"; advisors and board members included farmers, land use planners, ministers, attorneys, realtors, and a representative of the Blount County Chamber of Commerce. ABC voted to close shortly after FLC was incorporated in 1985, giving its resources to the new effort.[35] A membership

organization formed to change public policy was replaced by a public trust committed to "making use of the free enterprise system to achieve its goals."[36]

The Raven Society

In May 2000, the announcement of a proposed beltway southwest of Maryville
and Alcoa led to formation of The Raven Society. Several leaders of ABC and FLC
were involved in organizing opposition to the project, known as the Southern
Loop.[37] Leading beltway advocates were local governments, the Blount County
Industrial Development Board (later called the Economic Development Board),
and the Blount County Chamber of Commerce.[38]

Initial resistance came from property owners on or near the proposed route
of the beltway, but TRS's leadership and membership also included people who
wanted the county to remain rural and feared the project would encourage new
development and more roads. More significant was projection of how an interstate with commercial interchanges would irrevocably alter the serene foothills
of the Smoky Mountains. Unlike ABC, TRS explicitly sought political power and
intended "to raise money and support qualified candidates whose views are consistent with the goals that were expressed by the voters in the land use planning
survey, which was to keep the county rural."[39] Reflecting on ABC's history and
the formation of TRS, Gail Harris remarked, "If you give up at all, your battle is
lost. You have to keep the issues before the public."[40]

Encouraged by leaders previously frustrated by ABC's inability to influence
public policy, TRS became the county's first citizens' political action committee.
When the county commission in June 2000 adopted its first zoning plan, TRS
publicly commended commissioners who voted for zoning[41] and began to educate the public and support politicians who favored land use planning and rural
preservation.

Even after the Tennessee Department of Transportation (TDOT) declared the
Southern Loop too expensive to build "at the present time,"[42] for five weekends in
the winter of 2003–2004 members of TRS walked the proposed route and handed
out three thousand maps and phone numbers of elected officials. Residents who
opposed the project were encouraged to voice their opposition, but TRS members
neither circulated a petition nor took names of people who agreed with them.[43]
TRS wanted political power but at that time did not have an organizing strategy
to build that power; leaders believed people would take action once they had
sufficient information.

TRS has played a nonpartisan but aggressive role in local politics. TRS's treasurer put it this way: "The preservation of rural Blount County is the goal. That
appeals to both parties, both sides, and all factions of our society."[44] This diversity
is evident in TRS's membership, which includes middle-class professionals as
well as numerous farmers and rural working-class people. However, very few

members are under fifty, perhaps a reflection of the time commitment necessary and an awareness (from age and experience) that the county has changed in unsustainable ways. In local elections, TRS has endorsed and financially supported Republicans and Democrats for county mayor and county commission,[45] with some successes. TRS has sponsored public forums on farmland preservation and "smart growth" principles,[46] conducted public workshops on proposed revisions in county policies,[47] written and distributed analyses of proposed land use and zoning issues, and appeared at several standing-room-only public hearings and commission meetings.[48] TRS's analyses and participation in public hearings about zoning changes for the sports complex and to increase residential density in rural zones helped defeat those proposals[49] and raised awareness about the power of public pressure to influence policy.

Despite being nonpartisan, TRS is characterized by proponents of growth as a "Liberal, Left Wing" organization out to "kill our economy and take away our rights."[50] The controversies about land use mean that many people who support TRS will not do so publicly, and its board often talks about how and whether it should be less polarizing. The organization's identity remains in question: whether to continue as a PAC or to focus on educating the public and public officials about land use planning.

Citizens Against the Pellissippi Parkway Extension, Inc. (CAPPE)

Like ABC and TRS, CAPPE was organized in response to a precipitating event: a proposed interstate-grade highway through the largely agricultural and rural northeastern sector of Blount County. Like some founders of TRS, several people who formed CAPPE in early 2002 had a personal stake in the issue because their homes and livelihoods were threatened by the proposed highway. The majority of CAPPE supporters, a number of whom were also members of TRS, did not live near any of the routes under consideration; their engagement was based in concern about the broader impact of the new highway on the entire county.

The Pellissippi Parkway is part of a state program to promote economic development in Tennessee's rural counties. After the interstate between the Knoxville airport in Alcoa and Oak Ridge to the north was built, it was extended east to the corporate headquarters of a major employer and then another two miles to a state highway. Another segment, proposed as 4.4 miles curving through farms and the Little River valley and terminating a few miles north of the GSMNP entrance, became known as the Pellissippi Parkway Extension (PPE). The 2001 feasibility study that deemed the Southern Loop too costly to build as a single project recommended construction in segments; the PPE would become the northeastern quarter of the beltway.

CAPPE took shape in the living room of Susan Keller, a full-time farmer and life-long Blount County resident. Using a small ad in the newspaper inviting people to speak for or against the proposed highway, Keller convened a standing-room-only public meeting in the Blount County Courthouse.[51] After this meeting—at which only one person spoke in favor of the project—a small group of people, the majority of whom had never met, gathered at Keller's home to discuss their options. In a subsequent meeting they received pledges sufficient to retain an environmental attorney and decided to incorporate as a nonprofit organization with a mission to educate the public about the issues and impacts of the PPE.

From its beginning, CAPPE questioned the purpose and need for the highway. TDOT and advocates for the PPE (city and county governments, the Chamber of Commerce, the local newspaper, developers, and realtors) claimed, without any supporting analysis or data, that it would alleviate traffic congestion in the center of Maryville and be good for the county. CAPPE countered that the cities would benefit from sales tax revenues from commercial development at the highway interchanges, but Blount County would bear increased costs to provide services to the rural residential development that would inevitably follow the highway.

Dissatisfied with often repeated justifications that the PPE had been in regional transportation plans for decades, CAPPE developed a three-part strategy: influencing TDOT, governments, and the public. All three strategies came into play as CAPPE sued the Federal Highway Administration (FHWA), the U.S. Secretary of Transportation, TDOT, and the Tennessee Transportation Commissioner for failure to comply with the National Environmental Policy Act (NEPA), which required an environmental impact statement (EIS) for this type of federally funded project.[52] The circuit court issued an injunction halting all activity on the PPE until CAPPE's complaint could be heard.[53] Although no court ever ruled on CAPPE's complaint, both FHWA and TDOT agreed to conduct the EIS. CAPPE asked TDOT to include in the EIS's economic analysis an evaluation of the impact of PPE-induced growth on the county budget for schools, roads, and law enforcement, but TDOT refused, responding that the economic analysis for the EIS would consider only impacts on the private sector.[54] At the time of this writing, TDOT projects release of the final environmental impact statement (FEIS) in 2012. The FEIS must respond to all public comments on the draft EIS, which was issued in April 2010. CAPPE members dominated a crowded public hearing in July 2010, where they presented detailed analysis of the flaws and deficiencies in the DEIS, which included the economic impact analysis TDOT had earlier refused to do.[55]

CAPPE joined a statewide coalition focused on reforming TDOT. The agency was notorious for its dismissive attitude toward the public and for disregarding both state and federal regulations. The TDOT reform campaign was at the center of the 2002 gubernatorial election, and CAPPE, along with more than thirty other community groups, formed Citizens for TDOT Reform (CTR) to speak in a unified voice about changes expected from a new administration.[56] Candidate Phil Bredesen committed to "reform" TDOT if elected, and CTR shared credit for both Bredesen's election and a subsequent change in TDOT staff behavior and some agency practices.[57]

CAPPE's strategy to influence TDOT and local governments took several forms, including hosting a meeting with the new TDOT commissioner,[58] contracting with a transportation engineer for advice on alternatives to the PPE that CAPPE presented to TDOT, and presenting detailed analyses at TDOT's public workshops and hearings. CAPPE members maintained relationships with county commissioners, turned out in large numbers whenever transportation issues were on county commission agendas, and hosted a transportation issues forum with candidates for state Senate.[59] One notable early achievement was passage by the county commission, at CAPPE's request, of a resolution calling for TDOT to complete the mandatory EIS.[60] The county commission subsequently tabled a Chamber of Commerce resolution seeking the commission's support for the extension.[61]

CAPPE's visibility whenever transportation appeared on public meeting agendas paid off at a standing-room-only TDOT event in February 2008. A CAPPE member asked about the basis for TDOT's assurance that the PPE would alleviate traffic congestion in Maryville. The answer stunned both TDOT representatives and local officials; TDOT's analysis showing very limited and short-lived "improvements" in traffic flow assumed that the Southern Loop and two other proposed road projects—none of which was funded—would also be completed.[62] CAPPE responded that TDOT's credibility depended on new analyses with the current road system, not speculations about future projects.

Early on, CAPPE circulated a petition and held a series of "on the road" public meetings featuring county officials addressing transportation planning, costs of community services, and road maintenance. Later CAPPE worked with a coalition to ask the Tennessee congressional delegation to impose "fix it first" restrictions on transportation spending in the 2009 federal economic stimulus package. Annual events like the yearly membership meeting, Rural Preservation Party, Chili Fest, and a benefit concert received coverage by local media, attracted the general public, and provided opportunities to keep CAPPE's perspective in circulation. CAPPE has an extensive Web page and its supporters frequently contribute letters to the editor of the local newspaper (which repeatedly endorses the PPE).[63]

Place as a Feature of Local Organizing and Identity

Attachment to place figured differently in these organizations' formation. The founders of ABC were alarmed by a threat to "our mountains—we felt it [Smoky World] would ruin the county,"[64] and used Smoky World to call attention to dangers posed by unregulated growth. FLC depended on landowners' place-based affinities to put conservation easements on their own property. TRS consistently presented itself as a place-based organization. One leader, who took action after realizing the Southern Loop would pass close by her family land, said: "I am from here. My grandpa lived next to my father; my uncle and cousin lived across the street. You have only one homeplace."[65] Another TRS founder wrote, "My family has 400 acres of farm land . . . that my grandfather . . . bought and which will soon go to his fourth generation of descendants. We see ourselves as stewards entrusted with the responsibility to protect the land for future generations, not to exploit it for our personal financial gain."[66] The original route proposed for the PPE would have bisected CAPPE founder Susan Keller's farm; "farmers have a special connection to the land," she said, after admitting that if the proposed route had followed her farm's boundary she "wouldn't have liked it" but probably would not have become involved. "My primary motivation was our livelihood. I knew what roads did . . . and there is no way to replace lost farmland. I wasn't thinking about the future of the county as much as I do now."[67]

Though members of TRS and CAPPE have deep personal connections to place, these connections do not often rise to organizational consciousness, discourse, or strategy. TRS, which clearly articulated preservation of place in its mission, is better known for advocating smart growth principles and analyzing land use policy than for directly preserving Blount County. It has never, for example, recruited members based on family heritage as Blount Countians. CAPPE holds rural preservation parties, but is better known for interfering with the local power elite's plans for development. Even when connections to place have moved individuals to activism, there has not been an explicit or consistent relationship between those motivations, the organizations' missions and strategies, and perceptions of these organizations in the community.

Another dimension of place is strategy driven by the location of decision makers who determine land use and development. For ABC and TRS, state and federal agencies had some role; however, both groups focused on influencing local governing bodies with authority to regulate land use. CAPPE sued state and federal authorities, but the real contest remained at home because the PPE would die without local government support. Despite their common focus on influencing local decision-making bodies, TRS and CAPPE never formally linked their efforts.

Members of all three organizations, like most county residents, have tended to live in rural areas outside incorporated cities, but power is inverse to population: city residents have more influence because professionals, civic leaders, and institutions are based there. This membership/power division constrained both strategy and impact. For example, Susan Keller approached the Farm Bureau and the Blount Farmers Cooperative about opposing the PPE, but both declined to get involved. "No one would help me," she recalled. "Maybe we have to help ourselves."[68]

These orientations toward local opinion and governing bodies shaped how each organization related to broader movements and larger organizations. ABC leaders attended national Trust for Public Land (TPL) conferences and brought ideas home, but the relationship with TPL did not advance ABC's original public policy agenda. TRS promoted its objectives through "smart growth," a nationally recognized set of principles emphasizing confining growth to urban centers and encouraging the preservation of open spaces; however, advocacy of "smart growth" does not challenge the idea that growth is necessary and desirable. Although TRS's interest in smart growth does potentially put the organization in alliance with people all over the country who share common principles, this interest is strategically focused on how the concept can advance TRS's local agenda, not on how the organization can become part of something larger.[69]

Focus on place led to strategies directed toward local decision-making authorities. For example, CAPPE became part of a statewide coalition to reform TDOT because of the importance of TDOT in the 2002 gubernatorial campaign. The coalition enabled participating organizations to speak with one voice to agencies they were confronting in common, but offered little help with the hometown struggle.

As these examples show, local groups will join larger efforts when they can see how doing so will advance their own agenda. Until local groups understand the relevance to their own struggle of what is occurring elsewhere, they are unlikely to expend personal and organizational resources to form alliances beyond their community.[70] When regulatory bodies are local, the value of coalitions that cross geographic boundaries is not clear; people need principled reasons, more than place-based reasons, to form such alliances.[71]

Prospects for Change

Sociologist Xavier de Souza Briggs refers to the capacity to devise, decide, and act collectively to improve our lives as *civic capacity*.[72] Many components of civic capacity are present in Blount County, but local governing bodies and other institutional leaders do not want them exercised in concert. They welcome newcomers as positive evidence of growth while discouraging their participation in civic life. The county mayor referred to activists who challenged his agenda as "far-left loons. They've landed here in Blount County. . . . If you don't believe me, come to one of my County Commission meetings and you watch them perform."[73] The mayor's characterization of anyone asking questions as left-wing and a newcomer exploited historic suspicion of outsiders, even though he knew that many TRS and CAPPE activists have deep roots in the community and are life-long Republicans. The mayor was not alone in his sentiments about civic action; county government remains conservative, insular, and resistant to change and new ideas.

Traditional voting patterns combined with successful politicians' consistent views on growth make fundamental policy change unlikely: change in understanding and perceptions among those in power will be necessary before civic capacity can be tapped to address the hegemony of growth. The limited impact of citizen action on local governing bodies and the city-county divide raise the question of whether alliances beyond the county would provide citizens greater leverage. These community organizations did have impact, especially relative to their size and lack of conventional power, but becoming part of larger movements would not have appreciably altered the power dynamics in the communities where local decisions were made. TPL and Smart Growth America were vital sources of ideas but contributed no political clout locally. Greater leverage is more likely to come from civic leaders persuaded to consider ideas from forward-thinking counterparts elsewhere in the country—and the three community groups have pushed them in that direction. Blount County's participation in East Tennessee Quality Growth (ETQG), a sixteen-county organization formed in 2009 to "create a vision of quality growth, and promote and facilitate this vision through regional cooperation and local action,"[74] may do the same. For example, in 2010 Blount County representatives to ETQG led the creation of the Blount Green Infrastructure Network to generate public support for the county's adoption of a green infrastructure plan.

In analyzing a successful regional planning effort in Utah, de Souza Briggs emphasizes the important difference between "interests" ("what we want or think we want") and "values" ("principles that define who we are") and argues that a values-based constituency for contentious decisions is more sustainable than one based on interests.[75] The activists in ABC, TRS, and CAPPE, whose interests included slowing the pace of change and preserving family livelihoods, rarely attempted to articulate shared values like comprehensive public planning, a diverse economy including agriculture, and attachment to place that could have attracted people for whom Smoky World, the Southern Loop, or the PPE were not a major concern.[76] Envisioning sustainable communities would allow people with very different concerns and interests to identify what they have in common. Like clean air or water, the concept of sustainable communities and the values this concept represents extend beyond local places and issues.

If mainstream institutions like the Chamber of Commerce, the EDB, the U.S. Natural Resources Conservation Service, and the Farm Bureau worked with other local constituencies to define and endorse a vision of a "sustainable community," this would help shift the perceptions of those in power. Mainstream community organizations like Keep Blount Beautiful, the Little River Watershed Association, and FLC (all of which avoid any controversial land use issues) might join such a coalition. As Susan Keller speculated, "We need to come together instead of being our own little island. There is a lot we could do if we came together."[77] Steps taken in one location toward building a sustainable community—whether focused on transportation, land use, jobs, or housing—could be adapted to advance goals in Blount County. Perhaps more important for bridging issues, geography, and the locus of decision-making authority, "sustainable communities" invokes values and principles, not a fixed set of policies or models.

Organizing to ensure a sustainable community or planet is a global challenge that offers a way for community groups to be proponents of desirable and necessary visions. Taking up this position would be different from (but related to) organizing opposition to "growthmania" and its partners, consumerism and commercialism.[78] Deepening awareness and analysis of the relationship of their local issues to the hegemony of growth—if that analysis offered an alternative—could connect local groups to values and visions of what they wish to create instead of what they oppose. Opposition to the hegemony of growth is the flip side of promoting a sustainable planet; both projects can seem abstract and overwhelming, while providing ways to unite local struggles over growth and the economics of land use with values- and principle-based movements.

The challenge of transforming our consumption-based culture to a sustainable one has mobilized many young people across the globe, but very few young people were engaged in the three organizations featured in this chapter. The impact of poor land use planning—unless the threat is dramatic and visible, like mountaintop removal mining—is gradual. Older residents of the county have witnessed the insidious creep of sprawl and its consequences for a cherished way of life, but young people have not.

There is more attention now in Blount County than in the 1980s to the nature and merits of growth because of wider understanding of the planet's capacity to sustain our way of life, the economic advantages of a more intentional approach to planning, and the importance of viewscapes for the area's tourism. A series of events (planning commission discussion of ridgetop development, public seminars on "sustainable tourism," a county government–sanctioned study committee on purchase of development rights, and adoption of a green infrastructure plan) challenge property rights advocates and individualism. The hegemony of growth was and is sustained in part because there are few examples of viable alternatives. The cumulative impact of ABC, TRS, and CAPPE demonstrated the capacity of small, well-informed groups to bring formerly unscrutinized actions of local government to public awareness, create space for new ideas, and slow the pace of development, even as overall trends persist.

ABC tried to educate Blount Countians about alternatives that were unheard of in east Tennessee in the 1980s. The idea that growth itself (understood to mean increased population and development) is not sustainable or desirable occupies a similar place in the public consciousness as did "smart growth" a few years ago.

It may be possible to discuss making Blount County a "sustainable community" as long as this does not imply being "against growth."

To have sustainable communities, we need sustainable businesses and public services. A growing number of economists believe that the hegemony of growth must be challenged directly to meet human needs and avoid environmental disaster;[79] we will need a very different kind of economy. The solidarity economy, which aims to create sustainable communities, is a values-based movement better known in Canada, South America, Europe, and Asia than in the United States.[80] The solidarity economy could offer a scope beyond local experiences as well as values and principles to aid in overcoming conflicting interests. Though activists in Blount County were not motivated by a critique of capitalism, a values-based vision of alternatives to the dominant model of economic growth might bring these and other locally focused groups together. Few in Blount County would respond favorably to a critique of the profit motive, but many would endorse the values of the solidarity economy: reciprocity, democracy, sustainability, and equity.

Although the term "solidarity economy" itself would be a conceptual and rhetorical barrier to change, the institutionalization of solidarity economy principles in cooperatives, credit unions, and complementary supply chains is already familiar. The principles of sustainable communities and the values of the solidarity economy provide a platform for focusing on quality of life instead of growth of goods and wealth, and together could help Mr. Murray and the EDB reconsider their mission and answer the question, "What kinds of growth do we want and where?"

Notes

1. http://www.blountindustry.com/about.html.

2. *Daily Times* (Maryville), January 30, 2006, and Doug Gamble's notes.

3. "Growth" occurs when new factories, subdivisions and commercial/retail enterprises result in the quantitative increase in the production and consumption of goods and services that are subject to property and/or sales taxes. For economists' definitions of "growth," see James G. Speth, *The Bridge at the Edge of the World: Capitalism, the Environment, and Crossing from Crisis to Sustainability* (New Haven, Conn.: Yale University Press, 2008), 110.

4. Gamble was a member of Alternatives for Blount County and on the board of The Raven Society from 2005 until 2011. He has been a member of Citizens Against the Pellissippi Parkway Extension (CAPPE) since its inception, is on the board of East Tennessee Quality Growth, and helped form the Blount Green Infrastructure Network. Gregg helped organize CAPPE and is on its board.

5. *Blount County Green Infrastructure Plan* (Blount County, Tenn., July 23, 2009), 8.

6. Inez E. Burns, *History of Blount County, Tennessee from War Trail to Landing Strip, 1795–1955,* rev. ed. (Mt. Vernon, Ind.: Windmill Publishing, 1988), 232–33.

7. Environmental Health Action Team, Blount County, Tenn., *Action Plan and Issue*

Profile: Addressing Environmental Health Issues of Land Use, Growth, and Development, Outdoor Air Quality, and Water Quality (Blount County, Tenn., Jan. 2007), 2.

8. Hunter Interests, Inc., *Blount County Growth Strategy,* May 2, 2005, Technical Memorandum #1, 5.

9. Environmental Health Action Team, *Action Plan,* 2.

10. U.S. Census, 2000.

11. Blount County Planning Department, based on U.S. Census, 2000.

12. Murray said, "[y]ou can have growth and development two different ways: One, you can let . . . people do whatever they want to do, and then you can mitigate the problems associated with that growth. The alternative is to plan for growth. Play an active role in the front end in planning for the community's future." "Economic Official Urges Public to Guide Growth," *Daily Times,* January 30, 2006.

13. Darren Dunlap, "Growing Pains—Planning Commission Wrestles with School Growth," *Daily Times,* September 7, 2003.

14. *Cost of Community Services Study,* Blount County, Tenn., July 2006, http://www.farmlandinfo.org/documents/30993/BlountTN_COCS_final_report.pdf.

15. *Daily Times,* May 3, 2006.

16. Iva Butler, "City Manager: Growth Keeps Maryville Prosperous," *Daily Times,* May 13, 2008.

17. *Blount County Policies Plan,* adopted June 24, 1999, by the Blount County Planning Commission.

18. *Daily Times,* June 24, 2006.

19. *Blount Today,* April 19, 2007.

20. *Daily Times,* March 7, 2007.

21. *Daily Times,* August 26, 2008.

22. *Daily Times,* January 29, 2002; see also *Blount Today,* February 20, 2008.

23. David R. Bennett, "The Economics of Growth in Blount County," presented for CAPPE, May 23, 2005.

24. *Maryville-Alcoa Times,* October 20, 1977.

25. See http://www.smokymountains.org/.

26. *Maryville-Alcoa Times,* January 31, 1978.

27. *Knoxville Journal,* November 11, 1977.

28. *Knoxville Journal,* January 28, 1978.

29. *Maryville-Alcoa Times,* January 30, 1978.

30. Tennessee Water Quality Control, Knoxville Basin Office, *Environmental Impact Notice of Studies, Little River, Blount County, October 1979.*

31. *Maryville-Alcoa Times,* November 23, 1979.

32. *Maryville-Alcoa Times,* October 2, 1981.

33. Authors' interview with Gail Harris, December 22, 2008.

34. *Foothills Forum* 2 (May 1985).

35. Authors' interview with Gail Harris, December 22, 2008.

36. *Foothills Forum* 2 (May 1985).

37. *Daily Times,* May 16, 2000.

38. *Daily Times,* March 9, 2001.

39. *Daily Times,* May 16, 2000.

40. Authors' interview with Gail Harris, December 22, 2008.

41. *Daily Times,* June 22, 2000.

42. *Daily Times,* March 9, 2001.

43. *Daily Times,* November 3, 2003, and February 4, 2004.

44. *Daily Times,* October 31, 2004.

45. *Daily Times,* July 28, 2006.

46. *Daily Times,* October 3, 2007, and January 25, 2008.

47. *Daily Times,* March 6, 2006.

48. *Blount Today,* April 19, 2007; The Raven Society, "Analysis of Proposed Zoning Regulations and Their Relationship to Tennessee Public Chapter 1101 and Quality Growth in Blount County," March 2007.

49. "Proposed Sports Complex: Out for County, In for Alcoa?" *Blount Today,* June 13, 2007.

50. *Daily Times,* May 1, 2006, in a paid ad titled "Beware the Raven Society."

51. Joel Davis, "Citizens Speak Out Against Extension," *Daily Times,* January 30, 2002.

52. FHWA Code of Federal Regulation (23 CFR § 771.115).

53. "Judge Halts Pellissippi Extension," *Daily Times,* July 18, 2002.

54. Leslie Bales-Sherrod, "More Data Sought on Parkway Extension," *Daily Times,* October 11, 2006.

55. "Pellissippi Project Foes Speak Out," *Daily Times,* July 21, 2010.

56. "Group Calls for Changes to TDOT," *Daily Times,* March 14, 2003.

57. In 2011, a new governor whose family business depends on the transportation and highway sectors took office, a reminder of the fleeting nature of success in electoral politics.

58. "TDOT Head Hears CAPPE Concerns," *Daily Times,* February 7, 2003.

59. "CAPPE to Host Forum for Senators," *Daily Times,* October 9, 2004.

60. Board of Commissioners of Blount County, Tenn., "A Resolution Regarding an Environmental Assessment for the Proposed Pellissippi Parkway Extension," May 20, 2002.

61. Darren Dunlap, "Committee Tables (Chamber) Resolution Seeking Support of Parkway Extension," *Daily Times,* March 5, 2003.

62. "Parkway Packs 'em In," *Daily Times,* February 20, 2008.

63. www.discoveret.org/cappe.

64. Authors' interview with Gail Harris, December 22, 2008.

65. Authors' interview with Laurie Leslie, January 18, 2009.

66. "One Reader Ready," *Daily Times,* March 24, 2000.

67. Authors' interview with Susan Keller, January 13, 2009.

68. Ibid.

69. See www.smartgrowth.org. For limitations of "smart growth," see Edward T. McMahon, "Stopping Sprawl by Growing Smarter," *Planning Commissioners Journal,* no. 26 (Spring 1997): 3–5.

70. CAPPE supported RAIL Solution, a Virginia group focused on improving rail capacity along the I-40/I-81 corridor and WaysSouth, headquartered in Georgia, because both address Tennessee transportation issues.

71. In *Contesting Community: The Limits and Potential of Local Organizing* (New Brunswick, N.J.: Rutgers University Press, 2010), James DeFillipis, Robert Fisher, and Eric Shragge consider "how, if at all, local communities and their organizations can contribute to the process of social change" (13).

72. Xavier de Souza Briggs, *Democracy as Problem Solving: Civic Capacity in Communities across the Globe* (Cambridge, Mass.: MIT Press, 2008), 11.

73. "Cunningham Calls Commission Democrats 'Monkeys.'" *Daily Times,* May 10, 2008.

74. http://www.etqg.org/BoD-resources/ETQGprogramPlan20090812.pdf.

75. De Souza Briggs, *Democracy as Problem Solving,* 71–72.

76. In 2002 CAPPE resisted appeals to join a campaign against a state income tax. The board asserted the organization's mission and consistently avoids issues that would divide membership.

77. Authors' interview with Susan Keller, January 13, 2009.

78. For growthmania, see Speth, *The Bridge at the Edge of the World,* 46–49.

79. Ibid., 111–25.

80. Yvon Poirier and Emily Kawano, "Another Economy Is Possible! Visions Related to Building the Solidarity Economy and Related Alternatives in North America." Paper submitted to Alliance for a Responsible, Plural and Solidarity-based Economy (ALOE) and RIPESS North America, July 2008, 21; see http://www.populareconomics.org/ussen/ and http://aloe.socioeco.org/documents.php3?id_rubrique=51&lang=en.

CHAPTER 4

Identity Matters

Building an Urban Appalachian Movement in Cincinnati

Phillip J. Obermiller, M. Kathryn Brown, Donna Jones,
Michael E. Maloney, and Thomas E. Wagner

Ernie Mynatt was an early leader in the Appalachian identity movement in Cincinnati. The Hazard, Kentucky, native saw that low-income migrants to Cincinnati would not receive human services as long as they remained an invisible minority. He once jokingly suggested, "We ought to paint 'em green" before the migrants, many from the eastern Kentucky coalfields, crossed the Ohio River into the city.[1]

Others from the Appalachian mountains had been coming to Cincinnati since the early 1800s. Following World War II, mountaineers came by the thousands to find jobs in southwestern Ohio. A part of this Great Migration, Mynatt, a former schoolteacher, became a social worker and organizer in the city's Appalachian neighborhoods.[2]

Identifying the needs of Appalachian newcomers to social service providers based in heavily Appalachian neighborhoods such as Over-the-Rhine was a substantial part of Mynatt's job. A charismatic leader, he influenced the growing Appalachian community and reached out to other key constituencies as well, building strong working relationships with civic activist Louise Spiegel, philanthropist Stuart Faber, the Boy Scouts' Ted Parker, the Junior League's Diane Williams, Xavier University professor Frank Foster, and human-relations pioneer Virginia Coffey, among others. Mynatt's organizing efforts eventually led to the formation of a succession of Appalachian groups and organizations including the initial Appalachian Committee, the youth-oriented Appalachian Identity Center, and ultimately the Urban Appalachian Council (UAC), an advocacy organization that celebrated its thirty-fifth anniversary in October 2009.

Another dimension to Mynatt's concept of identity remains deeply embedded in Cincinnati's Appalachian movement and its various organizations.[3] Mynatt knew that *some* urban Appalachians needed help with basics such as food, clothing, housing, and jobs, but *the majority* needed help embracing their identity as Appalachians. He believed that to flourish in the city, newcomers and their

Ernie Mynatt began his career in Over-the-Rhine as a roving boys' worker. (Photo by Daniel J. Ransohoff, courtesy of Cincinnati Museum Center–Cincinnati Historical Society Library)

descendants—regardless of their class—needed the psychological security of knowing who they were.[4]

In this chapter we think of identity in terms of Appalachian heritage, rather than culture. For some, Appalachian culture infers a set of distinctive social characteristics by which a group can be clearly distinguished from the dominant culture—a tall order for mostly white, English-speaking Protestants with deep roots in the United States. By heritage we mean a shared sense of being a people, a self-identification expressed in the migrants' associational patterns—primarily in kinship networks and shared neighborhoods, then in churches, unions, worksites, and even bars. Early migrants did not use formal categories such as "migrant" or "Appalachian" (those would come later). They knew who they were, perhaps a "country girl" or a "good old boy," and sought out others like themselves. Attached to this sense of peoplehood were secondary traits such as a mountain dialect, or preferences in recreation, food, dance, and music, but these were more fungible than fundamental.

As Appalachian migrants replicated patterns of earlier ethnic immigrants, they were ostracized by Cincinnatians fearing competition for jobs, loss of home values, deterioration of the public schools, and rising crime rates. Many long-term residents saw the migrants as challenging the social order of the city, and responded with negative stereotypes and discrimination. Mynatt simply made the migrants' sense of peoplehood explicit with the term "Appalachian" and worked to create a positive group identity to counteract the labeling and bigotry.

Appalachians in Cincinnati were clearly a "group" both in their own eyes and in the eyes of the host population. But were they a "minority" group? Many Appalachians share the same class status as African Americans in Cincinnati—scientific surveys and census tract data collected in greater Cincinnati since 1970 show that many white Appalachian residents have job statuses, average incomes, and educational attainment levels much closer to those of African Americans than those of non-Appalachian white residents.[5] Other research has shown that black migrants from Appalachia identified more closely with the urban black community than with white Appalachians in the city.[6] Although class mobility was a possibility open to some members of both minority groups, only white Appalachians could aspire to assimilate socially because they were not subject to racism.

Though class mobility was an option for white Appalachian migrants, it was not a foregone conclusion. Upward mobility occurred on some indicators such as income, while not occurring on others such as education. Both the rate and degree of social and economic mobility among Appalachian migrants and their progeny were affected by variables such as location or socioeconomic status. Appalachian enclaves still exist all over southwestern Ohio, while poverty remains an issue for some urban Appalachians. Nevertheless, the majority of Appalachian migrants and their descendants discussed here now live in multiethnic, working-class neighborhoods in and around Cincinnati.[7]

Throughout this chapter we use the concepts of race, class, and gender to introduce some of the struggles of the Appalachian movement in Cincinnati over the last half-century. Underlying each of these concepts is the important subtext of Appalachian identity. Having a sense of identity has been an important element in building lasting Appalachian-controlled institutions; negotiating coalitions with other groups, especially African Americans; crossing class boundaries to further Appalachian interests; and standing up for health-related needs in Appalachian neighborhoods.

Establishing an explicit Appalachian identity was neither easy nor uniform. Many urban Appalachians preferred and still prefer standard class, neighborhood, or occupational identities. This is especially true for second-, third-, and subsequent-generation Appalachians for whom negative stereotypes have made these the easiest options. Even having a strong sense of one's Appalachian heritage does not necessarily guarantee all goals will be met when negotiating with government agencies, urban powerbrokers, or other advocacy organizations. Appalachian identity has both benefits and limits in creating social change.

In the first two sections we describe how a shared Appalachian identity among primarily first-generation migrants was instrumental in negotiating the difficult terrain of urban race and class relations. In the final section we show how second-generation migrants' gender and neighborhood affiliation combine with

Appalachian identity, increasing the group's effectiveness in organizing around neighborhood health issues.

Crossing Race Boundaries: Cooperation and Conflict

Urban Appalachians' efforts to organize a movement for recognition and inclusion in Cincinnati involved both cooperation and conflict with other minority groups. The first phase of the struggle involved control over community organizing and social service resources. In the 1960s Mynatt joined forces with African American leaders Paul Henry and Virginia Coffey to form the Uptown Basin Council, a racially integrated grassroots effort to improve the Over-the-Rhine community (O-T-R). However, when the War on Poverty came to town in the mid-'60s, O-T-R was not included as a target area. Using Kentucky political contacts, Mynatt secured a Pilot Cities project grant to establish Hub Services, Inc., one of the federal program's fourteen experimental urban social service centers, in O-T-R. As with the Uptown Basin Council effort, the Hub board and staff were racially integrated. For example, the CEO and head of intake were African Americans, while the deputy director was white. Michael Maloney, a white Appalachian leader, was head of outreach, with Mattie Sutton, an African American, as his assistant.

Sutton cautioned Maloney that, "You need to do some work with your own people. You can't tag along on the civil rights movement."[8] Her advice led Maloney, Mynatt, and Ted Parker to form United Appalachian Cincinnati, one of the Urban Appalachian Council's predecessors, which was active from 1968 through 1970.

By 1970 it was clear that Appalachians were forming and participating in interracial coalitions, but some neighborhood agencies proved unable to run integrated recreation programs for youth. This was a time of extreme racial tension and violence in Cincinnati. As racial polarization increased, Maloney found that Appalachian youth were angry at their exclusion from neighborhood youth centers because they were white. After confirming this perception, Maloney, Parker, and Mynatt opened the Appalachian Identity Center under the auspices of the Berea-based Council of the Southern Mountains. This center provided a place where Appalachian youth could "hang out" and interact with older, more settled members of groups such as Sons of Appalachia and Daughters of Appalachia.

In 1972 the Cincinnati Human Relations Commission (CHRC) hired Maloney as a research and Appalachian specialist. Under CHRC auspices Maloney, with the aid of Virginia Coffey, Stuart Faber, and Frank Foster, created the Appalachian Committee Maloney staffed.[9] In 1974 the committee merged with the Appalachian Identity Center to form the Urban Appalachian Council, with Maloney as executive director. This allowed CHRC to retain its primary focus on race relations, while Appalachians built a stronger, more independent organization to address their specific interests throughout inner-city Cincinnati and beyond.

The federal government and many American cities responded to the increasing political power of African Americans by setting up programs principally designed to address their needs. This made it harder for UAC to secure funding for youth programs and other services in low-income, white communities. The problem persists to this day when token contracts are doled out to UAC in a way that ironically resembles the way black leaders in Cincinnati were treated prior to the civil rights movement. When Maloney expressed frustration at this treatment to his friend Bill Mallory, an African American and former Ohio House majority leader, Mallory responded, "A majority will always act like a majority," indicating that African Americans held more political power than Appalachians and were simply acting accordingly.[10]

The mix of intergroup cooperation and conflict continued unabated. In the late 1970s a city bureaucrat proposed that Cincinnati "triage" inner city neighborhoods and withdraw all public investment from areas deemed too blighted to recover. UAC helped organize the interracial Inner City Neighborhood Coalition, which succeeded in making sure that this policy was not imposed on low-income Appalachians and African Americans.

During the same period, Appalachian leaders appealed to Cincinnati's first African American mayor, Theodore Berry, to reopen bidding on a federally funded employment and training program grant. After being presented with evidence that urban Appalachians were excluded from these programs, Mayor Berry summed up the Appalachian case: "What you are seeking is parity."[11] The bidding was reopened and UAC received a $250,000 contract.

A key example of interracial cooperation is the Charter Committee, Cincinnati's reform party founded during the Progressive Era to end ward politics and boss rule. Charter produced the first black and female members of Cincinnati's city council, as well as the first white Appalachian candidate for city council, Michael Maloney. Executive directors of UAC, excluded from Republican and Democratic inner circles, have regularly served on the Charter Committee board. Charter provided a framework for friendship and cooperation between Appalachian and African American leaders such as Marian Spencer, the first African American and Appalachian woman to serve on the city council. The Appalachian Political Action Committee (AppalPAC) organized support for Spencer and other Charter and progressive candidates.

Personal friendships shaped interracial alliances, too. Former Cincinnati Mayor Dwight Tillery, an African American, befriended AppalPAC member Charlene Dalton, who made sure that AppalPAC supported him when he ran for office. When he became director of the Closing the Health Gap program, Tillery included Appalachians, although never beyond the level of tokenism. In 2003, Tillery organized Black PAC to increase minority representation on the council. Black PAC and AppalPAC leaders developed a list of candidates both groups could support. Tillery was dissatisfied with the election-day results, and this kind of joint effort has not been repeated.

Since the 1990s Latinos have gained visibility on Cincinnati's social and political scene—leading to a mixture of intergroup competition and street violence, as well as instances of cooperation and mutual support. In the heavily Appalachian neighborhood of Lower Price Hill (LPH), for example, there have been incidents of drug-related violence between Appalachian and Latino youth. At the same time, the neighborhood saw the establishment of English for Speakers of Other Languages classes at the LPH Community School, as well as the inclusion of Latina residents in a women's health survey conducted by neighborhood women.

Crossing Class Boundaries: The Appalachian Festival

In the 1950s public perception of Appalachian migrants in Cincinnati was strongly—and negatively—affected by Berea College's Roscoe Giffin. He served as the principal speaker for a workshop on the southern mountaineer sponsored by the Cincinnati Mayor's Friendly Relations Committee. Following a behavioral model, Giffin maintained that southern Appalachian migrants (SAMS) were from a "dysfunctional mountain culture" with values contrary to "the modern 'rational' model of city living."[12] Although Giffin's remarks were meant to help urban professionals "understand" mountain folk in the city, they reinforced negative images of migrants characterized by such terms as "hillbilly," "briarhopper," and "ridgerunner."

Ten years later, Mynatt began to use identity-based organizing to build the self-esteem of the city's Appalachian population. Mynatt's approach was "let's teach Appalachians who they are."[13] Mynatt recruited cross-cultural ambassadors, including Diane Williams and other members of Cincinnati's Junior League, as allies in furthering Appalachian advocacy efforts.

Mynatt's outreach to the Junior League brought quick returns. In 1969 Williams and Sally Brush represented the Cincinnati League at a regional conference in Charleston, West Virginia, on the topic of Appalachian migrants living in midwestern cities. At the end of the conference each delegation was asked to present a plan for addressing the issues raised by Appalachian migrants. Williams and Brush decided, "we were going back and try to persuade our League to make a major contribution to raising the consciousness in the greater Cincinnati community to the cultural contributions that urban Appalachians have made in our community."[14]

The local League undertook sponsorship, according to Williams, ". . . of something that we called, at the time, an Appalachian Exhibition. We started out rather small scale, in the ballroom of Music Hall." Williams and other League members were determined that the exhibition would involve low-income craftspeople from the city's neighborhoods. However, local craftspeople were reluctant to become involved. Williams explained that "they didn't know what this event was, they thought the League was—none of them were discourteous and never stated this— but I'm sure they felt we were a bunch of do-gooder, white glove ladies . . . it was hard to persuade them that this, indeed, would be to their benefit."

The lack of involvement by Cincinnati's Appalachian community led Williams to solicit craft cooperatives in the mountains as exhibitors. She believed ". . . that if some of the mountain groups came . . . that people in, among the urban migrant population in Cincinnati would then feel more comfortable about participating and, of course, what we were after was instilling a sense of pride, not only in crafts that were made but in the music and the poetry."

The event became a success. By the third year it moved to a larger venue, where it was renamed the Appalachian Festival. Williams recalled that by then, ". . . the Appalachian community of greater Cincinnati, including Covington and Newport [Kentucky], a lot of those folks were just really, really ready to have booths and to make things and so it really was working." After the successful 1973 festival, the Junior League agreed to transfer responsibility for planning and managing the event to the Appalachian community. It first approached the Appalachian Committee about assuming responsibility for the festival. The committee declined, fearing the festival would be more than its members could handle and distract from other important program initiatives.[15]

Williams, Maloney, and CHRC's Virginia Coffey then convened a group to discuss how the festival could be continued as a community event. Out of these discussions came a new organization, the Appalachian Community Development Association (ACDA), to oversee the festival. A three-year transition plan was developed to allow the League to phase out its Festival responsibilities.[16] In 1975, Kathleen Sowders, a young migrant from Whitley County, Kentucky, was chairperson of the first Appalachian Festival fully sponsored by ACDA. Following that year's festival, ACDA provided grants totaling $9,600 from festival proceeds to Appalachian organizations and neighborhood groups.[17] The festival celebrated its fortieth anniversary in May 2010.

The Appalachian Festival is an important narrative in the building of an Appalachian advocacy movement in Cincinnati, offering a story of using the influence and power of cross-class allies to further the goals of urban Appalachians. One example of leveraging the Junior League's class power occurred in the late 1970s when the Cincinnati Convention Center tried to oust the Appalachian Festival in favor of "a more profitable group or convention." As soon as League members heard about this effort, they made personal phone calls to the mayor, city manager, and city council members. Within a week, the Convention Center's manager called the festival chairperson to say there had been a misunderstanding, and that ACDA was welcome to use the facilities that year and in following years.[18]

Women Organizing to Improve Neighborhood Health

In 2002 a group of women set out to improve the health of their community, Lower Price Hill, which had been adversely impacted by years of industrial pollution and unresponsive public health and environmental regulatory agencies.[19] Initially Donna Jones, a UAC outreach worker and community leader, and Maureen Sullivan, executive director of UAC, invited neighborhood women to form a women's group to share stories and concerns with the aim of stitching together the fraying social fabric of the neighborhood.

Sullivan, recalling experiences with the Daughters of Appalachia at the Appalachian Identity Center, supported Jones's outreach to local women with both personal and institutional backing. The women began meeting weekly at lunchtime, sharing home-cooked meals and personal stories, voicing their concerns about the neighborhood and exploring the potential for change. They named themselves the Women's Wellness Group (WWG) to reflect their decision to improve health and health services in the neighborhood.

The founders of WWG were residents of LPH or women who had close ties to the neighborhood. For some this was where they had grown up, gotten married, and raised their families; others were still raising children or caring for grandchildren. They knew from personal experience the history of the neighborhood and the networks of families and friends that made this community the place they called home.

They also knew, while not making a major point of it, that they were Appalachian. This sense of rootedness in a mountain heritage, coupled with their experiences in LPH and with UAC, served to reinforce their identity as Appalachian women. The city's media recognized the neighborhood as Appalachian, while the community itself supported activities such as an annual Appalachian mini-festival. Their self-awareness was reinforced by participating in Appalachian studies conferences and the Appalachian Women's Alliance.

Although fluctuating in size and activity, the fundamental objectives of WWG—mutual support, improved community health, and access to health care—have remained intact. Several other key principles—gender, autonomy, a sense of place, relationships, and experience—have guided the decisions and actions of WWG members as well.

Gender

Many of the WWG members had been active in a community leadership program supported by two federal grants administered by UAC.[20] They felt sidelined by men making decisions about operations of the Environmental Leadership Group (ELG), which represented neighborhood concerns and perspectives in the conduct of the grant programs. Although ELG struggled to create an identity and governance structure independent of the lead agency, it never achieved full independence. The women grew weary of their inability to affect change while drastic changes were taking place all around them: family members and neighbors diagnosed with strange illnesses; problem pregnancies becoming commonplace; and cancer deaths seemingly of epidemic proportions. They felt strongly that it was time for local women to take charge.

Autonomy

WWG set their own priorities, controlled their membership, created their own bylaws, and conducted selected programs. Although UAC supported WWG with funding for Donna Jones, members insisted on independence from the council. They did not want to be managed by UAC staff or any local social service agency. They saw firsthand that agencies' priorities shifted without neighborhood input, and that residents were used as tokens in the crossfire among local agencies and organizations. Self-determination was fundamental to the women's ownership and control of their organization. They fiercely protected their autonomy, seeing it as fundamental to maintaining pride in themselves and essential to their sense of power to effect change.

Sense of Place

WWG members were initially sensitive to attendance at meetings by outsiders, and self-determination was safeguarded by their discouraging attendance by individuals from outside the neighborhood. WWG membership decisions turned on two issues: absolute commitment to the community and the absence of perceived conflicts of interest. In part, membership was predicated on a shared experience of place. Allegiance to LPH, not an adjacent neighborhood even if it was largely urban Appalachian, was important. Likewise, the founding members were skeptical of extending membership to staff of agencies that operated in the neighborhood. WWG members were well aware of turf struggles between agencies that had less to do with their neighborhood and more to do with internal agency budgets and policies.

Relationships

Though residence in the community was an important criterion for membership, a few exceptions were allowed. For instance, two university-based researchers, Katie Brown and JoAnn Grote, were concurrently working with many members on a National Institutes of Health–funded women's health survey when WWG began, and were welcomed as founding members. The researchers had spent years working with neighborhood residents on two community-based participatory research health surveys, tutoring them in research methods and mentoring them in the analysis and interpretation of survey results.[21] Mutual respect and admiration were hallmarks of the relationship. A growing sense of empowerment among the neighborhood women bonded them to the researchers, who in turn respected the integrity and perseverance of the neighborhood women. The researchers stayed engaged for several years, providing WWG with organizational support and guidance.

Experience

Another criterion for membership was shared life experiences, which tended to exclude younger women. The founding members' average age was between forty and fifty. One purpose of the group was to provide support for one another, and the needs of younger women were seen as substantially different. Although women of all ages were encouraged to assist with and participate in the annual health fair and other scheduled events, their attendance at regular meetings was discouraged. WWG members saw themselves as the health elders of the community, responsible for their own well-being as well as the future of their neighborhood.

Since its founding the Women's Wellness Group has conducted educational programs in both community and academic settings, provided support and information to members and nonmembers alike, participated in the analysis and interpretation of the LPH Women's Health Survey using community-based participatory research methods, and sponsored an annual health fair.[22] WWG members are addressing problems at the local public health clinic by soliciting the backing of an assistant health commissioner and by meeting regularly with the clinic director to discuss these concerns. These efforts are intended to benefit all clinic patrons, including the growing number of Latina women and children residing in the neighborhood.

Discussion

Appalachian identity bridges race, class, and gender in Cincinnati's urban Appalachian movement. Clearly, there would be no Appalachian movement without that identity. As Ernie Mynatt understood, identity is both instrumental and personal. It is a useful political tool for negotiating the delivery of services and resources where public programs or their administrators are not inclusive of urban Appalachians. It also enables individuals to find their own places in a multiethnic society.

Race

Because race was consistently and incorrectly confounded with class ("blacks are poor, whites are not"), leaders in Cincinnati's low-income white neighborhoods, where many urban Appalachians lived, had to develop a strategy that challenged this false assumption. Instead of emphasizing racial differences, they chose to organize along lines of a common heritage and group awareness, allowing them to be racially inclusive while still addressing the needs of a largely white Appalachian constituency.

This made urban Appalachians a legitimate group negotiating for needed resources alongside African Americans instead of in opposition to them. Indeed, identifying specific Appalachian needs and concerns became the basis for alliances with African American organizations pursuing similar agendas. When the two groups were in conflict over a given issue, there was at least acknowledgment of, if not agreement with, the other group's position. This recognition was facilitated in part by the fact that African Americans were among the founding board members of the Appalachian Community Development Association; black Appalachians have served on the board, committees, and staff of the Urban Appalachian Council since its inception; and individual UAC board members, staff, and volunteers have been active members of the local NAACP, the Urban League, and the National Anti-Klan network.

Establishing a specific Appalachian profile in the community is, however, not a sufficient basis for acquiring or wielding political power. Earning recognition is one thing, achieving parity is another. The latter requires an ongoing strategy of diplomacy, moral suasion, and advocacy. Tactics include concrete political organizing efforts such as AppalPAC, promoting an Appalachian perspective through a community-based newspaper such as *The Appalachian Connection,* and backing effective grassroots initiatives such as community-based literacy and health advocacy.

Class

One of the major obstacles urban Appalachians face in Cincinnati is associated with identity, but it involves a false identity. Negative assumptions about "hillbillies" cause many urban Appalachians to shy away from group strengths and the self-respect inherent in being Appalachian.[23] The Appalachian Festival provides Appalachians and non-Appalachians alike access to a rich heritage of music, dance, food, literature, folklore, and arts and crafts. It celebrates the strengths of Appalachia as well and serves as the basis for a positive identity among Appalachians living outside the region.

A hallmark of Cincinnati's Appalachian movement was its inclusiveness. Mynatt, and later UAC executive directors Maloney and Sullivan, worked proactively across racial, ethnic, religious, and class boundaries. It was decided early on that non-Appalachians such as Stuart Faber, Louise Spiegel, and Frank Foster would be valuable allies in the movement.

The story of the Appalachian Festival is emblematic of this approach. Everyone recognized that the class gap between many urban Appalachians and Junior League members was wide and deep. But League volunteers were accepted and quickly put in key roles. Their advice and work were valued, especially their ability to open the doors of corporate, political, and agency leaders on behalf of Appalachian causes, and to act as proponents of those causes within their own social networks.[24]

Of critical importance here is not only the alliance formed across classes, but the respect the League showed for the dignity and autonomy of their Appalachian counterparts. The formation of ACDA, an independent, Appalachian-controlled organization, is testimony to that respect. Appalachian identity was manifest not only in the artifacts in the festival booths, but also in the autonomy of the urban Appalachians who organized and still run ACDA.

Although the festival has suffered ups and downs, it continues to be an annual celebration of what is positive about the lives of Appalachians in cities and in the mountains. Negative stereotypes still persist, but many in the urban community have come to a different understanding of Appalachians through the festival. Mini-celebrations funded by proceeds from the festival continue the promotion of Appalachian identity and pride in neighborhoods across the city. Both activities attest to the importance of cross-class collaborations and to the sustainability of organizations based on Appalachian identity.

Gender

The formation and work of the Women's Wellness Group adds an important dimension to the understanding of the Appalachian movement in Cincinnati. Although creating an identity is important, Appalachian identity alone does not provide a sufficient basis for community organizing. Early on, the UAC found the limits of what was then called "issue organizing" in the classic Alinsky style because it did not work well in Appalachian neighborhoods.[25] But attempts at "identity organizing" as exemplified by the Appalachian Identity Center were not completely satisfactory either. It took a combination of the two to finally succeed.

Today WWG members are not concerned as much with their Appalachian identity, which they simply assume, as with health-care issues facing women in LPH. They are motivated to identify concrete problems and devise solutions. Still, members of the WWG, their families, and their neighbors have not escaped the sting of disparaging comments and negative stereotypes. The women's experiences at the local health clinic provide an example of how second-generation migrants frequently negotiate between their Appalachian identity and a problem-oriented approach.

Blatant disregard for patient privacy and frequent gestures of disrespect kept many away from the clinic or delayed appointments, potentially damaging their health. Patients tired of the ridicule and stereotype of "dumb hillbillies" they encountered at the clinic. Although these insults were personal affronts to themselves as Appalachians, WWG members decided not to address them as matters of prejudice and bigotry, but as impediments to effective health care.

WWG members were dealing with an institution where being Appalachian was seen as a problem, not a point of pride. Their Appalachian heritage was affecting the quality of their treatment, but they chose to address the negative labeling as an immediate barrier to health care, rather than tackle the more tenuous issues of bigotry and discrimination. Carefully picking their fights, members have thus far opted to seek change in specific behaviors at the local clinic, rather than try to change the pejorative attitudes of the Cincinnati Health Department or local medical professionals toward Appalachian patients.

It is also important to note the role of community-based participatory research in WWG's work and success.[26] Several of the women in WWG mounted surveys of both children's and women's health in LPH. They did this with the assistance of researchers from the University of Cincinnati working with UAC to obtain grants to underwrite the surveys. Neighborhood residents designed, administered, analyzed, and communicated the results of their surveys. In addition to recruiting a scientifically random sample of respondents to the women's health survey (Latina residents were provided with survey instruments in Spanish), the women refurbished an unused building in the neighborhood to conduct interviews and administer the survey.

All of this—working with university personnel, learning research protocols, reaching out in the neighborhood through a health fair, and disseminating survey results locally and in academic settings—added to the women's self-confidence and willingness to take on new issues as members of WWG. Appalachian scholar and health activist Richard Couto has noted the importance of coalitions between university and grassroots groups in devising successful local responses to healthcare issues in the mountains.[27] The experience of WWG reflects a similar dynamic at work among urban Appalachians.

The learning that took place during the research and the successes that came with its completion helped WWG members develop a voice of authority backed, at least in part, by the data they collected. That voice is still heard in the annual health fairs they sponsor and in their ongoing negotiations with administrative personnel at the local health clinic.

In the end, identity awareness as a means of advocacy and organizing has proven its effectiveness among urban Appalachians in Cincinnati. Although many of the concepts employed in the 1960s, 1970s, and 1980s remain effective today, media cycles, political issues, societal values, and leadership styles have changed substantially. As the members of WWG have shown, the role of identity in community struggles must always be adapted to suit local conditions.

Notes

1. Many federal policies developed in the 1960s had the unintended consequence of ignoring urban white poverty. William W. Philliber and Clyde B. McCoy, eds., *The Invisible Minority: Urban Appalachians* (Lexington: University Press of Kentucky, 1981); Thomas E. Wagner and Phillip J. Obermiller, *Valuing Our Past Creating Our Future: The Founding of the Urban Appalachian Council* (Berea, Ky.: Berea College Press, 1999).

2. Wagner and Obermiller, eds., *The Invisible Minority*; Phillip J. Obermiller, "Migration," in *High Mountains Rising: Appalachia in Time and Place*, ed. Richard A. Straw and H. Tyler Blethen (Urbana: University of Illinois Press, 2004), 88–100.

3. These organizations include UAC; the political action group AppalPAC; the community-

controlled newspaper, *Appalachian Connection*; the Appalachian Community Development Association, which runs the annual Appalachian Festival; and literacy programs based in Appalachian neighborhoods.

4. This phenomenon arose among urban Appalachians during the latter half of the twentieth century when other identity-based movements among groups such as African Americans, Chicanos/as, and women were gaining momentum. Ernest N. Mynatt, "The Appalachian Experience," unpublished typescript in the files of Phillip J. Obermiller, Cincinnati, Ohio.

5. William W. Philliber, *Appalachian Migrants in Urban America: Cultural Conflict or Ethnic Group Formation?* (New York: Praeger, 1981); Michael Maloney and Christopher Auffrey, "The Social Areas of Cincinnati: An Analysis of Social Needs," 4th ed., 2004, at http://socialareasofcincinnati.org/.

6. Because of black Appalachians' preferred identification with the urban black community in Cincinnati, we use "Appalachian" and "white Appalachians" interchangeably throughout this chapter. William W. Philliber and Phillip J. Obermiller, "Black Appalachian Migrants: The Issue of Dual Minority Status," in *Too Few Tomorrows: Urban Appalachians in the 1980s,* ed. Phillip J. Obermiller and William W. Philliber (Boone, N.C.: Appalachian Consortium Press, 1987), 111–16.

7. Phillip J. Obermiller and Michael E. Maloney, "'We ain't agoin' back': A Retrospective Look at Urban Appalachians in Cincinnati," in *Appalachia: Social Context Past and Present,* 5th ed., ed. Phillip J. Obermiller and Michael E. Maloney (Dubuque, Iowa: Kendall/ Hunt, 2007), 94–99.

8. Michael E. Maloney, personal notes.

9. Virginia Coffey, Stuart Faber, and Frank Foster were cross-cultural allies who helped in urban Appalachian advocacy. Coffey, an African American born in Wheeling, West Virginia, had served as director of Memorial Community Center in Over-the-Rhine and was director of the Cincinnati Human Relations Commission. Faber was president of the Appalachian Fund, which supported Mynatt's outreach position. Foster, a former college president and professor of sociology at Xavier University, was a mentor to Maloney.

10. Michael E. Maloney, personal notes.

11. Ibid.

12. Bruce Tucker, "Transforming Mountain Folk: Roscoe Giffin and the Invention of Urban Appalachia," in *Appalachian Odyssey: Historical Perspectives on the Great Migration,* ed. Phillip J. Obermiller, Thomas E. Wagner, and E. Bruce Tucker (Westport, Conn.: Praeger, 2000), 69–95.

13. Interview with Michael Maloney, Cincinnati, Ohio, September 16, 1989. Transcript in the personal files of Thomas E. Wagner.

14. All quotes from Diane Williams Smart here and below are excerpted from an interview with Diane Williams Smart, Washington, D.C., February 14, 1992. Transcript in the personal files of Thomas E. Wagner.

15. Interview with Michael Maloney.

16. Ibid.; Interview with Diane Williams Smart.

17. Appalachian Community Development Association Papers, Urban Appalachian Council Archives. Box 11. Cincinnati, Ohio.

18. Thomas E. Wagner, personal notes.

19. Lower Price Hill became a predominantly Appalachian neighborhood in the 1950s when blue-collar migrants from eastern Kentucky, after a period of reorganization in

Over-the-Rhine, gravitated to Lower Price Hill because of the industrial jobs available in the area.

20. National Institute of Health Sciences grant #R25 ES7717-8; National Institute of Health Sciences grant #1-RZ5ESC7717.

21. M. Kathryn Brown, Linda Bryant, Pam Childress, JoAnn Grote, Donna Jones, and Karen Mayer, "Survey Results: Lower Price Hill Women's Health Survey." Brochure created by the Women's Wellness Group, supported with funding from the National Institutes of Environmental Health Sciences Grant No: R25 ES07717 (June 2005).

22. See M. Kathryn Brown and JoAnn Grote, "How To Do a Community Health Survey," Department of Environmental Health, University of Cincinnati (2002).

23. Phillip J. Obermiller, "Paving the Way: Urban Organizations and the Image of Appalachians," in *Confronting Appalachian Stereotypes: Back Talk from an American Region*, ed. Dwight B. Billings, Gurney Norman, and Katherine Ledford (Lexington: University Press of Kentucky, 1999), 251–66.

24. Cincinnati's Junior League chose to work with urban Appalachians for at least three reasons. First, Mynatt actively encouraged league members to work with Appalachians. Second, the late 1960s and early 1970s were a time of the emerging Black Pride and Black Power movements among African Americans nationally and in Cincinnati. Offers of assistance from affluent white women with traditional concepts of volunteerism would not have been easily accepted by progressive black leaders. Third, the leadership of the National Junior League had selected Appalachia as a focus area for its membership in the late 1960s.

25. Saul Alinsky, *Rules for Radicals: A Practical Primer for Realistic Radicals* (New York: Random House, 1971).

26. Richard A. Couto and Julia DeBruicker, "Lessons from Community-based Participatory Research in Appalachia," in *Appalachia: Social Context Past and Present,* 5th ed., ed. Phillip J. Obermiller and Michael E. Maloney (Dubuque, Iowa: Kendall/Hunt, 2007), 337–43.

27. Richard A. Couto, *Streams of Idealism and Health Care Innovation: An Assessment of Service-Learning and Community Mobilization* (New York: Columbia University Teachers College Press, 1982).

CHAPTER 5

Appalachian Youth Re-envisioning Home, Re-making Identities

Katie Richards-Schuster and Rebecca O'Doherty

I'm tired of being raised to leave [my home], I want you all to know that I'm going to school so I can stay home, here in the mountains.

—AMI intern speaking at 2008 Appalachian Studies Association conference

Young people in central Appalachia face significant challenges becoming active participants in their communities and in making the decisions that shape their lives. They grapple with confusing messages and experiences that both celebrate and denigrate their culture and communities, disconnecting youth from their homes and from positive individual and collective identities. To be successful, young people are told—sometimes even by their families—they have to leave their mountain communities. At the same time, the history of resistance, the desire to connect to culture, people, community, and land, and the richness of culturally based assets have the potential to position youth in central Appalachia as talented and innovative change makers.[1]

How do young people from Appalachia come to see their mountain homes as places of strength and resiliency, view themselves as key contributors to their communities, and develop identities as Appalachian activists? The first critical step is to deconstruct constricting roles and rules about youth's own potential and the prospects for positive change in the region. This process, combined with opportunities to develop skills and initiate action, can reinforce notions of possibility, strengthen belief in change, and build activist identities.[2] When identity is linked to notions of civic activism, the seeds for staying home and building movements are planted.

Over the last two decades, the Appalachian Media Institute (AMI) has been a place where young people (ages fourteen to twenty-two) in central Appalachia develop the skills and knowledge to understand, represent, and participate in their mountain communities. Through video documentary production, young people develop their own agency in the questions they ask and the critiques they raise. They begin to develop their own voice, disrupt received messages about themselves, and see themselves as activists with a role and responsibility to change the community. As veteran media educator Steven Goodman notes, "Taking a video camera into the community as a regular method for teaching and learning gives kids a critical lens through which they can explore the world around them. It helps them to defamiliarize the familiar taken-for-granted conditions of life.... [L]earning about the world is directly linked to the possibility of changing it ... [and] a prerequisite for self-representation and autonomous citizenship."[3]

This chapter explores the transformative media production process of AMI. It is based on archival materials from AMI, in-depth interviews with five current and past AMI participants, and firsthand knowledge of the AMI process from the authors—the director of the AMI program (O'Doherty) and a partner of the program (Richards-Schuster).[4] The authors utilized participatory methodology by engaging young people from AMI in developing knowledge for the chapter, responding to drafts, and contributing to the overall writing.

Appalshop and Appalachian Media Institute

AMI was founded in 1988 as part of Appalshop, a cultural, educational, and media arts center in Letcher County, in the southeastern Kentucky coalfields. Appalshop began in 1969 as an experiment in community-based filmmaking. The War on Poverty brought many television reporters and filmmakers into the Appalachian coalfields to document the rural poverty of the area, but there were few opportunities for local people to use media to tell their own, often very different, stories. These stories sought to transform popular understanding of the issues and people of Appalachia, often in direct opposition to stories told by those, such as corporations that profit from resource extraction and politicians in collusion with these corporations, who have an incentive to suppress and control popular resistance. Appalshop's work is grounded in the idea that local people are best able to tell their own stories, frame the discourse about issues that matter to their community, and move toward community-generated solutions.[5]

AMI is Appalshop's community engagement, youth media, and leadership training program. The majority of the young people who participate come from southeastern Kentucky—including Letcher, Floyd, Pike, Knott, Perry, Leslie, and Harlan counties. At least half of AMI's participants come from families whose annual income is less than $22,000, and nearly all, if they attend college, are the first in their families to do so. Often recognized by youth as a rare safe space for expressing nontraditional ideas about gender and sexuality, it is estimated that about 5 percent of youth in AMI are gay or in the process of coming out.

A team of four to five staff members runs the AMI program. They include past participants in the program, artists from the region, older interns who take on staff roles, and others who come from different fields (education, youth organizing, and so forth).

Each year, AMI selects approximately thirty young people (all of whom are referred to hereafter as interns) to participate in its intensive internship programs, the eight-week Summer Documentary Institute, and after-school Media Lab. AMI staff work with a network of social service providers, teachers, and community members to identify applicants. The program seeks to engage youth of all abilities, skills, and experiences, not just those predisposed to leadership and activism. Intern cohorts include valedictorians, youth on parole, the shy and the outspoken, those from low-income and middle-class backgrounds, youth with learning and behavior disabilities, and those who are proven leaders. Ensuring access to the program for young people of all backgrounds means staff often must respond to problems interns face outside the program, working within informal and formal networks to secure resources such as transportation, shelter, food, clothing, and a safe place to discuss problems. Intern cohorts are not age-specific, and the application criteria focus on identifying youth who want to take risks; have demonstrated an interest in learning new things; and are seeking new ways to live, work, and learn in school, home, and the wider world. Both the Media Lab and Summer Documentary Institute are structured as jobs; participants are hired as interns and paid a stipend for their work.

AMI's curriculum has been developed through experimentation and collaboration over years, with staff working constantly to respond to the challenges posed by this kind of educational practice in the coalfields. The program engages young people in researching issues, developing media pieces, and using the media production process to create outreach campaigns around specific social issues, including suicide, drug abuse, domestic abuse, and environmental justice.

Most youth development programs for low-income communities relate to youth as individual problems to be solved, not as important actors in creating comprehensive solutions to community problems. In the educational system, the messages youth typically receive tend to discourage inquiry and encourage low expectations and minimal effort. After being conditioned *not to participate,* youth face challenges building a different kind of learning community in AMI. It is easy to become disheartened by the failures and challenges they encounter when producing a video documentary. AMI staff mentor and closely engage with interns to provide the types of support needed as young people grapple with new, sometimes unsettling understandings about themselves and their communities.

Media Production and Civic Activism

Media has long been used as a tool through which identity and civic activism can be fostered. This process, which can be especially powerful for those who have been most marginalized from the mainstream and traditional access points of power, often leads to deeper examination of the world and critical questioning of the community.[6] Goodman argues that "Historically, the way in which poor and other marginalized groups managed to become visible, to demand political recognition and economic rights, has been through acquisition of literacy in the dominant medium."[7] In these cases, media become an alternative vehicle through which new voices are heard, new stories told, and critical discussions opened up to alternative ideas.[8]

Often referred to as critical media literacy, the process of media production enables young people to develop their own voice, build critical consciousness of the world around them, and learn skills that enable them to take part in understanding and making decisions about the issues that affect them most.[9] From a civic action perspective, critical media literacy also provides a space where young people can be radical—question authority, challenge dominant media constructions of young people and their communities, and re-imagine new possibilities for themselves.[10] This is especially powerful for Appalachian youth who are disrupting stereotypes of hillbillies, hopeless social problems, and a culture of poverty that have defined and limited them and their communities over the last century.[11] When they discover the power of their voices to counter these messages, youth reveal some of the myths that those in power work to create: for example, the problems facing their communities are inherent and cannot be solved; and injustice is the natural accompaniment to life in the mountains.

Finding and interviewing subjects for a documentary creates new connections between youth and adults, both of whom may feel isolated and frustrated in their individual resistance. As they edit a video documentary, youth get to imagine outcomes for themselves and their communities that differ from the usual refrain of "this is just how things have always been." When youth present their documentary in public screenings, they gain confidence to speak out on issues

AMI interns and staff at work in Letcher County, Kentucky, early 1990s. (Photo by Jeff Whetstone, courtesy of Appalshop, Inc.)

they care about and help shift community norms about the ability to speak freely on controversial matters. As young people explore their community and act to promote notions of change, they begin to see themselves as community activists, which reinforces their connection to community, use of voice, and identity as agents of change.[12]

The Media Process in AMI

AMI's internship learning process has three components that are reflexive and influence one another: youth explore themselves and their community; use media to understand, document, and act on issues; and develop positive identity and civic activism. Interns spend the first half of their internship developing skills and knowledge (for example, community research methods, learning to form and ask questions, teamwork skills, asset-based problem solving, technology skills, and crafting messages). In the second half, interns practice those skills by producing a short, culminating video documentary focused on a community issue and developing an outreach plan to use the video as a tool for participating in their communities.

Phase 1: Exploring Themselves and the Community

In the first week, interns adjust to AMI's learning environment, which presents radical challenges to passive and conservative modes of learning; explore the role representation and identity play in shaping their own experiences and opportunities; and practice forming and expressing their own opinions. This first week focuses on building capacity for inquiry and reflection, grounded in self-knowledge. Interns complete individual and group projects where they tell their own stories, visually interpret images they encounter in their everyday lives, and become acquainted with media arts skills about composition, visual literacy, and critical viewing. For example, interns critically consider photographs of Appalachia and how these pictures shape understanding of the region. Interns then start to gather their own modern photo archives—collecting images from such sources as the local and national press and their own family photos—and then finally make their own photos that express the way they see the region and their communities.

During these activities young people examine their identity in relation to how it is understood by other groups (their peers, parents, schools, people from other places). This leads to conversations about the power of media representation. In critically reviewing how others have depicted the region in contrast to their own experiences, young people often begin to question their own understanding of the community. Willa, an AMI intern, reflected: "I think for me, when everything got turned around was the very beginning of the program, when we had to watch films and we had to analyze did this filmmaker show your community in a positive light, did this picture represent where you live? And I think that changed everything for me because I started thinking about this place."

The realization that the stories of people from the region are not being told accurately often leads to personal exploration, in which young people are able to construct their own ideas about themselves and their region in contrast to the often negative and false representations of who they are and the challenges their communities face. As Derek, a former AMI intern and current Appalshop staff member, noted: "So, as kids, I would say the majority of people that I went to school with were really embarrassed to be from here. And that's just the reality of it. . . . And, in AMI when I came here and I saw some of the films and talked to people, it really hit me that outside perception of the area was really robbing me of my history and culture and making me to feel ashamed . . ."

For many young people, AMI offers the first opportunity to "sit back" and "think about where they are from." Instead of being passive recipients of media messages, young people begin to think about their personal stake in the community and the messages that they want to communicate about it. They begin to ask themselves, "What is our connection to these issues and to the region?"

> The reason I think AMI is so successful . . . [is] because you get kids in here who don't have a chance for a summer job and don't have an opportunity to work anywhere. They are given the chance to stop everything and just look at their community, really look at it. And I don't think they're ever given that chance in life to sit back and think about where they're from. And be told that it's okay to be proud of where they're from. And in AMI they are given that chance. And almost everyone who comes through leaves with more pride than they came in with. (Willa)

This process of learning about the community and region from a personal perspective seeds a transformation of perception: interns begin to embrace their community for its strengths. Mac observed:

> [F]or the longest time, I never really cared a lot about this place. It could blow off the map, and I wouldn't care. And [in AMI, through the video-making process] I learned to see this place for what it really is. It's an important place. It's my home. And I didn't really see it before that. I just saw it as a place to keep my stuff. . . . And I really liked it here. And after I realized that, I realized how much of the culture, and how much of the stuff there was here that, you know, I couldn't just give that all up just as easily as I wanted to.

Phase 2: Using Media to Document Issues and Take Action

In this second phase, interns draw on their understanding of their community as a place of resilience to develop documentary video projects, which are guided by interns' internal questions of "who am I," "why are things the way they are," and "what kind of people am I a part of." AMI staff challenge interns to examine these questions by seeking information through interviews with family members, academic and policy experts, archival materials at the local library, informal conversations with the interns' friends, and by calling on a variety of community-based and social service organizations.

Interns explore topics for final projects and complete a rigorous project proposal with mentorship from AMI and Appalshop staff. The participants select their own final production topics, with the only criterion that their production make a positive contribution to their community.

Interns spend the next four weeks in small groups producing a short video documentary. In developing their projects, interns use community-based research methods, an inclusive process that values knowledge, both informal and formal, from the community. This research builds on their earlier exploration and enables the teams to examine a topic in depth. Interns' final projects have addressed such topics as prescription drug abuse, water quality, the true costs of coal mining, youth activism, and gay rights, and have become well-known resources for activists, educators, governmental agencies, news outlets, and social service organizations. For example, a video about domestic violence featuring the candid voices of eastern Kentucky women produced by interns in 1988 continues to be used by area health services organizations in their prevention efforts.

When interns research and record information in the community, they test their ideas and opinions about issues that are central to their values and identity. They learn how to negotiate conflict as they attempt to craft less polemical dialogues about longstanding controversies, such as the value of coal production versus that of environmental protection. Youth and adults who share interests and passions create new relationships. And interns learn how different people practice action and resistance in Appalachia:

> Before, I thought I was separate from the community. I didn't try and participate in anything. And now I feel very much part of the community and very much attached to it. I met a lot of people in the community and knowing them makes me feel more attached to it. I guess it started with the interviewing process and going out and meeting with people who are doing important things . . . anything important. And feeling how they felt so strongly tied to this place made me start to think about what I cared about and what I was connected to. (Brittany)

This process is reinforced by the requirement to develop video outreach plans, which involve teams thinking critically about the stories they are telling, the voices they are creating, and the responses they want from their audience. Often these outreach plans engage the broader community and lead to action on multiple levels. For example, after youth produced a documentary on the environmental dangers of mining, they worked in partnership with a social justice citizens' group, Kentuckians For The Commonwealth (KFTC), to organize young people and adults to protest a permit for mining that was destroying a local watershed. After recruiting over forty youth and community members, the group held a two-hour meeting and protest with government officials, which they documented for future use. Through negotiation, youth and their adult allies succeeded in getting the permit pulled, ensuring the safety of their community's watershed.

WILLA'S STORY For Willa, AMI presented a much-needed opportunity to make sense of conflicting messages she received about her personal worth and the worth of her community: "Really you were learning about your community and the struggles here and you were able to realize what you believed instead of what you were being told to believe because you did get to hear everyone's point of view and you got to take from it your own thoughts and decide what you learned from it."

Willa worked with two other interns on her final video production project. The group wanted to learn more about the debate over turning coal to diesel fuel (a process made possible by new fuel technology that threatens the environment), which was happening in eastern Kentucky in the summer of 2007. As the group investigated the issue, two members became invested in challenging the coal industry. However, the third was uncomfortable with this, because many people in her family had been miners. Her complaint against making a "protest" video prompted other group members to consider their relationship to the coal industry and the industry's impact over time on eastern Kentucky families. The group began to develop a more nuanced view of their subject. When Willa went home in the evenings and talked to her family about her video, she started to connect their experiences to what she was learning at AMI. Her grandfather's efforts to save his land and garden from being destroyed by resource extraction, memories of coal company–caused floods that washed away homes, and her family's employment in the coal industry became part of the dialogue. Willa was soon speaking about coal issues from a place of strength, placing her questions about the coal industry in the context of concern for her land and people.

At the same time, the group was out practicing community-based research by talking with supporters and opponents of the liquid coal issue: families who had lost loved ones in the mines, citizens who questioned the actions of the coal industry, and local politicians. The group tried to speak with coal company representatives, but none of the individuals they contacted would agree to a recorded interview. When it came time to edit their video, the group had to make sense of all the conflicting stories, which helped them sharpen their critical inquiry skills, develop their own questions about the injustices they saw, and realize a more complex view of the region than just the duality of negative stereotypes and wistful nostalgia.

After reviewing the interviews and other materials and talking with coworkers, family members, and friends, the group came to the conclusion that the current debate about coal-to-liquid technology was unproductive, pitting environmental priorities against pressing economic concerns. The group decided to produce a video that considered the real costs communities would incur if this technology were brought to eastern Kentucky. After spending the first half of the program examining how the media shapes people's ability to identify and resolve persistent issues, the group felt a responsibility to represent the debate in a different way from mainstream media; if they did not do it, perhaps no one else would. They carefully considered production decisions, knowing they needed to tell the story in a way that would not scare locals off by being too strident, yet persuade national audiences of the extent of the problem. Thus the group worked to tell stories people would connect to, endeavoring to create a video that would provoke dialogue, not polemics, an essential skill for broad-based movement building.

Outreach meant working with a variety of organizations to screen their video for many audiences: at events intended to build youth activism, for academic and policy elites at film festivals, and at community screenings where legal aid lawyers challenged the group to be inclusive in their discussion about coal. With AMI's support the group has traveled with their video for the last two years, providing support for people and organizations that challenge the status quo in coal communities like their own.

Phase 3: Developing Positive Identity and Civic Activism

For Willa, the process of producing a video required many acts, small and larger, which allowed her to practice her new sense of self and realize a deeper desire to stay home and participate in movements for change. Small acts included asking questions at home about her family's long-held ideas about coal; larger actions included representing coal issues in Appalachia as a human rights concern at a presentation in New York City:

> When you know who you are you're more confident and you're able to believe. If you don't know who you are and you go in and fight for an issue, you don't really know what you're fighting for. You have to understand yourself before you can understand the issue. You have to understand what you believe before you can decide if you believe in a certain issue. You have to know yourself first. I think that's really important.

Instead of being isolated and "separate" from the community, the process of interviewing others and meeting people who are trying to create change draws young people closer to the community and strengthens their understanding of themselves:

> First of all, I learned that I am a capable person because I created something [a video documentary] and it's something that I'm proud of and it's something that other people see. I developed an identity as an Appalachian. Before I knew

where I was from, but I didn't have any feelings of pride. It wasn't an important part of my identity. It [the production process] gave me something to identify with and be passionate about. It gave me something to want to fight for and to want to make change for. (Brittany)

For AMI interns, the practice of re-imagining a new identity and changing the narrative of possibility for their communities and culture becomes a cause for activism in and of itself. All the interns interviewed for this chapter noted the need for resistance to mainstream narratives that limited their communities' worth. Even the smallest positive interaction or transgressive dialogue can build young people's resistance and commitment to their re-imagined ideas of their own potential and that of their communities. Natasha, an AMI participant and current AMI trainer, stated:

I was taught . . . something . . . was wrong with me because I was from eastern Kentucky. I was taught I couldn't be as good as anyone else. After being in the program I finally understood who I could be in a world where I was expected to be like everyone else. So the program empowered me, helped me learn that not only could I do things, but that I could change things. It was intense and scary to ask critical questions about my home, and think about how the answers affected my family. But by doing that I came to see that so much was possible. It's an amazing thing now to be helping a younger generation learn about their own potential, their own communities, and start to realize that if things are going to get better around here, we're going to be the ones who have to make the changes.

However, this process is not easy, and AMI interns report being targets of discrimination by those in power (for example, county government, school board, coal companies) or those who feel vulnerable to that power (for example, families, teachers) because of their alternative storytelling and ability to ask critical questions. Interns struggle to maintain new ideas about themselves and the world while also being connected to their families and friends, who may not support their new ideas. As a result, they sometimes find that their new identity leads them to feel more like "outsiders" because they can see new possibilities that their peers, families, and communities do not see.

As interns progress through the program, they begin to connect their new ideas and concerns to those of other oppressed groups, recognizing common experiences. In this way their ability to articulate their identity as Appalachian, activists, or eastern Kentuckians allows them to connect to national and transnational movements for change and imagine a role for their communities in these movements. For example, AMI intern Machlyn writes about this connection when considering the Appalachian experience of economic migration and the ongoing immigration debate in this country. In a commentary for National Public Radio, he noted, "Seeing the immigration debates and demonstrations on TV,

I understand that big companies look at our families as dollar signs, as people who can pack coal out or bring the tomato harvest in."

AMI is still working to formalize how interns transition from being leaders with the AMI program to acting independently within their communities. Some young people get involved in social justice organizations like KFTC. Others remain involved in Appalshop and stay on as trainers in the AMI program. Some have also started to organize their own group, working on movement building in the area. For example, throughout 2008 and 2009, a team of five current and past interns with varying levels of experience in AMI met with other young people in the region to make plans to bring together youth activists to strengthen their collective understanding of what it means to be Appalachian and the issues facing the region, and to work on skills and strategies for mobilizing regionally and in their home communities. They connected with other young people through informal networks, by reaching out to existing organizations that had connections with young people, and by mapping and cold-calling community programs throughout the region.

Although most of the work is community-rooted, AMI interns have had the opportunity to participate in national dialogues and workshops on youth engagement, youth media, and rural policy issues. A team of AMI interns has also participated in cross-site exchanges with filmmakers from Indonesia in which they critically examined transnational issues and movements for change. Working with their Indonesian peers to create videos that document daily life in Yogjakarta provided examples of the free speech and economic justice issues interns face at home in Appalachia. Seeing how another community dealt with related issues and the severity of resolving those issues in nondemocratic environments brought Appalachian issues into focus for the interns and shed new light on opportunities for action on issues previously regarded as unsolvable. Interns and adult staff returned home with a renewed commitment to justice movements and insight into what those movements need to activate their fellow citizens and create change.

The opportunity to connect with individuals and organizations from different communities is an essential part of the AMI learning process. These interactions enable interns to explore their identity beyond the boundaries of their own community. Through this exploration, interns are prompted to develop and deepen their language and understanding of who they are and what it means to be from their local communities, the Appalachian region, and the United States. This can lead to difficult individual discussions about the ways in which they both share an identity with other communities based on common concerns and the ways in which their sense of personal and Appalachian identity can inhibit cross-community collaboration. For example, when making plans for regional coalitions, youth must consider how a strict geographic definition of Appalachia could exclude willing participants who would offer much-needed support for issues like living wage campaigns and mountaintop removal. The majority never come to a conclusion; rather, the questioning and struggling lead to their own identity development. For AMI, the priority is that interns are allowed to create their own understanding of their personal identity and also be able to realize their interconnection to other places and movements in and outside the region.

Conclusion: Identity, Media, and Movement Building

> Identity is hard to define, I could make lists of things that make it up, but it is a really long list. The most important thing is that I can have one, make it up on my own . . .
> —Brittany

AMI interns' identity as Appalachians and as activists does not become definitely formed in AMI. Rather, youth learn that they can change how they are perceived and the opportunities they have to participate and act in their communities. The media production process can be a unique tool to support this change; when it is grounded in an exploration of identity and community, it can seed activism and inquiry among youth participants. Through sharing their media productions, youth participants also create opportunities for their friends, families, neighbors, and others across the region to re-imagine their own identities and relationships to Appalachia and recast their ideas about what is possible.

In the example of AMI, we have observed that these links between personal development and community development, individual resistance and collective mobilization, and the transition from youth-produced videos to important, credible commentaries are fragile. AMI works to connect interns to further opportunities to participate in movements for change, but two main challenges prevent the program from formalizing this strategy. First, although some groups have developed youth initiatives (for example, Highlander, High Rocks School for Girls), youth development programs in central Appalachia are rare; owing to rural geography, limited infrastructure, lack of funding, and lack of technology, there is no systematic structure for connecting those programs that do exist. Second, some social change initiatives and organizations in the region tend to be adult-centric, fail to invest in resources to prepare Appalachian youth for participation, and/or operate without authentic participation of local communities. Often youth find themselves doubly marginalized, first as Appalachians and second as youth, drawn into change efforts without the training or tools to participate fully or exercise their own agency.

AMI's program and the recent work by its interns can be starting points for youth participation in movement building, but ultimately needed are structures—informal networks and formal organizations—that build the ongoing capacity both of young people across organizations to work together for change and adult social justice organizations to engage young people. It is also necessary to examine the complexity that emerges as new activist identities develop and to support young people's efforts to build collective networks.

There is potential for movement building among young people in the coalfields, and media can play a critical role in its emergence. The act of telling an alternative story that challenges dominant understanding of Appalachian people and Appalachian issues begins with young people taking control of their own story and strengthening their sense of self within the context of larger social change efforts. When young people re-envision themselves and their communities, they begin to create a movement of youth activists staying home and reconstructing Appalachia.

Acknowledgments

The authors would like to acknowledge the following people who contributed to the development of the chapter: Beth Bingham, Maureen Mullinax, Libby Richards, Julia Taylor, and the editors of the book, Steve Fisher and Barbara Ellen Smith. In addition, we are deeply grateful to the AMI interviewees who were willing to share their stories and critical insight on the AMI process, as well as all of the AMI interns, AMI staff, Appalshop artists, and community members who have been and are a part of the program.

Notes

1. Stephen L. Fisher, ed., *Fighting Back in Appalachia: Traditions of Resistance and Change* (Philadelphia: Temple University Press, 1993); John M. Glen, *Highlander: No Ordinary School* (Knoxville: University of Tennessee Press, 1996).

2. Constance Flanagan, "Trust, Identity and Civic Hope," *Applied Developmental Science* 7, no. 3 (2003): 165–71; Katie Richards-Schuster and David Dobbie, *Youth Civic Spaces: Strengthening Youth Organizing and Promoting Democracy* (Ann Arbor: Michigan Youth and Community Program, 2009).

3. Steven Goodman, *Teaching Youth Media: A Critical Guide to Literacy, Video Production, & Social Change* (New York: Teachers College Press, 2003), 3.

4. Of the interviews conducted, three were taped and transcribed and two were done through written responses to questions. In accordance with Appalshop's values, the AMI interns and alumni who contributed to the chapter, all over eighteen years of age, were asked to read the chapter, provide feedback on content, and approve the quotes attributed to them in the chapter.

5. See Appalshop's Web site for more information: www.appalshop.org.

6. Stuart Hall, "Old and New Identities, Old and New Ethnicities," in *Culture, Globalization and the World-System: Contemporary Conditions for the Representation of Identity,* ed. Anthony D. King (Minneapolis: University of Minnesota Press, 1997); Clemencia Rodriguez, *Fissures in the Mediascape: An International Study of Citizens' Media* (Cresskill, N.J.: Hampton Press, 2001).

7. Goodman, *Teaching Youth Media,* 4.

8. Diana Coryat, "Challenging the Silences and Omissions of Dominant Media: Youth-led Media Collectives in Colombia," *Youth Media Reporter* 2, no. 4 (2008); Goodman, *Teaching Youth Media*; Rodriguez, *Fissures in the Mediascape*.

9. David Buckingham, "News Media, Political Socialization and Popular Citizenship: Towards a New Agenda," *Critical Studies in Mass Communication* 14 (December 1997): 344–66; Patricia Aufderheide, *Media Literacy: A Report of the National Leadership Conference on Media Literacy* (Washington, D.C.: Aspen Institute, 1993); Kathleen R. Tyner, *Literacy in a Digital World: Teaching and Learning in the Age of Information* (Mahwah, N.J.: Lawrence Erlbaum Associates, 1998).

10. A. A. Akom, Julio Cammarota, and Shawn Ginwright, "Youthtopias: Towards a New Paradigm of Critical Youth Studies," *Youth Media Reporter* 2, no. 4 (2008); Coryat, "Challenging the Silences"; Kevin Howley, *Community Media: People, Places, and Communication Technologies* (Cambridge, U.K.: Cambridge University Press, 2005).

11. Dwight B. Billings, Gurney Norman, and Katherine Ledford, eds., *Back Talk from Appalachia: Confronting Stereotypes* (Lexington: University Press of Kentucky, 1999).

12. Richards-Schuster and Dobbie, *Youth Civic Spaces*; Barry N. Checkoway and Lorraine Gutierrez, "Youth Participation and Community Change: An Introduction," *Journal of Community Practice* 14, no. 1/2 (2006): 1–9.

CHAPTER 6

Resistance through Community-based Arts

Maureen Mullinax

> Most small towns put on community plays to celebrate their founding
> by brave pioneers or a battle won by stalwart local soldiers. They
> commemorate 'little engine that could' determination that leads
> to inevitable civic success. In 2005, however, Harlan County was
> producing a community play about civic failure—about the county's
> battle with drug addiction, primarily the painkiller OxyContin. It was a
> struggle the county had so far lost.
> —Bill Bishop and Robert C. Cushing, *The Big Sort: Why the Clustering
>   of Like-minded America Is Tearing Us Apart*[1]

From their lifelong activism in the American South and the Appalachian coalfields, veteran cultural workers Guy and Candie Carawan learned that cultural
traditions of music, poetry, and drama can be used strategically to forge a shared
experience and develop a collective identity in social justice efforts: "singing
together, even in the face of terrible difficulties, can be empowering."[2] The Carawans emphasize, however, that these cultural responses do not arise naturally
but must be cultivated by individuals and organizations attuned to deliberately
strengthening resistance movements "by building on their own heritage and
adding contemporary expressions from the new struggle."[3]

In this chapter I examine the work of a coalition of students, residents, and
teachers in Harlan County, Kentucky, who are intensively using the arts and
community-based research to build community capacity for democratic practice
and, in the process, engaging in a subtle form of resistance to social and economic
decline in their rural communities. Institutionally based at the local community
college, the overarching goal of this long-term, community cultural development
project is to reflect creatively on and re-present the hard realities and unique
resources of Harlan County in the hope of building awareness of commonalities
among area residents across deeply entrenched divisions of class, race, religion,
and geographic community. It raises important questions about the role of culture
in movement building, transformative efforts guided by place-based pedagogy,
and the ability of civic organizations to be inclusive.

These questions are especially poignant as many rural communities in central Appalachia and beyond struggle with pervasive social, economic, and political challenges exacerbated by the concentration of corporate power and the dismantling of the welfare state. The newest challenge, prescription drug abuse, is seen by many as a response to these deeper issues and the consequent despair people feel about their declining communities.[4]

Some scholars and activists have questioned the ability of social movements, especially rural, localized efforts such as this project, to challenge effectively the hegemony of the neoliberal state, transnational corporations, and enormous media conglomerates. From this perspective, the market and capital determine the parameters of community decisions.[5]

Sociologist Janet Conway argues that new forms of social movements, different from prior oppositional efforts, *are* challenging the impacts of globalization and neoliberalism in their communities. Open-ended in orientation and centered on a respect for experimentation, these new movements embrace multiple perspectives and the *process* of identity formation, in contrast to movements that have a clearly outlined end point. Often controversial because of the emphasis on education and learning in place of direct action, these mobilizations are committed to a long revolution of continual cultural transformation.

According to Conway, this nonlinear approach to movement building has at its core a commitment to inclusiveness, receptivity to opportunity, and continual learning through action and reflection, or what she refers to as "knowledge arising from praxis"[6]: "The belief in and demonstrated capacity to act on provisional knowing, and to act together with others who think, live and dream differently, rely on a culture and politics of social learning and capacity building. They suggest notions of democracy, revolution and utopia as open-ended projects-in-process, worked out in practice, open to question and to new 'others,' and always needing renovation."[7]

The project explored in this chapter approaches organizing with a set of guiding principles focused on culture and capacity building similar to the efforts of the movements outlined by Conway. Grounded by a commitment to open-ended, long-haul cultural organizing, this project has been able to sustain its activities in ways that respect diversity and experimentation in a place where notions of insider/outsider and deep attachment to tradition endure.

The Harlan County PACT Project: Beginnings

Rich in natural resources, Harlan County is located in the rural eastern coalfield region of Kentucky. Initially settled by subsistence farmers, the county has been tied to resource extraction since the late 1800s, when outside interests bought up land for timber and mineral rights for coal reserves. Although violent strikes in the 1930s and 1970s drew attention to intense labor struggles in the area, at the turn of the millennium no unionized mines remained in the county. Defined by the Appalachian Regional Commission as a "persistently economically distressed county," 29.3 percent of its residents lived below the federal poverty line in 2007.[8]

By 2000, it was clear that the toll of poverty and economic decline on families and participation in civic life in this rural Appalachian county was exacerbated by the growing abuse of prescription painkillers by discouraged residents. Robert Gipe, a professor at Harlan County's Southeast Kentucky Community and Technical College (SKCTC), describes the backdrop against which he and his students began to document and discuss the challenges of their communities:

> The top local stories in the *Harlan Daily Enterprise* at the turn of the twenty-first century include state-subsidized relocation of the unemployed in the wake of welfare reform, a massive roundup of synthetic narcotic traffickers, threats to consolidate the county's high schools in the face of declining enrollment, gutting of the workers compensation law by Kentucky's coal operator governor, local struggles to limit strip mining near Kentucky's highest point on the south side of the county and its only National Historic Landmark on the north side, and widespread coal-company tampering with dust-sampling units designed to keep air in underground mines breathable. All of these events are happening in an environment where it is virtually impossible for organized labor to have the power to mediate such changes.[9]

When made aware of a funding opportunity through the Rockefeller Foundation's Partnerships Affirming Community Transformation program (PACT), Gipe saw the opportunity to engage his Appalachian Studies students in the process of writing a grant as an organizing strategy to build community dialogue. In the fall of 2001 Gipe's students began to systematically gather input from residents about what they saw as the assets of their place, as well as what they thought were their most pressing challenges. Having seen many faith-based, governmental, and nonprofit aid organizations come to Harlan County to provide community development guidance and resources without lasting, tangible benefits, the group wanted to raise funds to develop grassroots programs that would both create spaces for discussion about these challenges and build upon the county's cultural strengths of music and storytelling. After an intensive community planning process, they submitted a proposal to PACT, the goal of which was to build partnerships between communities and professional artists through projects that addressed a pressing community issue by the participatory production of art.

In addition to choosing artistic media and collaborating professional artists with whom to work, the group needed to identify the single pressing community issue they would address through the project. Earlier that year, SKCTC students participated in an Appalachian Regional Commission–sponsored project in which they were asked to "assess the assets of Harlan County, threats to those assets, and strategies for using assets to address the threats."[10] Having done this research, they were attuned to some of their neighbors' hard stories and loss of hope. Many of the students had personal experience with the addiction problem through family members or friends, specifically abuse of the narcotic painkiller OxyContin, and therefore chose the growing prescription drug abuse problem as their issue.[11]

Gipe and his students proposed an intensive, long-term engagement with community research and arts projects designed to promote trust, dialogue, and hope, while simultaneously creating processes for frank discussions of the deep challenges residents were facing. Their clarity of purpose must have shown through, because the Rockefeller Foundation awarded the group a three-year grant.[12]

The Harlan County PACT Project: Implementation

Thousands of Harlan Countians and nonresident artists and students have participated in this ongoing project. Because the strategy was to include as many people as possible, the group pitched involvement through community college classes, schools, churches, and by word of mouth across the county. In addition to permanent tile mosaics depicting local issues and traditions in several county communities, they have taken and exhibited locally thousands of photographs of places and people in the area. The group scripted and performed two community plays—*Higher Ground* and *Playing with Fire*. They have also taken numerous road trips, presenting their performances to other communities grappling with similar issues.

Throughout, the project's leadership has been simultaneously diffuse and concentrated. Because a key goal is to build the skills of participants, whether fundraising know-how, artistic skills, confidence in public presentation, or abilities to negotiate difference and understand commonality, consistent efforts have been made to position the many participants as experts of their own experiences and as learners and enactors of these newly learned qualities.[13]

Even given this ethos of valuing what all participants bring to the process, the driving force and decision-making center of the project has been the participating SKCTC faculty, including project director and Appalachian Studies professor Robert Gipe, music director and professor Ann Schertz, project coordinator and professor Theresa Osborne, and sociology professor Roy Silver. This team, in collaboration with participating professional artists and emerging leaders among the community participants, has shepherded the project as it developed, met new opportunities, and faced a variety of challenges. The issues of how much to institutionalize or organize the project, the makeup of its leadership, and the direction of its trajectory are ongoing dilemmas and points of conversation for the group.

Significantly, both the art produced and the experience of participating in the PACT project have been informed by systematic community research. To assess

Cast of *Higher Ground* at Southeast Kentucky Community and Technical College in Cumberland, Kentucky, September 21, 2006. (Photo by David Perry/*Lexington Herald-Leader*)

the depth of the drug abuse problem and its connection to economic conditions in the county, the group conducted a Listening Project, a longstanding organizing tool used to help disenfranchised members of communities negotiate polarization and increase understanding of their social situation and alternative courses of actions. Working with the Rural Southern Voices Project, participants were trained in the technique and then conducted four hundred confidential interviews with a wide range of Harlan Countians about the strengths and challenges of the county, including the extent and causes of, and possible solutions to, the drug abuse problem.[14] In addition, the community oral histories of SKCTC students as part of their course work are an ongoing contribution.

These interviews informed all of the art produced. Most intensively, they became source material for construction of scripts for community performances. Gipe describes how incorporating information from the Listening Project into the play *Higher Ground* helped ease audiences into tougher social issues of the county, particularly drug abuse among residents: "In many ways, the play was part of the community report on the listening project. It certainly put before nearly 2,000 people the issues surfaced by the listening project in a way that kept them (for the most part) from becoming too defensive. I felt like the play also demonstrated how addressing problems could be something that is in part affirming of our community."[15]

In her discussion of oral history as a tool for studying communities, historian Linda Shopes points out that a common impulse is to celebrate uncritically the past and wax nostalgic, rather than reveal and probe deeper problems and contradictions of a place.[16] However, because of the foundation of the Listening Project, the final script for *Higher Ground* is a complex weave of local stories that both celebrate the traditions of Harlan County and expose the wounds and scars. Illustrated through a wide-ranging mix of skits, songs, and dances, the stories in the play are about life in Harlan County in the past, the social impact of floods on community solidarity, the history of the county's illegal drug economy (first moonshine and then OxyContin), the discriminatory practices of white store owners toward African American residents, and a local poker game organized by a pair of orphaned children.

"There's a lot of pickin' and grinnin' in our first half,"[17] says director Gerry Stropnicky. As the play progresses, however, the damaging impact of prescription drug abuse on family and community relationships becomes evident, especially in the dynamic multi-act story of a father who gets hurt in the mines, becomes addicted to prescription painkillers, and eventually loses his family and then his own life to an overdose. In another act, a financially pinched older man who is prescribed OxyContin for a back injury he sustained in the mines "doesn't see no harm" in selling a few of his pills when approached by a local pusher. The price is right and he can get by with a little more pain, he figures. In yet another act, a young woman from "a good family" tells how addiction does not discriminate by class.

At this writing, the Harlan County group continues its complex work that incorporates deliberative dialogue, the arts, and community-based research. Though a detailed assessment of the multilayered impacts of the project is beyond the scope of this chapter, the continuing character of the PACT project is a testament to the power of this process. Although the group consistently faces challenges and struggles with questions of structure and direction, many participants and leaders affirm an ongoing commitment to continuing their efforts, in some cases referring to the project as a "godsend."

Movement Building and the Harlan County PACT Project

Citizen resistance in Appalachia has often taken the form of protest against unjust corporate acts or inadequate governmental enforcement of existing regulations.[18] These oppositional efforts have largely been mobilized against the actions of clearly identified adversaries or for specific social goals, such as black lung compensation. Though connected to and influenced by these efforts, the Harlan County project has eschewed a direct oppositional stance in favor of an intentional practice of cultivating tolerant relationships and building spaces for recognizing commonality. Listening coordinator Joan Robinette, a seasoned veteran of grassroots campaigns in the region, defines how the project is different from her past activist experience: " . . . the things I've been involved with before were always issue-driven. It was about getting clean water, or justice, or equal rights. But this project was about relationships and being a better individual. . . . A listening project to me is the grunt work, where you get to the root. You have to beat down the doors, get into people's lives to solve the problem of the community. And I have to be honest. It's a real emotional thing because we know all these people. They're our neighbors, our family."[19]

Conway argues that placing capacity building and knowledge production at the center of a movement is challenging. Groups struggle to balance organizing for direct action against organizing for education. The latter necessitates commitment to a long view of mobilization and social change because the focus is on forging relationships and developing the reflective agency of members through ongoing participatory processes.

Many factors have strengthened the PACT project's ability to negotiate these difficulties and to continue and deepen. However, three key factors aligned with Conway's discussion of a new democratic imaginary have been especially significant: the role of the arts in bringing people together through the physical practice of community, the focus on capacity building and continual learning that both honors and challenges traditional ways of being, and the institutional base and mission of the college.

Building Connections through Arts Practice

> It was moving together, physically moving together, that finally helped us get ourselves together in the music. This is the goal of uniting across fault lines and across barriers. We never achieved it perfectly. You know, you never do. Practicing moving together is a way to get to this kind of unity. That's why I keep coming back to this idea that if you are trying to establish community, you have to practice it all of the time.
> —Ann Schertz, Harlan County PACT Music Director[20]

The deliberate although at times meandering approach of the project illustrates the Carawans' point that cultural resources do not automatically become empowering, but must be cultivated. The Harlan County project has the distinct advantage of working with a seasoned veteran in the world of participatory, community-based arts.[21] In addition to intensive engagement in the fields of Appalachian Studies and place-based education, Robert Gipe has championed the cause of arts education through his work with the media arts center Appalshop, the Rural Trust,[22] and SKCTC. A charismatic organizer, Gipe is especially adept at engaging himself and others in a continual process of trying out, assessing what is working, and reinventing—Conway's "knowledge based in praxis." Because it allows a distancing from self and the ability to take on the roles of others, working with the arts adds a special dimension to group participation and learning. As participant Theresa Osborne observes, "Acting gives you the opportunity to step outside your own skin, and away from your problems for a while and become another person or character. It frees you to express emotions that you might not feel comfortable doing in everyday life. Through community theatre projects like *Higher Ground*, where the script is based on oral history interviews from within the community, the people get to tell their own stories, and face their own problems within a positive, supportive and healing framework."[23]

Music director Ann Schertz deliberately drew on this knowledge when she developed the score for *Higher Ground*. Her main goal was to incorporate three distinct musical traditions from the area: bluegrass gospel, black gospel, and white Pentecostal. To capture the essence of each tradition, she worked with performers who were aligned with each genre, in the process positioning them as experts of their own experiences. They helped her communicate to the musicians and performers the different cadences, tempos, and emphases of each tradition. This method of engagement and cultural sharing is based on a pedagogy akin to what Conway describes as a " . . . theory of knowledge [that] suggests in coalition, through dialogue, negotiation, practical acts of solidarity, and ongoing political collaboration, subjectivities can be transformed—not toward uniformity, but toward greater capability of producing fuller, more adequate knowledges with which to change the world in ways responsive to the diverse needs and desires of the many rather than an elite few."[24] By having the entire cast at some point inhabit the genre of others different from themselves, Schertz created an opportunity for them to assume those standpoints, at least musically.

Honoring and Challenging Tradition through Building a Learning Community

> "Cultural organizing" means placing culture at the center of an organizing strategy. It can be done to unite people through the humanity of culture and the democracy of participation. It can also be used to divide people through fear and polarization. . . . What is different are the values, principles, and vision for the future (and definition of whose future) that lie at the heart of organizing.
> —Caron Atlas, "Cultural Organizing: A Conversation at the Intersection"[25]

In addition to the tension between putting energies toward direct action or toward education, a central dilemma of activist efforts is deciding between the relative role of traditional knowledge about what the key issues are, how they should be approached, and who should be included and knowledge that is introduced to the group by a leadership informed by an alternative set of guiding values, principles, and vision for the future. Robert Fisher and Joseph M. Kling contrast two approaches to the role of ideology in community organizing: the more top-down, ideologically infused practice of the American Communist Party and the "non-ideological" approach taken by Saul Alinsky later in his career when he rejected deliberately applied external ideology. The authors point out that both traditional and critical derived ideologies need to be incorporated in movements to avoid the extremes of, on the one hand, the traditional as exclusionary and, on the other hand, the external as disconnected from the local. As they state, "In the development of progressive movements, free spaces must be understood as loci where popular and derived ideology can meet, interact and be reformulated."[26]

The Harlan County project exhibits a blending of celebration and critical examination of the local. The dance between the two is shepherded by the leadership, who encourage the honoring of democratic, participatory traditions such as storytelling and music making but challenge tendencies toward divisive or exclusive practices around personality, outsider/insider status, class, race, gender, sexuality, or whether or not someone is a drug user.

Based on her analysis of democratic civic organizations dedicated to bridging religious/political divides in Northern Ireland, Shaunna Scott warns of the exclusionary potential of community groups, especially along class lines, and she questions uncritical acceptance of the idea of the social justice promise of civil society in Appalachia.[27] According to the project's leadership, the task of helping participants become their best selves is a continual challenge. Gipe states, "The source of a lot of tension for me comes from the fact that we've been real explicit about creating a space where we relate to each other in a fair and open way and where everybody is tolerant and thoughtful of others and that standard becomes difficult to maintain."[28]

In spite of this ongoing challenge, continual learning is a central principle of the work of the PACT project. As an educational setting, the college provides a natural space for this focus. Students and residents learn about their community and traditions through original research—oral histories, community surveys, and photo documentation—and through discussing some of the many studies about Harlan County. The college might be viewed as providing a democratic "free space" where, in dialogue, residents develop a common vision of what they want their place to be.

Rather than offering an unmediated free space, however, the project leadership is committed to engaging the group in the practice of ideological principles derived from numerous social justice movements, including Freirian adult education, feminist and civil rights, community cultural development, and the loosely connected network of activist and scholarly groups that make up what some define as the "Appalachian movement." While seeing the cultural resources and traditions of Harlan County as key assets, they are attuned to focusing on challenges to the principles derived from these movements, including inclusiveness, attention to difference, and democratic decision making. Much of the reflective engagement with continual learning for both participants and leadership centers around how to address longstanding divisions of class, race, religion, and geography that had become a "natural" part of the community.

An example of this consistent deliberation is the determination of to what extent and at what point material that challenges traditional community divisions should be included in scripts. As the group began to move toward production of the second play, they grappled with potential divisiveness over the main themes of the script. In spite of a subtle point that increased flooding in the area has been exacerbated by intensive surface mining, *Higher Ground* never directly promotes this argument, implying that floods are beyond the control of individuals. Though the portrayal of the "flood of drugs" is pinned to the greed of doctors and pushers, addiction is linked to injury in the mines (another subtle critique of the coal industry). Some group members, especially those who joined the grassroots environmental group Kentuckians For The Commonwealth (KFTC) after personally experiencing the threat of damage to their homes and water sources, argued for a more direct critique of mountaintop removal. Gipe was wary, however, of the divisiveness of the issue, because the primary goal of the group was to document stories of their place and then find solutions based on what people have in common rather than what divides them. "I had in my head at one point that we'd be ready to talk about stuff like strip mining by about the fourth play. We started with drug abuse because it was such a forefront issue. It's really more a unifying than dividing issue. Nobody steps up and says they're for drug abuse in the way they step up and say they're for coal mining."[29]

His hesitation to include such a locally sensitive issue that is framed as a conflict between jobs and the environment illustrates the deliberate attention of the leadership to critical principles and the process of practice-based learning even when it slows the process of change. According to Gipe and others in the leadership, a persistent challenge in this work is addressing the various tensions of difference that continually resurface. By modeling behaviors of trust, respect, and openness to difference, the leadership strives to instill in participants a different way.

The Role of the Community College

Though much of the power and political potential of movements that emphasize education and cultural transformation are based on provisional knowledge and experimentation, Conway believes that having an "organizational permanence" can productively anchor a movement by providing consistency and space for shared reflection. "Permanence allows for a sense of change over time, including a historical perspective on one's own praxis, instead of the endless present that characterizes so much activist politics. It allows for the accumulation of shared memory and know-how, the collective generation and transfer of knowledge, and the production of questions, insights and practices that could not otherwise have been imagined."[30]

SKCTC is intimately intertwined with the viability of the PACT project. It provides numerous resources, including the nonprofit status necessary to apply for grants through the college-affiliated Southeast Education Foundation. It supplies creative spaces for performances, workshops, photography exhibits, screenings, music concerts, exhibits, and rehearsals. In partnership, the college and PACT actively cultivate connections to diverse regional, national, and international organizations engaged in sustaining communities.

According to SKCTC president Bruce Ayers, prior to 1994, when SKCTC joined the Rural Community College Initiative (RCCI)—a Ford Foundation demonstration project to address rural development and access to education needs of rural and tribal communities across the country—the college was not in tune with its diverse community. Participation in RCCI, says Ayers, re-energized the college by focusing it on the original philosophy of the community college: to address the economic, educational, and cultural needs of the local community. The first step was to re-examine who the college considered stakeholders. Upon reflection, says Ayers, though doctors, lawyers, and professionals were consistently consulted for input on the direction of the college's programs, the voices of coal miners, secretaries, and the unemployed were absent.[31] RCCI reoriented SKCTC toward development of leadership opportunities for a wide range of community members and established a receptive foundation for the PACT project's inclusive approach.

Initially, the expansive, open-ended style of the project's leadership was difficult to accept for a bureaucratic institution not known for radical leanings. The support and provision of "organizational permanence" grew, however, as the college's administration began to understand how thoroughly the project was connecting the school to a broad-based constituency in the community.

While not giving carte blanche privileges, the mostly hands-off support of the college has allowed the PACT project to radicalize this mission by supporting the work of staff who have become full-time cultural workers committed to transformational capacity building inside and outside the traditional classroom. The staff prioritize community engagement in their work and emphasize students and residents learning the history and current realities of the county through oral history research, survey research, documentary photography, and through reading and discussing some of the many studies about Harlan County.[32] The curriculum and community outreach now promote reflection upon and practice of both traditional and new principles and ways of being embedded in philosophies of social justice, inclusion, and participatory democracy. Place and identity in this conception, rather than static "things," are processes of becoming guided both by where the community has been and where it is possible to go.

Taking Stock of Capacity Building in the Harlan County PACT Project

> People in this holler or this town hadn't spent enough time with each other to realize how very much they had in common. . . . People feel like "we are the only people that has to deal with this," and so this project just blew a lot of those lies out of the way. That was refreshing. Cause most of us already knew all the same things. But we are not accustomed to sitting down saying the things we know and having someone who's not usually at the table say, "that's right."
> —Connie Owens, PACT participant[33]

The potential for a shift in power relations in Harlan County as a result of the ongoing PACT project and its capacity-building efforts is difficult to assess. To varying degrees, participants in the project have increased their appreciation and respect for the egalitarian cultural traditions of their communities, challenged the inherently limiting aspects of their heritage, and/or incorporated the social justice lessons encouraged by the leadership through consistent practice. It is clear, however, that the project has led to new relationships in the community and with other communities among people who would rarely have found a commonality of concerns and political positions.

A few examples of how participants were encouraged to sit down, listen to, and possibly agree with others who are "not usually at the table" illustrate these learning relationships. In October 2007, PACT participants joined representatives from Appalshop to form a regional coalition and participate in a national social justice conference in Oakland, California, that was forefronted by entertainer and civil rights activist Harry Belafonte. Among other social issues, participants in the "Gathering for Justice" learned about the challenges facing incarcerated youth, particularly youth of color, in U.S. prisons. Reflecting on his participation, seventy-seven-year old Rutland Melton, a retired African American coal miner from Lynch, Kentucky, described the experience of so many different people uniting around the same issue as inspiring. "It made me think about how we all need to hang together to address these problems that seem so far away, but are right here at home too."[34]

More locally, Harlan County youth worked with the Appalachian Center at SKCTC to develop Captain Crawdad's Social Experiment 119, which is a student-run, college-supported art and music festival. The project's initial call for participation by area youth echoes the emphasis on possibility and inclusiveness of the overarching PACT project of which it is an offshoot:

> We can imagine a festival involving many different forms of expression. Singing, songwriting, solo musical performance, bands, dancing, writing, photography,

digital art, film & video making, drama, drawing, painting, cartooning, graphic design, sculpture, pottery, fabric art, storytelling, tattoos, skateboarding—it's all good. This event IS NOT figured out yet. It doesn't even have a name. Some money is set aside for the festival, and staff in the Appalachian Center will help out in making it happen, but the name and exact shape of the festival is to be determined by the students who sign up to make it happen.[35]

While efforts to build just, equitable, and inclusive relationships in a specific place require intensive commitment and patience for the nonlinear, this form of long-haul cultural resistance can also lay the foundation for more directly oppositional engagements. It can instill the kind of "cultural confidence" the Carawans noted as foundational to standing up for one's rights. Although multiple factors were in play, the engagement of PACT participants as new members of KFTC in the 2009 fight against a permit that would allow mining above the Harlan County town of Lynch suggests that they felt emboldened to add to a collective oppositional voice.

The work of building the capacity of citizens to engage in collaborative, democratic processes is not without its challenges. It is messy, unpredictable, and requires incredible time and commitment. As music director Ann Schertz notes, however, there has been a shift in the community as a result. "I do think that there's been a critical stage reached that is making people here look for new ways of dealing with things. I think there's a flicker of hope and that's different than 'everything is going down the tubes and we're helpless to do anything about it.' It's like, 'okay things aren't right yet and there's no magic bullet or no magic pill, but you put one foot in front of the other.' Maybe this is showing one different way of putting one foot in front of the other. So practicing something different has started."[36]

Notes

1. Boston: Houghton Mifflin Harcourt, 2008, 136.

2. Guy Carawan and Candie Carawan, "Sowing on the Mountain: Nurturing Cultural Roots and Creativity for Community Change," in *Fighting Back in Appalachia: Traditions of Resistance and Change,* ed. Stephen L. Fisher (Philadelphia: Temple University Press, 1993), 259.

3. Ibid., 259.

4. In the late 1990s, prescription drug abuse emerged as a serious social issue in eastern Kentucky. See chapter 13 in this volume.

5. For example, sociologists Jeff C. Bridger and Theodore R. Alter suggest that, given the mobility of capital and the transitory character of communities like those in Harlan County, it is outdated to expect that voluntary associations will form to respond to these problems. Jeff C. Bridger and Theodore R. Alter, "Place, Community Development, and Social Capital," *Community Development* 37, no. 1 (2006): 5–18.

6. Janet Conway, *Praxis and Politics: Knowledge Production in Social Movements* (New York: Routledge, 2006), 21.

7. Ibid., 137.

8. U.S. Census Bureau, "State and County Quick Facts," (http://quickfacts.census.gov/qfd/states/21/21095.html).

9. Robert Gipe, "Foreword" to *Which Side Are You On? The Harlan County Coal Miners, 1931–39*, ed. John Hevener (Urbana: University of Illinois Press, 2002), xi.

10. Harlan County PACT Project, *The Harlan County Listening Project Report to the Community: A Community Response to Drug Abuse in a Historically Exploited Community* (http://www.listeningproject.info/resources, 2006), 1. The Appalachian Regional Commission convened a meeting in 2000 of higher education schools with Appalachian centers. The agenda was to think about how to coordinate research by higher education institutions in the region directed toward improved community life.

11. OxyContin is often prescribed for chronic pain from severe physical injuries or for pain management for terminal cancer patients. When crushed, the drug's time-release mechanism is rendered ineffective, so that when snorted or injected the user has a powerful and immediate high.

12. The group has continued to raise funds from foundations, the state arts council, and the Appalachian Regional Commission.

13. Participants, including students, professionals, retired coal miners, hourly employees at the community college, and others, range in age from the very young to senior citizens. They include African American, Asian American, and Caucasian residents, and they come from almost every community of the county.

14. For a detailed description of the technique and for examples of projects using this tool, see the Rural Southern Voices Project's Web site: http://www.listeningproject.info. For an analysis of the Harlan County Listening Project, see Matthew McCourt, "From a Place of Problems to a Place of Possibilities: Community Work and Collaboration in a Coalfield Community," Ph.D. diss., University of Kentucky, 2004.

15. Ibid., 13–14.

16. Linda Shopes, "Oral History and the Study of Communities: Problems, Paradoxes, and Possibilities," *Journal of American History* 89 (September 2002): 588–98.

17. Author's interview with Gerry Stropnicky, 2006.

18. For a list of organizations active in the region and a bibliography of the wealth of scholarship documenting and analyzing the approaches of those efforts, see "Directory of Organizations" and "Dissent in Appalachia: A Bibliography," in Stephen L. Fisher, ed., *Fighting Back in Appalachia: Traditions of Resistance and Change* (Philadelphia: Temple University Press, 1993), 339–62.

19. Harlan County PACT Project, 13.

20. Author's interview with Ann Schertz, 2008.

21. For detailed discussions of the community-based arts movement in the United States, see Jan Cohen-Cruz, *Local Acts: Community-based Performance in the United States* (New Brunswick, N.J.: Rutgers University Press, 2005) and Arlene Goldbard, *New Creative Community: The Art of Cultural Development* (Oakland: New Village Press, 2006).

22. Appalshop is a media arts and education center based in Whitesburg, Kentucky. Founded in 1969 as a War on Poverty training program for youth in eastern Kentucky, the organization has developed multidisciplinary community-based arts programs, including place-based art education efforts spearheaded by Gipe. The Rural School and Community

Trust (Rural Trust), founded as the Annenberg Foundation's Rural Challenge in 1995, promotes research, advocacy, and outreach to improve rural schools in the United States. Before coming to SKCTC, Gipe worked with Appalshop as a facilitator of place-based education projects.

23. West Virginia Prevention Resource Center, *Share the Vision* (West Virginia's annual statewide Abuse Prevention Conference, online conference program, 2006), 2.

24. Conway, *Praxis and Politics,* 31.

25. *Grantmakers in the Arts Reader* 17, no. 2 (2006): 2.

26. Robert Fisher and Joseph M. Kling, "Leading the People: Two Approaches to the Role of Ideology in Community Organizing," in *Dilemmas of Activism: Class, Community, and the Politics of Local Mobilization,* eds. Joseph M. Kling and Prudence S. Posner (Philadelphia: Temple University Press, 1990), 86.

27. Shaunna L. Scott, "Civics Lessons from Another Place: A Case Study of the Northern Ireland Women's Festival Day Project," *Journal of Appalachian Studies* 7 (Fall 2001): 187–225.

28. Robert Gipe, e-mail correspondence with the author, July 6, 2009.

29. Author's interview with Robert Gipe, 2008.

30. Conway, *Praxis and Politics,* 131.

31. Author's interview with Bruce Ayers, 2007.

32. Two other studies Gipe's students read are Cynthia M. Duncan, *Worlds Apart: Why Poverty Persists in Rural America* (New Haven, Conn.: Yale University Press, 2000) and Shaunna L. Scott, *Two Sides to Everything: The Cultural Construction of Class in Harlan County, Kentucky* (Albany: State University of New York, 1995).

33. Harlan County PACT Project, 10.

34. Author's interview with Rutland Melton, 2008.

35. Southeast Kentucky Community and Technical College's Appalachian Center Web site, http://www.secc.kctcs.edu/appalachiancenter/appal/stufest.htm.

36. Author's interview with Ann Schertz, 2007.

PART II

Where No One Stands Alone

Bridging Divides

CHAPTER 7

Organizing Appalachian Women
Hope Lies in the Struggle

Meredith Dean with Edna Gulley and Linda McKinney

> I hold my head high and my voice deepens with pride as I say "I am
> an Appalachian woman and I work with the Appalachian Women's
> Alliance." *This* is the work, and these are the women that I will speak of
> in my old age.[1]

More than two hundred women have played leadership roles in the Appalachian
Women's Alliance since our "Dawning Ceremony" in 1992. Thousands have been
touched by our work. Defying traditional stereotypes, the women among us have
been black, white, Hispanic, and Native American, poor, working, and middle class,
lesbian and straight, with and without traditional education, rural and urban, wage-
earners, and welfare mothers. This chapter represents the perspectives of three of
those women, Edna Gulley, Linda McKinney, and myself, each of whom has been
deeply and consistently involved throughout our twenty-year herstory.

> EDNA: I used to feel like I shouldn't be around middle-class white women. I
> didn't trust them. I knew they didn't care about the little people, they were
> all about themselves. They gave out rules but couldn't take them from us,
> because we weren't supposed to know what we were doing, or to think for
> ourselves. They were okay until they got called on, or challenged, then if they
> couldn't have their way, or figure out a way to control things, they would
> leave. I used to think I shouldn't even be at the table with those women, that
> I didn't know enough, that's the way I felt. I saw them as the women who had
> what I always wanted, the women with money and power. But then I studied
> them, and I saw that they needed me. They needed me so they could take me
> under their wings and control me. Of course I never knew I was under their
> wing till I saw my picture plastered all over their newsletters. They needed
> me, but I didn't need them.
>
> LINDA: I never would have believed it would be this hard to do organizing work
> with women on our own issues in our own way. I think I had some movie
> idea that everyone would be willing and happy to give up their time and
> energy and money to work and create projects together. But all the women
> I knew were overwhelmed with their day-to-day lives and demands. Asking

them to meet and talk, much less write and work on an issue, was just asking too much. Now more than ever, I am thankful to those women who didn't have cars, or computers, or good health, and still gave themselves to get the vote, birth control, and health care, to get divorce laws changed, and domestic violence laws enforced. I think middle-class women should be aware that the more they've been given the more important it is for them to work to improve the lives of all women and children. Class is everything and class awareness is a must. Otherwise, it's just too easy to blame the victim.

MEREDITH: I came into this region idealistic and strong. I had marched with millions of Filipinos to protest a violent dictatorship. I'd linked arms in solidarity with strangers to face tear gas and water cannons. I'd witnessed a National People's Congress and experienced the seeds of an alternative government. I'd seen organizing that had made a difference. I didn't come to Appalachia to "help" anybody. I chose to live here because my dad was from here, and because I thought it was one of the most beautiful places in the country. I came to "walk my talk," to live out what I had learned from Filipino organizers, plantation workers, and peasants, from Paulo Freire and the New Testament. When I moved to Appalachia, I had an unconditional respect for the women who were organizers in their communities, women I considered to be my peers. Although my job was to facilitate volunteer missions for a regional church organization, my aspiration was to turn such efforts inside out. At the time, I didn't realize all the things that would get in the way of that. I didn't fully understand internalized oppression, and I definitely didn't understand class.

The Dawning

> No way to count the light she adds to the day,
> no way to measure the warmth she has spread.
> It is enough to know that the warmth and light
> that were passed to her
> are shared and invested,
> held in trust
> for those who follow.[2]

Two hundred years before the Appalachian Women's Alliance, our foremothers scratched homesteads out of the mountain wilderness, birthed, fed, and clothed huge families, founded churches, worked the land, educated children, and always, always, struggled to make ends meet. Ninety years ago, our Appalachian mothers rallied strikers, organized picket lines, closed down boardrooms, and shot it out with company thugs as they watched their husbands, fathers, sons, and brothers die in the mines. Forty years ago, our Appalachian sisters packed pistols, blocked bulldozers, flooded courthouses, and went to jail as they watched their mountains being stripped and destroyed. These were the Christian Temperance women, the settlement school women, the women's auxiliaries, women coal miners, hillbilly women, sisters, and laywomen of just about every Protestant denomination. They were the women of Bloody Harlan, the Daughters of Mother Jones, the Mud Creek women, the domestic violence groups, Women and Employment, the women of Yellow Creek, Mountain Women's Exchange, and hundreds of other women who joined forces at one time or another to help their families and communities. And so it was that the Appalachian Women's Alliance took our place within a long line of strong, committed, mountain women. Only this time we were fighting for ourselves, attempting to organize in an explicitly "women's" kind of way, to bring a women's voice, agenda, and culture to the various patriarchal contexts within which each of us worked and lived.

> 1987: A year of nonstop travel down mountain roads, endless conversations in community centers, diners, cars, and living rooms. Finally, I trudge into Linda McKinney's aging trailer at the entrance to the Appalachian South Folklife Center. There I find a political and spiritual soul mate. Although we came from disparate worlds, Linda and I immediately recognized a shared passion, vision, and proclivity for action. Together, we initiated a regional gathering in St. Paul, Virginia, for women "to share stories and explore common struggles." In 1988, two more womanist soul mates joined us to organize a second gathering "to explore women's styles of leadership." Out of that event, *From Structures of Fear to Structures of Hope,* we organized an official Women's Task Force within the Appalachian People's Service Organization (APSO), the Episcopal ministry with which I was a staff person at the time.[3]

Owing to its church backing and base, the APSO Women's Task Force[4] had to maintain a careful balance between Episcopal volunteers and grassroots Appalachian organizers. Nevertheless, the group quickly published the first issue of the *Mountain Women's Journal,*[5] despite the conflicts in perspectives and agendas inherent in our composition. Primarily conceived by grassroots activist Teri Vautrin, the *Journal* was and is written by, for, and about women of the Appalachian mountains. Teri was adamant that women in isolation be provided with a way to speak out, often for the first time, telling their own stories in their own words. And, according to our grassroots members, countless women and communities had experienced academics and church people coming in, taking their stories, and exploiting the community's hard work for their own advancement.

> They wanted my story, and if they didn't get it, they moved on to the next low-income person or community who might give them what they wanted. You must understand, this is how I saw these people, people who took from low-income people but gave nothing back. They came into your community and sucked up all the information they needed from you, and then you never saw them again. Later on, someone would come up and tell you they had seen your story in a book.[6]

Over the next three years, the Women's Task Force established the *Mountain Women's Journal* as a significant regional voice, and hosted two powerful exposure tours for national church leaders during the 1989–1990 Pittston coal strike of the United Mine Workers of America (UMWA) in southwestern Virginia. However, our position as a class-conflicted "minority" task force within APSO, attempting to operate within a patriarchal structure, eventually wore us down.

> Class is the hardest issue of all. I have always experienced middle-class white women as being mean. I would try not to engage them in a discussion. If they asked me a question, I would answer briefly, then turn my attention away. Again and again I have seen those women watch and wait, looking for a vulnerable area to attack. Only now that I am much older do I have the knowledge to defend myself and sometimes attack back. I have watched them repeat this same pattern over and over again. I did not understand why they were so mean, until I saw how they treated each other. They are just so competitive, and low-income women briefly make them feel better about themselves. "Do no harm" should be the first goal for middle-class women.[7]

In 1991, the Women's Task Force took a next step by bringing together Appalachian women from a grassroots base "to explore a more unified way for women to work in a regional context." Calling for a "Gathering of 30," we invited women from across the region who we knew to share our vision and considered to be sisters in our work. Our hope was to provide neutral turf where women from very different class, ethnic, and spiritual backgrounds might come together on equal footing. Included were members and organizers from UMWA locals and grassroots community groups, staff with regional organizations, and laywomen involved with regional and local church efforts. The goals emerging from that initial gathering ranged from "listening to each other without animosity" to forming a women's union with a national health-care agenda. Our first collective action was for each member to inscribe, "I believe Anita Hill" on every dollar bill that passed through her hands. Some of us saw the group as a venue in which to articulate and practice a justice-oriented womanist spirituality. Others pushed for radical feminist action.

On the following goals, we could all agree:

- To provide opportunities for Appalachian women to come together to share stories, struggles, and strategies,
- To engender a proactive, creative, and diverse plan of action through which to promote a new vision empowering to women,
- To conceive new strategies for making our voices heard in bastions of patriarchal power (church, government, academia),
- To work toward economic self-sufficiency,
- To honor the women who came before and take responsibility for nurturing those who will come afterward.[8]

Daybreak

> We call each other to celebrate, to be inclusive, to redefine democracy,
> and to accept the gifts that each of us brings to the table.[9]

In the beginning, we spent an inordinate amount of time building a small core of feminist leaders, a mix between a support group and a think tank. Only two of our group of twenty-two were women of color, half were middle-class organizers, ministers, or social workers, and the other half were low-income women who had risen up as leaders in our communities. Together, we struggled to articulate an inclusive, Appalachian, feminist agenda while creating and practicing nonhierarchical models of power emphasizing every woman's right and responsibility to be heard.

> I came in thinking I had nothing to offer this group and wondering why I was there. I listened to them talk about this and that, throwing those big words around, while the tape is playing in my head, "what in the hell am I doing here, I don't understand a thing they are talking about." The next meeting I was still listening to them make decisions for me and letting it happen, so I began to talk. Only then I got talked over and looked over, until I got upset and talked real loud, the way poor people always have to do before people listen to us.[10]

Even as we struggled with substantive issues of class and race within our circle, we were united by our desire to organize around our own issues as women, outside the male-dominated institutions, communities, churches, and families in which we operated day to day. At last freed from banging our heads against a myriad of patriarchal walls, we joyfully created a proactive manifesto including a Women's Bill of Rights and an all-encompassing definition of economic, cultural, physical, and spiritual violence against women. We learned to use consensus as our model of decision making and struggled to hold ourselves accountable for the voices of all the women in our circle, including ourselves. We spent a whole evening discussing the feminist implications of *Thelma and Louise,* and fell into an easy rhythm of sharing stories, poems, songs, and dance as our Saturday night ritual. It was a time of excitement and growing commitment, and we wanted to share our "good news"[11] with others. That desire led us to the idea of organizing a Women's Caravan.

And so it was that the first Appalachian Women's Caravan wound its way through the mountains during the summer of 1994, carrying our message to end violence against women in all its many forms. The response was overwhelming. We held events with twenty different communities in cooperation with fifty local organizations. That summer, we touched more than one thousand women with our message about violence; but even more important, they touched us with theirs.

The violence we seek to name
to flush from its hidden lairs
to challenge in all its formless forms
to bring down where it is openly destroying us
is cultural, spiritual, economic.
But the face of the violence we find,
the face that looks for us,
is the real and the dangerous.
   Bruises, cuts, burns, deaths.
   Broken bones, broken hearts, broken dreams.
   The terrorism of personal violence.
   Women held hostage in their own lives.
   This is what comes to meet us on the roads of Appalachia.[12]

In one community we had to lock the doors and put tarpaper on the windows when women made t-shirts depicting experiences of violence in their lives, for fear their husbands would find out. . . . When women held Caravan events in their communities, they came together in a way they had never done before. They started talking about what was happening in their homes, things they'd been ashamed to share. Women stopped asking their husbands for permission to go to meetings, started . . . talking to other women. Some women ultimately left abusive and controlling relationships. We called that "directly confronting power." We called it organizing.[13]

We called it organizing, but we were not quite sure what to do with it. We had one office with one staff person and we were uncertain how to respond to and utilize the enormous energy we had created. Women were looking to us to provide direct services, support groups, legal advice . . . but we were not equipped to do so. Nor were we sure that we wanted to.

I didn't know what I wanted at the time, but I knew I wanted us to be something different from a domestic violence group. I think I saw myself as finding out who I was and where I fit in with a group of white women whom I didn't trust and really didn't care about. I was trying to figure out how to keep myself from looking crazy or standing out until I found someone I could talk with. I started holding other women's hands as they cried and told their stories, which didn't seem right because then they went back to their homes to the husband or boyfriend who was causing all the problems in the first place. It was the same thing over and over again and I was drained from listening. Somewhere in there I tuned everything out.[14]

Following the first Caravan, divisions began to deepen between women looking for a support group, founders who saw us as an intellectual think tank, and those interested in multi-issue organizing in their own communities. We adopted the theme "Women Rising Up" for our second caravan, and had lengthy, complex conversations about our role as "the yeast." Our group of core leaders took seriously complaints that we had become a clique, and struggled over how, when, and why to expand our membership. At the same time, there was a move to make issues of race and class more central to our work by explicitly incorporating them into our mission statement.

> I feel awful, my lower back hurts. I'm clumsy, unsure of my movements, . . . exhausted. . . . [S]till, I sit here in this circle of women, working on "hard thinking" issues: violence, dismantling racism, welfare reform, and classism. . . . As we struggle to discuss and plan we rub up against each other and sparks of anger and raw emotion fly around the room. Sometimes a woman walks out of the circle, sometimes there are tears, but always there is a "hanging on," a continuing to work in consensus, a piling up of creative work, meaningful work.[15]

Despite expectations we may have raised among other women in the region, we instinctively realized that we needed to continue to organize for ourselves, around our own issues, if we were to survive. Our plan was to reproduce what we had created on a regional level in each of our local communities, but when we got alone in our home contexts we found the process almost impossible to replicate, causing us to become even more isolated until our next regional meeting. As individual volunteers, we lacked the skills, constancy, or functionality to do the work required to build local circles; and as an organization, we lacked the capacity to provide what was needed on a local level. So we continued to direct our energies and resources into building and maintaining the regional group, where our analysis, network, and process were strong. Nevertheless, for several years we attempted to build the fund-raising, managerial, and communication capacities to hire local organizers, even as our organizational strength remained centralized and our funders were quick to point out the logistical nightmares of spreading isolated staff people over six states. The one exception was in Clinchco, Virginia, where our earlier work, our ability to hire one more staff person, and our growing attention to racism melded into a perfect union.

High Noon

In the midst of struggling with tough philosophical and organizational questions, a small group of us attended a Dismantling Racism workshop facilitated in 1996 by the Exchange Project of the Peace Development Fund. That workshop and our subsequent relationship with the Exchange Project trainers were to change the face of the Appalachian Women's Alliance for years to come. At the end of 1995, 10 percent of our twenty core leaders were women of color. By 2003, we had increased that number to 45 percent. Correspondingly, our number of low-income leaders increased from 40 percent in 1995 to 55 percent in 2003. In 2009, both figures stood at 85 percent.[16]

When we began to seriously address issues of race and class, the power dynamics of the group started to shift. It made all the white women uncomfortable when we could no longer define ourselves as the "poor" white person, or the "abused" white person, or the "good" white person in the group. All of us had to start owning up to some privilege and power, no matter who we were. I think we lost some women at that point—when it started to get more real.[17]

The racism trainings were a turning point for the Alliance. They showed us the work we needed to do to make the Alliance an equal place for women of color. And it was a turning point for me. Before that, I just didn't like white people, and I blamed them. But then I began to understand that society had set it up that way, that it was all set up for women like me to fall flat on my face. The workshops helped me see that I had a choice. I could accept it or I could move out of it, and take responsibility for working with Meredith and other white people to change things.[18]

It did not take long for us to translate our newfound awareness into action. In 1998, the Alliance hired Edna Gulley, an indigenous black Appalachian leader from the coal-mining community of Clinchco, Virginia. By 1999, Edna had organized two local circles, young and "old,"[19] based on the Alliance's previous work in Clinchco and our growing anti-racist agenda.

The Clinchco Circles elected baptism by fire when members decided their premiere project would be to organize an anti-racism rally in Dickenson County, the first in the community's collective memory. As word of the rally spread, the Alliance office received disturbing communications from the Klan. Refusing to be intimidated, Circle members contacted a neighboring police department for protection and proceeded to organize an outstanding event. Others in the community took notice—they had to. As one observer noted, "There you were, a group of women not afraid to put it out there, to say it like it is."[20]

For the very first time, there was support from the local United Mineworkers, local churches, the local police, even the local merchants.[21]

The day the Alliance had our first racism workshop in Clinchco, the one at the elementary school, was the day my baby son learned about the work I was doing. He began to understand racism for what it was, and he cried. At the age of twenty-three, he cried. The second workshop made people angry. They finally got it that they were not to blame for white folks' problems. After that, we had lots of meetings to talk about racism and how another person does not have the right to take away your dignity and make you think you are nothing, all because you are black.[22]

During the next four years the women in Clinchco put on annual Black Her/history events, organized a local march for economic human rights, educated and registered voters, hosted a national Poor People's March on its way to Washington,

D.C., sponsored two more dismantling racism workshops, and provided weekly tutoring and computer classes. In 2004, the Clinchco Center of the Appalachian Women's Alliance proudly opened its doors. When asked why the women in her community had gotten involved in such a big way, Edna offered, "Because we didn't give up. We kept at it. Even when people closed their doors and talked about us, we stood up for what was right, and kept asking other women to stand with us, and they did."[23]

Meanwhile, the regional Alliance turned its attention to the arts. Reaching out to Appalachian women musicians, poets, dancers, and storytellers, we held our first Ironweed Festival in September 1997. As women came together across barriers of class, race, and sexual orientation "without even thinking about it,"[24] the festival became one of our most diverse events. For several years, the Alliance was energized by the presence of a talented collection of Appalachian artists who helped us create new interest among constituencies we had not previously reached. Though we were never able to offer these artists a huge performance venue, we provided them with a space and incentive to come together to exchange visions and inform and energize each other's work.

Ultimately, Ironweed grew into a unique venue for artists, activists, *Journal* authors, community members, and institutions such as universities and colleges

Appalachian Women's Alliance Ironweed Festival, Pipestem, West Virginia, 1997. (Photo by Meredith Dean)

to work together to develop innovative approaches for lifting up the authentic voice of Appalachian women. However, developing relationships with institutions meant that we were also building our middle- to upper-class, well-educated constituency. And despite the fact that we had become much more savvy about the dynamics of power and oppression, we found the work to be as difficult as ever. To keep our focus and base of power with our primary and original constituents, rather than get swept up or sidetracked by the energy and needs of our institutional partners, demanded constant vigilance.

One voice we found missing in most Appalachian communities was that of Appalachian lesbians. So in 2004, the Alliance officially adopted homophobia as one of our priority issues. Not surprisingly, the new focus provoked a response. Some reacted strongly, including conservative college students, rural community groups, and at least two church funding sources. Others left more quietly. As we fielded the fallout, our overriding concern was how to stand by our lesbian sisters without losing our local Circles. We need not have worried.

> Our community was afraid of the word homophobia. They didn't know what it was. I never heard the word until I got into this work. Lesbian was a word we had never heard before, either. I thought it was something you might catch. Of course, being a lesbian was out of the question. It's a man and a woman or your soul is hell-bound. At least that's what our preachers tell people every Sunday. As for me if you didn't tell me you were a lesbian I didn't know, but when I found out I would pull back remembering what my preacher said, and wondering what I was going to do if you tried to hit on me. Of course no one ever did. One of our local churches stopped giving us money after reading on our flyers that the Alliance didn't support homophobia. That took me off guard—it had never happened before. I'm not a fast thinker, so I said okay and left. Years down the road, after talking a lot more about homophobia in the Alliance, I went back to that church and asked the preacher for a donation. I started talking about the Bible and got the upper hand on him. We got a donation that year, and every year after. Our community is strong in their beliefs when it comes to the church, but they were open-minded about homophobia. As my mother always said, treat people the way you want to be treated and you have done your best.[25]

Dusk

> We need to envision the world we want and then express it in ways that touch the heart as well as the mind. It has worked before, it can work again.[26]

Through our next regional endeavor, *Mountain Women Rising,* the Alliance successfully united the issues, interests, and needs of all of our various constituencies. By creating a script of poetry and prose from our *Appalachian Women's Journal* with original music from our network of Appalachian songwriters, we were able to convey a strong sense of culture and place, while addressing issues of race, class, gender, and the environment in Appalachian communities. Beginning in 2004, the performance has served as a microphone for Appalachian women's voices, a venue for Appalachian artists for social change, an organizing tool for Appalachian communities, and an educational tool for universities and other institutions.

> The Appalachian Women's Alliance is building an educated and informed con-
> stituency of women and girls from Appalachian communities who have the
> skills, confidence, and political analysis necessary to challenge the prevailing
> patriarchy under which we all suffer and participate fully in the institutions,
> from the family to the government, that affect our lives.[27]

Our hope for each performance of *Mountain Women Rising*, that we might educate and inspire people to move from complacency to action, may actually be the simplest, most inclusive way to describe the twenty-year intent of the Appalachian Women's Alliance as a whole. Whether women are taking their first steps toward personal and political analysis by writing their stories for the *Appalachian Women's Journal*, or sharing their experiences with others through *Mountain Women Rising*, or showing up at our Clinchco Center to participate in local events, or pounding the streets with voter education materials, or taking part in regional workshops on race, class, and gender issues, or attending school board or town council meetings for the first time, women are stirring, getting up off their porches, and becoming involved in their lives and communities. And by that measure, the Appalachian Women's Alliance has much to celebrate.

> EDNA: My journey took me from being a black woman in Clinchco, not know-
> ing there was so much more out there for me, to traveling, driving, flying,
> and meeting people I never thought I would meet. It taught me how to trust
> the women that I was working with, to open up and break down the walls of
> anger that I had built up for so many years. Most importantly, the Alliance
> opened up my eyes, and gave me the tools and skills to bring together a com-
> munity that has so much to give—my own. I learned how to understand, to
> trust, to love and to give back. I learned how to listen to people, to process,
> to give up some of my power to other women, and to be an organizer rather
> than a leader all the time. I learned how to face racism and talk about it—
> I'm sure the anger and hate I used to have would have driven me out of my
> mind—and now nobody can ever make me feel ashamed of being a black
> woman ever again.
> LINDA: The Alliance pushed me to be a part of the work that we created, and it
> demanded my commitment to the process. Having been in isolation in one
> form or another most of my life, it was painful to try to find my voice and
> express my views. But Meredith and others really wanted to know what I was
> thinking, and they listened. I had never experienced that before. I used to just
> walk out of a group and not say anything. I was only there to hear or learn

what I wanted to know. I had no concept of responding to other people, or that my presence and my words could have a healing and empowering effect upon them. Finally, I realized that I had an impact on the group process, that my speaking and my reactions were important. In twenty years the one thing I am sure of is that no matter what the issues are or how many resources we have, it's our humanness that gets in our way. The struggle is to be able to stay with it and work through the personal to reach the social justice goals.

MEREDITH: I'm white, I'm middle class, and I'll never be able to divest myself of all that comes with that status. At the same time, much of what I've contributed to the Alliance's journey has been a direct result of the associated privilege. My journey has been to understand and own my privilege, then utilize it for the benefit of a movement within which I've experienced considerable isolation and alienation as a person who has it. My hope has come from the transformative personal relationships I've developed with Edna, Linda, and others who have truly engaged with me in that struggle. And for them I am forever thankful. In the Philippines, they talk about a Theology of Struggle, rather than liberation. After one hundred–plus years of organizing, Filipinos from all sectors, including the middle class, forced a repressive, U.S.-backed dictator out of power. But in the end, very little actually changed. The oppressive structures remained the same. I'm not sure I believe that governments or institutions anywhere can ever really change. What I do believe is that there is hope for all of us in the struggle. That's where the transformation happens. It's all about the struggle.

Notes

1. Linda McKinney, "Good Grief! Why Do I Do This Work?" *Appalachian Women's Journal* 8 (Summer 1996): 25.

2. Debbie Seagraves, written for the Appalachian Women's Alliance *Dawning Ceremony,* Appalachian South Folklife Center (November 14, 1992). Recorded in the minutes of the meeting that are part of *The Herstory of the Appalachian Women's Alliance, 1987–1991,* which was compiled by and is in the possession of Meredith Dean.

3. Meredith Dean, personal journal entry, 2009.

4. Women's Task Force members from 1988 to 1991: Linda McKinney, Teri Vautrin, Dorothy Kincaid, Judy Pace, Debbie Seagraves, Gaye Evans, Mollie Blankenship, Marilyn Logan, Mary Williamson, and Meredith Dean.

5. The publication was renamed the *Appalachian Women's Journal* in 1994 to include urban Appalachian women and is still published under that name.

6. Edna Gulley, interview with Meredith Dean, 2009.

7. Linda McKinney, interview with Meredith Dean, 2009.

8. From the *Gathering of 30 Minutes,* Southwest Virginia 4-H Center, Abingdon, 1991, in *The Herstory of the Appalachian Women's Alliance.*

9. Appalachian Women's Alliance minutes, Appalachian South Folklife Center, November 13–15, 1992, in *Core Leader Meetings 1991–2005,* which was compiled by and is in the possession of Meredith Dean.

10. Edna Gulley, interview with Meredith Dean, 2009.

11. Barbara Greene, founding leader, at a core leader meeting in 1993.

12. Gaye Evans, from "The Caravan," *Appalachian Women's Journal* 6 (Spring 1995): 31–32.

13. Meredith Dean, "Appalachian Women Rising Up," *RESIST Newsletter* 10 (May 2001): 3.

14. Edna Gulley, interview with Meredith Dean, 2009.

15. McKinney, "Good Grief," 23.

16. Appalachian Women's Alliance core leadership from 1992 to 1995: Jo Davenport, Meredith Dean, Jean Eason, Gaye Evans, Barbara Greene, Edna Gulley, Pauletta Hansel, Diana Hays, Carol Honeycutt, Dianne Levy, Marilyn Logan, Linda McKinney, Carolyn Murdock, Judy Pace, Debbie Seagraves, Jean Stone, Maureen Sullivan, Teri Vautrin, Winnie Vautrin, Grace Wanamaker, Carol Williams, and Marty Zinn.

Appalachian Women's Alliance core leadership from 1996 to 1999: Jackie Cook, Joletta Crowe, Meredith Dean, Gaye Evans, Patricia Gillikin, Christie Green, Barbara Greene, Edna Gulley, Diana Hays, Peg Hill, Carol Honeycutt, Lisa Justice, Terry Kessinger, Jean Korkisch, Libby Lindsay, Linda McKinney, Carol O'Brien, Kem Short, Alice Smith, Melissa Tuckey, Phillis White, and Marty Zinn.

Appalachian Women's Alliance core leadership from 2000 to 2003: Amber Adams, Liza Jane Alexander, Cynthia Babb, Joletta Crowe, Sunale Crowe, Meredith Dean, Helen deHaven, Edna Gulley, Kiya Heartwood, Peg Hill, Lisa Justice, Deborah Kerwood, Terry Kessinger, Sam Kraft, Sue Massek, Linda McKinney, Jennifer Mock, Paula Nelson, Carol O'Brien, Karen Shaffer, Kem Short, Alice Smith, Maureen Sullivan, and Anna Suter.

Appalachian Women's Alliance core leadership from 2004 to 2007: Carla Hatfield Barrett, Viney Charles, Meredith Dean, Helen deHaven, Edna Gulley, Frankie Gulley, Donna Jones, Rema Keen, Deborah Kerwood, Robin Lambert, Karen Mayer, Linda McKinney, Jennifer Mock, Coraline Norris, Linda Petrie, Karen Shaffer, Maureen Sullivan, Martha Venatoe, Laura Weaver, Sandra Whittaker, Faye Williams, and Megan Williams.

Appalachian Women's Alliance core leadership from 2008 to 2009: Tracy Byrd, Viney Charles, Joyce Gains, Edna Gulley, Raven Gulley, Craig Mickens, Jennifer Mock, Coraline Norris, Justin Preston, Brenda Stanley, Martha Venatoe, Sandra Whittaker, Faye Williams, and Megan Williams.

17. Meredith Dean, personal journal entry, 2009.

18. Edna Gulley, interview with Meredith Dean, 2009.

19. The two Clinchco Circles divided themselves between the women and girls who were under twenty-five and those who were older.

20. Kisha Milgram, who soon after became a leading member of the Clinchco Young Women's Circle, 1999. In Dean, "Appalachian Women Rising Up," 4.

21. Dean, "Appalachian Women Rising Up," 4.

22. Edna Gully, interview with Meredith Dean, 2009.

23. Ibid.

24. Ironweed Festival participant, 1998.

25. Edna Gulley, interview with Meredith Dean, 2009.

26. Candie Carawan, "Appalachian Artists and Activists for Social Change: Scenes and Reflections from Ironweed, 2004," *Ironweed Newsletter* 5 (Winter 2005): 2.

27. Appalachian Women's Alliance purpose statement, 2009, found at http://www.appalachianwomen.org/join.html.

CHAPTER 8

The Southern Empowerment Project
Homegrown Organizing Gone Too Soon

June Rostan and Walter Davis

The Southern Empowerment Project (SEP) was a unique community organizing school created in 1986 by five southern and Appalachian community-based groups.[1] The founders sought through SEP to address a problem confronting many urban and rural community groups in the region: the difficulty of finding and training organizing staff.[2] Volunteer leaders (not staff) of the member groups comprised the board of directors, thereby ensuring that they, along with the professional organizers, would direct and shape the programs as well as govern this new regional intermediary organization. Over the lifetime of SEP, the member groups changed, but the core idea of a training network rooted in community groups themselves persisted.

SEP affirmed membership-based, multi-issue organizing and helped community leaders internalize organizing concepts and reach beyond their own constituencies. It broadened the pool of potential organizers and improved the qualifications of organizing staff in a wide range of organizations. Between 1987 and 2007, SEP trained 337 people in multiple-week community organizing and fund-raising schools, hundreds in leadership gatherings and retreats, nearly two hundred in workshops conducted in Spanish, and many others in short workshops and through onsite technical assistance.

Our experience spans the entire history of SEP. June Rostan, the first staff person, served seventeen years as coordinator and director. Walter Davis served as recruiter and training coordinator for fifteen years and director for the final years beginning in 2004. We examine what made the school unusual, its strengths as well as its weaknesses and limitations, turning points in its development, and the factors and circumstances that led to its closure in May 2007.

Goals and Organizational History

The Southern Empowerment Project believed in its name. *Empowerment* was not an abstract concept: the community, the organization, and individuals must grow and learn from the organizing. Goals, campaigns, and issues were important but so were the *means* to the ends. Thus, SEP's organizing goals included winning issues, building organizations, empowering individuals, changing institutions, fostering democratic values, and overcoming racism, classism, sexism, and homophobia. SEP taught the mechanics of organizing, but the power analysis training and strategy development focused on institutional change in a new way. We believed that "power plus oppression" produces "isms" that are preserved in oppressive institutions—not just elite institutions, but also potentially our own organizations.

As a regional organization SEP had some advantages. It covered Appalachia and the upper South—West Virginia, Kentucky, Tennessee, and North and South Carolina—and later brought in a group from Louisiana, states whose population diversity varied widely. Its membership always included majority African American groups, such as North Carolina's A. Philip Randolph Institute, the Charlotte Organizing Project, and Just Organized Neighborhoods Area Headquarters (JONAH). SEP board meetings and other gatherings were frequently the first time black and white community leaders worked together as equals. Blacks and whites shared leadership on the board of directors and valued working together, learning from each other, and developing friendships. Those relationships helped the board take on tough topics and challenges. Stronger groups usually sent leaders who clearly understood their role as board

---

SEP MEMBER GROUPS*

Carolina Alliance for Fair Employment (CAFE), South Carolina
Charlotte Organizing Project (CHOP), North Carolina
Citizens for Justice Equality and Fairness (CJEF), Tennessee
Citizens Organized to End Poverty in the Commonwealth (CO-EPIC), Kentucky
Community Farm Alliance (CFA), Kentucky
Just Organized Neighborhoods Area Headquarters (JONAH), Tennessee
Kentuckians For The Commonwealth (formerly Kentucky Fair Tax Coalition) (KFTC)
Kentucky Fairness Alliance (KFA)
Louisiana Labor-Neighbor Project (LLNP)
North Carolina A. Philip Randolph Institute (NC APRI)
Save Our Cumberland Mountains (SOCM), Tennessee
Solutions to Issues of Concern to Knoxvillians (SICK), Tennessee
South Carolina Fair Share
Tennesseans for Fair Taxation (TFT)
Tennessee Hunger Coalition (THC)
Tennessee Valley Energy Coalition (TVEC) (evolved into the Southern Alliance for
    Clean Energy [SACE])
West Virginia Organizing Project (WVOP)
Western North Carolina Alliance (WNCA)

*Member groups varied at different moments in SEP history

members and how to govern an organization. They helped educate and train less experienced board members. Staff valued the board members' role and looked for ways to help develop additional skills, such as how to design and conduct training. For a number of years, SEP Leadership Gatherings, conferences of leaders from SEP member groups, were planned and conducted almost totally by the leaders themselves.

As an intermediary organization, SEP did not engage members day-to-day in organizing. Rather, it provided outreach and training for its member groups, and they did the daily organizing. That provided some elbow room to experiment, develop theory, and push the envelope on certain aspects of organizing, such as overcoming the "isms," which some organizers considered risky to do in their own organizations. For the African American leaders on SEP's board, challenging racism was not a choice; it was a way of life that was integrated into their organizing. They pushed their white colleagues to take on overcoming racism in their organizing and organizations.

While SEP viewed overcoming racism, classism, sexism, and heterosexism head-on as part of community organizing, some organizers argued this would divide members of community groups. SEP felt that refusing to face internal as well as external oppressions allowed existing divisions to sharpen, subjecting community members to outside exploitation through wedge issues. SEP's mission statement reflected this commitment: "SEP stands with the oppressed challenging racism and social injustice. SEP recruits and trains community leaders to become organizers to assist organizations in the South and Appalachia to solve community problems."

The SEP Organizing School

The Organizing School began as an eight-week endeavor, but quickly evolved to a six-week combination of residential training and field placements. It required considerable commitment from both individuals and the organizations that sent them, but produced organizers who had a good understanding of the theory of membership-based community organizing, a solid exposure to the region's organizing groups, and strong bonds with one another. SEP incorporated the history and culture of organizing in the region into its curriculum. Documentary films, music, readings, and role-plays conveyed the stories of civil rights, community, and labor struggles in the South and Appalachia. Community organizing set in this context is inspirational and politically progressive.

For the first eight years the training program moved to a new location each residential week, sharing the training with member groups and their leaders. Usually the lead trainer was an experienced organizer from a member group. SEP respected and drew upon both rural and urban organizing models, approaches, issues, settings, and scenarios. Families involved in organizing welcomed SEP trainees to mountain hollows, family farms, and inner-city neighborhoods. A discussion of an organizing campaign such as repealing Kentucky's broad form deed (which allowed strip mining without a landowner's permission) was followed by a visit to an actual strip mine. On one memorable occasion, coal company employees pushed the truck holding SEP training participants away from a massively stripped section of land in an attempt to prevent the group from seeing a hillside being dynamited. It was one of many dramatic convergences of theory and practice.

The commitment to addressing racism, sexism, classism, and heterosexism was lived out in the community organizing curriculum and organizer and leader development. The theoretical and philosophical framework of training on "isms" in the context of organizing was grounded in organizing scenarios and problem solving. One whole day was spent on "Overcoming Racism in Organizing." The session always had a biracial facilitation team and primarily dealt with institutional racism. Part of the day was spent in separate caucuses by race. For many of the white trainees it was their first exposure to the idea of "white privilege."

Community organizing and membership-based fund-raising were woven together as "sisters in the struggle." SEP developed the theory and practice of integrating fund-raising from members and donors with organizing via the Fundraising School for Community Organizing (FSCO), which consisted of a full week of the Organizing School, training "clusters," and freestanding training with community groups. In the "clusters" fund-raisers for groups met on a regular basis for three years, learned new skills, and developed specific goals for their organizations via tasks and assignments between training sessions. They developed, implemented, and evaluated fund-raising plans and held each other accountable. It was peer learning at its best. Some participants institutionalized and systematized member and donor giving in their organizations. Via the Fundraising School organizers began to see that raising funds from members and donors was an integral part of their jobs.

In sum, SEP was innovative in the types of people it brought together for training, the format and focus of its training, and the targets of its outreach. For example, workshops brought together leaders from Appalachian, Latino immigrant, and African American groups with leaders from gay and lesbian groups. SEP added new forms of learning. In addition to FSCO, these included Leadership Gatherings, education in planning and conducting training, and retreats and advanced training for alumni and experienced organizers. In addition, SEP joined with the Center for Third World Organizing to create the Grassroots Institute for Fundraising Training (GIFT), an organization that trains and develops fund-raisers of color and provides fund-raising training and consulting to groups of color.

New Initiatives That Faltered

SEP's willingness to experiment, take risks, and develop new initiatives may have contributed to its demise. During its last few years, SEP made two significant departures from its initial role and mission that, in combination with powerful cultural forces, led ultimately to its closing. Both projects were worth doing; however, they presented difficulties not fully anticipated and not sufficiently managed.

The first of these initiatives was the Southern Organizing Cooperative, established in 1997 by SEP, its member groups, and other organizations in the region, including the Alabama Organizing Project, Greater Birmingham Ministries, Federation of Child Care Centers of Alabama, Alabama Arise, Southern Echo, and the Virginia Organizing Project. These groups joined with key program officers of foundations that funded community organizing to develop an analysis and critique of foundation funding patterns and policies. They pursued an organizing approach designed to get foundations to give more money to community organizing. This effort ultimately led to the formation of the Southern Organizing Cooperative and more than one million dollars in funding from the Ford Foundation.

Two purposes shaped the Cooperative. One was to improve the organizing and organizational development of the twenty-two groups from West Virginia to Louisiana. The other was to bring new money into the South and Appalachia for community organizing. In its first years much of the Organizing Cooperative's work involved holding conferences and workshops. Governing the Cooperative also involved regular meetings of staff and volunteer leaders from member groups. The demands of additional meetings, conferences, and workshops convened by the Cooperative exhausted the leaders and staff of SEP's member organizations, especially in the smaller groups, and adversely affected participation in SEP meetings, Leadership Gatherings, and other events.

Every organization must weigh the cost of creating coalitions. Building the Cooperative weakened SEP. There was confusion among foundation program officers about the difference and delineation of roles between SEP and the Cooperative. Both were intermediary or "umbrella" groups and it was difficult to understand the distinction between them, except that SEP trained community organizers and fund-raisers. Tensions around resources and money grew. Some of the directors who looked out for the interests of their organizations first and foremost were successful in snaring new money. Others like SEP, which helped a number of groups access money, lost out. SEP received $1.2 million from the W. K. Kellogg Foundation for eleven groups to pursue innovations in organizing. Some of the groups would never have been able to obtain funding from Kellogg on their own, but SEP's spirit and practice of sharing access to foundations was not reciprocated by other groups in the Cooperative.

The second new initiative was the establishment of Latinos Unidos, a group that addressed the problems of Latino immigrants in the region. SEP's role had been to train and advise organizers and member organizations. So actually organizing and building a membership organization was a major departure from SEP's previous history and work. The demographic changes and influx of Mexican and Central American immigrants into North Carolina, Tennessee, and Georgia were obvious, although the implications for community organizing were less so. Progressive activists and groups were thinking about how to assist these immigrants at the same time that community organizations in the region were struggling with how to diversify their memberships. SEP's staff was familiar with the multiracial Center for Third World Organizing in California, which trained organizers and developed several multiracial organizing groups. In 2000, SEP's board of directors approved hiring an experienced Latino organizer from Mexico to do outreach with recent Latino immigrants in east Tennessee. Within several months groups of immigrants were meeting in four different locations to talk about their problems. Eventually they began to demand better services from local governments and immigration reform from Congress and the Bush administration.

The monthly meetings of the four chapters and the regional training sessions of members and leaders were conducted in Spanish. A core of leaders learned the basics of community organizing and/or built on organizing and mobilizing experiences they had in Mexico. Latinos Unidos subsequently helped found the

Latinos Unidos' lobbying trip to the U.S. Capitol, 2003. (Photo by Wendy Romero, courtesy of Archives of Appalachia, East Tennessee State University)

Tennessee Immigrant and Refugee Rights Coalition (TIRRC) and hosted the Los Angeles buses of the Immigrant Worker Freedom Ride at a picnic and march for immigration reform in Morristown, Tennessee, a city where several thousand Latino immigrants live. The march was the first time Latino immigrants had taken any kind of public action in the city.[3]

Latinos Unidos was an exciting and challenging development in SEP's work, but it consumed a great deal of time and energy by program staff, who never numbered more than five. Moreover, not all of the staff, board, and member groups were committed to organizing undocumented Latino immigrants. In retrospect, there should have been more debate and deliberation on the decision to do direct organizing. The demands of Latinos Unidos on SEP's time, energy, focus, and resources, especially when combined with dwindling foundation and church funding, led to serious problems in communication and trust within and between the staff and board that ultimately led to crisis and weakened the organization.

Understanding SEP's Decline

On March 31, 2007, the members of the board voted unanimously to disband SEP. We point to a number of factors that contributed to the demise of the organization. The first was the loss of key relationships between SEP and member organizations. During the first years of the Organizing School, the directors of key member groups, particularly the founders, had a close relationship with SEP. They attended board meetings and served as lead trainers in the Organizing School. As the years passed, that changed and directors and organizers left SEP work to volunteer leaders and newer staff. Gradually, the trusted relations with seasoned leaders gave way to the personal interests of individual volunteers, and the views and interests of the member groups played less and less of a role in SEP meetings. To get good volunteer leaders on the SEP board there had to be staff of member groups committed to identifying those leaders, asking them if they would serve, and making sure they knew what was expected of them. As the relationship with the director and/or key staff weakened, so did the group's relationship with SEP unless its representative to the SEP board was very conscientious, even insistent, in reporting back to the member group.

A second reason for SEP's demise was decreased participation by member groups in the Organizing School. Over the years, SEP staff assumed more of the training role, particularly after the school stopped holding the training with member groups in different states. After eight years of training sessions hosted by member groups, fewer leaders participated. This was the primary reason for holding the training at one site—Maryville College, located in the same town as the SEP office. In addition, the resources (travel time and costs, housing, food, and time to coordinate logistics) required to move to a new location for each week of residential training were tremendous. This further weakened the relationship with member groups.

Even though these groups were member-led, staff is a critical element in making sure there is follow through, communication, participation in the organizers school by new staff, and involvement of SEP in their organization's development.

Over time, some member groups did not make full use of the Organizing School. In the latter years, SEP's training in grassroots fund-raising was the most popular program, while basic organizing and anti-oppression sessions were increasingly neglected. Weakened participation of member groups was also a product of these groups' decline. One after another, the Tennessee Hunger Coalition, Citizens Organized to End Poverty in the Commonwealth, West Virginia Organizing Project, Charlotte Organizing Project, Citizens for Justice, Equality and Fairness, JONAH, and Solutions to Issues of Concern to Knoxvillians became fragile shells or closed outright. As a result, representative leadership in SEP withered. Only a few groups continued to discuss their annual renewal of membership. "Election" of SEP representatives often became a decision of member groups' staff. In the end, the board that closed SEP did so with no objection from member groups.

An additional factor in SEP's decline involved the contradiction between its emphasis on anti-racist transformation in both individuals and organizations, which required years of ongoing effort, and the short-term funding cycles of foundations, which seldom exceeded three years. Foundations often would stand up for diversity and even demand anti-racist education, only to change priorities a short time later.

Powerful cultural and political forces also contributed to the decline of SEP. The events of September 11, 2001, and the development of a climate of fear and suspicion, a rightward political shift, and the war in Iraq created a difficult environment for community organizing and single-issue groups. Millions marched, sent e-mails, and called the White House, but their organizing and activism did not stop the war. People began to feel powerless. Financial losses and shifts in foundation funding priorities, along with the focus on Gulf Coast recovery from the devastating effects of Hurricane Katrina, meant there was less money for organizing. Funding decreases and the sense of futility created unhealthy organizational dynamics. These did not happen overnight. It took a couple of years for these conditions to set in. Wherever people could find some power, they seized it, and in some cases organizations and individuals in them started to turn on each other. Some of this organizational dysfunction eventually surfaced at SEP.

Finally, personal factors also contributed to the decline of SEP, in particular the deaths of two important people associated with the organization. In 2001 staff member Rosemary Derrick died unexpectedly. Rosemary had been an organizer and the director for JONAH before joining SEP's staff. Her organizing experience enriched the training program and her leadership development capability strengthened the SEP leaders. Her death was a great loss to the organization, its board, and to her colleagues on the staff. Rosemary had helped make sure that

SEP was a healthy organization. Her death rent a tear in the fabric of SEP that never was mended. In 2004 Vicki Quatmann, a consultant who worked closely with SEP in developing the fund-raising curriculum, teaching in the Fundraising School, and providing on-site training and technical assistance, died unexpectedly in Bolivia. She had just completed a creative, user-friendly fund-raising training manual called *You Can Do It!* that SEP published in English and Spanish.[4] Vicki's death was also a shock and loss to the organization and her friends on the board and staff. There are no guidebooks on how to heal groups and individuals from such tragedies, and they take their toll.

Lessons Learned

SEP's antioppression training is one of its proudest legacies. The fact that the board, staff, and participants in the training program were diverse and came from oppressed groups made it easier to take on the "isms." For example, a board member sitting with other board members at one of the early Leadership Gatherings revealed that she was a lesbian. SEP began to address the issue of homophobia because gay organizers who worked for member groups were encountering problems. Those organizers and other staff encouraged SEP to take homophobia on, to pave the way, so they could then follow. The board's curriculum committee affirmed the addition of overcoming homophobia, later called overcoming heterosexism, the system of privileges given to "straights."

From the start SEP made anti-racism the centerpiece of training on oppression. The power structure uses racism and white supremacy to divide people who otherwise would be allies. Even in communities that are primarily of one race or ethnic group, understanding racism is part of building community power. SEP put forth the concept that racism was prejudice plus power. Only whites could be racist in a system that rewarded them for preserving the status quo. Blacks and Hispanics could be prejudiced and biased but they did not have the power to impose their will on the community. SEP did not force people to accept this definition, but just presenting it led to intense, often life-changing, learning moments. Resistance to the concept of racist power was not limited to whites. In caucus groups, people of color also examined how internalized oppression disempowered them.

Member organizations did not always go along with challenging racism. Some sought to avoid anti-racism training by sending staff to some weeks but not the full course. This tended to diminish the overall impact of the training upon individual participants and to take the heat off the groups back home. White people who did not come to terms with racism were blocked by it. In response, SEP made sure that the entire curriculum was anti-racist, thus fusing traditional organizing methods with anti-racist concepts. However, most groups that resisted SEP's early anti-racist work came to embrace anti-racism in word and deed. That is one of the living legacies of SEP. Nonetheless, a few walked away from the conversation permanently.

Classism was also a profound barrier in itself and to the anti-racism work. Classism exists among elites but it is also present within community organizations. Classism blocked many solid people's organizations from succeeding because poor and working-class people frequently deferred to the middle-class "experts" or the more educated leaders and members. Many white organizers who came to the field were from middle-class or upper-class backgrounds. They often did not see themselves as racist and resisted the fact that they enjoyed white privilege. Nor did they see their own class privilege.

SEP's unusual origins and structure make it a model worth emulating. Frequently intermediaries constitute themselves and then ask the community organizations to partake of their offerings. Community groups often are concerned that they will be competing with intermediaries for resources, both from foundations and individual donors. But the member groups formed SEP based on a need they identified. SEP's governance structure reflected its origins. The group was accountable to its member organizations via their designated volunteer leaders who served on the board of directors.

A representative structure is particularly hard to maintain over the long haul in an intermediary organization. The first ten years of SEP's life cycle were the best for engagement of member groups, including both leaders and staff. The degree of communication with and accountability to the member group varied, depending on the experience level of the leader and the interest by the staff liaison from the member group. We struggled with the issue of whether the staff of groups should sit alongside volunteers in decision making as they did in the early formation of SEP.[5] Other networks have had a life cycle curve leading to periodic crisis and renewal or end. We know too well that many "coalitions" turn into meetings of paid staff rather than community leaders.

SEP believed that community organizers must be actively accountable to a constituency. Passive membership cannot build the power of the group. One can gauge how strong a group's membership is by watching when there is a mobilization, lobbying event, or direct action. If the same handful of leaders and staff or a small number of familiar activists turns out, the politicians may be polite but they will not change. It takes membership numbers and strength as well as deep community relationships to alter how public officials relate to the community organization. It is a waste of people's time to do actions in front of empty buildings where no public officials are present to answer people's demands.

We learned that you fail to train your leaders at great risk. You cannot do a class in organizing only with staff. Nor can you teach Organizing 101 to leaders and think you have accomplished the job. Both staff and members need resources and training regularly and consistently. The fundamentals of organizing remain the same in an Internet age: Go to the ground. Build the movement, one person at a time within organizations. Do not get so mesmerized by an issue that you fail to prepare people for building the democratic power to win. There is no substitute for confronting power. You cannot sweet talk your way to winning.

Toward the Future

There is still a need for well-trained, anti-racist, politically savvy community organizers in Appalachia and the South. The framework and conditions for community organizing have changed, however, particularly with the successes of the 2008 Obama campaign in using the Internet to provide nonhierarchical access to participation in a presidential campaign and to raise money.

We can no longer afford our isolation. We must build political power, not just be moral witnesses. Coalitions and networks must be renewed with true and open acknowledgment of shared self-interest, and the reasons for the existence of current and future coalitions need to be periodically assessed. Any new efforts at training organizers need to analyze what has changed in organizing and what that means for a training program and curriculum. The world is very different today from what it was in 1986.

We still believe that the basics are vital: build organizations, train leaders, analyze power, form strategies, mobilize the power of the people to force those with decision-making power to fulfill our demands and dreams. Share information and ideas. Trust the people to lead.

Notes

1. The founding members were the Charlotte Organizing Project; Kentucky Fair Tax Coalition; North Carolina A. Philip Randolph Institute; Save Our Cumberland Mountains; and Tennessee Valley Energy Coalition.

2. The various discussions and meetings that ultimately led to the formation of SEP are described by Melanie A. Zuercher in her *Homegrown Organizing—Southern Empowerment Project, Training for Organizing and Fundraising: The First Ten Years* (Maryville, Tenn.: Southern Empowerment Project, 1996), 1–4.

3. See chapter 11 in this volume for additional information about organizing Latinos in Morristown.

4. Vicki Quatmann, *You Can Do It! A Volunteer's Guide to Raising Money for Your Group in Words and Pictures* (Maryville, Tenn.: Southern Empowerment Project, 2002). Now distributed by the Appalachian Community Fund. Spanish information the same.

5. Richard Couto and SEP alumna Catherine Guthrie point to the significance of cooperation among organizations: "The experience of staff members is another important and obvious source of ideas that is especially valuable when there are multiple staffs, as in the case of the Southern Empowerment Project." See Richard A. Couto with Catherine S. Guthrie, *Making Democracy Work Better: Mediating Structures, Social Capital, and the Democratic Prospect* (Chapel Hill: University of North Carolina Press, 1999), 258.

CHAPTER 9

Center for Participatory Change
Cultivating Grassroots Support Organizing

Craig White, Paul Castelloe, Molly Hemstreet,
Yaira Andrea Arias Soto, and Jeannette Butterworth

Since 2000, the Center for Participatory Change (CPC) has helped organize, support, or train thousands of grassroots leaders in more than 150 community groups, grassroots networks, and worker-owned cooperatives in western North Carolina. As the five staff members of CPC, we have written this chapter to share some lessons we have learned about organizing in Appalachia in the twenty-first century.

When we first started our work, there was no blueprint to follow. We borrowed techniques from community organizing, approaches from popular education, and the philosophies of participatory rural development. From there we made the road as we walked it, learning by doing, listening to people, trying new approaches, and making mistakes. As we grew, we connected with other organizations in Appalachia and the Southeast that had come to do similar work, but from different directions—sustainable agriculture, economic development, multiracial coalition building. Despite the differences, there seemed to be patterns to the processes of building, supporting, and connecting—but not leading, directing, or controlling—the grassroots organizations that are central to any change effort. Out of those conversations, we coined the term "grassroots support organizing" and began to define this model, which we believe holds great promise for building a diverse, multi-issue, decentralized, and sustainable movement for justice and social transformation.

Grassroots Support Organizing
and Social Transformation

Grassroots organizations are the fundamental vehicle of social change. People on the social, political, and economic margins of a society, when they get organized, become the basic force that drives the society toward greater inclusiveness and equality. That social transformation includes shifts in attitudes and behaviors, revisions of laws and policies, redistribution of money and other resources, and changes in social and economic structures. For all of these, the fundamental moving force is the people at the grassroots.

Grassroots Support Organizing (GSO) is a model of community organizing developed out of this principle. Rather than organizing around an issue and building a base of people who develop a related campaign, GSO concentrates on building the skills, capacities, and critical analysis of people who belong to grassroots groups. These groups apply their abilities to a number of different projects and efforts, affecting a wide range of issues over a long time span. The key organizing principle is that the decisions of each group and the direction of its work are controlled by the members, which keeps power, ownership, and accountability at the grassroots level.

Across a region, these groups connect with each other—sometimes formally in coalitions and partnerships and sometimes informally through networks and personal relationships. This web of grassroots leaders, groups, and networks is the "grassroots infrastructure" of the region. Power, decision making, and resources are not centralized, but distributed throughout the grassroots infrastructure. The connections among people and groups are often informal, based on shared values rather than concrete partnerships. For these reasons, the grassroots infrastructure is largely intangible and difficult to define precisely, compared with, say, a formal coalition of organizations working on a particular advocacy campaign. The decentralized, informal nature of the grassroots infrastructure is also its greatest strength, however, because it allows for a level of inclusiveness, diversity, flexibility, creativity, and responsiveness that would be impossible in any single, centralized effort. In one region or around the globe, the grassroots infrastructure serves as the foundation of the long-term social justice movement.

The purpose of a grassroots support organization is to strengthen a region's grassroots infrastructure—to help those leaders, groups, and networks become more effective, resourceful, resilient, and connected. Over time, the work of many grassroots projects and advocacy efforts has a cumulative impact: creating alternative social and economic systems, improving communities, changing attitudes and behaviors, and making mainstream systems and institutions more inclusive, responsive, and accountable to people who have historically been pushed to the margins of their society.

The Center for Participatory Change:
History and Approach

The Center for Participatory Change is a grassroots support organization that provides support to community-based groups, organized and led by Latino, African American, Cherokee, Hmong, and white Appalachian grassroots leaders, in the twenty-five counties of western North Carolina. CPC's mission calls us to work with community groups and organizations that are focused on racial or economic justice. Our partner organizations' work varies greatly, including advocacy for workers' rights and immigrant rights, workshops on dismantling racism, preserving Cherokee culture and traditions, sustainable agriculture, improving educational opportunities for people of color, worker-owned cooperative businesses, and much more. CPC also prioritizes working with groups that are organized and controlled by people on the social, economic, or political margins of society. About 75 percent of the grassroots leaders we work with are women, and about 70 percent of these are women of color.

Since its inception, CPC's approach has merged popular education, community organizing, and participatory development. We looked to several Appalachian organizations, particularly the Highlander Research and Education Center, as models for community organizing and popular education. CPC took what we saw as the better of these two approaches and integrated them with the strengths of participatory development approaches being created in India and sub-Saharan Africa. The Grassroots Support Organizing approach outlined in this chapter combines heavy doses of the thinking and practices of people like Myles Horton and Paulo Freire (popular education), Saul Alinsky and César Chávez (community organizing), and Robert Chambers and many participatory development practitioners in the Global South. The combination of these three approaches has resulted in an organizing model that stresses grassroots participation and power, values reflection and critical analysis, and is capable of both organizing for short-term advocacy goals and concentrating on long-term human and community development.

Organizational Structure: Collective Authority and Responsibility

CPC began as a conventionally structured nonprofit organization, with two co-executive directors and a board with a chair, vice chair, secretary, and treasurer. In practice, however, we did not follow that formal structure; both staff and board were more collective and nonhierarchical. During 2005, while our board and staff were engaging in a long-term training and reflection process around race, privilege, and oppression, we realized that our organizational structure did not reflect our values. Over the course of a year, CPC developed a new staff structure. We listed all of our pieces of work, rated the ones that held the most power organizationally, and then divided up those roles more fairly. We looked at informal power, too—who talked the most in our meetings, whose ideas and comments usually held sway in decisions, how issues were framed, what was valued within the organization. We also talked about race and gender privilege and how they play out in organizational contexts.

By the end of 2005, we formalized our new nonhierarchical, collective structure. CPC no longer has an executive director; organizational decisions are made by consensus, and all staff share authority and responsibility. Each staff member acts as a "point person" for particular pieces of CPC's work (for example, external work like supporting a grassroots group, or internal work like financial management, grassroots fund-raising, or grant writing). The point person is not responsible for doing all the work in that area; rather, he or she is responsible for overseeing and coordinating that work. Inherently powerful roles, such as liaison with the board and financial management, are rotated among the staff every two years, so that skills, knowledge, and power are widely shared. CPC's board also changed its structure, getting rid of conventional officer roles and replacing them with small, multiracial teams that carry out the same responsibilities.

This collective organizational structure has come to work very well for us. We have a small number of staff members, all highly motivated and self-directed, who have the power and freedom to determine and carry out their best organizing. We are accountable to each other, and the questions of organizational power, influence, and authority are always on the table for discussion. Most important, this structure lets us be transparent, both claiming and practicing our values of equality and participation.

Core Principles of Grassroots Support Organizing

Though the content and pace of CPC's work vary from group to group, we believe that certain core principles are essential to grassroots support organizing.

BELIEVE IN PEOPLE   We start from the fundamental belief that the people in a community are those who best know what that community needs; the people who are affected by an issue are those who most deserve to have a voice on that issue.

POWER RESTS WITH PEOPLE   It follows that the people in a community group must retain their own power and decision-making authority. This can be tricky, because the very experiences, skills, knowledge, and connections to resources that make the CPC staff useful to the group also carry an inherent authority. CPC staff must be explicit and transparent about remaining in a support and advisory role.

WALKING ALONGSIDE   CPC organizers conceive our role as "walking alongside"—we are not out in front leading, and we are not in back pushing. We are walking alongside the members of each grassroots group, learning together, taking risks together, supporting each other for as long as the group wants and needs our support. Walking alongside also means being there for grassroots leaders and groups over the long haul.

RECIPROCITY   CPC believes that every relationship with a grassroots organization is an exchange—there is giving and giving back. What CPC provides to a group may be tangible—training, facilitation, technical or personal support, even a small grant. However, it is not more important than what we receive in return: learning, relationships, stories, and the opportunity to be part of meaningful social change.

FOLLOW THE ENERGY   CPC staff put time, energy, and resources into the issues, projects, and tasks that are priorities of the grassroots leaders we support. This helps keep the group in control of the relationship and means that CPC's resources are used as effectively as possible.

PEOPLE LEARN WHAT THEY ARE READY TO LEARN, WHEN THEY ARE READY TO LEARN IT   Effective adult learning comes from experience. It does not work for CPC to come in with an agenda of what we think the group needs, whether it is effective group decision making or how to engage the media. When the members' work brings them to a place where it is useful for them to develop those skills, they will ask for CPC's support if they want it. This requires our approach to be responsive and reflective, rather than directive.

RACIAL JUSTICE AND HUMAN DIGNITY   We work with a deep commitment to racial justice and human dignity. As an organization and as individuals, we recognize that our region and society have been shaped by gross inequalities and injustices. Our analysis of power, privilege, and oppression shapes everything that we do, particularly in our recognition that the "helping" relationship has historically been a major contributor to inequality, oppression, and privilege.

The Practice of Grassroots Support Organizing

CPC's grassroots support includes community organizing, leadership development, capacity building, advocacy assistance, help in forming networks, and micro-grants. In practice, the support that CPC provides is different in every case, specific to the needs, culture, opportunities, and challenges of each group. However, there are general patterns to that work, which we outline below in three sections illustrated with stories from different grassroots groups and organizations.

Supporting Grassroots Groups and Organizations

Because grassroots groups are the fundamental vehicle of social change, as well as the basic building blocks of the grassroots infrastructure, CPC's primary mission is to help strengthen grassroots groups and organizations in western North Carolina. Sometimes we train and support organizers as they first pull people together to form a fledgling group or cooperative. Other times, we work with a group that has been around for years and needs help in revitalizing its programs, membership, or mission. Regardless of the group's stage in its life cycle, our work usually involves technical support, interpersonal support, or assistance with their organizational structure. CPC also has a micro-grants program, the Self Development Fund, which provides groups with both funds and targeted capacity building.

TECHNICAL SUPPORT   Many grassroots groups and organizations request training and support on the technical aspects of creating and building an organization. Questions that come up include: What does a board of directors do? How do we write a grant proposal? How do we make our first budget? Should we incorporate as a nonprofit? What are bylaws? How do we plan a new project? How do we manage money?

Technical questions like these are especially common in the beginning of our work with an emerging group and often spark the initial connection with CPC. Grassroots leaders frequently have a deep, personal knowledge of local issues. They may not, however, have much experience in the nonprofit sector, and the technical aspects of creating and funding an organization can be very intimidating. This is a key stage: members of a new group may get discouraged and give up; they may limit their growth before reaching their full potential; or they may feel obligated to develop into a mainstream nonprofit organization and fall apart trying to box themselves into an organizational structure that does not fit their culture, mission, or work.

For example, CPC works with the Pisgah View Community Peace Garden, organized and run by residents of a public housing community in Buncombe County. Much of CPC's work with the group has been technical: helping them develop a board of directors; assisting in writing bylaws; developing a financial system; and working step by step through the process of incorporating a nonprofit organization. However, before that technical assistance began, CPC staff had been working alongside the group for more than a year, helping with raising money, going to community celebrations, lending a hand with building a greenhouse, and just hanging out. We also spent time talking with people at Pisgah View about important topics like dreams and faith and poverty and race relations. So when the technical work began in earnest, the Peace Garden was not just seeking nonprofit status to qualify for grant funding, rather, because it was the right step in the natural growth of the organization. Because of the personal relationship, CPC's assistance was not just another case of a professional coming in to help; rather, our presence rounded out a diverse group working together to master the complicated nonprofit systems that typically discourage inexperienced people from forming their own organizations.

INTERPERSONAL SUPPORT   The second key piece of CPC's assistance is interpersonal support: all the ways in which members of a group learn to work effectively together. Support in this area helps group members find answers to questions like: How do we make decisions where everyone has a voice? What do we do when conflicts or disagreements arise? How do we build and maintain participation? Over time, as the group develops a shared history of working together, deeper questions emerge: What are our group's identity, vision, and values? How do we avoid getting burned out? How do we keep this work fun and fulfilling? How do we effectively bridge racial, cultural, gender, language, or class differences within our group?

Support for a group's interpersonal development is critical, because relationships are almost always at the core of why a grassroots group succeeds or fails. They may not be the apparent cause of failure—often it seems like programs fail, money runs out, or there are not enough volunteers—but all of these problems are rooted in whether the group takes care of its people, whether people work effectively together, and whether they are able to reach their full potential in the group. Success, likewise, is rooted in interpersonal relations: a group that has fun together, handles conflict productively, and gives its members meaningful leadership opportunities is much more likely to be high-functioning and effective.

Although every group is different, there are two common elements that CPC staff observe in most effective, successful groups. One is the practice of "facilitative leadership," a style of leading that is focused on recognizing and cultivating the leadership potential of the other members in the group (in contrast with more traditional forms of leadership, which focus on authority and power). The other is a "culture of nurturing," a group dynamic that creates a sense of welcome, encouragement, and mutual support among members. CPC promotes both practices, in the belief that a person's experience in a grassroots group should be enjoyable, encouraging, and fulfilling.

ORGANIZATIONAL STRUCTURE   The third form of support is helping the group create a structure that reflects the values, cultures, and talents of its members. In U.S. society, there is considerable pressure for groups to assume a traditional nonprofit organizational structure: a board of directors with formal officers, overseeing a staff headed by an executive director. Frequently, people have been taught that this is the only kind of structure it is possible to create. This kind of nonprofit structure, however, has a particular context; it was developed during the nineteenth century, largely by European American men, in imitation of the business, military, and government structures that were most familiar to them. The characteristic "chain of command," centralized authority, and hierarchical nature of this structure are not inherently good or bad, but they often are not a good fit for a grassroots organization that is organized and led by women or people of color who value equality and freedom of participation. Thus a key part of CPC's work involves helping groups explore alternative organizational structures to find one that reflects their own values.

For example, CPC is involved in a partnership that was approached by Maggie's

Functional Organics, a leading U.S. producer of organic clothing, about forming a sewing cooperative. In 2008, CPC helped a group of eight Latino and Hmong workers form a small sewing plant, called Opportunity Threads, which produces organic cotton stuffed animals and garments. With CPC's help, the workers structured the business as a worker-owned cooperative, where the worker-owners have an equal wage structure and equal voice in decision making. They have created a micro-manufacturing plant that they own and control, thus creating jobs that are fairly paid and a workplace that is safe and humane. As far as we know, Opportunity Threads is unique as the only worker-owned, environmentally friendly textile production plant in the United States.

THE SELF DEVELOPMENT FUND　　Since 2001, CPC has operated a micro-grants program with the purpose of helping grassroots groups access funds while strengthening their fund-raising skills. CPC staff help group members with the application process for one of two grant programs: Seed Grants, which provide start-up funding of $1,000 for newly emerging grassroots groups, and Grassroots Fundraising Matching Grants, which match up to $500 of income for a grassroots organization that is trying a new or creative fund-raising activity. In both cases, the groups receive not only the financial resources but also develop stronger skills in grant writing or grassroots fund-raising. Funding for the Self Development Fund comes primarily through individual donors, who like to see their gifts have a direct, grassroots impact. Decisions about funding are made by a review committee consisting primarily of people from organizations that were former Self Development Fund recipients, giving these grassroots leaders the chance to experience both sides of the grant review process.

Supporting Grassroots Leaders

At CPC, we consider a leader any person who provides direction, inspiration, guidance, encouragement, or support to others. Nearly every member of a grassroots group plays such a role at some point, either formally or informally, so we at CPC tend to think of every person in a group as being on a journey of developing or strengthening their leadership skills.

ENCOURAGEMENT AND REFLECTION　　Members of grassroots groups often tell us that the most important form of support CPC offers is just being there, walking alongside them, and believing in them. An essential part of our role is to listen deeply, ask questions, reflect back what we are hearing, and offer encouragement.

　　CPC has worked for four years with the Cherokee Healing and Wellness Coalition, based on the Qualla Boundary of the Eastern Band of Cherokee Indians. The Cherokee people here, like indigenous peoples all over the world, suffer from a high incidence of health problems. The Healing and Wellness Coalition helps health professionals, tribal leaders, and community members to understand and address the root causes of those problems. The Coalition helps people recognize that although the problems affect individuals, they do not begin with individuals, but with hundreds of years of grief and trauma. Genocide through war and disease, the Indian Removal of the 1830s, Indian boarding schools, the outlawing of traditional language and culture, forced assimilation, and many other historical experiences did a great deal to destroy the cultural and spiritual identity of the Cherokee people and the family and clan networks that kept them strong. The Coalition seeks to honor and restore the seven traditional Cherokee values and encourage practices that can heal the people and make them well again. CPC supports the Coalition by facilitating retreats and advising on events, but the Coalition is largely made up of skilled and experienced grassroots leaders who do not require much technical support. Our primary role is to listen and encourage, honor the stories and the histories we hear, and be a consistent voice of affirmation and support, especially when other local leaders resist the Coalition's historical analysis and community work.

BUILDING TECHNICAL AND INTERPERSONAL SKILLS   CPC's capacity-building approach is hands-on, focused on learning by doing: people learn how to run a meeting by stepping up and running a meeting; people learn how to make a budget by drafting a budget. The first few times a leader is working on a new skill, CPC staff are right by their side, for support, and we help them reflect afterward on what went well and what could have gone better. The next few times, CPC staff are there when needed, and continue to offer a chance for reflection. Eventually, that leader is working independently and passing on their skills to other members of the group.

SUSTAINING LEADERSHIP FOR THE LONG HAUL   Working at the grassroots level is hard—the issues are complex, the needs are enormous, and there are rarely enough resources. Grassroots leaders face the constant threat of burning out. A key part of CPC's support is to help leaders keep a perspective on their work that will sustain them for the long haul. We open up opportunities for reflection about individuals' hopes and dreams, personal goals for their own leadership journey, and daily experiences being a leader in a grassroots group. CPC advocates the principle that "if you don't take care of yourself, you won't be able to do much for the movement." These conversations help leaders structure their work so that they do not get burned out, and make sure the group gives time and energy to celebrations, reflection, and relationship building.

DEVELOPING AN ANALYSIS   It is equally critical to recognize that grassroots social change does not happen in a vacuum, and so we also help grassroots leaders develop their analysis of how power, privilege, and oppression function at the local, national, and global levels. Nearly all of the grassroots leaders that CPC supports have experienced the impact of privilege and oppression in their daily lives, but many of them have had limited opportunities to reflect on and analyze those patterns.

CPC has developed an analysis that gives us some understanding of how society's structures and institutions give power and privileges to certain groups of people while denying those opportunities to others. We talk about this as our "racial justice and human dignity" commitment. While racial justice is central to our mission, we recognize that oppressions related to race, gender, immigration status, ethnicity, language, age, sexual identity, ability, and other identities are connected and reinforce each other in complex ways. We try to do all of our work with an awareness of our own privileged and oppressed identities, so that we honor the full human rights and dignity of all people. CPC is open and transparent about our analysis, even when it may not be popular (such as talking about white privilege with a mostly European American group, or sexual diversity with a group based in a conservative faith community). However, we do not offer a particular anti-oppression training model, and we do not expect or require that any group we work with share our particular analysis. What is important is that they have their own analysis, rooted in their own experience, which can help them keep perspective and carry on when they face resistance and repression from the mainstream society.

Supporting Grassroots Networks

No grassroots organization carries out its work in isolation, so the third level of CPC's support involves networks and partnerships. This includes helping groups in three primary ways.

ENGAGING MAINSTREAM SYSTEMS AND INSTITUTIONS   Grassroots organizations frequently need to work with mainstream organizations, agencies, or government institutions that are not especially interested in connecting with grassroots leaders. CPC's role here borrows from more traditional community organizing and advocacy work. We help groups strategize about finding potential allies, building relationships inside the system, analyzing how power works and how decisions get made, and setting concrete objectives on the way to a long-term goal.

When the Cooper Boulevard Mobile Home Park in Buncombe County was slated to be sold and replaced with a commercial development, a CPC staff member was part of a team who helped the Appalachian and Latino residents of the park get organized. Their initial efforts, to either purchase the park or prevent the sale, turned out to be legally and financially impossible. During the process, residents organized, learned to make plans and set goals, worked across cultural and language differences, and developed their skills at public speaking. They also caused the City of Asheville to hold its first public meeting with Spanish-language interpretation. After the first setbacks, the Cooper Boulevard Support Network targeted the businesses buying and selling the property. Although the sale did eventually go through, it was delayed several months, the businesses making the deal were forced to pay residents more than $70,000 in relocation assistance, and the City of Asheville started to include manufactured housing as part of its affordable housing plans.

SPARKING NEW GROUPS AND PROJECTS   A successful, established grass-roots organization can have a ripple effect in its community. As it provides more and more opportunities for participation, it helps more grassroots leaders develop confidence and skills. Eventually, some people may have a need that cannot be addressed by the existing organization, so they may start their own group or project. The original grassroots organization can then take a support role in encouraging the new group's development.

Centro de Enlace, the immigrant and Latino resource and advocacy center in Yancey County, is an excellent case in point. During a six-year period when CPC staff were working with Enlace, on three occasions grassroots Latino leaders connected to Centro de Enlace sparked new groups and organizations, which CPC and Enlace both supported in various ways. The majority of immigrants in Yancey County come from one state in Mexico, and most are members of an indigenous group, the Purepecha. In 2005 several of the leaders formed a cultural group, Renacimiento Purepecha (Purepecha Renaissance), which performed traditional Purepecha dances and made sure that young people had a chance to learn their cultural traditions. The immigrant community is also fragile eco-nomically, so a group of immigrant women formed the Tortilleria el Progreso, a worker-owned cooperative that makes money by meeting the community's demand for fresh, traditionally made tortillas. A third organization developed when the mobile home park where many Latinos lived was going to be sold. The residents organized an association called Vecinos Unidos (Neighbors Together) that, with assistance from CPC, Enlace, and a number of other organizations, sparked the creation of a land trust called Burnsville Land Community, which allowed the residents to purchase the property and manage it collectively. This project, which received national attention from housing organizations and pro-vided an important and replicable affordable housing model, was the first mobile home park conversion in North Carolina.

BUILDING NETWORKS AND COALITIONS   Many challenges marginalized people face are not local but stem from state and federal laws and the practices of large institutions. For grassroots groups to have an impact at this level, they must work together in networks and coalitions.

One aspect of this network building is primarily informal and involves simply providing opportunities for people and groups to come together across the lines of race, language, culture, geography, and class—all of which historically keep grassroots groups isolated in Appalachia. Every year, CPC invites all the people and groups we support to a "grassroots gathering." Some years the gathering has a technical focus, such as building fund-raising skills; other years, we concentrate on developing a justice analysis and talk about building a movement. We include time for people to share traditional foods, music and dance, and stories, and we provide simultaneous interpretation so that people can speak and listen in their most comfortable language. Every year, participants tell us that the most valuable part of the event is the chance to talk with someone different, someone Cherokee or Latino or Hmong or African American or Appalachian, whom they never had a chance to talk with before. Sometimes, connections made at the gathering have sparked new partnerships. Our primary purpose, though, is simply to give grassroots leaders a chance to know they are part of something bigger than what they see every day.

CPC staff also work hard to help groups with similar needs and interests come together in more structured networks and coalitions. As always, we follow the energy, and do not push networks that are not generated by the groups themselves. However, especially when people are facing systemic oppression or unjust laws, there is a natural inclination to come together and address the root causes of the problem.

The primary example of this work in western North Carolina is the regional Latino coalition, the Coalicion de Organizaciones Latino Americanas (COLA). COLA formed in 2002, when CPC hosted a gathering, or Encuentro, for Latino groups across the region. This event led to three more Encuentros in 2003, and then several more the next year. CPC staff member Andrea Arias Soto worked intensively on COLA's development, helping members of the groups take more and more leadership in planning and running the Encuentros. Eventually, the network created permanent committees, started raising and managing its own money, and began new projects on advocacy and leadership development. Andrea's work shifted to organizational development assistance, and by 2006 COLA developed into an independent organization, with its own staff, programs, and leadership structure. CPC and COLA continue to work very closely together, both on supporting grassroots Latino groups and leaders and on advocacy and education related to immigrants' rights. As a result of regional coalition building, COLA members have taken leadership roles in the national immigrant rights' movement.

Lessons Learned

This outline of Grassroots Support Organizing focuses on the successes and strengths of this approach. But we have also faced challenges, failures, setbacks, and problems. Some of the major lessons learned from the challenges we have faced are:

MULTILINGUAL SPACES ARE NOT OPTIONAL   Most of our immigrant rights organizing has been done in partnership with Latino-led grassroots groups. Early in our work we did not know how to use simultaneous interpretation to create spaces where everyone can speak in their first language. Our work with immigrants and our larger movement-building efforts both suffered as a result. Working with the Highlander Center, we developed the capacity to create multilingual spaces, using interpretation headsets and skilled interpreters. Creating and fostering multilingual spaces is now a core component of our grassroots support organizing.

AN ANALYSIS OF MULTIPLE OPPRESSIONS IS ESSENTIAL   When we started our work, CPC was working across lines of race, class, and gender, but had done little organizational analysis of issues related to systemic forms of power, privilege, and oppression. As many organizations have found, this practice produces work that may be technically and superficially useful while perpetuating larger, long-term injustices and inequalities. We have come to see that it is absolutely critical to develop and share an analysis of the ways that power, privilege, and oppression affect us all at the individual, organizational, and systemic levels if we are to make any progress toward genuine social transformation.

SUPPORT ORGANIZING RATHER THAN ORGANIZE   Early in our work we acted as community organizers: knocking on doors, bringing people together around shared concerns and hopes, organizing meetings, and creating new groups. Eventually we realized this practice often fostered dependency on CPC. Our primary practice now is to support local, grassroots organizers as they organize their own communities.

DO NOT PUSH STRUCTURES   Another early mistake was to encourage grassroots groups, often implicitly through our capacity-building support, to form as nonprofit organizations. In time, we realized that the 501(c)(3) structure does not work for many groups, and indeed may impede movement building. We now encourage groups to think deeply about the pros and cons of forming as a nonprofit.

DEVELOP MANY LEADERS   Grassroots organizations frequently operate under the control of a single, charismatic leader. This pattern is encouraged by the dominant society—an individual leader is far more vulnerable to threats, rewards, and manipulation—and it often serves to limit the power and resilience of the organization. We have found that grassroots groups are far more resourceful and effective when they are intentional about sharing power and developing many individuals as leaders.

Grassroots Support Organizing and Movement Building

The web of grassroots leaders, groups, and networks forms the grassroots infrastructure. Every region in the United States—and around the globe—has some level of grassroots infrastructure, because it is part of human nature to organize ourselves and shape our world. The grassroots infrastructure may be underground and largely fragmented, or it may be strong, powerful, and openly supported by the general public. It may exist in isolation, or it may be tightly connected with, and even obscured by, other institutions, such as the nonprofit sector. But the grassroots infrastructure is always there, and it provides an important foundation for grassroots participation and ownership in the expanding global movement for social transformation.

At this historical moment, there is considerable social momentum around many issues, including immigrants' civil rights, environmental protection, equality for same-sex couples, the creation of more fair and accountable economic systems, and sustainable agriculture and food security. People and groups connected to CPC are engaged in these and many other issues, and they bring their leadership and organizational skills to the work of building these emerging movements.

The broad and inclusive nature of grassroots support organizing is one of its essential strengths—and, in terms of movement building, also one of its most important weaknesses. The networks and coalitions formed among grassroots groups create an opportunity to come together across issues—but there is no guarantee that coming together will actually happen. The trade-off of having a bottom-up, inclusive organizing model is that no single issue or message causes a movement to crystallize and mobilizes a massive number of people. Many effective activities and change strategies are taking place across our region, but given the severely limited time and resources available in the face of overwhelming injustices, there is a persistent tendency for leaders and groups to remain disconnected, focused on their immediate issues and needs. Rather than a single, comprehensive social movement, we see a number of diverse justice strategies running parallel to each other, connected both by values and individual relationships.

Yet in the end, we have found it a mistake to underestimate the transformative power of those relationships. In the abstract, it is easy to say that every issue affects us all, but that idea is often more paralyzing than mobilizing for progressive politics, considering that there are so very many issues to address. Relationships seem to be the force that overcomes that paralysis: when someone I care about is affected by injustice, then I feel that injustice myself, and I am moved to speak and to act. A social movement happens when a critical mass of people, because of those relationships, begin to speak out or take action, and when the people most directly affected by the issue are able to channel that growing social energy to effect a permanent transformation of attitudes, behaviors, laws, and institutions. Grassroots support organizing, as it makes connections among individuals and groups working on different issues and goals, creates the ground for those transformative relationships to grow.

CHAPTER 10

Faith-based Coalitions and Organized Labor
New Forms of Collaboration in the Twenty-first Century?

Jill Kriesky and Daniel Swan

In the current political era, the centrality of religious belief and the institutional power of organized religion are undeniable. From international acts of terrorism to local school textbook controversies, people moved by their religious beliefs and guided by their church leaders have mobilized political and social movements that have changed the course of history. Most familiar in the United States at the turn of the twenty-first century are examples of right-wing religious influences—both evangelicals and Muslims—that profoundly influenced presidential elections and foreign policy. But also in this era, progressive mainline denominations and even traditionally conservative evangelical churches have endorsed liberal agendas, including federally funded health-care coverage, strict enforcement of regulations limiting mountaintop removal, and tax reform that maintains benefits for the poor.[1]

The relationship between churches and social movements has been particularly complex throughout the Appalachian region. This chapter seeks to consider how faith-based coalitions have provided crucial support for workers in some of the more important recent labor struggles in central Appalachia. Close examination of their role produces an interesting conundrum: The clergy's petitions, public and private meetings with management, and encouragement to union members often contribute significantly to the success of issue campaigns and the resolution of strikes. Yet the collaboration between unions and churches usually lasts only as long as the particular struggle. Hence any potential for united action to improve the economic conditions of parishioners and union members over the long haul remains unrealized.

This chapter examines three pieces of this puzzle in the context of contract campaigns waged by the United Mine Workers of America (UMWA) and by the Kentucky and West Virginia Nurses Associations (KYNA and WVNA) in collaboration with the Commission on Religion in Appalachia (CORA) and its successor organization, Religious Leaders for Coalfield Justice (RLCJ). It first identifies the strengths and weaknesses of a successful collaboration between the UMWA and

CORA during the Pittston strike of 1989–1990. Next, it examines the extent to which lessons learned at that time were incorporated into the partnership between unions and religious organizations in the 2005–2007 Justice at Peabody campaign and the 2007 nurses' strike against the Appalachian Regional Hospitals (ARH). Finally, it reflects on the lessons of these collaborations to identify the strategies and actions necessary if labor and faith-based coalitions are to reach their full potential in central Appalachia in the twenty-first century.

The Commission on Religion in Appalachia's Commitment to Labor

Although CORA began in 1965, its roots were decades older. Many of CORA's founding denominations entered the region in the late 1800s through mission churches and settlement schools. After World War II, there was renewed interest in missionary work in the mountains by the Presbyterian Church (USA), the Catholic Diocese of Covington (Kentucky), Christian Church (Disciples of Christ), Lutherans, American Baptists, Brethren, Episcopalians, Mennonites, Quakers, and other denominations. The Council of the Southern Mountains (CSM), which had sponsored poverty programs in various forms for decades, eventually organized networking opportunities for these churches. CSM coordinated fund-raising for local projects, programs for Appalachian migrants to northern industrial cities, and "work camps" or "immersion trips" by suburban youth into the region.[2] With that structure in place and the inspiration to step up efforts in response to and in coordination with the newly declared War on Poverty, eighteen denominational and other faith-based organization members established CORA to address "the religious, moral, and spiritual implications inherent in the economic, social, and cultural conditions in the Appalachian region."[3] Fulfilling this mission included funding for local development projects, coordination of work camps, and advocacy around public policies related to health, environmental degradation, and land use issues.[4]

CORA's commitment to economic justice was clearly established in the 1982 publication *A Theological Reflection on Economic and Labor Justice* and an accompanying guide prepared by its Social Economic and Political Issues Task Force (SEPI) for congregational social justice study groups. Based on the premise that Jesus' "message speaks most strongly wherever God's creation is abused, and especially where any members of the human family are denied their dignity and worth," and on CORA members' witnessing of working people's struggle for justice in Appalachia, the document concludes that "the *labor process* (and the economic system or context in which it happens) is a place where we can discern if a society worships or denies the creative and liberating power of the living God. JUSTICE IS TRUE WORSHIP; INJUSTICE ULTIMATELY IS IDOLATRY."[5]

Armed with such justification, CORA staff lent its support to textile and hospital workers and, most important, coal miners. Former CORA director Tena Willemsma recalls that some ministers hesitated to get involved in a few of these campaigns. But the ministers' recognition of the mine owners' power and importance of mining jobs in their communities meant that their support for coal miners in the region was always strong.[6] Thus CORA supported UMWA contract struggles at the Jericol, Stearns, Scotia, Brookside, and Massey mines throughout the 1970s and early 1980s.[7] Leaders of member congregations signed CORA letters in support of fair and timely settlements and collected money and food to support striking workers.

While support for the UMWA and other union causes in Appalachia built a foundation of trust with labor, CORA's actions were not without detractors. Recent statistics on church attendance in the entire Appalachian region rank Baptist (21 percent of the population), Catholic (13 percent), and Methodist (9 percent) as the major religious affiliations.[8] All were represented in CORA's membership. However, these are considered "county seat" churches of the region's middle class because they are found primarily in larger population centers, while independent Baptist and nondenominational and charismatic churches predominate in many rural areas, particularly in central Appalachia. Congregations are small and pastors frequently have a second job—sometimes in the local mine—to support their families. Because miners and their families more likely attend these latter churches, mine owners and other industrial leaders were able to dismiss CORA positions as those of misinformed outsiders.[9]

UMWA and CORA Solidarity in the Pittston Campaign

UMWA Tactics in the Pittston Strike

The essential elements of the UMWA strike against the Pittston Coal Company are well documented.[10] After years of negotiations with the UMWA as a member of the Bituminous Coal Operators Association (BCOA), Pittston unilaterally pulled out of the organization in 1987, citing the need to respond to increasing pressures of international competition. The company proceeded first to withdraw from the long-established industrywide fund for retired miners and widows, and shortly thereafter to cancel health insurance coverage for 1,600 active miners. Fourteen months after the 1988 contract expiration, fruitless negotiations dragged on. Finally, on April 5, 1989, the company made a "take-it-or-leave-it" offer that included a refusal to contribute to the BCOA pension and health funds, changes in retired miners' health insurance benefits, required overtime and Sunday work, and employment of nonunion workers at unionized mines.[11]

Over the next ten and a half months, the UMWA instituted a strike strategy that stood in stark contrast to the violence (from both sides) that often marked previous work stoppages. Led by then–Vice President Cecil Roberts, the membership engaged in nonviolent protest. Pittston responded by hiring the private security firm Vance International to supply armed guards to escort trucks and protect its property. Virginia Governor Gerald Baliles ordered hundreds of state troopers to the southwestern coalfields to keep order. Approximately four thousand members and supporters were arrested for blocking traffic and other misdemeanors. Many reported enduring rough physical treatment at the hands of the arresting officers. Others, transported to local jails on buses, were denied food, water, and restroom facilities for hours on unnecessarily circuitous routes.[12]

The union also organized a widespread outreach campaign that brought fifty thousand supporters to communities where Pittston mines were located. Coal miner family members and clergy carried to the Pittston boardroom, the U.S. capitol, and the world their message of outrage over Pittston's plans to abandon care for widows and children of deceased miners and retired miners and their families.[13] By most accounts, the settlement that concluded the strike was a victory for the UMWA. The union accepted more flexibility on work rules and failed to ensure that all members could return to work immediately. But retaining health-care benefits for retirees, preserving the leading role of the BCOA in negotiations, and ensuring the union's continued existence were achievements that most union members and pundits did not believe possible when the strike began.[14]

Sit-down by UMWA miners at McClure #1 mine, McClure, Virginia, during the Pittston strike, April 24, 1989. (Photo by Don Prange, Ministries in Economic Justice)

CORA's Contribution to Success at Pittston

Though, by the late 1980s, enlisting churches both regionally and nationally to support their cause was not unusual for unions in Appalachia, the relationship between CORA and the UMWA during the Pittston strike was extraordinary in scope and depth. Recognizing the important contribution that faith-based leaders could make to a struggle focused on nonviolent tactics and the care of retirees and widows, UMWA staffer Ken Zinn built on the union's previous relations with CORA by asking for help in organizing clergy support.

CORA staffer Tena Willemsma directed regional and national churches' support activities in consultation with the UMWA throughout the strike. She organized fact-finding meetings for a small delegation of national church leaders with both management and union leaders that led to a clergy report condemning Pittston's actions and the state's heavy-handed interventions. Appeals went out to church leaders across the country to sign resolutions and letters, such as "God Calls on Us to Speak on Behalf of Striking Miners."[15] When Pittston reacted by labeling the hundreds of religious supporters as "outlanders," CORA responded by encouraging striking miners to invite their local "mountain clergy" to sign the ministerial support letter, and nearly fifty did.[16] CORA also convened a meeting of twelve local independent church leaders to encourage and advertise their support of the workers.[17]

When UMWA strategists concluded that their nonviolent tactics had been shut off by the courts and the National Labor Relations Board, they hatched a plan to take over Pittston's Moss 3 coal preparation plant both to slow production and to keep focus on the miners' plight. Among the ranks of one hundred men selected to participate was CORA director Jim Sessions (a Methodist minister) and several "bi-vocational" miner/preachers. Prayer was an important and regular part of the occupiers' daily routine.[18] Further integration of CORA into UMWA actions occurred when Sessions participated in UMWA corporate campaign actions aimed at stockholders and corporate leaders at Pittston's Connecticut headquarters.

Lessons Learned from the CORA-UMWA Collaboration at Pittston

Despite their shared commitment to justice, faith-based organizations and unions both recognized that their relationship often was not a full partnership. At a conference sponsored by the national AFL-CIO and several faith-based organizations just months prior to the Pittston strike, John DeConcini, president of the Bakery, Confectionery and Tobacco Workers International Union, criticized "the labor movement for not reaching out more, for not communicating more, for not being part of an ongoing dialogue with the religious leaders in the cities and towns where we are." He also urged labor leaders to develop "a year-round relationship with the religious community," rather than communicating with them only during a strike or plant closing.[19] CORA had faced a related criticism that it represented "mainline" or "county seat" churches while failing to establish regular interactions with working-class churches in the region.[20]

During the Pittston strike, the relationship changed. The union and CORA worked together to connect more closely with local churches. CORA director Sessions noted that "local congregations added a lot of credibility to the strike. It wasn't just liberal, progressive outside theologians at work. . . . It wasn't religion coming to 'deal' with the labor issues. It was not a rent-a-collar attitude."[21]

But once the contract was settled, the relationship faded. The UMWA focused its strike follow-up on an investigative commission and legislative actions that strengthened health-care protections for retirees and widows. Despite the value of working in concert with faith-based organizations during the strike, the union chose not to continue this partnership in pursuing this national health-care protection policy. Moreover, the kind of ongoing interaction with CORA and independent churches that might have kept the union in conversation with the religious community about *their* issues in the region never materialized.

Most union and CORA leaders interviewed declined to discuss the specific reasons for this. But through their general reflections about the post-strike period, it appears that CORA learned important lessons about working with the UMWA. Despite their collaboration during the strike, the UMWA did not seek to build on the mobilization of community partners once it was over. CORA also learned that, in keeping with earlier criticism of union-initiated collaboration with churches, the UMWA was not going to give such relationship building high priority because it was not required to meet immediate union goals.[22]

For its part, the union learned that framing its strike around justice for retirees and widows and its strategic emphasis on nonviolence eased recruitment of local, regional, and national faith-based supporters. In the process, it also learned that developing ties with independent mountain churches was significantly different from the process required to work with mainline churches. Reaching out to the former required "county by county, church by church, and pastor by pastor," relationship building to overcome economic class and cultural differences.[23] Surely CORA, independent churches, and the UMWA all learned that their counterparts' divergent goals made the process of effective, long-term coalition building challenging.

The UMWA and CORA Take On Peabody Coal

The Labor-Faith Strategy Revisited

In the late 1990s and early 2000s, the largest coal producer in the world—Peabody Coal—was shutting down its unionized, Appalachian mines and then selling them to consortiums of buyers in which it represented slightly less than 50 percent interest. Once the deal was completed and the union dismantled, Peabody purchased enough stock to become again the majority holder.[24]

Other unionized coal companies were also employing similar practices to rid themselves of the UMWA. Additionally, mining technology continued to reduce significantly the number of jobs in the industry. As a result, the UMWA faced dwindling membership and increasing difficulties in organizing. The union saw its 2006 contract negotiations with Peabody in their remaining nine union mines in the Midwest and Appalachia as an opportunity to expand membership in Peabody's nineteen nonunion mines by securing neutrality and card check provisions that would allow it to launch organizing drives without facing intense anti-union campaigning.

In December 2005, the UMWA established its "Justice at Peabody" campaign. Enlisting help from national AFL-CIO community organizing staff, the union also hired one of its own "bi-vocational" members, Joel Watts, to recruit community leaders, especially leaders of local churches and CORA, to pressure Peabody to accept neutrality and card check. As it had in the past, CORA stepped up to assist. Understanding the importance of gaining support from independent mountain churches for the campaign, it created an umbrella organization called Religious Leaders for Coalfield Justice (RLCJ) under which both CORA members and nonmembers could participate.[25]

For more than a year, clergy supported the call for a level playing field in UMWA organizing. A petition, signed by more than seven hundred church leaders, urged Peabody to "refrain from intimidating, threatening, and firing miners who are working to organize a union . . . [and] to be truly neutral with respect to employees' rights to form or join a union and to voluntarily recognize a union when a majority of their employees sign authorizations."[26]

Many also joined other union supporters in lobbying coalfield town councils to pass resolutions urging Peabody to accept neutrality and card check provisions. In April 2006, hundreds of clergy and other union supporters gathered outside Peabody headquarters in St. Louis, Missouri, to publicize their demands.

In July 2006, union staffers organized a public information-gathering session in Madisonville, Kentucky, led by a panel that included Catholic, Protestant, and Jewish clergy. Together with the national organization Interfaith Workers for Justice (IWJ), RLCJ issued *Peabody Energy: Rights Denied and Promises Broken,* which outlined Peabody's strategies to avoid hiring former union members, instill fear in its non-union work force, and disregard miner health and safety. The clergy concluded: "We were overwhelmed by reports of abuses endured by non-union miners and their families. We were appalled by reports of company intimidation in the communities where they operate. The issues here are profoundly moral. We concluded that Peabody's actions assault the foundations of human dignity, and must be addressed by America's people of faith to preserve the credibility of our religious traditions and the integrity of American civil society."[27]

Buoyed by the visible support for the campaign by so many community leaders, "bi-vocational" miner/preachers and other independent mountain church leaders spoke openly about their support for the UMWA for the first time. Their experiences either in the mines or with miners' struggles inspired actions that championed the UMWA's battle to secure dignity at work. Clergy organized prayer vigils and discussed their support of the union with their congregations. They also helped combat the company's anti-union fear tactics during organizing campaigns. One organizer commented that "we got [authorization] cards, we got workers on the inside, and they knew that the community was with them."[28]

Peabody responded to these actions by sending personalized letters to involved clergy characterizing their involvement as naïve and the union as manipulative.[29] But by the time the large RLCJ, IWJ, and union member delegations converged on its corporate headquarters, Peabody was no longer dismissing their role. CEO Greg Boyce agreed to an off-the-record meeting with a few of the leaders. Participant Rev. Dennis Sparks of the West Virginia Council of Churches left the meeting "feeling that [company representatives] had been respectful and willing to listen to the clergy's point of view."[30] An AFL-CIO organizer pointed out that "even getting a meeting with Peabody is hard to do. It had to make a difference."[31]

From the perspective of current and retired Peabody employees, the five-year contract agreement reached in February 2007 was fair. It contained the same provisions as the deal negotiated between the BCOA and the UMWA in 2006, including a 20 percent pay increase spread over five years, a $1,000 bonus, and improved pensions for current (though not for new) miners. It also retained previous health-care provisions for active miners and added some health-care improvements for retirees.[32] However, the neutrality and card check provisions for which the clergy mobilized and that would have eased the way for further organizing were not part of the agreement.

Comparing Labor-Clergy Relations

A comparison between the UMWA's relationship with CORA and independent churches in the Pittston strike and the Peabody contract campaign fifteen years later suggests that both forward and backward steps were made toward the goal of building effective coalitions. On the positive side, the UMWA and CORA both incorporated independent churches into their strategies from the start. The UMWA used its "bi-vocational" organizer to undertake the painstaking work of one-on-one meetings to garner support of independent churches in both Appalachian and the midwestern Peabody mine communities. Likewise, CORA leaders created the RLCJ "umbrella" to facilitate cooperative actions including CORA and non-CORA members. To draw even greater attention to the working conditions that created the need for new union organizing, the UMWA enlisted AFL-CIO community organizing staff. Similarly, the national clergy alliance IWJ joined with RLCJ actions to involve churches from across the country. All of these tactics worked remarkably well.

But at the same time, a major weakness emerged. At least in the short run the UMWA simply abandoned the neutrality/card check demand and the religious leaders who were moved to act in support of it. After the contract settlement, UMWA President Cecil Roberts characterized the contract as a "victory . . . [achieved] largely due to the strength and unity of our members." Roberts added: "Without [member] solidarity, Peabody would not have gotten the message that we were serious about getting the national agreement. . . . But the company eventually got that message, and they understood that our members were willing to stand together and do whatever it took to get a new agreement."[33] There was no mention of Justice at Peabody, neutrality, card check, or the support of clergy.

The reasons the UMWA decided not to pursue neutrality/card check as aggressively as it did retirees' health-care benefits in the Pittston strike are undoubtedly multiple and complex.[34] But the impact on coalitional strategy is likely to be more straightforward and negative for future collaborations. None of the clergy, AFL-CIO, or UMWA faith community organizers interviewed indicated that the union ever met with church leaders to explain why it withdrew the Justice at Peabody campaign. Privately, some observers noted that supportive independent preachers whose congregations were split over support of union organizing were "left hanging" when the UMWA gave up on neutrality and card check, and that it may be impossible to regain their support for labor issues in the future. A CORA commissioner and longtime UMWA supporter was understanding but also resigned to the status quo in communications. He concluded that union leaders "jump around and so do we. . . . We needed to develop a strategy, but instead we got worn down."[35] In short, the ongoing local dialogue that would have allowed both union and religious leaders to share what was at stake for their members and the communities in which they live and to craft a strategy that could pursue joint goals never emerged. Coupled with the failure to gain the demand that mobilized clergy, the relationship between churches and the UMWA weakened.

RLCJ and Justice for Appalachian Regional Hospital Nurses

Labor Strategies for Nurses' Rights

Another tough contract negotiation in central Appalachia came on the heels of the Peabody campaign. In fall 2007, approximately 750 nurses—members of the West Virginia Nurses Association and the Kentucky Nurses Association, who worked at nine Appalachian Regional Hospitals in the two states—faced an uphill battle during more than a month of negotiations on issues including pay, mandatory overtime, staffing levels, and increased insurance premiums.[36] Interestingly, ARH was created by the UMWA in the mid-1950s to serve rural central Appalachian communities. In 1963, with the UMWA unable to shoulder the financial burden of running the hospitals, CSM-affiliated churches provided funding to purchase the hospitals and created a nonprofit organization to manage them.[37] Despite the hospital's union roots, the need to update and expand service options and growing demand for uncompensated care stiffened management's resolve in contract negotiations.[38] Early in the year, the United Steelworkers of America (USWA) local, representing hospital workers other than nurses, struck for twenty-five days before settling with ARH.[39] ARH hired consultants Yessin and Associates, who were reputed to be counseling the hospital organization on how to break unions during the course of the contract negotiations.[40]

In late September, the nurses rejected the contract proposal and ARH refused to return to the bargaining table. The strike began on October 1, 2007, four days before the contract expired. Management hired replacement workers, housing them on vacant floors within the hospitals. The union began to solicit support from community organizations, including other unions (the UMWA, American Federation of Teachers, Communication Workers of America, and Service Employees International Union), county and state political figures, and religious leaders. Although CORA had recently ceased operations, Michael Spock, an AFL-CIO community organizing staff member assigned to the strike, pursued clergy support by meeting with former CORA directors Tena Willemsma and Jim Sessions and other longtime clergy allies. They agreed to elicit support for the nurses under the RLCJ label created during the Peabody campaign.

As an informal affiliation of faith-based leaders, RLCJ began to seek the kinds of support offered by clergy in previous mineworker and other union campaigns. They focused on the issues that the nurses repeatedly claimed were most important—mandatory overtime and staffing ratios that were impacting patient care. They researched ARH trustees to determine how best to approach each of them about the strike. Some RLCJ members regularly attended rallies in local communities where ARH hospitals are located. At one such event in Hazard, Kentucky, Fr. John Rausch of the Catholic Committee on Appalachia and Lon Oliver of the Christian Church (Disciples of Christ) in Kentucky caught the attention of both a local minister who served as a chaplain in the hospital and the local ARH hospital president. The minister criticized RLCJ leaders for failing to involve local church leaders in the struggle. Coincidentally, the hospital president contacted Rausch and Oliver and asked them to meet with him, which presented them the opportunity to involve the minister/chaplain in the discussion. Although the meeting began with tension, the RLCJ offer to help if they could and to leave if they could not impressed both local representatives. The minister invited RLCJ to meet with the local ministerial association to keep them abreast of strike support developments.[41]

By late November, with no end in sight and 150 nurses permanently replaced for their role in the strike, RLCJ began collecting signatures for "An Open Letter by Religious Leaders to the President and CEO Jarry Haynes; Members of the Board of Trustees of Appalachian Regional Healthcare; Kentucky Nurses Association; and West Virginia Nurses Association." The letter highlighted the importance of both sides bargaining in good faith. But its strongest language was written in support of the nurses:

> Nurses who feel like they cannot provide proper care to patients . . . end up leaving the nursing profession. Our communities cannot afford to lose these nurses.
> From a moral and ethical perspective, the permanent replacement of striking nurses at Appalachian Regional Healthcare must stop; and permanently replaced workers should be reinstated . . . [42]

By the time the letter, signed by more than 105 clergy, was released to the press, further strife was evident. ARH had offered another contract that increased pay but failed to address patient care and staffing ratios. The nurses rejected it by a 455–5 margin.[43] Rhetoric by both sides escalated in public media. Nurses from across the nation rallied at ARH's Lexington headquarters, where RLCJ members spoke in support of the struggle. Ultimately, the West Virginia and Kentucky governors brought both sides to the bargaining table, exploring options for a "cooling off period" and substantive discussions excluding participation by management's consultants and outside union supporters.[44] Neither proposal was adopted, but within five days the parties approved an agreement.

Nurses and union officials interviewed after the contract vote were ambivalent. They recognized that the contract was better than the previous offers. But there was no guarantee that all nurses would be called back, though ARH said it would try to return 80 percent to their previous assignments by the end of January.[45] Moreover, union nurses were required to work alongside remaining replacement workers, and contract language prohibited informational pickets criticizing ARH. Union representatives believe that managers regularly violate the contract, including terminating workers without just cause.[46]

A Setback for Labor-Clergy Relations?

Comparing the ARH strike with both the Pittston and Peabody campaigns produces a mixed record in terms of labor-religious coalitions' influence on the outcome of union struggles in Appalachia. The most promising aspect of the collaboration was the ease with which it started to function. Less than a year before the strike began, CORA had ceased to exist. Yet AFL-CIO organizer Spock had sturdy enough relations with its former members that an informally constructed RLCJ began organizing church support shortly after the strike began. Although the group was small—six to eight active members—they were able to capture the attention and support of churches across the country.

But despite long-term relations that made this clergy presence at rallies and strongly endorsed open letters to ARH possible, day-to-day communication between unions and RLCJ prior to the strike that would have allowed the partners to frame the issues in ways that would have appealed to local community churches did not occur. Messages carried by clergy to their communities were more diffuse than in either the Pittston or Peabody campaigns. Religious leaders talked about patient care endangered by low staffing ratios and long hours, the union's original strike issues. Sometimes they focused on the immorality of using replacement workers. Occasionally they discussed specifics of day-to-day complaints, such as the lack of proper equipment to lift obese patients.[47] This range of grievances related at least in part to broader issues of health-care delivery in the country. Though the hospital did not respond directly to these complaints, it emphasized in public comments its efforts to deliver both high-quality health care and services to the uninsured under the difficult circumstances created by existing national health-care policy.[48]

One RLCJ member noted that people in the small communities where the ARH hospitals are located are keenly aware that they are the life support system in regions where the nearest health-care facility may be miles away over hazardous roads. The recognition that a hospital without its nursing staff might not be able to provide lifesaving services left many fearful. However, as Sally Maggard and others have documented, women's work, especially in "caring professions," has been historically undervalued in the Appalachian region and nationwide.[49] One RLCJ member reported that such traditional professional and gender role stereotypes surfaced here, too. Several local clergy expressed surprise that nurses would ever strike. This translated into a failure to express support for striking nurses from the pulpit or even to engage parishioners who might support similar stereotypes into discussion about the strike. A union supporter summed it up: "Always the patient is first!"[50]

Finally, as the Hazard rally events illustrate, RLCJ leaders again faced the criticism that they were outsiders who had not involved local churches in the campaign. The validity of this charge is not clear. Rausch and Willemsma reported that RLCJ went to great lengths to be sure local churches knew about their support strategies. Many clergy involved in the campaign reported that local churches did not get involved because their members were either split on support for nurses or feared that an extended strike would result in loss of hospital services.[51] Still, the *perception* by local ministers that the "county seat" churches were excluding them from strike support actions is one that longtime CORA members should have been prepared to address.

Analysis and Conclusions

The successes that emerged from the coalitions between CORA and RLCJ and the UMWA and Kentucky and West Virginia nurses associations during the contract campaigns and strikes suggest that three ingredients are key to meaningful clergy involvement in Appalachian-based labor struggles. First, where the strike issue around which religious leaders rally can be framed in terms of church teachings, the "moral authority" of clergy is nearly impossible for management to discount. Thus the UMWA's focus on contractual guarantees for health care for retirees and widows in the Pittston strike and on the right to organize against unjust working conditions in the Peabody campaign was further legitimized by clergy, who framed the issues in theological terms. The right of a hospital to hire replacement nurses to care for patients during a strike is undeniably unjust in the eyes of workers who have walked out in an effort to force the employer to change their patient-staff ratio. But to the Christian who believes all human beings have the right to access health care, the judgment is less clear.

Second, religious leaders' support for worker causes is more difficult for management to deflect when they are speaking on behalf of their congregations. This is particularly evident in Appalachia, where CORA long faced criticism from management and mountain churches alike for their "county seat church" intervention into the struggles of "mountain church members." Relatedly, twentieth-century union organizers, accustomed to "top-down" or staff-led organizing and representing of workers, found collaboration with mainline churches through their institutional structures more familiar and comfortable than the church-by-church, pastor-by-pastor organizing required to enlist the support of independent mountain churches. When CORA and the UMWA engaged "bi-vocational" and local church leaders in actions on behalf of Pittston workers, they enhanced the morally "high road" campaign that nonviolent tactics created. Similar actions with the Justice at Peabody campaign, in its early stages, appeared to have the same impact.

The third and most evasive ingredient is promotion of union-religious collaborations on a scale that can significantly influence a struggle's outcome. For example, even though the Pittston strike ended with the restoration of retiree health benefits, long-term success on this goal emerged from legislative reform in which CORA and independent churches had no part. If labor and religious institutions in Appalachia had a mechanism for engaging local supporters with national policy-making efforts in which local communities clearly had a stake, perhaps the partnership would have continued to develop. Likewise, had local Appalachian and midwestern pastors who passionately endorsed the rights of miners to organize been educated on the national campaign to ease onerous restrictions that favored employers during union organizing drives, the unsuccessful effort to change Peabody's contract language could still have made a positive contribution to ongoing struggles. Finally, for those ministers hamstrung by their own professional and gender stereotypes and congregational divisions over whether nurses should leave their patient care responsibilities to strike, linking the local impasse to a national campaign around the right of all people to access health care may have channeled energy in a direction productive to all.

The three campaigns support the view that in Appalachia, organized labor and its religious allies have identified the first two ingredients for successful collaboration, though they have not consistently employed them in their campaigns. Religious and labor leaders interviewed understood the importance of the third ingredient. They acknowledged the importance of governmental oversight of retiree miner and survivor benefits; of creating a more equitable playing field for unions in organizing campaigns; and of health-care reform, in solving the underlying issues of the three disputes respectively. In each campaign, some attention was given to the faith community's attempts to influence corporate or public policy making in relation to the underlying issues.

But more intentional, strategic coalition development is needed for this third key strategy to succeed. The partnering organizations have not yet formulated the mechanism that can transfer their commitment to fight for justice for local workers and the communities in which they live to a campaign that ultimately plays out on a national or international stage. To create this process intentionally will require ongoing dialogue between labor and churches. Union and religious leaders admit that regular communication would improve their coalition efforts. One method of achieving this would be for such leaders to endorse and implement regular communication at the national level to set the example for regional and local relationship building. Alternatively, labor and church leaders would agree to cultivate a few regional "greenhouse" or pilot projects in which both unions and faith-based organizations agree to commit staff and financial resources necessary for long-term relationship building and strategic planning.

Leaders should consider central Appalachia, with Pittston, Peabody, and ARH in its recent past, as a site for such an experiment. The potential obstacles may be significant. The unions must accept the importance of relationship building beyond what is required to pressure management in a strike. Mainline and nondenominational churches must bridge the geographic, economic class, and theological gaps that divide them before they can build efficient labor-faith community communications. But given the critical social and worker justice issues in the region and the importance of both the union and the church in the lives of many Appalachian people, it would be hard to imagine more fertile ground in which to plant the seeds of this experiment.

Notes

1. See, for example, Jim Wallis, *God's Politics: Why the Right Gets It Wrong and the Left Doesn't Get It* (New York: HarperCollins, 2005) and the WV Council of Churches policy statements, available at http://www.wvcc.org/?content=policy2009.

2. Ronald D. Eller, *Uneven Ground: Appalachia since 1945* (Lexington: University Press of Kentucky, 2008), 119.

3. James Sessions, "The Commission on Religion in Appalachia: Empowering the

People," in *Christianity in Appalachia: Profiles in Regional Pluralism,* ed. Bill J. Leonard (Knoxville: University of Tennessee Press, 1999), 166.

4. Ibid., p. 168.

5. Social, Economic and Political Issues Task Force of the Commission on Religion in Appalachia, *A Theological Reflection on Economic and Labor Justice* (Knoxville, Tenn., 1982), 1.

6. Jill Kriesky, interview with Tena Willemsma, May 14, 2009.

7. Ibid.; Social, Economic and Political Issues Task Force, *A Theological Reflection,* 1.

8. Daniel Swan, interview with James Sessions, October 10, 2008.

9. Ibid.

10. See Richard A. Brisbin Jr., *A Strike Like No Other Strike: Law & Resistance during the Pittston Coal Strike of 1989–1990* (Baltimore: John Hopkins University Press, 2002) and "'A Strike Like No Other Strike:' Pittston Strike Holds Lessons for Today," *United Mine Workers Journal* 120 (March–April 2009): 4–12.

11. Karen Beckwith, "Hinges in Collective Action: Strategic Innovation in the Pittston Coal Strike," *Mobilization: An International Journal* 5 (Fall 2001): 180.

12. John Bookser Feister, "Crisis in the Coalfields: The Church Calls for Justice," *St. Anthony Messenger* 97 (December 1989): 24–25; Joyce Hollyday, "Amazing Grace," *Sojourners* 18 (July 1989): 15.

13. Brisbin, "A Strike Like No Other Strike," 7.

14. Jim Sessions and Fran Ansley, "Singing across Dark Spaces: The Union/Community Takeover of Pittston's Moss 3 Plant," in *Fighting Back in Appalachia: Traditions of Resistance and Change,* ed. Stephen L. Fisher (Philadelphia: Temple University Press, 1993), 222.

15. Brisbin, *A Strike like No Other Strike,* 185.

16. Daniel Swan, interview with Tena Willemsma.

17. Daniel Swan, interview with James Sessions.

18. Ibid.; Sessions and Ansley, "Singing across Dark Spaces," 210, 215.

19. American Federation of Labor and Congress of Industrial Organizations, *A Dialogue between the Religious and Labor Community on Social and Ethical Concerns in a Changing Society* (Washington, D.C., 1989), 18.

20. Daniel Swan, interview with James Sessions.

21. Ibid.

22. Daniel Swan, interview with Tena Willemsma.

23. Daniel Swan, interview with James Sessions.

24. Religious Leaders for Coalfield Justice and Interfaith Worker Justice, *Peabody Energy: Rights Denied and Promises Broken,* Report of Fact Finding Mission, July 16–17, 2006, Madisonville, Ky., 7–8.

25. Jill Kriesky, interview with Tena Willemsma.

26. www.justiceatpeabody.org/rlcjprayervigils81406.html.

27. Religious Leaders for Coalfield Justice and Interfaith Worker Justice, *Peabody Energy,* 3.

28. Jill Kriesky, interview with Joel Watts, December 20, 2007.

29. Ibid.; Jill Kriesky, interview with Dennis Sparks, December 19, 2007.

30. "Church Leaders Dig in for Miners," *Joplin Globe,* April 30, 2006.

31. Jill Kriesky, interview with June Rostan, December 19, 2007.

32. http://justiceatpeabody.org/ blog/2007/02/.

33. Ibid.

34. Jill Kriesky, "Big Coal: Faith and Labor Coalitions in Appalachia," *Perspectives on Work* 12 (Summer 2008-Winter 2009): 41.

35. Daniel Swan, interview with Dennis Sparks, September 26, 2009.

36. "More Than 750 ARH Nurses Strike," *Lexington Herald-Leader,* October 1, 2007.

37. Eller, *Uneven Ground,* 120.

38. J. D. Miller, "ARH Offers High-Quality Care despite Strike," *Lexington Herald-Leader,* December 17, 2007.

39. "More Than 750 ARH Nurses Strike," *Lexington Herald-Leader.*

40. Daniel Swan, interview with John Rausch, March 3, 2009, and Mannix Porterfield, "Governors Meet with Striking Nurses, ARH Officials," *Glasgow Daily Times,* December 19, 2007.

41. Daniel Swan, interview with John Rausch; Daniel Swan, interview with Tena Willemsma, February 20, 2009.

42. Jim Sessions and Tena Willemsma, Letter to Friends and Colleagues in the Religious Community, Re: An Open Letter by Religious Leaders to President and CEO Jerry Haynes; Members of the Board of Trustees of Appalachian Regional Healthcare; Kentucky Nurses Association; and West Virginia Nurses Association, November 27, 2007. Available at http://www.peaceandjusticeky.org/openletReligLeadARH.pdf.

43. Suzanne Higgins, "ARH Strike Update for WVM," *West Virginia Public Broadcasting,* December 10, 2007. Available at http://wvpubcastnews.wordpress.com/2007/12/10/nurses-strike-negotiations-remain-at-impasse/.

44. Porterfield, "Governors Meet with Striking Nurses, ARH Officials."

45. http://blog.aflcio.org/2007/12/23/striking-nurses-approve-new-pact.

46. Daniel Swan, interview with Dewey Parker, March 2, 2009.

47. Ibid.

48. J. D. Miller, "ARH Offers High-Quality Care despite Strike."

49. Sally Ward Maggard, "Gender, Race, and Place: Confounding Labor Activism in Central Appalachia," in *Neither Separate nor Equal: Women, Race, and Class in the South,* ed. Barbara Ellen Smith (Philadelphia: Temple University Press, 1999), 190.

50. Daniel Swan, interview with Tena Willemsma.

51. Ibid.; Daniel Swan, interview with John Rausch.

CHAPTER 11

Talking Union in Two Languages
Labor Rights and Immigrant Workers in East Tennessee

Fran Ansley

Like every part of Appalachia, east Tennessee has been deeply affected in recent decades by global economic transformation. Social justice activists there have been struggling for years to understand and respond to these developments and to the difficult social divides they have created and exposed. This chapter recounts from the perspective of a participant-observer the story of one local response and suggests lessons for future social justice efforts in the region.

A rapid increase in the movement of industrial capital from east Tennessee to countries of the Global South constituted the early leading edge of the corporate-led, "free trade" brand of globalization that swept so powerfully into local lives in the 1980s and thereafter. A number of projects launched by groups in east Tennessee attempted to use the moment of crisis created by plant closings to open local windows onto the global scene and construct bottom-up internationalist channels of communication and action between working-class Tennesseans and their counterparts in other countries. For example, during the 1990s, the Tennessee Industrial Renewal Network (TIRN) collaborated with unions and other allies to organize worker-to-worker exchange trips to the *maquiladora* region of Mexico, where many U.S.-based multinationals had opened branch factories in burgeoning export-processing zones along the border.

Travelers returned home to lobby energetically against the North American Free Trade Agreement and similar trade measures. They did not block passage of these pro–big business trade deals, nor did they manage to save much of the state's manufacturing base, which continues hemorrhaging to this day. But they did learn a great deal about the global economy, educate many of their fellow citizens about what they had seen in their travels, and take part in the growing national and international movement to challenge the new global rules designed to protect large international investors. Some veterans of the exchange trips eventually represented TIRN at the 1999 "Battle of Seattle," where labor unionists, environmentalists, and others hit the streets and changed the future course of the World Trade Organization.[1]

It soon became clear that many of the same global and corporate dynamics that had sent jobs and capital streaming from Tennessee to Mexico were also pushing Mexican and other Latin American people out of their home countries and north to the United States. These new international migrants (some of them with papers, but many without) were arriving not only in traditional receiving states like California and Florida but also in new places like Appalachia, deep in the nation's interior. Tennessee woke up at the turn of the century to find itself home to one of the fastest-growing Latino populations in the country.[2]

Astonishingly rapid demographic change had brought, directly into the state's own backyard, the U.S.-Mexico border that TIRN delegations to the *maquiladoras* had once traveled long days to reach. In the presence of that strange new local-global border, issues of racism and xenophobia, the reasonable and unreasonable fears of U.S. workers about competition for scarce employment, and scores of questionable assumptions about America and its role in the world bubbled quickly to the surface. Such matters had been difficult enough for social justice activists with an internationalist bent to take up effectively when the conversation focused on far-away places, but when the situation involved a sudden bloom of new backdoor neighbors marked as "different" in terms of race, language, and culture, the challenges became even greater. At the same time, the volatile atmosphere created by the surge in immigration presented opportunities for extending and deepening some of the cross-national bridge building initiated earlier. The case described below represents one moment when this opportunity was seized.

In 2005 a labor-community alliance between Jobs with Justice of East Tennessee (JwJET) and the United Food & Commercial Workers (UFCW) put the new issues of immigration and immigrants' rights front and center. The collaboration was formed to support an organizing drive by the union at a chicken processing plant whose workforce had become virtually 100 percent Latino. After months of intensive organizing, the workers at the plant voted overwhelmingly in favor of the union, despite the factory's location about an hour north of Knoxville in Morristown, a small, anti-union town that is hardly exempt from racism or xenophobia, in a portion of the state where precious little labor organizing of any kind had been seen for years.

The first aim of this study is simply to demonstrate that even under such austere conditions, labor-community coalitions with a focus on immigrant workers can win substantial victories. They can advance the rights and well-being of immigrants, strengthen organized labor, educate native-born members of the larger community, and alter power relationships at immigrant-heavy work sites—at least when a strong combination of favorable elements is present or can be brought into play. The story also reveals, however, that after the election, significant ongoing challenges continued to face the union, the workers, and community partners of the campaign, thereby suggesting some of the persistent obstacles likely to confront those who hope to bridge divisions of race and nation within the increasingly multinational labor markets of global Appalachia.

Jobs with Justice in East Tennessee

Based in Knoxville, Jobs with Justice of East Tennessee (JwJET) is part of a larger national JwJ network. Sharing a conviction that labor unions and collective bargaining are necessary elements for a just and healthy democracy, JwJ coalitions also believe that labor and progressive grassroots groups will both be stronger by joining forces to support each other's goals.

Our JwJ coalition in east Tennessee dates back to the mid-1990s. Buoyed by a wave of optimism about labor-community cooperation that followed the 1995 election of reform candidates John Sweeney and Appalachia's own Rich Trumka to the top leadership of the AFL-CIO, JwJET's founding partners set out to get a local chapter underway. We recruited member groups, developed plans and structures, and announced that we were in business, waiting in eager anticipation for the new era to begin and for the invitations we thought we would receive from east Tennessee labor unions, asking us to support their initiatives.

We did find that some unions in east Tennessee were interested in this kind of approach. What we did not find, however, was any real degree of substantial, sustained, proactive organizing by unions in our area. We were ready to be in solidarity, but there was depressingly little to be in solidarity with!

No doubt some of the problem was our own failure to find effective ways to get out the word to individual unions and their members about JwJ's goals and capacities, a task that remains an ongoing challenge. Some of the problem was also rooted in the inertia of old habits on the labor side. Few unions in our area have had much experience with labor-community coalitions, and some are not yet convinced that community allies can be trusted to understand labor issues or that collaboration will prove worth the time and risk of messy conflict that such work requires.

For the most part, however, the lack of union response to our presence was a question of power and resources. Manufacturing jobs were in steep decline, union organizing in the burgeoning service sector was slow, and union membership and morale were slipping fast. This lack of energy, growth, and vision was precisely the downward spiral we had hoped to help interrupt with our JwJ activities, but it was hard to see how to achieve that goal when opportunities for active solidarity seemed so few.

We were not idle. Occasionally a local union asked for support in a dispute. We helped with consumer boycotts called by distant farmworkers in North Carolina and Florida. We joined the fight for a city and campus living wage, and then supported efforts by progressive students and public employees to build a union presence at the University of Tennessee, Knoxville. We convened Worker Rights

Board hearings where panels of local leaders received testimony on workplace problems. All of this was fine work, and we were happy to do it. But with the exception of the organizing at the university, it did not really reflect the kind of revived and expanding labor movement that JwJET had envisioned.

Meanwhile, like others in the state in this period, we were witnesses to the upsurge in Latino migration.[3] The arrival and reception of Latino newcomers were noteworthy to all kinds of people for all kinds of reasons, of course. But for worker rights activists, the trend was especially salient. After all, the main magnet pulling this mass migration into Tennessee was the chance for employment, and the flow of new immigrants was mostly heading straight into low-wage jobs where the potential for old and new forms of exploitation and abuse was all too clear.

Although some of the new arrivals were citizens or lawful residents, a large number were undocumented. Their precarious legal status, often coupled with other problems such as low English proficiency, or lack of literacy in any language, rendered many Latinas and Latinos in Tennessee extremely vulnerable to mistreatment on the job and discouraged them from coming forward with complaints. This handed employers a heavy threat to hold over the head of any worker who might get out of line. All these dynamics intimidated unions, many of them already beleaguered on other fronts and with little experience operating in the shadowy world of undocumented employment. Thus a social actor that should have been, at least by JwJ's logic, a leading ally in any fight by or for immigrant workers' rights, sat sidelined and silent in a disappointing number of cases.

Further, as anti-immigrant fervor was whipped up across the nation by the likes of television commentator Lou Dobbs and worse, and as the post–September 11 Department of Homeland Security ramped up its immigrant enforcement activity at the border and elsewhere, native-born union members were bombarded with negative images of immigrants and with the idea that "illegal aliens" were taking the jobs and pulling down the labor standards of U.S. workers. Of course, not all workers fell for these divisive claims or for the assumed master narrative of labor market competition. But many did, and the overall climate of hostility toward immigrants affected the thinking of many native-born workers, both in and out of unions.[4]

As a result of these complex factors, when it came to labor initiatives aimed at immigrant workers or their concerns, we did not find much action underway. We did undertake small steps of our own as we could identify them. For instance, JwJ looked for ways to do educational presentations about immigration and globalization, and we were welcomed by some unions to do so.[5] But new organizing to reach new immigrant populations was seldom on the agenda in the venues where we spoke.

I describe this gloomy state of affairs in some detail because case studies too often focus on high points in the development of both individual campaigns and larger social movements. Useful knowledge of how change actually occurs can only be produced through research that also includes the long daunting periods of listening, groping, and experimentation in which most of us are destined to live the major portion of our time on this earth. This explains why it was so exciting for the organization when at last we were contacted about a possible break in the weather: the opportunity to support a union-organizing drive at a poultry plant in Morristown—a city with the highest percentage of Latinas and Latinos anywhere in east Tennessee.

The Campaign

A number of factors contributed to Morristown's attraction for the mostly Mexican immigrants who had been streaming into the small factory town for years, but the presence of a large chicken-processing plant was high on the list. JwJET had long been aware of this Morristown enterprise, once a local business but eventually acquired by one of the nation's largest poultry producers and processors. We knew that, like similar operations in other parts of the state, it had expanded in recent years and had begun aggressively hiring Latino immigrants. Our organization was also aware that conditions in the industry nationwide were brutal and barriers to union success substantial. In Morristown and surrounding Hamblen County, anti-immigrant activity and xenophobic rhetoric were evident, both in the seats of power and at the grassroots. Organizing by a union there would require a degree of optimism and a readiness to commit major resources that, frankly, we did not expect to see in east Tennessee.

In early 2005, however, we learned that the UFCW had decided to launch an organizing drive at the Morristown plant and that they were eager to identify community allies. They put two organizers on the ground in Morristown, and JwJET sent a small delegation to attend the union's first open community meeting with workers from the plant. Even our partisan crew was genuinely surprised at the degree of excitement we saw and felt at that first meeting.

When we arrived, the large room the union had rented in a local community center was packed. Mothers and fathers with children in tow, young women talking in animated clusters, groups of single men leaning against the back wall of the room—all these people filled the space with energy and anticipation. The organizers—a black man from Alabama and a Latino from Arizona—stood at the front explaining their mission. But as the conversation proceeded, the organizers faded back and the people in the room took center stage.

One worker after another rose to tell about an injustice or to describe another objectionable fact of life in the plant. The room bubbled up with laughter as one woman jumped to her feet to demonstrate the behavior of her supervisor. Narrowing her eyes and throwing back her head, she channeled his hateful, denigrating words and tone: "Shut up! Do you hear me? Shut your mouth! You have no rights here. This is not your home. I am the one who speaks here!" Her portrait quickly provoked additional performances, revealing a world in which worker humiliation had become a supervisory norm. People talked also about wages, punishing line speeds, and threats to worker safety and health. But it was the disrespect and personal degradation that inspired the best theater and generated people's greatest anger and indignation. Our JwJET delegation was moved and impressed by what we saw and eagerly jumped into the campaign.

JwJET's activities in the effort were wide ranging. For instance, we showed up at meetings of the workers' organizing committee in Morristown to demonstrate that they had supporters among the native-born community and in faraway places like Knoxville, Mississippi, and Chicago. Given that the lead union organizer and many of us supporters spoke no Spanish, we located resource people to help the union with interpretation for meetings and with translation of documents. We shared our small but growing knowledge of immigration issues and immigrants' concerns with the organizers assigned to the campaign on occasions when it seemed that some of these things were new to them.

We also reached out to the broader community. For example, we organized a Worker Rights Board hearing in Knoxville on the right to organize as a fundamental U.S. labor standard and an international human right. We worked with multiple community and religious groups to provide opportunities for workers to speak from podiums and pulpits, through interpreters if necessary, about their lives in the plant and why they were seeking to organize a union. Building from those contacts, we recruited Knoxvillians to Morristown for a support rally as the election drew near. The group found one Morristown church willing to host a low-profile discussion about the campaign. We cultivated contacts with local media, and found some interest. JwJ collaborated with regional and national allies, who contributed various kinds of advice, worker education, and general support. During the campaign, which went on for months, we also worked hard to maintain regular and active contact with the unions' organizers and with district and international union staff.

One of the union's most urgent goals was an agreement with the company that it would refrain from mounting an active campaign against union recognition, and instead allow the workers to decide for themselves what they wanted to do. JwJET fully understood why winning such an agreement was crucial and was likely to be difficult. U.S. employers and their attorneys have honed to a fine edge their ability to resist union recognition campaigns. Dancing deftly around and often over the edges of legal rules that are already weighted heavily against workers and their organizations, anti-union consultants succeed in defeating labor initiatives in a huge number of cases, even when the workers are native-born and do not have the specter of immigration enforcement hanging over their heads. When undocumented workers are added to the mix, the ability of the employees at a work site to win a union through the traditional mechanism of a National

Labor Relations Board (NLRB) election is even more severely compromised. So we understood the union's desire to get a neutrality agreement, and we did what we could to advance that goal.

For instance, in pursuit of this aim we connected the union with Anne Lewis, who was happy to include the organizing drive as part of a documentary film she was shooting about local impacts of globalization. She brought a crew to town, and footage they captured of workers' concerns was later used by the union to prove to company management in Chicago that workers' complaints were not a figment of some deranged organizer's imagination. In addition, the instant the company took the tried-and-true union-busting step of firing two of the worker leaders, we protested that move, and we cheered with the union when we learned that the company had made the surprising move of agreeing to hire the workers back—perhaps a sign that the wind was beginning to shift. Throughout this period, we also coordinated a letter-writing campaign to the management of the factory, urging the company to agree to a neutral stance.[6]

Eventually the company acceded to this demand and promised to remain hands-off during the organizing drive. This represented a momentous development and one that undoubtedly affected the outcome of the campaign.[7] There were some subsequent troubling reports from workers about continued backhanded comments and innuendos from supervisors, but the company did honor its agreement to the extent of refraining from overt intimidation or reprisals against union sympathizers.

Despite the neutrality agreement, however, none of us rested easy for a minute during the remainder of the campaign. Members were painfully aware of many reasons immigrant workers might still vote to continue living with the status quo: for example, they might well be fearful of later reprisals from the company, doubtful about the union's own promises of benefit, or worried about attracting attention from the immigration authorities. We were not living in a time when optimism came easy, and we also knew that the cold probabilities were not in the workers' favor.

So when the date set for the election finally rolled around, we were definitely on edge. Our organization had recruited as many people as we could muster to stand outside the gates in support of the union for each of the different shift changes. When some of us arrived for the night shift (which was to cast the opening ballot), we could see that as workers pulled their passenger-laden cars into the company parking lot, they were being greeted by teams of leaflet-wielding, Spanish-speaking men and women enthusiastically urging them to vote "Si!" for the union. We learned that these people were UFCW organizers and members from other plants around the country who had been flown to Tennessee to help in the final blitz of home visits prior to the election. As we watched the cars rolling up to these teams, it seemed we were mostly seeing windows opened gladly, faces spread with friendly grins, leaflets taken with welcoming interest. But then again, we hated to trust our eyes. We knocked on wood and were trying hard to keep our expectations low.

In the bright sunshine of the next day, a motley group of JwJET members and other supporters stood outside the main plant when the last shift still to vote had all gone inside. Election monitors from the NLRB were inside the plant, counting ballots under the watchful eyes of company and union observers, while those of us outside were craning our necks and straining our eyes for any sign of the result of the months-long campaign.

Standing along the highway that morning, together with our JwJET delegation from Knoxville, there were black, white, and Latino organizers and union members from the UFCW, and a couple of guys from the Nashville local union to which the Morristown chicken plant workers would be attached if the election went for the union. There was a faithful young intern from the Highlander Research and Education Center whose highly skilled interpreting and translating services had been integral to the organizers' efforts and workers' comprehension, involvement, and morale. There was a union painter from Morristown who had learned about the election at a recent Labor Day event in Knoxville and who showed up at the factory gates to lend his support. There was an Appalshop film crew diligently working the crowd for interviews and impressions. There was the president of a dying union local at a soon-to-close chemical plant in Morristown who, throughout the organizing drive, had opened the doors of his aging union hall to the workers from the chicken plant, welcoming its use for meetings, rallies, child care, buffet suppers, and workshops, and who had now come to stand with them on this fateful day.

The wait seemed interminable, but at last we made out the sound of cheering. Spilling down the hill toward our waiting crew came an elated group of union-designated election watchers. "Ganamos! We won! Ganamos!" We gathered around this jubilant group and pressed for details. Blinking and smiling with dazed pride, they announced the startling news. The workers had scored not a mere victory, but a landslide. In an era when most unions would be relieved and delighted to eke out a bare majority, the workers that day voted for union recognition by a startling margin of 465 to 18. Amazing.[8]

Elements of Success

Labor unions all over the country do win victories sometimes, and immigrant workers do come together in effective ways to organize, whether in unions, community organizations, or the varied "worker centers" that have emerged as a vehicle for worker rights in situations where union organizing is impractical, inappropriate, or undesired.[9] Nevertheless, the victory we tasted that bright day in Morristown was far from the norm. It therefore seems appropriate to reflect on what contributed to its success.

First and most foundational were assets brought by the workers themselves. During the campaign, powerful leaders emerged from within the plant, people willing and able to step forward, speak out, and take responsibility. It was evident to JwJET and union organizers that these leaders and their skill sets, connections with other workers, and personal character were a key motor for the campaign. Many brought experiences from Mexico that translated into the organizing drive. For instance, some had been active in local community mobilizations, others had learned from watching parents who were educators and social activists. During the union drive, we saw all kinds of resources mobilized that we would not have thought to imagine. Pickup trucks magically arrived with mammoth sound systems when amplification was needed. Extensive informal grapevines far outstripping the power of any e-mail lists were activated in the service of turnout. Delicious homemade dishes became the norm at large events, supplanting the lame hotdogs that the organizers had provided at the start. Stacks of signed union cards were delivered by member volunteers to paid organizers, who sat in a local motel room amazed at what they were witnessing.

The contributions of the union were also crucial. When the drive first began, some of us were skeptical that the union would invest the kinds of resources that were likely to be needed for a victory in Morristown. In fact, the union came through with a substantial commitment. It sent in a pair of organizers for many months, assigned others who rotated in to relieve them periodically, and bolstered the basic team with additional troops from other locations for occasional bursts of more intensive work. Although the lead organizer assigned to the project was an African American who spoke no Spanish, he knew a great deal about the poultry industry and about racism, and he knew the importance of recruiting immigrant workers into the UFCW and the labor movement in general. The second organizer assigned full-time to the campaign was a Spanish-speaking Mexican American, and virtually all the other staff and union members who rotated through the campaign were Latinas or Latinos.

Beyond simply investing resources, the union was generally smart in how it used them. Once on the ground, the initial organizing team recruited active participation from workers and helped them build an in-plant committee. The organizers and the committee made multiple calls on workers in their homes to initiate conversations about workers' concerns at the plant. They logged this outreach activity on computers, kept track of workers' responses and feelings about the union, and conducted regular formal assessments of their progress rather than relying on memories and informal impressions to gauge the strength of their support. Organizers listened to workers and discussed ways a union presence could improve conditions that bothered workers most. With help from two poultry justice educators, they hosted a training session where workers could learn about occupational hazards and ways that union pressure could reduce them. They fought like tigers to defend pro-union workers from retaliation. These union staffers struggled to understand community allies and make good use of the resources we offered, even though such close collaboration with outsiders was new for them and there were times when their frustration at our different ways was evident. Finally, the organizers and those above them in the union structure, together with the workers' committee inside the plant, succeeded in the tricky task of managing the pace and trajectory of the campaign so that it came to a crescendo just in time for the election.[10]

Although the workers themselves and the union provided the most important pieces of the campaign's success, the community support stimulated and coordinated by JwJET also made an important difference. For the most part our role in the campaign was directed outward to the larger community to win more supporters and allies; we also initiated communications to management to urge their neutrality. But to do either of these things well, we had to build relationships of trust with both the union and the workers. As to the former, the organizers and other union staff could see that we genuinely respected their work and appreciated many of its difficulties. That respect built trust with the union people and helped both sides toil more patiently through rough spots in communication.

Similarly, the workers could see that we were excited to be engaged with poultry workers in general and with Mexican immigrants in particular. We showed our eagerness to learn from them about their lives and experiences. Often, we voiced our convictions about the importance of solidarity between immigrant and native-born workers and about the strategic importance of the poultry industry and other low-wage, high-exploitation sectors. In addition, several members of JwJET were involved with non-workplace issues of importance to immigrants, such as lack of access to a driver's license, racial profiling by local law enforcement, and the need for federal immigration reform. We discussed these issues with workers from the plant and provided information about groups in the state that were trying to do something about them. Although a better model would be one in which the union itself was already involved in issues of civil rights and community concern and could use that involvement to show prospective members the union's relevance for a broader range of social concerns, JwJET's demonstrated interest was a second-best way of integrating these community justice issues into the life of the campaign.

Beyond our visible commitment to both labor justice and immigrants' rights, we allies contributed in other ways. Thanks in large part to help from the nearby Highlander Research and Education Center,[11] we were able to bring some knowledge about language issues to bear in the campaign. Highlander provided a staff interpreter and lent interpreting equipment for a large union-community rally prior to the election. A Highlander intern volunteered to translate documents on demand, both for JwJET and the union, allowing JwJET to keep workers more fully informed about some of our activities. Even more important, this intern did one-on-one simultaneous interpretation for the lead organizer during all union meetings. As a consequence, the organizer was able to observe and digest what was going on at meetings without having to choose between being left out entirely or interrupting the flow of discussion for repeated translation breaks. These interventions and contributions were all part of an important learning curve about language practices in bilingual environments that were instructive both for JwJET and the union.

Several other elements provided by JwJET were helpful to the campaign. Working in concert with Interfaith Worker Justice of East Tennessee, we had the ability to identify people who were willing to speak out on workplace justice as a religious value. Of all the resources we mustered during the campaign, this was most often mentioned by the union as our key contribution. Religious voices carry weight in east Tennessee, and we took this part of our mission seriously.

As we started to reach out both to religious groups and secular progressives in Knoxville, we came to see that many people had been wanting a way to connect with the new immigrant community. There was a hunger among many people to learn more about immigration and what immigrants themselves were really like. In JwJET's assessment, our decision to bring activist workers from the plant to speak with groups of native-born non-Spanish speakers led to some of our best work. Giving congregations and other groups a chance to hear directly from some of the impressive leaders who had emerged during the campaign created real energy and interest.

Finally, some elements contributing to the success of the organizing drive cannot be credited to any of the main players above. One was provided by two young women who took the first steps of resistance to everyday norms. The first, Antonia Lopez Paz, a young Latina working in the plant, took action when the company denied her permission for bathroom breaks.[12] The company's refusal violated law and common decency in any context, but it was particularly outrageous given that she was pregnant, had been diagnosed with a bladder infection, and had even provided the company with a letter from her doctor requesting the company's cooperation.

The second pioneering individual who helped open the door to what followed was Jennifer Rosenbaum, a young lawyer whom the pregnant poultry worker contacted for help. Together these two framed a complaint to state health and safety authorities, triggered an inspection of the factory, and then initiated another complaint against the state agency itself after the inspection was botched. Most important was their decision to reach out to others in the plant. In the weeks that followed their initial contact, what could have been treated as an individual matter affecting one pregnant worker became a plantwide agitation about a whole range of health and safety problems. When workers met to talk and explore their legal options, they soon understood that many of the problems they were uncovering had no workable legal remedy but required organization and the exercise of collective power inside the plant. This is the point at which the UFCW was invited by the workers to visit Morristown and talk with them about what a union might have to offer.

So the micro level was important to this case: at its opening juncture and beyond, individual agency mattered. But the macro level was also at work, and the larger context mattered as well. One piece of that larger context was the climate around immigration policy at the time these events took place. All of the major work on the organizing campaign at the chicken plant in Morristown occurred in 2005, culminating with the election in early September of that year. The postelection campaign for a contract involved negotiations that stretched into the spring of 2006. Those months are precisely the period during which an unexpected and unprecedented mass movement in defense of immigrants' rights was simmering beneath the surface, then bubbling, and eventually spilling over into the great outpouring of protests and street processions seen in places large and small all over the United States.

Without our knowing it, the campaign at the chicken plant was riding a current of human feeling and social movement that would only break the surface in March through May 2006. Throughout the period, there was both escalating frustration and rising hope, a feeling in the immigrant community that the pressure had become intolerable and that something had to give, the conviction that it was time to move. This was also a time when the fear of immigration raids, though always present, was less intense than it was later to become in the waning days of the Bush administration, after the failure of comprehensive immigration reform, and after the Department of Homeland Security began to stage repeated raids that were large-scale pieces of political theater aimed most often at high-visibility targets like poultry processing.[13]

During the organizing drive, the union chose to focus almost exclusively on workplace issues, and it talked very little with workers, at least as far as I am aware, about the large policy debates then raging among immigrants and nonimmigrants alike. Nevertheless, in my judgment workers were more ready to take risks to gain a union because they were breathing the air of that preparatory time. For its part, the company too may have been affected by these still-submerged currents. It may have been less ready to provoke a public conflict with its employees because it had the sense that some kind of immigrant revolt might be in the air. Conversely, the company may have feared becoming the target of anti-immigrant community backlash if visible disputes arose, given that anti-immigrant sentiment was also simmering.

The worker leaders from the plant were thoroughly tuned in to the debates over immigration reform. One of the highlights of my life that spring was standing on a sidewalk in Knoxville outside then-Senator Bill Frist's office, along with thousands of others who had assembled to show their outrage at the regressive anti-immigration legislation that had passed the U.S. House of Representatives in December and to urge Frist to support comprehensive immigration reform when that issue reached the Senate. As I watched the crowd of festive, joyous, chanting people parading six-deep around the federal building, all decked out with their flags and baby strollers and T-shirts and protest signs, I looked up and saw walking toward me all of the key leaders from the workers' organizing committee at the poultry plant. We greeted each other in delighted surprise, and they jubilantly informed me of two things. First, they had just succeeded in beating the odds by obtaining a first contract, and, second, management had shut down the plant for the day to allow workers to be present at "la gran marcha."

Postelection Challenges

We rejoiced with the poultry workers from Morristown, both on election day at the plant and later during the astonishing week when they won their first contract and thousands of brown-skinned people poured into the streets of Knoxville for the largest protest in that city since the Vietnam War. But, of course neither of those events represented the resolution of all the problems that had led people to mobilize. The victory in Morristown, though exhilarating for many of us, did not change the fact that unions in the food-processing industry had suffered tremendous losses in membership and social power in recent decades, or that wages and conditions in poultry were dismal even with a union contract.

In the days, weeks, and months after the campaign, many remaining challenges became evident. The union structure into which the newly organized group was to fit was a Nashville-headquartered local made up primarily of native-born retail grocery workers. Its officers and staff had to start from scratch learning to competently represent this new group of non-English-speaking immigrant poultry workers who were located several hours away from the main office. Providing interpretation in contract negotiations or union workshops, for instance, was something they had not thought about before. The strong need and desire of many immigrant workers for help from their union with individual and social problems outside the plant was a dynamic with which the local was unfamiliar. The challenges of education and leadership development in an immigrant workplace were likewise new.[14]

As community allies, we were faced with our own difficult adjustment. We were not clear what our role might or should be in the aftermath of the election. The organizers we had gotten to know so well had been pulled off to their next assignments, and those responsible for negotiating the crucial first contract clearly felt that the need for working with community allies was over, at least for a time. Our own language resources were slim, so it was not easy for us to maintain regular communication with the workers in the plant across physical and language distances. And, in any case, we were aware that the main relationship that needed to be built and strengthened was between workers and the union, and we did not want to be a hindrance to that process.

The workers too had difficulties with the transition. Those who had been most active in the campaign had many questions about what it meant that they now "had" a union. They did not know what to expect from the company or union staff. Those without papers wondered if their immigration status would interfere with what the union was supposed to do for them, or what they could do for the union (both complex questions that few in the union in Tennessee were well qualified to answer). They had no real idea of U.S. labor law, or how a collective bargaining agreement worked, or what their or the union's authority was during negotiations. And of course all day every day the company was ready to take advantage of every sign of weakness or uncertainty. Meanwhile, union leaders faced brush fires on many fronts. Doubtless these challenges and more will continue to face unions, workers, and their allies in labor organizing efforts in the future. Easy solutions are few.

Conclusion

This story has no tidy ending. The union at the Morristown chicken plant continues to exist and to face challenges. Here, as across the nation, many questions about the future of the labor movement and the future of efforts to win and implement significant immigration reform remain open.

JwJET entered this campaign with the conviction that labor unions, for all their considerable weaknesses, are crucial to a genuinely democratic society. They constitute one of the rare institutions in our divided social order that can provide space for horizontal dialogue and exchange between native-born and immigrant workers. Granted, there is no guarantee that labor unions will be able and willing to provide or help build this kind of space. History shows that unions have sometimes played exactly the opposite role with regard to immigration, choosing instead to scapegoat immigrants and push an exclusionary agenda. But unions today have not embraced that anti-immigrant path. Although the outcome is not yet certain, they are at least struggling to find another way.[15]

Having experienced both the elation of this rare union victory and the ambiguities of its aftermath, JwJET activists appreciate more deeply how much about normal union practice will have to change if labor is to rise to the challenges now facing it. But we are also more convinced than ever that labor rights and immigrants' rights are mutually dependent and inextricably intertwined. We see local workplace organizing as key for any progressive response to immigration because it has the rare capacity to create a space where workers themselves can explore the intersection of these two sets of rights and interests and can move toward the solidarity that is key to the advance of both.

The questions that linger for the workers, the union, and their allies show that all of us still have much to learn about building organizations that bring native-born and immigrant workers together on reciprocal terms that increase their mutual power in relation to employers and the state. Whatever the remaining challenges, those of us who worked on this campaign with JwJET are still convinced that we were onto something big and promising. We do not intend to stop.

Notes

1. Eve S. Weinbaum, *To Move a Mountain: Fighting the Global Economy in Appalachia* (New York: New Press, 2004); Fran Ansley and Susan Williams, "Southern Women and Southern Borders on the Move: Tennessee Workers Explore the New International Division of Labor," in *Neither Separate nor Equal: Women, Race and Class in the South,* ed. Barbara Ellen Smith (Philadelphia: Temple University Press, 1999), 207–44.

2. Fran Ansley and Jon Shefner, eds., *Global Connections & Local Receptions: New Latino Immigration to the Southeastern United States* (Knoxville: University of Tennessee Press, 2009).

3. During JwJ's early days, those witnesses did not include any immigrants' rights organizations in the state. The Tennessee Immigrant and Refugee Rights Coalition (TIRRC) emerged in 2001 and eventually placed an organizer in east Tennessee, but not until after events described here. For more on TIRRC, see Fran Ansley, "Constructing Citizenship without a License: The Struggle of Undocumented Immigrants in the USA for Livelihoods and Recognition," in *Inclusive Citizenship: Meanings and Expressions,* ed. Naila Kabeer (London: Zed, 2005), 199–215.

4. The literature on what effect the presence and reception of immigrants may have on nonimmigrants is voluminous. Debates abound. Though studies reporting no or slight effects predominate, most note that the likelihood of negative impact is greater for low-wage nonimmigrants. Two excellent resources are: Barbara Ellen Smith, "Market Rivals or Class Allies? Relations between African American and Latino Immigrant Workers in Memphis," in *Global Connections, Local Receptions,* ed. Ansley and Shefner, 299–317; and Jennifer Gordon and R. A. Lenhardt, "Conflict and Solidarity between African-American and Latino Immigrant Workers" (Berkeley, Calif.: Earl Warren Institute on Race, Ethnicity, and Diversity, 2007).

5. Anne Lewis was then at Appalshop, an arts center in Whitesburg, Kentucky, and she had already begun work on *Morristown: In the Air and Sun,* not released until 2007. In the interim, she produced a set of English/Spanish interviews (or "video letters") with U.S. and Mexican workers, and we screened these for some union audiences. *Morristown Video Letters* is available from Highlander Research and Education Center.

6. Stephen Greenhouse, "Union Organizers at Poultry Plants in South Find Newly Sympathetic Ears," *New York Times,* September 6, 2005; and "Victory for Immigrant Workers' Rights at Koch Foods in East Tennessee," *I'll Be There* (national newsletter of Jobs with Justice), March 2006, 2.

7. Such an agreement can make all the difference. An organizing drive at a chicken plant in Morganton, North Carolina, went down to bitter defeat not long after our own victory, despite long years of labor struggle by generations of workers. For more on the earlier history, see Leon Fink, *The Maya of Morganton: Work and Community in the Nuevo New South* (Chapel Hill: University of North Carolina Press, 2003). The most obvious difference between their recent effort and ours was the winning of a neutrality agreement in Morristown, contrasted with the vicious antiunion campaign waged by the company in Morganton.

8. Rebecca Ferrar, "Working Hard for a Better Life: Koch Food Employees Fight for Fairness," *Knoxville News-Sentinel,* November 20, 2005, C-1. Some scenes described above appear in Anne Lewis's 2007 documentary, *Morristown: In the Air and Sun* (Whitesburg, Ky.: Appalshop).

9. Janice Fine, *Worker Centers: Organizing Communities at the Edge of the Dream* (Ithaca, N.Y.: ILR Press, 2006).

10. In a planning aid developed by Cornell researchers Kate Bronfenbrenner and Robert S. Hickey, the authors identified ten recurring elements in successful drives they studied. *Blueprint for Change: A National Assessment of Winning Union Strategies* (Ithaca, N.Y.: Office of Labor Education Research, New York School of Industrial and Labor Relations, Cornell University, 2003). In our case, the union managed to incorporate all ten.

11. The Highlander Center's Multilingual Capacity Building Program trained interpreters, educated groups about how to be linguistically inclusive, and provided interpretation for grassroots events.

12. Steven Greenhouse mentions Antonia in *The Big Squeeze: Tough Times for the American Worker* (New York: Knopf, 2008), 2–3.

13. See "Postville Raids Symposium," *DePaul Journal for Social Justice* 2 (Fall 2008): 1–100.

14. UFCW has invested more than most unions in organizing immigrants and opposing ICE raids. See, for example, National Commission on ICE Misconduct and Violations of 4th Amendment Rights, *Raids on Workers: Destroying Our Rights* (Washington, D.C.: UFCW, 2009).

15. See Janice Fine and Daniel J. Tichenor, "A Movement Wrestling: American Labor's Enduring Struggle with Immigration, 1866—2007," *Studies in American Political Development* 23 (April 2009): 84–113.

PART III

Climbing Jacob's Ladder

Scaling Up

CHAPTER 12

Virginia Organizing
The Action Is at the State Level

Joe Szakos and Ladelle McWhorter

For decades, community organizations in West Virginia and the Appalachian sections of Kentucky, Tennessee, and Virginia have struggled to determine the best level or "place" to push for economic and social justice and environmental reforms. Should they work exclusively in their home communities? Should they develop regional—geographically and economically based—alliances across state lines, or should they concentrate their efforts inside their own states, disregarding links that cut across government-imposed boundaries? Some groups have focused on their Appalachian identity and fashioned plans without worrying about political boundaries. Others have worked exclusively on local issues while hoping someone else would push for change at a higher level. A few have participated in national alliances. And some have chosen the vehicle of a statewide organization to pursue their dreams of a better world.

In the 1980s, this question of where to focus organizational effort took on new urgency as President Ronald Reagan engineered a massive "devolution" in the United States. National government was slated to downsize as spending on domestic programs was cut and "states' rights" emphasized. Responsibility for public welfare—including the environment, human rights, and labor—shifted to state capitals. Thus, it would seem logical that community groups would shift attention to state government as well. However, through much of the decade few Appalachian groups joined statewide organizations to work for change in their communities, and few statewide groups reached out to people in Appalachian areas, even though many of those people were significantly affected by cuts in domestic programs.

In this chapter, we examine some reasons for this initial failure of statewide organizing in central Appalachia, looking at four interrelated obstacles to effective statewide organizing. We believe the best way to overcome these obstacles is by shifting focus from issue campaigns to development of what we call, borrowing from sociologist Richard L. Wood, "strategic capacity."[1] To illustrate this claim, we draw on our experience with Virginia Organizing[2] since 1994.[3]

Obstacles and Challenges of Statewide Organizing

The first challenge for statewide organizing anywhere in the United States is developing an appropriate organizational scale. This challenge is especially acute in states with Appalachian counties. Consider, for example, the difficulties of including residents of Lee County, Virginia, in any statewide organizations, networks, and campaigns. Lee County, bordering both Tennessee and Kentucky, is closer to six other state capitals than to Richmond. Many of Virginia's statewide groups in 1994 did not, and still do not, have enough money and staff to build connections far from their base of operations with people in Lee County or other Appalachian counties. To maximize resources, the vast majority choose to work in densely populated communities closer to Richmond. Similarly, most Appalachian groups do not have the resources to reach out to a distant state capital and organizations headquartered there.

Even if statewide groups had the resources to get people like those in Lee County involved in their work, they would face another problem: how to bridge the rural-urban divide. This divide involves differences not just in concerns and perspectives but also in work schedules, leisure and family time commitments, and access to various forms of transportation and technology, all of which make a logistical difference in how people connect to an organization and how lasting their connections are. This leads to challenge number two: building an organizational structure that will allow diverse people different entry points into the organization's work and a variety of ways to stay involved over the long haul. Not everybody can speak at a subcommittee hearing or attend a rally at the capital; other forms of participation must be regularly available and valued.

The wider the reach of the organization, the greater the differences in potential participants' backgrounds, perspectives, concerns, skills, financial resources, values, and sense of self and community. An inclusive statewide group must be effective in working on identity politics (for example, race, sex, sexual orientation, class) where issues can sometimes be intense and personal as well as crucial to campaigns. At the same time, it must be ready to make adjustments in approach and strategy as the political landscape changes; it must be able to introduce different methods (such as nonpartisan electoral participation) when needed and know when to link to national groups when strategic opportunities arise.[4] Cultivating adaptability with a diverse constituency is challenge number three. Though the word *adaptability* suggests change rather than stability, preparing an organization to be adaptable requires laying firm groundwork that includes both reliable long-term staff and clear and enduring understanding by all members about the organization's purpose and priorities and the importance and value of its own internal diversity. This brings us to the fourth challenge: how to reflect democratic practices within a growing—and often fast-moving—organization. Democratic processes can be slow; adherence to them can conflict with the need for quick adaptation to new situations. But they are part of that firm ground that holds a grassroots organization together and enables growth; democratic processes ensure that everyone feels—and *is*—welcome, respected, and valued.

By the end of the 1980s, just as some statewide groups realized they had to include Appalachians in their organizing, central Appalachian community groups realized that, while affirming a cultural identity across political jurisdictions is important, they also had to look to their state capitals—Frankfort, Nashville, Richmond, and Charleston—for meaningful change. This meant connecting to statewide organizations. The reach went both ways; statewide organizations needed the diversity of perspective and grassroots power that resides in rural and outlying areas, and Appalachian communities needed the resources, experience, and access to state political leaders that centrally based organizations had to offer. But how could groups with different histories, approaches, beliefs, and concerns come together?

In some states, alliances were forged between existing statewide and community groups—as when Kentuckians For The Commonwealth and Tennessee's Save Our Cumberland Mountains began to address these obstacles to organizing in Appalachian counties.[5] But in Virginia, Appalachians faced a preliminary obstacle even greater than the four listed above: There simply was no statewide organization with which to ally.

Shifting the Frame from Campaigns to Strategic Capacity

From August 1994 to July 1995, Joe Szakos traveled more than forty thousand miles, crisscrossing Virginia to talk with people about what they wanted to see changed. These conversations revealed how much need there was not only for change but also for community organizing infrastructure. Most so-called statewide groups had only one or two staff people; based in and focused on Richmond, they typically did not know where Lee County was. Undaunted, Joe arranged two meetings: one of a group of ten brave souls willing to serve on the initial Organizing Committee of Virginia Organizing and another of about a dozen experienced organizers from across the country.

In August 1995, the first Organizing Committee meeting set the groundwork for a truly inclusive statewide group. Participants acknowledged the usual list of differences—race, class, gender, religion, sexual orientation, age, ability, country of origin—but also added geography to make sure nobody in any part of the state was excluded. The group called what developed the "outside-in strategy." The idea was to get everyone traditionally left out (like Lee Countians) involved *first* and *then* move in toward the capital. In addition, the group decided to be "for" things, not just against them, and to embody what it was "for" in a "Statement of Beliefs" that still guides the organization today (see sidebar).

VIRGINIA ORGANIZING
STATEMENT OF BELIEFS

. . . we believe that all people should be treated fairly and with dignity in all aspects of life, regardless of race, class, gender, religion, sexual orientation, age, ability or country of origin.

. . . we believe that every person in the Commonwealth is entitled to a living wage and benefit package that is sufficient to provide the basic necessities of life, including adequate housing, a nutritious diet, proper child care, sound mental and physical health care, and a secure retirement.

. . . we believe that every person is entitled to an equal educational opportunity.

. . . we believe that community, economic, social and environmental policy should be developed with the greatest input from the people it is meant to serve, and that the policies should promote, celebrate and sustain the human and natural resources of Virginia.

. . . we believe in the elimination of the extremes of wealth and poverty, in a progressive tax system based on the ability to pay, and in making the nation's financial systems, including the Federal Reserve Bank, more responsive to the average citizen's needs.

. . . we believe that we should enhance and celebrate diversity in our communities and in our state.

. . . we believe that those who have positions of authority in our governmental bodies, law enforcement agencies and institutions of learning should reflect the diversity of our communities.

. . . we believe that our public officials should be held accountable for their actions and decisions.

. . . we believe in the rights of workers, consumers, shareholders and taxpayers to democratic self-organization.

. . . we believe in the elimination of the death penalty in all cases because it is fundamentally inhumane, ineffective as a deterrent to crime, and disproportionately and unjustly applied against people of color and those who are economically or educationally disadvantaged.

. . . we believe that physical and mental health are parts of personal and community well-being; we believe that Virginians have a broad public health and economic interest in ensuring that adequate care is available to low- and moderate-income residents.

The second meeting consisted of experienced organizers who had been re-thinking their approaches to community organizing since the Reagan years. Previously, the standard approach was to mount a series of issue campaigns. Organizers identified an issue people wanted to tackle by asking two questions: "What do you want, and who can give it to you?" Usually unstated was another question: "How will this campaign lead to the next and make our organization stronger?" Organizations were built one campaign at a time, growing bigger through each in preparation for the next. But by the 1990s, many organizers were thinking differently. Just getting local officials to pave a road, build more public housing, or stop a hazardous waste incinerator was not enough, even if each victory left their organizations better positioned to win the next campaign. Without *structural* change, they would face a succession of tough issue campaigns with no guarantee of long-term improvement in people's lives. Organizers began to seek lasting changes that could give communities more access and a stronger voice over the long haul. Hence, they added another question: "How does our present campaign push for long-term structural changes?"

Of course, community organizing has always been about power; the main challenge is to achieve sufficient power—real and/or perceived—to get what the organization wants. Building power was the point of developing organizations through issue campaigns, and power took on even more importance when organizers prepared to work for structural change. But our meeting participants were not interested in just seeing Virginia Organizing moving power from one institutional site to another. They believed that to be broadly effective, organizing in Virginia would have to involve lots of people dealing with local as well as statewide problems and long-term, sustainable solutions involving fundamental structural change. For that work, Virginia Organizing would need what Richard L. Wood calls "mobilizing capacity," the ability to turn out people for direct actions or generate calls and letters to key political leaders on short notice. And more important, it would need to develop "strategic capacity," the ability to adapt to take advantage of changing circumstances—including opportunities not only for forging new relationships with political leaders but also involving new groups of people and incorporating new resources and technologies.[6] Each organizational move, therefore, had to contribute to the systematic accumulation of political capacity.

Virginia Organizing thus began as an experiment in organizing dictated by geographical, political, and historical circumstances whose far-reaching implications only became clear to its founders as the organization took shape. The experiment was affected by the ways its organizers and members confronted the four challenges outlined above: expanding to scale, creating and maintaining broadly open organizational structures, preparing to adapt to changing circumstances, and ensuring that decision making is transparent and inclusive. Given historical contingencies in Virginia, these four challenges emerged as matters to be resolved among existing groups *and* as issues to be addressed within a single, extremely diverse, rapidly growing statewide organization. All four have had an impact, in both positive and negative ways, on our ability to build strategic capacity.

Scale

When Denise Smith met Joe Szakos for the first time, her family had just begun to recover from the financial devastation the Reagan recession wreaked in

Appalachia. She had worked with neighbors in Bland County to fight a medical incinerator and a power line. She even went to Richmond but, she recalls, "It took so much. Who cares about a little backwoods county called Bland?"[7] When Joe asked what change she wanted to see, she said she wanted the invisible state line at Roanoke to disappear; she wanted leaders in Richmond to recognize southwest Virginia as part of their own state. But how could a handful of activists in Bland County make that happen? Joe responded with a parable, which Denise remembers fondly:

A large rock is blocking a highway. Twenty-five people are pushing as hard as they can on the rock, but it will not move. Someone finally says, "Why don't we figure out how many people we really need to move this rock?" The group analyzes the situation and determines that one thousand people are needed; the twenty-five they have now can push and push, but they will never move that rock. So instead of pushing, they figure out how to recruit 975 additional people. Once the one thousand are gathered *and brought to understand why they are there,* the rock is moved quickly. (Or they see that their analysis was inaccurate, so they set up to recruit more people.)

Joe's point, which Denise knew all too well from experience, was that the typical organization relies on a few activists who push on a rock they cannot move when they should invest time analyzing their needs and building sufficient strength to tackle the job. In other words, most organizations simply refuse to confront the issue of scale—how big the job is and how big the organization has to be to do that job. Instead of stepping back to analyze, they invest all their energy confronting the forces that oppose the change they seek. Denise and the others who came together in those initial meetings knew they were up against a very large rock and needed to step back and think strategically about how to move it. None of them wanted to waste any more time in a "typical organization." They were sure Virginia Organizing would not be typical.

First of all, it would involve a lot of people spread across a lot of territory. That meant a lot of organizers had to be hired who would stay around for continuity, so Virginia Organizing had to offer decent salaries and benefits. Fund raising—both grant writing and seeking major and grassroots donors—had to be a priority. Communication would be crucial. Investing a lot of money (and training time) in new technology was not feasible initially, so Virginia Organizing's leaders encouraged people to donate old laptop computers and found someone to set them up with e-mail to keep members connected. In ensuing years Virginia Organizing has embraced advances in communications technology whenever they could be used to keep members in touch and get Virginia Organizing's message out.

More important, what helped Virginia Organizing continue to grow to scale was its insistence on honesty, clarity, and member education. We must be honest about what is really needed to do the job we want to do and in our assessment of

Virginia Organizing Board Members Janice "Jay" Johnson and Denise Smith talk about the origins of Virginia Organizing at the group's fifteenth anniversary celebration, August 2010. (Photo by Cynthia Hurst)

whether our approach is working. The issues are serious—a crumbling economy, violations of human rights. We cannot pretend we are making a difference if we are not. Not only will refusal to face facts make us politically ineffective; it will cost us members and material support. We are also committed to combating the negativity that can arise from efforts to get to scale. Rapid growth can create internal conflict, failure to raise sufficient funds, and inability to adapt and stay creative as new challenges present themselves. We have to address these issues as they arise, before they also scale up and impede our growth.

Clarity is essential in every aspect of our work. We must have a clear and regularly updated analysis of power in the state—who can make things happen and where power relations may be shifting. At least once a year, we gather to do a power analysis. Most meetings are open to any member able to attend because we know that crucial information comes from many sources and that diversity of input is a major organizational strength. We also have clarity about our principles and goals. For years we published our "Statement of Beliefs" on the back page of every news-letter, and we display it prominently on our Web site. We keep it in mind when we decide not only which issues to tackle but also how to tackle them.

Clarity about our principles is part of education as well. If Virginia Organiz-ing is really "for" economic justice and civic democracy, we must be sure that all members—especially those who have been excluded from political participation and consequently have few civic skills—have the opportunity to learn how to make their voices heard and become leaders in their communities. To that end, we created a wide range of leadership workshops to train members in political activism and a large internship program to bring young people into the work of community organizing. And we make sure individuals from diverse constituencies understand how our principles apply in our treatment of each other. Everybody's issues matter to the organization; nobody is asked to sacrifice their own concerns indefinitely while they work on issues that primarily benefit others.

Another crucial aspect of education within Virginia Organizing is learning what we mean by "borrowing and sharing power." Each community and issue group has something the others need. What southwest Virginia has that groups in Richmond need is access to powerful legislators who represent the southwestern counties. This need for help creates an opportunity for reciprocation between Appalachians and those other groups. This means that residents of Appalachian counties do not have to wear out their vehicles making long trips to the state capital; these trips can be made by those who live nearer to Richmond. Appalachians just have to wear out their telephones (doing phone banking) and their shoes (doing door-to-door canvassing) to get neighbors to contact their legislators on targeted issues. In return, centrally located groups press legislators from other sections of Virginia to support issues of importance to southwest Virginians. This is "borrowing and sharing power." It works, but only if members understand how power works, trust each other enough to place their issues in each others' hands, and respect others enough (even others who are very different) to give time and attention to their concerns. Each of us must grow—in abilities, knowledge, and relationships with others—if Virginia Organizing is to grow to scale.

Organizational Structure

Closely related to scale is organizational structure. A big, widely dispersed organization must be open at a variety of points to differently situated people. Virginia Organizing starts at the bottom, building one-to-one relationships to identify issues and implement strategies that break down traditional divisions as well as achieve concrete results. Members identify potential members with whom to talk about Virginia Organizing and their concerns. After weaving a strong fabric in communities, Virginia Organizing brings everyone together as a network to push for reforms. We also ally with other organizations whenever possible, drawing their members into our power analyses and workshops and working on their issues in return for their work on ours. Many people's first encounter with Virginia Organizing occurs as an issue partnership; we use those partnerships to inform allies of our principles and organizing strategy and develop relationships with them that outlast their issue campaign.

This approach is time-consuming. Newcomers to Virginia Organizing may wonder why their energy is diverted from their pressing concerns and toward developing relationships with people who appear to have nothing in common with them. To allay that confusion, we tackle current community problems—that is, we run traditional issue campaigns—while we simultaneously work to build lasting networks of cooperation and leadership. We mobilize people for issues, but we also integrate them into a long-term network of cooperation to "borrow and share power."

Virginia Organizing's leadership development focuses on cultivating strategic thinking. Members figure out together how to go after what they want rather than only react to issues as they come up. Developing strategic plans and acting on them are major attractions for those who feel they have spent years "in the trenches" without getting what they really want. Moving from a reactive to an initiating stance is a major step toward creating the capacity to accomplish goals.

Not everyone can plunge into a day-long power analysis or serve on the governing board. People need choices about how to get and stay involved, so Virginia Organizing must have multiple entry points. One person may attend a community forum. Another might do phone banking or door knocking. Some people first connect via the Web site or a forwarded e-mail from a friend. Regardless of the point of contact, a statewide group must be welcoming, with communications and training systems that allow people to feel part of what is happening.

But we cannot stop with just making connections with people where they are. We have to push them beyond their comfort zones by asking them to see the links between (for example) poverty, labor issues, sexual orientation, and health care. We use each issue campaign to deepen members' understanding of the workings of power, locally and statewide. As Wood notes, "Done systematically, this has gradually built a deeper reservoir of power analysis within the organization, thus heightening the group's strategic capacity."[8]

Adaptability: The Changing Nature of Organizing

Shifting power in any state is a gigantic task, especially if a high priority is including marginalized constituencies in the change work itself. In Virginia, where there is little history of full citizen participation, many sectors are not organized, and statewide constituencies such as environmentalists and gay rights activists often choose a narrow, single-issue approach, shifting power is even harder.

After our first serious power analysis in 1995, we saw these obstacles, but we also saw some opportunities. Here is some of what we learned then and in subsequent analyses:

Marginalized constituencies—people of color, gays and lesbians, poor, disabled, rural, and more—were not organized.	Virginia Organizing set out to organize them, and they are now included in the organization's fabric.

Virginia's governor is limited to one term in office, so a lot of power resides in the legislative branch. We realized we needed to bring pressure to bear primarily on the General Assembly.	By developing a multi-issue, multiconstituency approach that encourages and enables more groups to work together, Virginia Organizing has been able to conduct dozens of constituent meetings with legislators in their home districts. Over time we added major civic engagement activities (conducting voter registration drives, promoting get-out-the-vote activities, distributing nonpartisan voter guides, and holding candidate forums) to our repertoire, because they got the attention of candidates as well as incumbents.
Statewide organizations were under-resourced.	We set out to build a strong statewide organization, piece by piece, knowing that we had to continue to grow for a long time before major changes would happen. We invested in our future rather than placing all our resources in current campaigns.
Statewide groups would not play in the same sandbox together.	Even if we did not always agree with their strategies, we set out to work with everyone who wanted progressive long-term change.

We began by identifying opportunities and seizing on as many as we could to build our organization for the future. Whereas most attempts at creating statewide organizations have been linear—running successive issue campaigns, bringing together established players (unions, seniors, progressive legislators), or focusing on electoral politics—Virginia Organizing experimented with ways to build a broad constituency and an infrastructure able to respond to alterations in the playing field from a variety of quarters. Capacity for rapid adaptability must rest on a solid foundation, and Virginia Organizing's structure, staff, and internal relationships provide enough stability to enable us to tolerate the friction that is a natural part of any rapid shift in strategy or issue.

However, although we borrow heavily from models that start with relationship building, we differ in one major way: we look outward more than inward. Most relationship-based models are very controlled: tight timelines, specific demands of specific targets; win, celebrate, and move on to the next issue campaign. Though some include leadership development, few tackle prevalent "isms" in a deliberate way. Because Virginia Organizing set out to build relationships across a wide range of constituencies, our people had to learn how to interact with others very different from themselves. When the first Organizing Committee met in August 1995, their decision to build a political force composed of low- to moderate-income people, people of color, and others traditionally excluded from Virginia political life brought the young organization up against the difficult issue of racism. In Virginia obvious patterns of racism and classism have long served to separate African Americans from whites and low-income people from those higher in socioeconomic status. These divisions run so deep that they are hard to examine, let alone overcome. But for Virginia Organizing to succeed, explicit discussions of racism and classism were essential.

We began by requiring that all Virginia Organizing chapters be racially diverse. To make that possible, we provided "tools"—workshops, materials, and ongoing support. We dedicated substantial resources to Dismantling Racism workshops and, eventually, workshops on heterosexism and classism. We included exercises that would make sense to community groups wanting to tackle race on personal, local, and broader levels. Participants developed openness, confidence, and a sense of empowerment across boundaries. These experiences have increased our achievements on various issues immeasurably and have enabled members to look outward, not only inward, as we work together to choose our issues and strategies.

As we learned to work across our differences, we tackled issues such as racial profiling, discrimination based on sexual orientation, and unfair wages. Later we took on unfair lending practices, health care for the un- and under-insured, and state tax reform. Issue campaigns are vehicles that people can rally around, and they energize our organization. But we use them as learning tools. We want people to join us to fight racial profiling, for example, but in the process to learn about power, recognize it, change it! We never look just for a victory but always also look for opportunities to bring a wide range of constituencies together to make a difference, no matter where that might be—locally, regionally, statewide—because by doing so we build capacity within Virginia Organizing that can be put to use down the road. Building understanding and depth within the organization is a way of building the capacity to adapt as conditions change.

This variability in focus may sound too loose, but our "Statement of Beliefs" offers direction to our organizing, and our "Annual Organizing Plan" gives us specific direction in a given year. We provide an overall framework (multi-issue, multiconstituency, long-term change, moving people to action) and we pay attention to all the elements of organizational development (power analysis, strategic thinking, continual expansion, fund raising/resources, leadership development, public education). Our relationship-building approach allows us to agitate, nurture, challenge, and promote social change in ways that are enriching, not limiting. We have built relationships with marginalized constituencies, staff, and leaders of other statewide groups, politicians and other important actors in the political arena, and key actors in national networks that have a presence in Virginia. We are in a position to formulate and carry out appropriate responses to changing political conditions at every level in every region of the state. Through all its work, Virginia Organizing has built "strategic capacity."

Here are some important lessons we have learned over the years about adapt-
ing:

- Do not be afraid to start over if things are not working. Initially we tried to
  mix home-grown chapters with the power of existing groups (calling them
  affiliates), but that failed because the affiliates did not buy into the mission of
  structural change through a multi-issue, multiconstituency approach. Instead
  of "you scratch my back and I'll scratch yours," many groups favored a "put all
  your energy into what we want" approach.
- Grow your own. Leaders. Staff. Interns. When there were no leadership programs, we started them. When we could not find enough experienced staff
  people, we started apprentice programs and recruited people of color. We
  learned it is easier to sponsor fifty internships than just two or three because
  a big commitment meant that we had to make sure there were resources and
  systems to make it work and that our interns were well-utilized and incorporated into the real work of the organization.

Democratic Decision Making

Grassroots members are volunteers; if they do not feel valued, they walk away.
People want to work cooperatively with others, contribute to something bigger
than themselves, and believe their concerns are important to that larger whole.
Many want to learn new skills. Organizations must give something back to the
individuals who serve them, not just in terms of issue-campaign victories but
also in terms of personal enrichment.

Statewide organizations need a system of local units—chapters, branches, committees—that brings new people into the network and gives members a forum to
develop their knowledge and leadership skills. Regional trainings and workshops
help build organizations and connect people across them. Newsletters, e-action
alert systems, text messaging brigades, and conference call briefings all help, but
communication must be a two-way process if people are going to make long-term
gains and deepen their commitment to the organization and its many different issues and constituencies. Virginia Organizing constantly stresses the need for local
groups to work on local issues that are important to them, yet develop and maintain
a sense of the whole, a greater purpose of the "common good," by contributing to
statewide campaigns. Many members quickly learn that they can "borrow and
share power" by using the leverage of the statewide group to push for local reforms.
Local politicians often pay attention when they learn that a local group is part of a
statewide organization with staff, lawyers, and media contacts. Virginia Organizing sees the cares of ordinary people as central and is able to link these cares to the
broader issues of public life. We do not speak *for* people; we welcome, encourage,
and train all our members and incorporate them into the heart of the organization
so that they can speak for themselves.

Virginia Organizing at the Center
of Statewide Organizing in Virginia

Having recruited members in every legislative district in the state, Virginia Organizing took on a new role, that of "convener." There are many examples of this role—bringing together two dozen groups to work on distributing radio spots throughout the state, working on statewide affordable housing and minimum wage campaigns, coordinating efforts of various groups through the Health Care for America Now campaign. But the clearest example of Virginia Organizing's role in bringing groups together is the Virginia Civic Engagement Table, a group that works on nonpartisan civic engagement.

Based on strong relationships we had with other statewide groups, Virginia Organizing convened a meeting in December 2007 with representatives of the Virginia AFL-CIO, Virginia NAACP, the Virginia Interfaith Center for Public Policy, the Service Employees International Union (SEIU), the Virginia ACLU, Equality Virginia, the Virginia League of Conservation Voters Education Fund, and the Virginia Conservation Network to develop a strategic plan for civic engagement in 2008. The following January, the Virginia Sierra Club and the Virginia Education Association and, shortly thereafter, Tenants and Workers United and Democracy South joined the table. Together, these groups coordinated their nonpartisan voter registration activities and determined the key areas to distribute action flyers for statewide issue campaigns. These activities were coordinated with local as well as national groups, such as the Center for Community Change, the Advancement Project, and the Lawyers' Committee for Civil Rights Under Law. A key component of this plan was a door-to-door canvass by Virginia Organizing. We hired fifty interns to work alongside hundreds of volunteers. They distributed a thirty-two–page nonpartisan voter guide, which included a one-page contribution from each statewide group at the Civic Engagement Table on its most important issue campaign. More than 300,000 copies of the voter guide were distributed in 2008—140,000 through door knocking and the others at events. Canvassers also distributed flyers in key areas on statewide issue campaigns such as health care and climate change.

In addition to the canvassing effort, participating groups worked on a wide range of activities: voter registration, voter contact, training and leadership development, issue identification, get-out-the-vote, and election protection. Many of the groups were part of civic engagement activities for the first time. The Virginia Civic Engagement Table provided a mechanism for groups to learn from each other and from other experts outside the state (especially State Voices), as well as to identify more ways to "borrow and share" power. These activities continue, with participating organizations (twenty-one groups)[9] thinking through power dynamics and learning the same thing that Virginia Organizing has learned, namely, that collaboration and cooperation lead to more effective results in state-wide policy reform.

What Next?

Although we believe Virginia Organizing is on the correct path, we know there are challenges ahead. The key to effective organizing is recognizing challenges and having a plan to deal with them. We still need to develop a more refined power analysis, enlist more statewide groups to join coalitional efforts, dramatically increase grassroots fund raising, and connect to more people who are directly affected by the issues we are tackling so that they can find their public voice. We need additional experienced staff. There is also a need to involve more social service providers in long-term change efforts. We need to know more about using the media to get our messages out. Our organization is looking for ways to take advantage of national realignments that might afford opportunities to move on some of our health care and financial reform issues. New alliances currently forming across state boundaries on these and other issues may cause us to rethink our approach to our own legislature. Though we have made much progress, many big rocks standing in the way of change are still beyond our capacity to move. But whatever happens, Virginia Organizing can experiment, adapt, and grow as circumstances demand or permit, because, over the years, we have carefully cultivated both our mobilizing and strategic capacities.

Denise Smith—still living in southwest Virginia and deeply involved with Virginia Organizing's State Governing Board—reminisced. "I look at what was built from those early days," she writes, "and I am amazed. Ordinary people can make extraordinary change when they join together for a common goal. Virginia Organizing is living proof."[10] Appalachian activists like Denise are living proof that statewide organizations can work effectively in rural areas, overcome the rural-urban divide, and establish strong networks of diverse people across a range of progressive issues. Because of her work and the work of many thousands of people across the Commonwealth, decision makers in Richmond are learning that Virginia's citizens include African Americans, Native Americans, working people, queer people, the disabled, and the uninsured, among others, and that Virginia's western boundary lies a lot farther west than the city of Roanoke.

Acknowledgment

We would like to thank Ellen Ryan for some important concepts used in this essay.

Notes

1. Richard L. Wood, "Raising the Bar: Organizing Capacity in 2009 and Beyond," research report written in 2009 for the Neighborhood Funders Group; available at http://hdl.handle.net/1928/10675; and "Higher Power: Strategic Capacity for State and National Organizing," in *Transforming the City: Community Organizing and the Challenge of Political Change,* ed. Marion Orr (Lawrence: University of Kansas Press, 2007), 162–92.

2. Known for fifteen years as the Virginia Organizing Project, the organization changed its name to Virginia Organizing in August of 2010. The word *Project* sounded transitory or ad hoc and did not reflect the group's status, growth, and long-term commitment.

3. Joe Szakos is executive director of Virginia Organizing and has been since its inception. Ladelle McWhorter joined Virginia Organizing as a member in 1995 and has served as secretary and vice chairperson of the State Governing Board.

4. See, for example, Kristin Layng Szakos and Joe Szakos, *We Make Change: Community Organizers Talk About What They Do—and Why* (Nashville, Tenn.: Vanderbilt University Press, 2007).

5. Joe Szakos served as coordinator of Kentuckians For The Commonwealth from 1981 to 1993.

6. Wood, *Raising the Bar.*

7. Denise Smith, e-mail communication to Joe Szakos, May 19, 2009.

8. Wood, *Raising the Bar,* 8

9. The groups in the Virginia Civic Engagement Table, as of August 1, 2009, were: Advancement Project, Chesapeake Climate Action Network, Clean Water Fund, Democracy South, Environment Virginia Policy and Research Center, Equality Virginia Education Fund, Fair Elections Legal Network, Lawyers Committee for Civil Rights Under Law, Project Vote, Student PIRGs, Tenants and Workers United, Virginia Association of Personal Care Assistants, Virginia Conservation Network, Virginia Education Association, Virginia Interfaith Center for Public Policy, Virginia League of Conservation Voters Education Fund, Virginia Organizing, Virginia Sierra Club, Voice of Vietnamese Americans, Women's Voices/Women Vote, and Working America.

10. Denise Smith, e-mail communication to Joe Szakos, May 19, 2009.

CHAPTER 13

OxyContin Flood in the Coalfields
"Searching for Higher Ground"

Sue Ella Kobak

The last time I saw Little Paul alive, he was halfway under his trailer fixing his water line. It was mid-August 2008, and his dad was nearby, "supervising." Little Paul ducked his head out and gave me a nod with a smile that reminded me he was his father's son. A few weeks later my husband and I attended his funeral.

On an otherwise beautiful September evening, the first impression is, how do so many cars park safely to allow access to the church and let other vehicles drive past? We parked to the side, leaving the car jutting out into the already narrow road. When I was growing up there, the road was dirt and gravel. Back then and even now, the road is so narrow in places that cars often cannot pass. We all know where the wide places are and who is supposed to pull over for oncoming traffic.

Almost all my old friends who went to Poor Bottom's one-room school with me were at the funeral. Some left home after high school to get jobs or join the military, but have come back for their retirement. They are active in the community and important to this little Free Will Baptist church. The underlying theology is Baptist, with focus on the experience of the Holy Spirit through prayer, song, community, and reading the Bible.

At the front of the church, Little Paul lay in the coffin in his favorite ball cap, jeans, and shirt. The law decided it was a self-inflicted .45 bullet, but we all knew it was drugs—sixty Lorcets and sixty Xanax on a recent visit to the doctor in Williamson, West Virginia—that killed Little Paul at the age of twenty-seven. There were stories at the funeral of the line of people running out into the parking lot at the doctor's office he had visited. It seems that the federal Drug Enforcement Agency gets rid of one doctor who is a greedy pill pusher and another will pop up somewhere else.

It was a hot day and still very warm as the evening service started. The church was not air-conditioned. There were fans and the windows were open. It was not uncomfortable, but the texture of the air hung like sadness in the room. The holler community, cousins, uncles, aunts, friends, and neighbors, were there. We all said hello and hugged each other. We approached the parents, Paul and Carol, with such a sense of pain for their loss.

The singing started with very expressive voices conveying the loving nature of a just and good God. The songs urged this family that lost so much to cling to the Lord for help and strength. That seemed the only hope left in the room. Pastor Richard talked to all of us without judgment. His theology is that we hope we will receive eternal life through the redemption of the savior, Jesus. We were all wondering whose child would be next.

The minister announced that the congregation would provide a meal for the family at 3:00 the next afternoon. After the service friends informed me that the previous day, a young boy, who should have been a man except for the arresting effects of addiction that delayed his physical, emotional, and intellectual development, died in a fire on the hill where he lived in a camper trailer. He was a heavy drug user. Nobody knew exactly what happened, but nobody doubted the killer was his addiction to prescription drugs.

History and Background: Mine and Theirs

Very few families in central Appalachia have not been directly touched with the tragedy of addiction. I have feelings of anger and frustration from the impact that prescription drug abuse has had on the culture I treasure.

I was born and raised in east Kentucky. My husband, Art Van Zee, has been a primary care doctor in Lee County, Virginia, for more than thirty years. My history as an organizer, teacher, and attorney goes back more than forty years. It had been common knowledge for years in our community that prescription drug abuse was a problem, but the introduction and aggressive marketing of OxyContin by Purdue Pharma dramatized the problem in all sectors of the community. Resources of families, agencies, and government entities were hit really hard, really fast. Art and I were and still are active in attempting to identify both the problems related to addiction and ways to confront those problems effectively, especially within the culture of central Appalachia. However, we are by far not the only people or even the most effective people or organizations who have committed their lives to this very important issue. I am writing this because I was there and I was involved and I have been given this opportunity to tell the story.

Prescription drug abuse became very serious in 1996, when OxyContin was introduced by Purdue Pharma, its Connecticut-based manufacturer. The first, anecdotal evidence of OxyContin abuse surfaced shortly thereafter. OxyContin, a high-potency oxycodone sustained-release preparation to be taken twice daily for moderate to severe pain, is a federal Food and Drug Administration (FDA) designation. Those who use the drug illegally crush the tablet and inhale or inject it for a heroinlike high. A number of people are now also smoking the drug.[1]

Purdue Pharma relied on an unprecedented and heavily financed promotional and marketing campaign for the new drug. Thousands of doctors were treated to all-expenses-paid pain-management conferences in resort communities. An additional twenty thousand other pain-related educational programs sponsored by Purdue Pharma between 1996 and 2002 were available to doctors free of charge. The company sent out mass mailings of promotional materials to physicians and paid lucrative incentives to its sales representatives. Free starter vouchers and coupons for OxyContin were made available for doctors to give to their patients. The company provided doctors logo-branded OxyContin fishing hats, tote bags, clocks, plush stuffed toys, and music compact discs. OxyContin sales accelerated from $48 million in 1996 to a blockbuster $1.1 billion in 2000.[2]

Dr. Vince Stravino, who worked for the local Stone Mountain Health Center, first began talking about abuse of OxyContin after caring for overdose patients in the Lee County hospital emergency room. In addition, Sister Elizabeth Vines and Sister Beth Davies, who for more than twenty-five years have provided local addiction education and counseling, began seeing the growing tragedy as OxyContin became the drug of choice for addicts; together, they began to share their concerns. In 1999, Dr. Stravino called the FDA and Purdue Pharma regarding the incidents of abuse. He got little to no response.

The Lee Coalition for Health

The Lee Coalition for Health ("the Coalition"), a nonprofit Virginia corporation, is composed of people from local government agencies, churches, health-care institutions, and the community at large. Stimulated by Dr. Van Zee and other health-care providers in the county, who became actively involved in preventive health care, the Coalition sponsored health education; community health events, such as cancer screenings, prenatal care promotion, and smoking cessation campaigns; and community health assessments.

The St. Charles Clinic, now part of the Stone Mountain Health clinic system, was a key institution in the formation of the Coalition. This community-owned-and-operated health clinic was organized with the help of volunteers from the Vanderbilt Student Health Coalition, but with the vision and hard work of the retired coal miners of Lee County. The Stone Mountain Health Clinic system is still owned and operated by the same type of community-based board. People within the community had often talked about local problems, who had power, and what their motives were. In the last thirty to forty years these same community people learned the need to gather and use evidence-based information to plan for action, which working with the Coalition enabled them to do.

With the rising tide of addiction, associated deaths, and significant anecdotal information, the Coalition decided to focus on OxyContin-related issues. One of their first actions was to post a petition on their Web site, which ultimately drew about ten thousand signatures, demanding that Purdue Pharma recall Oxy-Contin. In addition, Van Zee obtained an assessment questionnaire, designed to gather information about the health habits of adolescents within a community, from the Centers for Disease Control. The Coalition obtained permission from the school board to administer the questionnaire to all Lee County public school students in grades seven through twelve, a process that was completed in the early spring of 2000. Through the East Tennessee Medical School Appalachian Summer Program, Van Zee recruited a student, Garrett Key (now Dr. Key), who collated the data collected through the questionnaire and prepared a report.

Key organized the effort, which drew on significant community support and resources, to put information from the completed questionnaires into a database. He obtained use of the school computer labs and support of the computer teachers as volunteers. Kevin Carson, president of the Lee High School student body, recruited student volunteers, who were supervised by the volunteer teachers. Someone in the community even provided pizzas for the crew. Because of the Coalition's prior activities, people trusted their efforts and were generous to help with the work.

After the database was established, Key and Van Zee began the analysis. The pervasiveness of prescription drug abuse, including the drug OxyContin, was astounding: 9 percent of seventh graders and 24 percent of eleventh graders in Lee County had used OxyContin at least once. As Art, Garrett, and I looked at the bars and graphs, we thought about Claude Brown's autobiographical work, *Manchild in the Promised Land,* and his story about the impacts of heroin on the culture and lives of African Americans in Harlem.[3] His experiences, so distant in some respects, named the changes, forever, of the cultures of both his community and ours! The comparison was dramatic.

Even though the information from the questionnaire was informal, it did support the anecdotal stories and helped us design a plan to do something about the problem. The Coalition's next project was a public forum held at the Lee High School auditorium. More than eight hundred people attended, including many parents, preachers, church members, teachers, law enforcement officials, and professionals who worked with addiction issues. Out of this effort, several focus groups formed to plan for action. Those who continued to meet were primarily the parent and family support groups. Sisters Beth and Elizabeth worked not only with these groups but also with their members' loved ones in the local jail.

Coalition members also met with other doctors and the staff of hospitals and area mental health agencies to communicate about the problems. As a result of these meetings, the group planned an educational seminar focusing on the identification and treatment of addiction. They pooled funds to obtain a location, catered meal, and approval for accreditation from relevant professional organizations. The group identified Drs. Richard Schottenfield and David Fiellin from Yale Medical School, well-known national authorities on addiction, as potential speakers, but members felt intimidated about contacting these men; however, when asked, the doctors graciously agreed to come for the price of a plane ticket, meal, and hotel room.

The resulting event was a successful, widely attended, informative, areawide discussion of the problem. The prestige of the speakers gave significant attention to the meeting. However, missing were the grassroots people, which included the addicts, parents, and families devastated by the use of the drug. The ultimate plan of action by the people and agencies who sponsored the meeting and those in attendance included: 1) treatment and support for the people addicted; 2) drug courts designed to work with addicts to aid rehabilitation; 3) accountability from the drug company; 4) major efforts to control the availability of the drug; 5) on-going public education regarding the disease of addiction; and 6) state, regional, and national policies and plans to address addiction and change attitudes toward the victims of this disease.

Coincidentally, Beverly Enterprises, a California corporation, closed a local nursing home in Dryden, Virginia (located in Lee County), and gave the facility to the Coalition. Built in the late 1970s, the building was in good shape, except for some needed repairs in the plumbing, electric wiring, and roof. The property included more than four acres of land and was accessible but private. The Coalition and the community now had a project that was concrete and could provide a long-term residential treatment facility for addiction victims. This service was not available on an affordable basis to people within a one hundred–mile radius. The new not-for-profit corporation was named New Beginnings. It took three years and a lot of sweat equity, but finally on opening day the facility was introduced to the community that had put so much into its creation. The policy was to take anyone if their addiction qualified them for services and there was space, whether or not they could pay. As a result, fund-raising was and remains a major challenge. The facility continues to operate and has served more than 450 people.

There was a lot of community support for the facility, but local officials refused to back it with economic development money. With information that local coal companies were having trouble hiring drug-free miners, we argued that the facility would help ensure sober workers for jobs that economic developers were trying to attract and, in the case of coal mining, already had in the region. In my view, negative attitudes regarding addicts as bad people, not diseased people, had a lot of influence on this decision. Ron Flannery, director of the local planning district, who had significant influence on all local development efforts, told me directly, "Addiction is not an economic issue."

Our efforts in Lee County drew attention from Purdue Pharma. Corporate headquarters contacted Dr. Van Zee and others to inform us that company representatives were coming to Lee County to help with the problems related to addiction. They requested a private meeting with Dr. Van Zee but would not tell him why they wanted to talk with him alone. He therefore asked several community persons, including myself, to attend with him. When we arrived, medical representative Dr. David Haddox, corporate counsel Howard Udell, CEO Michael Friedman, and various other public relations people were present.

After we ate dinner, the parent of a son who was addicted to OxyContin gave a most sensitive story of his family's horrors with Purdue Pharma's drug. The others present tried to share with company officials their professional and personal experiences with the easy availability of the drug. Company representatives continued to assert that the availability of the drug was not the problem; addicts were the problem. They even offered us $100,000 to spend as we saw fit to work with these poor addicts, if only the Coalition would take down from its Web site the petition to recall OxyContin, which the company apparently credited Van Zee for initiating. The bribe did nothing but make the group mad.

Greg Stewart, a local pharmacist, left the room. Mr. Udell pulled out of his briefcase an open letter to the public from Dr. David Haddox to be placed in area newspapers as a way of sharing their compassion for our problem. I started to read the letter, which began, "as a fellow Appalachian [Dr. Haddox was born in West Virginia] he . . ." That was the last word I read. I told Dr. Haddox he had his nerve; he had done more to destroy Appalachia than probably the entire coal industry. I walked outside, intending to pay for our meal because I was not going to take anything from them. Greg Stewart met me on my way out and told me not to bother; he had already paid it.

Politicizing OxyContin

Abuse of OxyContin appears to have started in the Appalachian coalfields and parts of rural Maine, then spread throughout the country.[4] What these two areas have in common is the demanding physical labor of their major industries—coal mining and logging. In central Appalachia, many people have been physically injured working as coal miners and suffer chronic pain as a result; in northern Maine, people working in the logging industry have had similar experiences. In this sense, OxyContin abuse is no less an occupational safety and health problem and sign of workplace exploitation than, for example, black lung disease, which did become the focus of a mass movement in Appalachia. Both areas also share a high incidence of chronic pain patients, much higher volume of prescribed pain pills, high levels of rural poverty, and high dependence on Medicaid. This was not lost on Purdue Pharma.

The history of negative stereotyping of Appalachia contributed to the stigma that OxyContin addicts faced and made it more difficult to target the systemic roots of addiction. OxyContin abuse was defined as the fault of the individual, evidence of the moral failing of a bad person. Like Harlem, New York, with its reputation for drugs, crime, and poverty, central Appalachia became identified as a rural ghetto. The problem was addicts, not regional exploitation and impoverishment, much less the availability of the drug, the manufacturer's deceptive marketing, or the suppression of evidence regarding its highly addictive qualities. Further, media use of terms like "hillbilly heroin" gave the impression that OxyContin addiction was only a poor people's problem, and that perception persists. However, the disease of prescription drug addiction crosses economic, cultural, and social lines throughout the country.

The response of most government entities to OxyContin abuse was to beef up law enforcement on the consumption side. Crime rates for breaking and entering and for grand and petty larceny in Lee County and surrounding areas were increasing exponentially. Federal enforcement agencies like the Bureau of Alcohol, Tobacco, and Firearms Control, Federal Bureau of Investigation, Drug Enforcement Agency (DEA), and U.S. attorney's office became alarmed by criminal problems resulting from addictive use of OxyContin in particular, but also other drugs' illegal sale and use. Local law enforcement agencies began to investigate and prosecute drug traders, doctors for illegal prescribing, and individual addicts who sold one or more tablets to get drugs for themselves. Jails and prisons were filling up fast at both federal and state levels. As a result of this criminal activity, social service agencies saw a significant increase in the number of children in foster care. Meanwhile, OxyContin was selling for $1.00 per milligram on the streets and was easily available.

Identification of the OxyContin problem and the relatively rapid community response may have occurred in Lee County because people had a history of working together to assess and identify problems for quick action. Through the years, many people in the county worked together to stop private landfill development and unregulated strip mining, and to support improved water quality, among other campaigns. As the problem with OxyContin abuse became more dramatic, people from various social, economic, and professional groups took direct action. There was not, however, a coordinated regional or national grassroots effort to address the issue of addiction. Several Appalachian groups, such as Kentuckians For The Commonwealth (KFTC), Save Our Cumberland Mountains (SOCM) in Tennessee, and the Virginia Organizing Project (VOP), operated statewide and had skills, people, and resources to mount a comprehensive campaign around this problem, but they did not take on addiction as an issue. However, all these groups had local chapters and some, such as the Lee County chapter of VOP, selected this problem as a local focus.

By the time Lee County began challenging OxyContin abuse, VOP had employed an organizer, Jill Carson, who lived in Lee County, and she was encouraged by state VOP staff to be part of that challenge. However, the entire board of directors for VOP planned their statewide agenda and campaigns a year in advance, and none of the board members other than those from the southwestern part of the state recognized the problem as an issue with statewide, regional, or national interest. Laura Lawson and Kathy Rowles, board members for VOP from southwest Virginia, and Jill Carson, the organizer, could not convince VOP's full board of directors or the executive director that this issue needed immediate statewide and perhaps regional support. I requested that we be allowed to make a presentation to the VOP board of directors to attempt to influence the board and staff to put the issue on their statewide agenda. I was denied that opportunity. My thinking was that VOP and other statewide grassroots organizations could have an impact on policies and programs regarding addiction. I still think that the refusal of these grassroots groups to take on this issue resulted in the failure to address addiction fully. Because addiction has had such a devastating effect on the culture and lives of people within the region, these groups' refusal also failed the people who created them and who hoped thereby to have a statewide and ideally a regional voice.

Whereas VOP and other grassroots organizations chose not to define prescription drug abuse as a political priority, the Appalachian Substance Abuse Coalition for Prevention and Treatment, an organization of professionals working in addiction treatment and mental health programs, did form to address abuse of OxyContin and other drugs. As a community board member during the early establishment of the organization, I tried to encourage regionwide planning and inclusion of grassroots groups. The people involved with the organization did not seem to know about or understand that several statewide grassroots organizations existed in Tennessee, Virginia, Kentucky, and West Virginia. For example, in communities like Gilbert, West Virginia, and surrounding areas, there were very aggressive, community-based efforts. The Appalachian Substance Abuse Coalition, like the grassroots organization VOP, did not see the potential benefit in an alliance. To me, there was a need for grassroots community organizers and professionals like those in the Appalachian Substance Abuse Coalition to join in planning a regionwide conference to educate broadly about the disease of addiction, move from criminalization to proactive treatment, advocate for drug courts, and develop at least a regionwide policy for addressing the problem.

An additional approach to organizing around OxyContin abuse emerged when many people from all across the country started to be connected by the Internet. These were most often people who had family members who were addicted or died because of prescription drug use or abuse. Several Web sites were created for people to share information, learn as much as possible, and provide support for victims, families, and loved ones. Greg Wood, a chief health-care fraud investigator with the U.S. attorney's office in Roanoke, Virginia, regularly sent out via e-mail reports about OxyContin that he gathered from the media. This information was shared across the country. Although this Internet community communicated regularly, they, too, did not have a clear and organized plan for affecting policy regarding the disease of addiction. Nonetheless, the Internet is the hero of this story. It allowed all kinds of people to communicate immediately about happenings all over the country. Many are still connected electronically and communicate opportunities and information. They still attend state and federal legislative committee meetings and federal agency hearings on these issues and talk with their individual legislators whenever they can. The Internet also helped show that prescription drug abuse crosses all social and economic groups and places. Even as the negative stereotype of "hillbilly heroin" prevented the country from seeing this as a serious problem in Appalachia (and elsewhere), we were hearing from people of wealth and influence all over the United States who had lost a child or had a child who was addicted. On May 26, 2009, National Public Radio aired a report on this escalating problem. The circle of prescription drug abuse, particularly of OxyContin, was growing.

A final approach took place through the courts. In 2003, the U.S. attorney's office out of Roanoke—after years of dedicated hard work—was able to obtain criminal indictments against Purdue Pharma and its three top executives, Harold Udell, Michael Friedman, and Dr. Paul Goldenheim, the former medical director. The parties eventually pled guilty to criminal charges of misbranding OxyContin by claiming that it was less addictive and less subject to abuse and diversion than other opioids and had to pay $634 million in fines, none of which was allowed to be used for addiction treatment.[5]

VOP's Lee County chapter, through their new southwest Virginia organizer, Brian Johns, helped make the sentencing of Purdue Pharma and its executives a special event for people throughout the country. Many had been connected to each other by the Internet, and they came to watch the sentencing hearing in federal court in Abingdon, Virginia. Judge Jim Jones, a sensitive jurist, allowed everyone who wanted to speak about the sentencing to have their say in court. The executives of Purdue Parma asked to enter the courthouse by a back door, but Judge Jones required them to come through the front like everybody else. People stood on the sidewalk as the men did the "perp walk" into the courthouse. It was a rainy day, but members of the local community, with the help of VOP's organizing, found each other and expressed their hurt and loss in appropriate ways. However, this was not the end of OxyContin problems or of Purdue Pharma's aggressive marketing. Having kept a low profile in their promotion and advertising for months before the plea and sentencing, Purdue Pharma launched a new marketing campaign in a number of prominent medical journals within months of the sentencing day.

Where We Are Today

Appalachia has been forever changed by the availability of OxyContin. Sales of the drug and deaths resulting from its use continue beyond any of our expectations, even though there is no scientific evidence that sustained released medications are a more effective treatment for pain. Since the release of OxyContin, several other sustained release opioid medications have come on the market. The FDA has made efforts to educate doctors about prescribing these medications and to investigate ways to limit their availability. These are met with assertions by many professional associations, drug companies, doctors, and pain management advocates that pain management is a serious problem and that pain is under-treated. Though true, they ignore the tremendous social, economic, and health problem of addiction resulting from the ready availability of these medications. In response to considerable pressure, Purdue Pharma did eventually develop an abuse-resistant formulation of the drug.

Those of us who organized around issues related to OxyContin abuse, spe-cifically addiction problems, missed a major opportunity for a regional and/or nationwide influence on policy regarding treatment for addiction. Community-organizing groups in the region were unable to forge cross-state and cross-orga-nizational alliances to build a regional grassroots response to the problem, and this remains true today. Their capacity to send out mass e-mails to government representatives and provide support for changes in attitudes toward addiction would be powerful tools to add to the many other efforts.

Mental health agencies and all levels of health-care professionals within the central Appalachian region are clearly aware of the problem of OxyContin abuse and the continued proliferation of addiction problems in general. Several profes-sional groups in Virginia, Kentucky, West Virginia, and Tennessee formed efforts similar to those of the Appalachian Substance Abuse Coalition for Prevention and Treatment. However, they have all been working in their own states and communities to obtain as many resources as possible, and at times have become rather protective of their turf. Being involved with grassroots organizations and professional efforts, it became clear to me that both needed to form a more in-clusive group.

Class differences have been a major barrier preventing more inclusive orga-nizing, not only on OxyContin and addiction but also on many other issues. My own experience illustrates this. I became an organizer when I was a student at Morehead State University and a poor person from Pike County, Kentucky. As I became educated and moved into the middle class as a professional, I was not considered by some grassroots organizers as a grassroots person. In their thinking, if you were not poor or if you developed personal power, you were not a candidate for their organization; I felt that my presence in grassroots meetings was thought to taint their organizing efforts. This never made sense to me. I always have and still do consider myself part of the general Appalachian culture. Because of my heritage and experiences moving up from poverty, I believe that I and others like me have a sensitivity that could help bridge the class gap between people who are organizers, particularly people who did not come from the culture, and grassroots people. Additionally, I feel that one of the major features of personal power is not to be intimidated by people no matter their class or profession. This type of personal power comes from learning how the system works, who has the power, how to find information, and how to use all three skills to communicate your problems or needs effectively. I have always felt that if my skills, education, or professional status could give credibility to a grassroots group, then that is an effective use of my changed status.

This class gap could be bridged if state and regional grassroots organizations evaluated their organizational structures and developed training techniques for grassroots people to work effectively with professionals and people in power as equal partners. Organizations like VOP, KFTC, and SOCM do function as grassroots organizations with decision-making processes through which a large number of grassroots people speak effectively. However, these organizations need to have a more inclusive mechanism by which local chapters or other community-based groups or persons can come to a board meeting to make a presentation to obtain that organization's participation in issues like OxyContin abuse. Similarly, in professional organizations seeking to address local problems, grassroots input and planning would assure that any policies and programs truly reflect the needs and culture of the people.

The struggle continues. The Appalachian Substance Abuse Coalition for Prevention and Treatment group in southwest Virginia received a $200,000 share of the OxyContin Civil Settlement Funds from the Virginia attorney general's office. Their award is being used "to implement an information dissemination and social norm marketing prevention campaign to increase the awareness of the use and abuse of prescription drugs, such as OxyContin . . ."[6]

The approach in Kentucky, which has had major success obtaining wide support to move beyond criminalization of the disease of addiction, offers a hopeful model. The state surpasses Virginia and other central Appalachian states in establishing drug courts (a court system that takes nonviolent addicts and provides treatment and other services so that they have the potential of returning to the community as healthy, contributing citizens). The state has also supported short- and long-term residential treatment facilities. Community organizations called Unite, supported by federal and state money acquired by their congressman, Hal Rogers, exist in every county. Most of the funds go to police support, but community involvement and education are also a significant emphasis. At one point five thousand people walked through the streets of Pikeville, voicing their concerns and supporting efforts to stop the tide of addiction.

In the absence of such statewide programs, appropriate treatment for addiction remains an important need in Lee County and throughout Virginia. We continue to take steps to change attitudes regarding the disease of addiction and to provide appropriate treatment that will return people with the disease to the community as working, contributing citizens.

Notes

This chapter is dedicated to Paul Holland Jr., 1981–2008.

1. Drug Enforcement Administration, Office of Diversion Control, *Action Plan To Prevent the Diversion and Abuse of OxyContin* (Springfield, Va.: Drug Enforcement Administration, 2001).

2. Art Van Zee, "The Promotion and Marketing of OxyContin: Commercial Triumph, Public Health Tragedy," *American Journal of Public Health* 99 (February 2009): 1.

3. Claude Brown, *Manchild in the Promised Land* (New York: Touchstone, 1965).

4. Theodore J. Cicero, James A. Inciardi, and Alvaro Muñoz, "Trends in Abuse of Oxy-Contin® and Other Opioid Analgesics in the United States: 2002–2004," *Journal of Pain* 6 (October 2005): 662–72.

5. http://www.usdoj.gov/usao/vaw/press_releases/purdue_frederick_10may2007.html.

6. McConnell Awards OxyContin Civil Settlement Funds. Press release, January 30, 2009. See www.vaag.com.

CHAPTER 14

Not Your Grandmother's Agrarianism
The Community Farm Alliance's Agrifood Activism

Jenrose Fitzgerald, Lisa Markowitz, and Dwight B. Billings

> Nobody should cry because of lower consumption of a product that
> kills half the people who use it.
> —Danny McGoldrick, "Smoking Declines as Taxes Increase"[1]

> Yes, it is carcinogenic, and generally grown with too many inputs, but
> tobacco is the last big commodity in America that's still mostly grown
> on family farms, in an economy that won't let these farmers shift to
> another crop. If it goes extinct, so do they.
> —Barbara Kingsolver, "Foreword" to *The Essential Agrarian Reader:*
> *The Future of Culture, Community, and the Land*[2]

The story of Kentucky's farm economy is a story about tobacco. Tobacco has not
only been a key source of income for small farmers in the state, it has long been
a way of life and source of pride for those producing it. For more than seventy
years, Kentucky's tobacco farmers depended on the federal tobacco program,
which aimed to "spread the wealth" among growers by limiting the amount of
tobacco each farmer could grow and guaranteeing them a set price for their
product. Primarily because of the success of this program, Kentucky had one
of the highest numbers of family farms in the country in 1997.[3] Thus when U.S.
tobacco companies reached their Tobacco Master Settlement Agreement with
states in 1998, essentially acknowledging the health consequences of smoking,
reactions in Kentucky were mixed. While some saw this as a great victory for the
health and well-being of Kentucky's citizens, others saw it as the beginning of
the end for family farming in the state. If tobacco farmers were to avoid "going
extinct," something would have to be done to mitigate the decline of what was
then Kentucky's number one cash crop. Though the tobacco settlement presented a significant problem for Kentucky agriculture, it ultimately provided
a partial solution as well. In the process, it brought together a surprisingly
diverse group of actors—including farmers, foodies, environmental activists,
and public health advocates—who have collectively worked to define a unique
kind of agrarianism in the state.

Through the tobacco settlement, Kentucky was awarded more than $3 billion over a twenty-five-year period. Nearly half of this money—$1.7 billion—was ultimately to be invested in the state's agricultural economy, with a focus on supporting family farmers through crop diversification and marketing infrastructure for local farm products. This novel approach differed from most states, where tobacco settlement money simply went into the general fund to balance state budgets. Although many organizations and individuals were involved in shaping Kentucky's approach, the contributions of one small grassroots organization have been largely overlooked in official accounts: the Community Farm Alliance (CFA). In this chapter, we argue that CFA was surprisingly influential in the process, despite its philosophical differences with numerous more powerful players at the table. We examine how it used this legislative moment to garner support for building a more sustainable and locally integrated food economy (LIFE) in Kentucky and identify and assess the relevance of its key strategies and challenges for other movements for sustainable development in Appalachia and beyond.

To understand CFA's role in the tobacco settlement process, we must first discuss the organization and our collective experience working with its members. The Community Farm Alliance is a statewide organization of family farmers and allies established in 1985 amid the farm crisis. A central mission of the organization, then as now, was to preserve family farming in Kentucky in the face of an increasingly industrialized agricultural economy. One of CFA's key accomplishments was shaping Kentucky House Bill 611, passed in 2000, which set up a farmer-driven process for the investment of tobacco settlement funds. The path leading to this legislative victory and subsequent accomplishments was by no means inevitable or smooth. We draw on our collective experience with CFA, including participant observation and informal interviews with members and constituents over a ten-year period, 1999–2009, to understand and recount the organization's effectiveness and glean lessons for other grassroots organizations working toward similar goals. We rely heavily on interviews conducted with then–executive director Deborah Webb, considering her long history within the organization and her strong leadership during the period in question; however, our analysis is equally shaped by our conversations and interactions with CFA's grassroots players. Although we are CFA members, our account reflects our roles as participant-observers and social scientists, rather than as members; the perspectives put forward here are ours and should not be mistaken for an official organizational account.

Envisioning Post-Tobacco Agriculture

During the summer of 1999, the Community Farm Alliance held a series of public meetings to strategize about how to secure some tobacco settlement money for farmers. Deborah Webb described the mood of those meetings: "People were scared. There was a lot of anxiety about how fast tobacco quotas would be cut, could they salvage that year's crop. . . . So the tension, the fear, the anxiety was just sky-high. And we did a lot of meetings that summer too, and they were not fun. These were some of the roughest public meetings I think that CFA had held."[4] Once the tobacco agreement was reached, farmers feared (rightly, it turns out) that the tobacco companies would pressure the government to end the federal tobacco program. Tobacco farmers would then have to figure out how to make up for that lost income, or get out of farming altogether. CFA leaders realized that if tobacco farmers did not transition to other crops, the end of the tobacco program would end their operations. The public meetings acted as catalysts, channeling farmers' tension into a call for action. One CFA meeting boasted 250 attendees, some of whom showed up with signs and tractors demanding the attention of Kentucky Governor Paul Patton and other public officials. CFA used this opportunity to get more small farmers involved in the tobacco settlement debate.

Convincing farmers that new directions were possible required both emotional and intellectual efforts. Emotionally, CFA had to counter the pessimism of farmers, especially older ones, who did not "see why pursuing any of this [a new course] makes any sense, because if you can't make a living, you can't make a living."[5] Intellectually, it had to challenge agricultural scientists and economists who reinforced farmers' doubts by arguing that small farms were inefficient, ineffective, and destined to disappear. Thus in structuring public meetings, the mobilization of counterexperts became a key strategy. Webb states: "'Where are the good-guy economists?' is the question we often ask ourselves, because most of the stuff we'd gotten out of UK [University of Kentucky] agriculture economists is basically a long list of why you can't do what you want to do. . . . They don't even do studies on our stuff. . . . [T]hey just want to tell you that it can't ever be any differently. And that the train is leaving the stations towards more industrial farming, even when you want to go in the opposite direction."[6] Learning how to push back against the negative "habits of feeling and judgment" that social theorist William Connolly contends impede the "politics of possibility" was an early challenge. Grassroots meetings proved an effective venue for this sort of communicative action.[7] Through this process, tobacco farmers were encouraged to see themselves as agricultural experts in their own right, insofar as they were in a unique position to represent the concerns of small farmers in policy discussions about the tobacco settlement and the future of Kentucky agriculture. During the summer of 1999, CFA slowly built support for the idea that tobacco farmers could indeed transition away from tobacco—but only if they had considerable help in doing so.

The CFA was not alone in its perspective that some tobacco settlement money should be invested in agriculture. Because tobacco was the state's top cash crop, many were concerned about the impact of its decline on the state's farm economy. During that same summer, then-Governor Patton revived a group called the Kentucky Agricultural Resources Development Authority (KARDA) to strategize about channeling tobacco settlement funds toward Kentucky agriculture. The players included representatives from the Kentucky Farm Bureau, Kentucky Department of Agriculture, Burley Growers' Cooperative, Commodity Growers Cooperative, Cattlemen's Association, and other commodity groups. Despite its active engagement with the tobacco settlement process, CFA was not asked to participate. According to John-Mark Hack, then–executive director of the Governor's Office of Agricultural Policy, CFA was not brought into the group in part because the perceived confrontational style of some of its leaders "threw up a red flag."[8] Whatever the reasons, Webb noted, "We were not invited and we were very insulted."[9] The CFA responded by continuing to hold public meetings and define their own vision of how tobacco settlement funds should be invested.

"Standing Up for the Little Guy"

A key difference between CFA's and KARDA's approaches to the tobacco settlement process was the grassroots nature of CFA's meetings and the focus on small farmers who would be most affected by the decline in tobacco. KARDA invited representatives from a range of agricultural interest groups to the table, and those representatives spoke on behalf of their diverse constituencies. Although some of KARDA's initiatives were helpful to smaller producers, most did not specifically target tobacco farmers; rather, they addressed "agricultural development" in a generalized way and increased funding for commodity groups' favorite programs.[10]

In contrast, CFA targeted small tobacco farmers. During the summer of 1999, the overwhelming message coming from CFA's rural constituents was that tobacco farmers, not just politicians or commodity groups, should decide how to invest tobacco settlement funds. There was also concern that agricultural players in western Kentucky, who had key political and institutional allies in the state, might skew the allocation of funds to benefit larger farms and agribusiness interests in that region, despite the fact they would not be most impacted by the decline of tobacco. In September, CFA developed a vision for allocating part of the tobacco settlement funds to counties, specifying that the process needed to be "farmer-driven." This phrase signaled the larger ideological difference between CFA's and KARDA's visions: the former emphasized the survival and prosperity of family farms, while the latter was more focused on industry and commodity groups' interests. One farmer who attended those meetings said, "There were lots of folks trying to get money for agriculture, but these people [CFA] were the ones standing up for the little guy."[11]

In October, CFA members testified before the legislature's Tobacco Task Force, where they emphasized the importance of small farmers' representation in debates about tobacco settlement funds. They voiced support for the idea of channeling tobacco settlement funds through farmer-led county councils to ensure small farmers in each county would receive a fair share of funds—an approach championed in the legislature by Representative Pete Worthington. Webb remembers the initial reaction from a key legislator: "Roger Thomas . . . said with some surprise in his voice, 'That's very democratic. That sounds like democracy.' And I think we all laughed and said 'Yes, it does.'" When asked how they were received at the meeting, Webb replied: "[T]hey got a standing ovation. That was the first time that I had ever seen a legislative body give their presenters a standing ovation" (laughs).[12]

According to John-Mark Hack, though the governor's office did not initially endorse the "farmer-driven" approach, they ultimately came to agree that it was a good way of bringing farmers into the process.[13] Within six months of that October meeting, the farmer-led county councils were written into House Bill 611, with 35 percent of the Agricultural Development Fund distributed to counties proportionate to their level of tobacco dependence. Through their grassroots organizing efforts and persistent policy work on behalf of and in partnership with small-scale farmers, CFA played an important role in bringing about this shift.

Even when it came to defining tobacco dependence, CFA was a key player. One approach was to rank counties solely on pounds of tobacco per county. This was the starting point for discussion, but CFA felt this put too much weight on counties in western and northern Kentucky. They formed a tobacco committee to figure out how to create an allocation more in line with need and impact. Recognizing that adequately representing small farmers meant showing the number of farms impacted, CFA worked on an alternative map depicting, by county, the number of farms, percentage of per-capita income represented by tobacco, and amount of tobacco grown.[14] This map, which targeted the counties most impacted by the end of the tobacco program, was a big hit with legislators. With 118 counties represented and poised to receive at least a small portion of the money, legislators quickly identified with CFA's definition of tobacco dependence, and its formula was ultimately incorporated into House Bill 611.[15]

From Blueprint to Greenprint

Another point of contention among different stakeholders in the state was whether tobacco settlement funds should be channeled toward biotechnology. While county councils met to develop plans for their pieces of the pie, state-level players were strategizing about how to spend the other 65 percent of the Agricultural Development Fund. In December 2000, Governor Patton announced that he would put together a "think tank" to come up with a blueprint for investing this money. In July 2001, sixty participants were invited to discuss the future of Kentucky agriculture. The governor hired agribusiness expert and Harvard law professor Ray Goldberg, who had coined the terms "agribusiness" and "agriceuticals," to join the meeting. Because of Patton's interest in drawing "new economy" businesses to the state, some feared this move was motivated by an interest in building a biotechnology industry in Kentucky. This concerned CFA leaders because the meeting was invitation only, led by someone with no firsthand knowledge of Kentucky agriculture, and the original list of invitees included only one farmer: Kentucky author and environmentalist Wendell Berry. Berry protested and persuaded planners to include a broader range of participants, including a few farmers. Nevertheless, CFA members feared this closed meeting would result in a blueprint that represented biotechnology and agribusiness interests over those of small farmers.

The week before the meeting of Patton's "think tank," CFA staff convened a planning group that, according to one account, included twenty-one of the sixty participants chosen by Patton.[16] Only a few of these invited participants were farmers, but because of its diverse membership, CFA had allies in unexpected places. Through its work on H.B. 611, the organization had built alliances with environmental and health groups who shared concerns about the potential hazards of biotechnology, as well as with restaurant owners, church groups, and nutritionists with vested interest in healthy food and the survival of Kentucky's family farms. During this planning meeting, CFA leaders sought common ground among invitees who were also allies of CFA. Organizers informed this group that strategic plans drafted by county councils identified support for marketing and value-added processing as primary goals and that biotechnology, mentioned in only two county plans, was barely on the radar. By the time these CFA allies went into the two-day meeting, they had created an informal shared vision for the future of Kentucky agriculture that reflected the interests of the county councils and the common ground forged among the group's diverse members.

Although excluded from the closed meeting, CFA leaders went to the hosting hotel and made documents detailing the counties' strategic plans available to participants. Between the first and second days of the meeting, members and allies met in participants' rooms to discuss the day's events, strategize, and inform those outside the meeting about what was happening. Largely because of these organizing strategies, feedback from participants at the official meeting was informed more by the interests of county councils than by biotechnology or other interests. Thus when Patton and Goldberg ended the meeting with an announcement that investments in biotechnology should be one focus area of Kentucky's long-term plan for agriculture, many participants were upset and a backlash ensued. In the aftermath of the meeting, CFA members and allies raised concerns about the process and whether it really represented the interests of farmers. In the view of John-Mark Hack and others in Patton's office, CFA leaders were making a mountain out of a molehill, because this pool of money was controlled by the state and not the counties.[17] Indeed, Hack suggests that this oppositional posture was one of the reasons they were not brought into the process in a more sustained way, ultimately hurting their cause. In the view of CFA leaders, agitation was necessary to make sure the interests of small farmers were fairly represented in a climate where more powerful players dominated the debate.

Although CFA leaders acted as agitators at times, the organization was by no means confined to an oppositional stance. As the governor's office and the Agricultural Development Board drafted their blueprint, CFA members initiated a participatory planning process that created *The Greenprint: A Long Term Plan for Kentucky's Agricultural Economy* (hereafter, the Greenprint).[18] They held meetings throughout the state and based their report on priorities identified in the county councils' strategic plans. The Greenprint, released in October 2001, called for the creation of a local food economy, arguing that "strong local economies are the foundation of a strong state economy." In contrast to the state's blueprint, CFA's Greenprint was founded on the belief that tobacco settlement funds should be invested solely in family farms and local foods—not biotechnology or large agribusiness. The next month, the governor's office released the first draft of *Cultivating Rural Prosperity: Kentucky's Long-Term Plan for Agricultural Development*.[19] This incorporated significant portions of CFA's Greenprint, while including new tax incentives for out-of-state agribusiness and biotechnology research and development. Following a series of citizen input meetings where CFA members accounted for nearly half of all participants, as well as a campaign resulting in 1,500 postcards addressed to Governor Patton that read "*Support CFA's Greenprint. No tobacco settlement funds for biotech!*", many of those incentives were dropped. When the last version of *Cultivating Rural Prosperity* was released, the vast majority of the plan mirrored CFA's Greenprint.[20]

Planting the Seeds of LIFE

CFA's work on House Bill 611 and the *Cultivating Rural Prosperity* report expressed the organization's broader vision regarding the future of Kentucky agriculture. As early as 1990, the group had focused attention on building a local food infrastructure.[21] With this goal in mind, in 2001 CFA started to look at how to use tobacco settlement funds to build vital, sustainable agrifood systems that would maximize the amount of food produced, processed, distributed, and consumed within the state while minimizing the distance food travels "from farm to fork." CFA leader Bonnie Cecil coined the phrase "Locally Integrated Food Economy" or "LIFE" to convey this model. LIFE's vision calls for networks of farmers, processors, distributors, and consumers to work collaboratively to institutionalize a new set of environmentally friendly agricultural practices. Although CFA had for years supported farmers' markets and cooperatives, sound use of the Agricultural Development Funds could permit expansion and multiplication of these networks, in effect "scaling up" local food systems.

To this end, CFA formed a Research Oversight Committee in 2002 and hired a staff researcher and external consultant to investigate the barriers to and opportunities for creating a more locally integrated food economy. Its study, *Bringing Kentucky's Food and Farm Economy Home,* concluded that Kentucky farmers can and should produce a much larger proportion of the food consumed in the state.[22] That same year, CFA initiated an "urban rural development plan" and got an active Jefferson County/Louisville chapter off the ground—where membership five years later would reach 250.[23] In 2005, CFA helped pass legislation easing restrictions on home processing, helping farmers market certain value-added products such as sauces, salsas, jams, and jellies. Between 2003 and 2006, CFA worked with dozens of farmers to establish a regional marketing and processing center in Bath County, providing infrastructure for institutional buying opportunities in public schools for farmers in eastern Kentucky. Such initiatives were part of a larger effort to link producers with markets. Most dramatically, CFA opened an office in west Louisville and hired two full-time urban organizers.

Creating urban-rural market linkages was a central component of LIFE; its antecedents stretched back to the 1980s in CFA's work "to forge links with urban consumers and low-income groups."[24] Though by the early 2000s, upper-end farmers' markets had fostered relationships between low-income producers and relatively high-income consumers, connections with low-income consumers were more difficult. With a metropolitan population of 700,000 people (20 percent of the state's population), Louisville represented a significant opportunity to demonstrate the viability of the LIFE model, yet many obstacles could impede building markets there, especially in low-income and predominantly African American neighborhoods. Success there, CFA leaders believed, would help counter the myth that farmers' markets were viable only in high-income, niche markets. Deborah Webb recalled: "You do have high-end markets generating themselves and they don't really need our help. But CFA believes that this food system has to be universal. . . . That's why west Louisville, which is the poor end of town, was chosen. A 38 percent poverty rate for twelve neighborhoods that we're working in, and a large percentage of the African-American population for the state. That's why we chose west Louisville and that's the importance of west Louisville: the universality."[25]

For a rural organization, addressing the needs of people in urban food deserts was a stretch. Indeed in the past, antihunger and alternative agriculture activists, mirroring the fragmentation of the U.S. agrifood system, rarely recognized mutual interests.[26] In the 1980s, CFA members had recognized that farmers and urban consumers share common ground, an understanding today expressed in the Community Food Security movement. But actually working in poor neighborhoods and catalyzing new alliances entailed outreach to diverse communities, notably: African American neighborhood groups, churches, and businesspeople; social justice and environmental activists; foodies; public health agencies and organizations; the metro government; and the private sector. CFA would later release a community food assessment, *Bridging the Divide,* which showed west Louisville and east downtown were "food deserts" with limited food stores, high prices, poor quality, a narrow range of food items, especially fresh produce, and limited consumer buying power.[27] This document, which has since served as a policy tool to assert the need to bring food into Louisville's poor neighborhoods, grew out of and contributed to CFA's organizing during this period.

New Markets, New Ventures, New Connections

By the middle of 2003, CFA, operating out of a new office in Louisville's Portland neighborhood, was working with business and community leaders to build farmers' markets. Spearheaded by an African American organizer, CFA started Portland-Shawnee, the first explicitly low-income farmers' market in the state. Ultimately, this effort failed. Recruiting farmers, generally unfamiliar with Louisville, especially its African American neighborhoods, proved a challenge. The farmers had to adjust pricing and volume to their new customers, who could spend much less than those in more affluent areas.[28] Over the next two seasons, market organizers tried to overcome these difficulties by partnering with community groups and city agencies to sponsor special events and festivals, and ultimately moved the market to a better-traveled west Louisville location provided by a Baptist church. In spite of the congregation's promotional assistance, a sufficient customer base never materialized. Nonetheless, the process of market building—the many conversations with residents, businesspeople, and local institutions—was instrumental in fostering subsequent food work, including the creation of another low-income neighborhood market.

The Smoketown/Shelby Park Market, established in the summer of 2004 in response to requests from African American community leaders, burgeoned in popularity the following year, in part because of emergent collaborations. A local bank, for instance, donated an Electronic Benefits machine to accommodate food stamp users. A Robert Wood Johnson Foundation–supported health program (ACTIVE Louisville) and the Metro Health Department initiated a voucher project so WIC eligible women could receive food vouchers that Kentucky did not otherwise fund. Each voucher permitted purchase of ten dollars worth of fruits and vegetables.[29] The Annie E. Casey Foundation funded the purchase of farmers' unsold produce for donations to homeless shelters.

Other collaborations were also important. Friends of the Market, a volunteer organization, helped orchestrate special events to draw shoppers, while chefs from the county extension service offered cooking demonstrations, taste tests, and recipe cards to encourage use of fresh foods. The market also served neighborhood children via the Presbyterian Community Center, which runs a summer Kid's Café for nutritionally vulnerable children. The café, which had formerly relied on donated food—ironically, mostly fast food—began to use the market to acquire and promote fresh food for its young clientele. Furthering youth engagement was the market's location on school grounds. Students painted a magnificent mural on the school wall to publicize the market and, led by a science teacher, developed a youth community garden on land remediated with Metro Health Department funding. Though all this was not the doing of CFA alone, its original market organizing stimulated an array of community-building activities that heightened awareness of the benefits of local food and the need and possibilities for increasing access to it. Such collaboration was not without tensions, however; at times some of these partners competed for scarce grant monies. Even so, farmers' markets have blossomed all over Louisville in the past few years, numbering twenty-two in 2009, and CFA staff report a steady flow of requests for their assistance in establishing new markets.

Beyond Farmers' Markets: Scaling Up

Farmers' markets offer a visible starting point for the creation of LIFE, but feeding a city and region requires bulking, distribution, and commercialization systems that will reliably supply a wide customer base. The challenge is how to build, as rural sociologist Jack Kloppenburg notes, something between corporate food suppliers like SYSCO and individualized farm share subscriptions, commonly known as Community Supported Agriculture (CSA).[30] CFA members began to contemplate how such efforts at scaling up could realistically be pursued through conversations among urban residents, area farmers, city chefs, and grocers about the logistics and economics of distributing local food. Both buyers and producers had expressed frustrations and concerns about making connections with one another. For individual farmers, finding buyers willing to pay an acceptable price for high-quality fresh food can be daunting and time-consuming. Chefs and grocers, for their part, require a reliable volume of properly processed (washed and packed) items. Finding regular supplies of local food for value-adding processing also interested a number of potential urban food entrepreneurs who had met farmers via the market-building work. Creating an intermediary institution emerged as the solution, one that would allow farmers to farm, not sell, and chefs to cook, rather than source and worry.

These conversations eventually evolved into plans for a bulking and distribution center in west Louisville. Originally, twenty-two farmers were interested, but as discussions brought to light individual investment costs, the number fell to four farmer-partners (all CFA members), who incorporated themselves in 2006 as Grasshoppers, a limited liability company.[31] This distribution business is intended to bring farmers and consumers together. Purchasing food from small producers, the majority of whom employ low-input practices, facilitates their access to the urban market and rewards environmentally friendly resource use. Simultaneously, Grasshoppers can offer a steady supply of many foods to cooks and grocers who currently depend upon large national or transnational distributors. Institutional purchase by city agencies and institutions also becomes feasible when large volumes are available; such contracts in turn generate reliable demand for producers. In 2009, Grasshoppers purchased food (produce, eggs, cheese, meat) from some seventy-five regional farmers and made weekly deliveries to more than thirty businesses, including local supermarkets, and a few city institutions. It also established a CSA and expected to supply more than three hundred households in the 2009 growing season.

Grasshoppers relies on business practices commensurate with those found in fair-trade models: long-term relationships with producers, payment of fair prices at delivery (critical to small-operation cash flows), and support of environmentally sustainable farming techniques. The Grasshoppers partners at the onset openly voiced doubts about this venture, but in just two years, bolstered significantly by receipt of USDA and tobacco settlement grants, they became contenders in the Louisville food sector. They have entered discussion with the city school system and the University of Louisville about supplying some of these institutions' food needs. Maturation of the city's still nascent local food system remains likely to benefit from CFA's political prowess at the state level as well as the initiative and energy of its staff and membership at the grassroots (or more accurately, sidewalks and boardrooms). Institutional buying, a stage of scaling up, viewed as a logical and necessary expansion of LIFE, will likely require further legislative intervention to address barriers posed by food safety regulations that, while designed to protect consumers from the dangers of large-scale operations, handicap smaller producers and distributers.

In addition to tackling these political challenges, CFA members have directed energy to activities aimed at generating enthusiasm and spawning innovative infrastructure for LIFE. CFA has expanded the market-building work by initiating or supporting the creation of small farmstands, micro-markets, and institution-based food delivery projects designed for low-income consumers. CFA staff and members continue to engage in the city's policy arena, participating in metro committees and working with representatives of city agencies to coordinate public, nonprofit, and private sector food work, especially as it pertains to the interests of low-income consumers and producers. They also continue to be involved in educational and community work. Stone Soup, for example, is a monthly communal supper in which diners collectively prepare a meal based on seasonal items, purchased from farmers and gleaned from farmers' market leftovers. Although considerable challenges remain for a truly locally integrated food system in Kentucky, all of these endeavors help create both institutional and social infrastructure for the "scaling up" of local foods markets.

Lessons

The Tobacco Master Settlement Agreement did not call forth the CFA. Rather, after fifteen years of community-based organizing, CFA found itself in position to take rapid advantage of a unique opportunity to influence agricultural policy and public funding in Kentucky. In the years prior to this conjuncture, CFA had already learned the value of local community building. When many farm organizations' response to the 1980s farm crisis was to exert pressure on federal policy makers, CFA went local. It did so because the farm policies that national organizations championed did not address the needs of small farmers. Consequently, CFA built strong county chapters across the state. Notably, it made the development of leadership skills among its farmer-members its highest priority. Its first director wrote: "The real goal of community organizing, however, is not so much to help people solve . . . immediate problems as it is recruit new leaders for long-term change."[32] CFA had attained some notable accomplishments during its first fifteen years of existence (addressing credit problems, for instance), but none would compare with its subsequent influence over the allocation of tobacco settlement monies. Thus a first lesson is that CFA's eventual success rested on long-term commitments to grassroots organizing and leadership development that were locally based but statewide in scope. Without strong local chapters and effective leaders already dispersed across the state, CFA would not have been in position to mobilize quickly and broadly to influence the debate about Kentucky's use of tobacco money.

A second lesson concerns the relationship between citizen knowledge and expert knowledge. Deborah Webb reports: "From the very beginning, CFA members held the notion that those who have the problem should be in charge of the solution. University experts and [credit] lenders were not hanging themselves in the barn [during the 1980s farm crisis]. . . . Therefore, for the next 14 years CFA built an organization of rural people dedicated to the notion that they were the experts—they knew their problems and together we would find solutions."[33] Part of CFA's success in framing issues and suggesting strategies to promote its vision of equitable and sustainable agricultural development can be attributed to how it nurtured citizen, that is, farmer, knowledge and incorporated it into a range of policy tools. These tools effectively countered the expert knowledge produced by corporate agribusiness, state officials, and university agricultural scientists and economists. For example, CFA's Greenprint systematized years of grassroots debate and study about local food systems (including trips to learn about policy and planning models in Europe).[34] Its community food assessment systematized the knowledge of local residents regarding the availability of healthy food in west Louisville, simultaneously winning allies among city officials and community activists. Finally, its tobacco map drew on farmers' and organizers'

knowledge of tobacco dependence, ultimately shaping the allocation of a significant proportion of tobacco settlement funds. Perhaps most notable, the vision
of farmer-led county councils provided a mechanism through which farmers in
all 118 counties that received settlement funds were given definitive authority as
agricultural experts. This democratic strategy institutionalized CFA's vision that
those who live the problem own the solution.

A third lesson is that scaling up necessitates bridging divides. By recalibrating
the allocation of tobacco settlement funds to benefit most legislative districts, CFA
effectively bridged regional and party divisions in the state legislature by making
it easier for more lawmakers to support their strategy. In its formative years, CFA
had already gained experience working with legislators and state officials. In the
same period, it adopted organizing models from Appalachian organizations such
as Kentuckians For The Commonwealth and Save Our Cumberland Mountains.
It went beyond networking with other farm organizations to build alliances with
environmental organizations such as the Kentucky Rivers Coalition and the Kentucky Resources Council and religious organizations such as Kentucky Catholic
Rural Life, the Kentucky Appalachian Ministry of the Disciples of Christ, and the
American Friends Service Committee. These religious groups especially helped
early CFA activists recruit African American members and become a biracial
organization—a commitment that would come to fruition in CFA's more recent
urban organizing.[35] This effort, in particular, has required overcoming traditional
divides among rural white farmers and low-income, urban African American
consumers as well as learning how to work with churches, businesses, neighborhood leaders, the media, health and social justice activists, and city officials in a
complex urban environment.

Finally, CFA's success can be attributed in part to its focus on organizing not
only *against* questionable practices (such as particular agricultural biotechnology
investments) but also *for* viable alternatives. Though grassroots movements can
sometimes be effective in organizing against practices they oppose, these efforts
are often limited if viable alternatives are not also developed and pursued with
equal intensity. A great strength of CFA's strategizing was its concerted effort to
develop specific and concrete plans for creating a coherent alternative vision for
the future of Kentucky agriculture. CFA's ability to promote this vision rested on
years of grassroots organizing, leadership development, and relationships built
with legislators and allies across the political spectrum. Even when not invited
to the table, CFA leaders pushed forward with public meetings, gathered input
from members and constituents, and continued to pursue their vision. Although
success in these arenas is always partial and tenuous, CFA's efforts resulted in
a surprisingly successful campaign to democratize a key piece of legislation in
Kentucky and to create a more equitable distribution of tobacco settlement funds
than most would have imagined at the outset.

CFA's success in community organizing and leadership development, crystallizing and publicizing grassroots knowledge, and bridging divides to build a powerful base for reform provides important lessons for other groups working for sustainable development in Appalachia. Admittedly, CFA's success in part owes to unique circumstances. If the opposite of a "perfect storm" is a perfectly sunny day, then the tobacco settlement agreement afforded Kentucky farmers just such a rare but perfect day. An important question is whether democratic coalitions can likewise tap into other sources of public funding and begin to develop comprehensive and compelling models of investment for sustainable development. Such efforts might include having a say in the investment of newly promised federal funds to build a "green economy," democratizing decisions about how coal severance taxes are used (now largely in the hands of local political elites) or, as Erik Reece has suggested, using the millions of dollars in the Abandoned Mine Land Fund "to train a generation of local men and women to reforest and manage abandoned strip mines."[36] Initiatives like Coal River Mountain Watch's proposal to build a wind farm as a concrete and viable alternative to mountaintop removal in West Virginia also provide compelling examples of innovative development solutions that grow out of grassroots organizing efforts.[37] Finding ways to channel federal funds into these kinds of projects is an important challenge. In any case, a major lesson from CFA's success in Kentucky is the promise that much can be accomplished when broadly based, citizen planning processes move beyond mere opposition to construct positive, comprehensive, and visionary models, that is, "greenprints" for sustainable development in Appalachia. Another point is that for this to happen, activists must not wait to be invited to the table.

Notes

1. *USA Today*, August 10, 2007.

2. *The Essential Agrarian Reader: The Future of Culture, Community, and the Land*, ed. Norman Wirzba (Lexington: University Press of Kentucky, 2003), x.

3. Only Texas and Missouri had significantly more family farms than Kentucky in 1997. http://www.agcensus.usda.gov/Publications/2002/Volume_1,_Chapter_2_US_State_Level/st99_2_008_008.pdf.

4. Deborah Webb, interview with Jenrose Fitzgerald, October 10, 2004.

5. Quoted in David F. Ruccio and Dwight Billings, "Everyday Economics and the Kentucky Community Farm Alliance: An Interview with Deborah Webb," in *Economic Representations: Academic and Everyday*, ed. David F. Ruccio (New York: Routledge, 2008), 262.

6. Quoted in Ruccio and Billings, "Everyday Economics," 265.

7. Quoted in J. K. Gibson-Graham, *A Postcapitalist Politics* (Minneapolis: University of Minnesota Press, 2006), 3.

8. John-Mark Hack, interview with Jenrose Fitzgerald, September 14, 2010.

9. Deborah Webb, interview with Jenrose Fitzgerald.

10. "Burley's Moment of Truth," editorial, *Louisville Courier Journal,* December 23, 1999, 10A.

11. Steve Smith, interview with Jenrose Fitzgerald, September 13, 2004.

12. Deborah Webb, interview with Jenrose Fitzgerald.

13. John-Mark Hack, interview with Jenrose Fitzgerald.

14. CFA member John Logan Brent worked with economist Will Snell on this formula. This was a prime example of how grassroots members and allies drew on their own agricultural expertise to advocate for small farmers.

15. Jenrose Fitzgerald, "Citizens, Experts and the Economy: The Grassroots Takeover of Kentucky's Agricultural Future" (Ph.D. diss., Rensselaer Polytechnic Institute, 2006).

16. Deborah Webb, interview with Jenrose Fitzgerald. While this number comes from Webb's interview, similar accounts were given in later conversations with John Logan Brent and Carol Gunderson, both of whom were key organizers during this period.

17. Paraphrase of John-Mark Hack, interview with Jenrose Fitzgerald.

18. Community Farm Alliance, *The Greenprint: A Long Term Plan for Kentucky's Agricultural Economy* (Frankfort, Ky., October 2001).

19. Kentucky Agricultural Development Board, "Cultivating Rural Prosperity: Kentucky's Long-Term Plan for Agricultural Development" (Frankfort, Ky.: Governor's Office of Agricultural Policy, 2001).

20. Fitzgerald, "Citizens, Experts and the Economy." According to Deborah Webb, after the report was released, Agricultural Development Board member Sam Lawson approached CFA and asked if they were aware of this fact.

21. Hal Hamilton and Ellen Ryan, "The Community Farm Alliance in Kentucky: The Growth, Mistakes, and Lessons of the Farm Movement of the 1980s," in *Fighting Back in Appalachia: Traditions of Resistance and Change,* ed. Stephen L. Fisher (Philadelphia: Temple University Press, 1993).

22. Community Farm Alliance, *Bringing Kentucky's Food and Farm Economy Home* (Frankfort, Ky., October 2003).

23. Ivor Chodkowski, CFA fellowship proposal (January 2002). In the personal files of Lisa Markowitz.

24. Hamilton and Ryan, "Community Farm Alliance," 143.

25. To the satisfaction of the CFA, the viability of low-income markets had already been proven in Appalachian Kentucky counties (see Ruccio and Billings, "Everyday Economics," 269).

26. See Anne C. Bellows and Michael W. Hamm, "U.S.-based Community Food Security: Influences, Practice, Debate," *Journal for the Study of Food and Society* 6 (Winter 2002): 31–44; also see Patricia Allen, *Together at the Table: Sustainability and Sustenance in the American Agrifood System* (University Park: Pennsylvania State University Press, 2004).

27. Community Farm Alliance, *Bridging the Divide: Growing Self-sufficiency in Our Food Supply* (Louisville, Ky., 2007).

28. Daily purchases tallied only five dollars at Portland-Shawnee in contrast to twenty dollars at the city's best-known middle-class market. See Lisa Markowitz, "'Sure Beats Krogers': Shopping for Change at Farmers' Markets," American Anthropological Association Annual Meeting, Washington, D.C., November 2005.

29. Natalie A. Halbach, *Building Health and Wealth: Assessing Potential Benefits and Raising Awareness of the WIC FMNP in Louisville Metro, KY* (Frankfurt, Ky., 2006), 11–12.

30. Brian Halweil, *Eat Here: Reclaiming Homegrown Pleasures in a Global Supermarket* (New York: W.W. Norton, 2004), 114.

31. Lisa Markowitz, "Produce(ing) Equity: Creating Fresh Markets in a Food Desert. Hidden Hands in the Market: Ethnographies of Fair Trade, Ethical Consumption, and Corporate Social Responsibility," *Research in Economic Anthropology* 28 (2008): 195–211.

32. Hamilton and Ryan, "Community Farm Alliance," 138.

33. Quoted in Ruccio and Billings, "Everyday Economics," 258.

34. See Hamilton and Ryan, "Community Farm Alliance," 146.

35. Ibid., 134.

36. Erik Reece, *Lost Mountain: A Year in the Vanishing Wilderness: Radical Strip Mining and the Devastation of Appalachia* (New York: Riverhead Books, 2006), 219.

37. Evan Hansen, Alan Collins, Michael Hendryx, Fritz Boettner, and Anne Hereford, "The Long-Term Economic Benefits of Wind versus Mountaintop Removal Coal on Coal River Mountain, West Virginia" (Morgantown, W.Va.: Downstream Strategies, 2008), ii–52.

CHAPTER 15

Mountain Justice

Cassie Robinson Pfleger, Randal Pfleger,
Ryan Wishart, and Dave Cooper

In July 2005, a traveling horde of sixty Mountain Justice Summer (MJS) activists crowded into an old general store on Route 3 in Naoma, in the Coal River Valley of West Virginia. The sagging brick building was not air-conditioned but had electricity, Internet access, and some filthy old sofas. Most activists slept on the floor and ate food salvaged from the dumpster of a supermarket in nearby Glen Daniels. The oven quit working, and the overpacked refrigerator started to die. Flies, the stench from an overflowing septic tank, and the steaming West Virginia summer quickly made life for the activists almost unbearable.

To make matters worse, near-constant harassment from local coal miners added to their misery. The back window of one activist's truck was shot out. Paintballs were splattered against the storefront windows. A dead fish was hurled from a passing vehicle. But worst of all, every night beginning at 3:00 A.M., as miners got off the "hoot owl" shift, they would blare their truck horns as they drove by.

After weeks of harassment, MJS activists were sleep-deprived and cranky; tensions were running high. Their solution to the problem later became an MJS trademark of simplicity and ingenuity within nonviolent resistance: one evening, someone tacked a big plastic sign to a telephone pole in front of the store: "HONK IF YOU LOVE MOUNTAINS." The honking stopped that night.

Origins of Mountain Justice

Since 2004, Mountain Justice (MJ) has evolved into an extensive network of anti–mountaintop removal (MTR) activists; however MJ did not start with the intention of becoming the movement, organization, or the network that it has become. Initially, MJ envisioned a strategically targeted summer-long campaign to raise awareness, encourage action, and ultimately ignite a chain of events leading to the abolition of MTR. However, that summer campaign in 2005 has evolved into a year-round network connecting rural coalfield communities to college campuses and activists in metropolitan areas across Appalachia and the country. In late 2007, organizers decided to modify the group's name from Mountain Justice Summer to Mountain Justice to reflect this expanded orientation. Both names are essentially interchangeable and refer to the same organization at different times in its history. Much of this chapter is based on our active participation in the MJ campaign from that first summer to the present.

From the beginning, Mountain Justice has been less a formal organization than a web of informal and pre-existing relationships among several environmental justice activist networks and coalfield groups.[1] A tragic mining accident in the fall of 2004 in the community of Inman in Wise County, Virginia, was a catalyst that solidified these relationships into the network that later became MJ. Three-year-old Jeremy Davidson, asleep in his bed, was killed instantly when a half-ton boulder rolled off a MTR mine above his house. A month later, nearly one hundred people gathered in a nearby town for a protest march to Inman honoring Jeremy's memory. Protesters came from a range of backgrounds reflecting MJ's current constituency of local community members and activists from across Appalachia. Inspired by the march and speeches, Virginia Tech graduate student Sue Daniels organized a trip to visit MTR sites in West Virginia in early November 2004. Katuah Earth First! (KEF!) activists, coalfield residents, and filmmakers toured MTR-ravaged Kayford Mountain with resident Larry Gibson and historic union battlefield and proposed MTR site Blair Mountain with Kenny King. These informal relationships laid the foundation for MJ. The founders drew inspiration from Mississippi Freedom Summer, an instrumental moment in the civil rights movement when young people from across the United States joined local activists in voter registration and political organizing with the immediate goal of voting rights for African Americans; and from Redwood Summer, an early 1990s environmental campaign in the Pacific Northwest to save old-growth forests, which focused on environmental defense, direct action, and civil disobedience. They envisioned a multistate campaign to bring new activists and resources to the coalfields, which founding activist Sue Daniels coined as a "Mountain Justice Summer."

The original MJ activists met throughout the winter (2004–2005), starting in the Coal River Mountain Watch (CRMW) office in Whitesville, West Virginia, then rotating around the region to accommodate various groups' involvement. In January 2005, the first official MJS meeting took place in Knoxville, Tennessee, and included representatives of informal networks of activists from CRMW, the Sierra Club, Appalachian Voices, and KEF!, plus several students from colleges across the Southeast. Reflecting the anarchist organizational preferences of KEF!, MJ was envisioned as a single, decentralized "summer of action," without hierarchy or leaders. The group adopted consensus-based decision making, requiring participation by all present. They agreed that MJ would support and strengthen existing campaigns and organizations in the coalfields, following the lead of coalfield residents when operating in their communities, and would resist MTR with nonviolence and without destroying property.

From the beginning, participants in meetings, actions, listserv discussions, and training camps attained a memberlike status. There are no membership rolls, regulations, or dues. MJ only requires that anyone participating in the MJ movement, regardless of political ideology, religious beliefs, or other personal ethics, adhere to the mission statement, particularly: *"Mountain Justice is committed to nonviolence and will not be engaged in property destruction."* The first MJ summer campaign was largely directed at raising the public profile of MTR and reframing discourse around the issue, rejecting, for example, a "jobs versus the environment" frame. Protests sought to build publicity around community grievances and use the increased attention as leverage on public and private institutions involved in extracting, processing, regulating, and consuming MTR coal. On March 31, 2005, Bo Webb of CRMW organized the first MJ protest at the West Virginia State Capitol, counterposing it to a rally organized by Friends of Coal, a nonprofit organization created by the state's coal industry.

MJ held its first training camp in May at the Appalachian South Folklife Center in Pipestem, West Virginia. The camp included workshops, trainings, and panel presentations that provided a baseline of knowledge and skills necessary for the upcoming summer of protests, rallies, and nonviolent direct actions throughout the region, and became a model for future training camps. At the end of the camp, sixteen activists were arrested for trespass while attempting to deliver a list of demands to Massey Energy. This set a precedent for actions following a training camp: give newcomers hands-on experience in planning, media outreach for, and execution of direct action or protest events.

Some examples from the first summer illustrate our scaling up MTR resistance.[2] In West Virginia, events centered around Marsh Fork Elementary School, where children are exposed to dust and chemicals from a Massey Energy processing facility and sit below a 2.8 billion-gallon toxic coal slurry impoundment. MJ and CRMW organized a march of more than one hundred people and dozens of acts of civil disobedience to draw attention to the environmental injustices caused by coal companies like Massey and amplify demands from students' families that the governor ensure children a safe place to learn in their community.[3] Linking injustice at Marsh Fork to power relations in the region and globe, hundreds marched outside Massey Energy headquarters in Richmond, Virginia, closing off its main entrance, as part of an international day of action on climate change coinciding with a meeting of the G-8.

In retrospect, Mountain Justice Summer 2005 was an action-packed but perhaps overly ambitious summer of events that left many activists burned out and exhausted. Some left the movement, never to return. Constant travel, shortages of resources, and the emotional and cognitive effort necessary for the consensus process took their toll. But the spirit of Mountain Justice Summer refused to die.

Having brought more regional and national attention to MTR, MJ's focus shifted from organizing large actions to utilizing heightened public scrutiny and pressure to effect change at the local level. Organizers decided to move away from the model of MJS 2005, which required a "traveling horde" across long distances, and instead ask that MJ members in each state host one major event in their home area. Former Greenpeace activist Hilary Hosta relocated to Rock Creek, West Virginia, and helped create the first MJ campaign house, a key event that inspired commitment and provided infrastructure for future campaigns as activists in other states also established campaign houses. Campaign houses provide basic living necessities and housing for visiting activists and residents who are working closely with community members and community organizations. Adding campaign houses to areas of concentrated activity has been a strategic move that both strengthens community ties and recruits help from activists outside the local community. Activities in 2006 focused on assisting local grassroots groups organize opposition to new mining permits, document industry violations (particularly water contamination), and pressure consumers like the Tennessee Valley Authority (TVA) to stop purchasing MTR coal. Time invested in training visiting volunteers and integrating them into local groups' community projects produced more payoff when volunteers stayed put in the same area. Although MJ has continued to support large demonstrations across the region, its local campaigns have been increasingly important.

Internal Structure

From the beginning, MJ was designed to provide much-needed support to coal-field community members and grassroots organizations fighting MTR in Appalachia. As a result, its structure is built around and in relation to other groups. MJ's nonhierarchical, horizontal environment empowers people to develop new initiatives without excessive meetings and bureaucracy. This organizational structure reflects MJ's philosophy that all individuals have valid experiences to share and all members are potential leaders. Leadership is developed through a tradition of encouraging those who contribute ideas for projects to take on or "bottom line" their implementation. Decentralization also allows for quicker response to urgent situations and regional disasters. For example, when the TVA dam in Kingston, Tennessee, failed on December 22, 2008, United Mountain Defense (UMD) members, representing the Tennessee component of MJ, were on the scene of the disaster with cameras, laptop computers, and a Geiger counter the same day. Despite the Christmas and New Year's holidays, MJ activists worked independently and without a day off for more than a month, documenting the disaster and attracting national news coverage.

MJ's primary deliberative forums are monthly meetings that rotate among states, training camp gatherings, and the organizers' e-mail listserv. Decisions are made and revisited in a collaborative manner, with all major agreements reached by consensus and working groups making less important decisions. When a proposed action or press release requires use of organizational resources or its name, all MJ activists are encouraged to provide input. If a local affiliate wants to do a small action, it is encouraged to do so, as long as members comply fully with the mission, goals, and tactics posted on the MJ Web site. Violence, sexual harassment, and substance abuse are not tolerated at MJ meetings, actions, or training camps, and may result in expulsion from the event and subsequent MJ activities. Measures developed to hold people accountable within MJ include: reference checks before an individual is allowed to participate in training camps; a required signed agreement promising compliance with the MJ mission statement; and a mediation process, facilitated by a conflict resolution team, in the event of internal problems. Individuals may face public censure from the group when actions go too far or do not reflect the spirit of MJ. Conflict mediation and enforcement of the conduct code at events have become more structured in response to occasional difficulties with ad hoc implementation as MJ has grown.

MJ is an all-volunteer movement with a budget of less than $10,000 a year. Some critics see the volunteer nature of MJ as evidence of stereotypical wealthy activists who do not have to work for a living (a characterization often perpetuated by the coal industry), but many people organizing for MJ in fact have very little money. Some who volunteer for MJ on a full-time basis have balked at taking money for their work out of fear that it would disrupt MJ's flat/horizontal organizational structure. Many full-time MJ organizers are students or people with limited and/or flexible work schedules—the self-employed, journalists, tradespersons, and part-time workers. It is difficult to provide a detailed description of activist demographics because there are no official membership rolls and those involved in meetings and events vary by time and place. In general, MJ activists from outside the region tend to be young, white, and middle class, while those within the coalfields tend to be older, working-class people. Successful outreach and recruitment among college students have increased their representation in MJ and brought positive results; however, there has been a simultaneous loss of sustained involvement by some of the train-hopping, dumpster-diving, eco-anarchists from MJ's first year. Nonetheless, the strong current of radical ideologies persists, due in part to the effects of witnessing social and environmental exploitation by business and the apathy or subservience of government officials in the coalfields, as well as the strong connection between EF! and MJ.

This model does have its challenges. Recording and filing meeting minutes and documenting collective decisions have been complicated, because there are no designated officers and different individuals volunteer for record keeping at each meeting. MJ has taken steps to remedy this problem by compiling a complete notebook of all meeting notes, newspaper clippings, and related documents, and by archiving its listserv. Still, these records can be difficult to reference and maintaining institutional memory with high turnover and lacking bylaws, officers, or staff has often proved difficult. Much of MJ's institutional memory is carried by individuals, but some is transmitted through songs, stories, and performances.[4]

Periodic problems responding to requests and following through on tasks have also occurred; the volume of communication via the listserv, in particular, complicates this process. Use of the listserv also makes it difficult to achieve active consensus; decisions by default tend to occur in that forum. However, some of the difficulties arising from MJ's internal structure are offset insofar as MJ functions as a support network for an array of ally organizations that creates a sort of external organizational structure. Activists can plug into campaigns that most appeal to them.

Regional, National, and Transnational Connections

Many if not most MJ activists are members, volunteers, staff, and leaders with a range of other organizations in the region. Some are local community groups, such as UMD, CRMW, and Southern Appalachian Mountain Stewards (SAMS), primarily fighting MTR and coal-related problems. Others, such as the Ohio Valley Environmental Coalition (OVEC), Christians for the Mountains, Kentuckians For The Commonwealth (KFTC), and chapters of the Sierra Club operate on a broader range of environmental and social issues at a state or regional scale. MJ members are also active in student environmental organizations on college campuses and regional collectives with anarchist principles, such as Three Rivers Earth First!, Rising Tide North America (RTNA), and Blue Ridge Earth First! (BREF!). The emergence of BREF! and SAMS in Virginia are examples of how MJ has helped incubate new local groups. Following listening projects in the area, MJ and Sierra Club organizers collaborated with community residents to support development of the community-based group SAMS in Wise County in 2006.

Since 2005, MJ has contributed to the creation of a collaborative space across Appalachia to work on coal issues on a scale not seen since regional mobilization leading to passage of the Surface Mine Control and Reclamation Act of 1977. This was made possible by perseverance and years of effort by coalfield residents like Larry Gibson, Judy Bonds, and Maria Gunnoe and by advocates like Dave Cooper, who created the "Mountain Top Removal Roadshow," a lecture and slideshow presentation about MTR that has traveled extensively across Appalachia and the United States. Appalachian Voices' years of research and advocacy on MTR also has played a huge role in creating this space. The Alliance for Appalachia was created within three years of the founding of MJ. It is a coalition of organizations with more structured and traditional frameworks that share the goals of abolishing MTR and creating a new sustainable economy in the region.[5]

Many activists involved with MJ have worked with national and international organizations such as the Energy Action Coalition, Greenpeace, and the Rainforest

Larry Gibson being arrested in West Virginia Governor Joe Manchin's office during a Mountain Justice nonviolent protest, March 2007. (Photo by Dave Cooper)

Action Network (RAN). These collaborative efforts have brought new resources, such as experienced trainers for workshops and financial and legal support for civil disobedience actions, to the anti-MTR movement. These connections also resulted in collaboration with the RAN Global Finance Campaign, targeting the coal industry's most important international financial supporters, including Citi Group and Bank of America, in both the Appalachian region and cities across the country.[6] Throughout this campaign, MJ activists collaborated with numerous other organizations to condemn Bank of America, Citi Group, Chase, Merrill Lynch, and other financial institutions for bankrolling coal companies using MTR on indigenous lands in Colombia; Black Mesa, Arizona; and across the coalfields of Appalachia. Referring to one episode in this campaign, Appalachian scholar Ronald D. Eller commented: "[It] symbolized an important change in the way America understood Appalachia . . . the region now had become a symbol of the larger dilemma of people's relationship to the land and responsibilities to each other. . . . The Appalachian experience reflected the social, environmental, and cultural consequences of unrestrained growth, and it echoed the voices of powerless people struggling to survive in a changing world. Saving Appalachia now meant confronting the larger structures of global injustice as well as challenging local power brokers, corporate greed, and government apathy."[7]

Despite numerous contacts and expressions of solidarity with groups fighting strip mining in New Zealand and various Latin American countries, to date there has been little coordinated international activity. One exception is MJ activists' collaboration with The Beehive Collective, a nonhierarchical nonprofit best known for its work on Latin American issues, to facilitate participation from coalfield residents and organizers in the Bees' "True Costs of Coal" visual storytelling campaign centered around an intricate mural print.[8] The Bees have shared updates to the mural and travel experiences from their speaking tours on their Web site. Because of their campaigns in Colombia and Mexico, many activists and allies in Latin America follow the "True Costs of Coal" campaign. The diverse backgrounds of MJ activists contribute to a common perception that coal and MTR are only a small part of local, regional, national, and international social and environmental problems. Though some community-based organizers work on specific, localized campaigns to improve life in communities affected by MTR, many agree that ending MTR is only one step in creating a more environmentally just world.

MJ Outreach and Organizing

Although the MJ campaign is directed toward empowerment and support of coalfield residents opposing MTR and all forms of surface mining, the campaign has also sought willing and capable volunteers from outside the region. There are three main categories for MJ outreach: 1) college campuses and youth-focused public events; 2) conferences focusing on energy issues specifically related to MTR, such as Power Shift and the Southeast Student Renewable Energy Conference, or on the global left/anticapitalist movements, such as the annual meeting of the National Conference on Organized Resistance (NCOR) and the U.S. Social Forum; and 3) regional academic scholarship.

MJ organizers have represented the campaign at NCOR in Washington, D.C., each winter. Outreach to young, radical, social and environmental justice organizers has benefited the campaign by producing new recruits and organizational allies to work in Appalachia. In 2007, MJ organizers, along with OVEC, KFTC, and CRMW, hosted two events on coal and MTR at the U.S. Social Forum in Atlanta. In academic circles, since 2005 MJ activists have presented at the Appalachian Studies Association's annual conference, where they have strengthened connections with scholars studying and teaching about the land, people, and culture of Appalachia, and received critical feedback that has informed the work of MJ.

A central venue for training new activists and organizers is the annual summer camp. Significant resources, including long hours and major fund-raising efforts, are necessary to create the camps. To increase accessibility across incomes, participants are fed three meals a day and pay on a sliding scale to attend. Activities include film screenings of recent documentaries on MTR, guest speakers from coalfield communities, Appalachian cultural sensitivity training, and sessions on nonviolence, direct action, contemporary surface mining, water testing, media work, networking opportunities, community listening projects, and much more.

Since 2007, MJ has hosted "alternative spring breaks" similar in form to the summer camp. Mountain Justice Spring Break (MJSB) activities in 2007 ended with a dramatic sit-in at the office of West Virginia Governor Joe Manchin, in which more than one hundred MJSB protestors and leaders of community groups demanded a meeting with Manchin and fulfillment of his promise to build a new school for students of Marsh Fork Elementary. Although their demands were unmet, the action attracted statewide attention to plans by Massey Energy to build a second silo next to the school. According to a previously submitted air quality permit application, plans for the second silo involve a doubling of the amount of coal dust in the air; many residents worry about students' increased exposure, while Massey representatives, school officials, and many "pro-coal" parents deny any threat.[9]

Organizing via the Internet

Since 2005, listservs have become increasingly crucial for sharing information and planning activities. The MJ organizers' list has approximately 185 members and is used to communicate with individuals across the globe working on MTR, coal, and climate issues. Hyperlinks to current news articles, upcoming events and actions, and discussions relevant to MJ's campaigns circulate on the list. Six volunteers moderate the listserv, address spam problems or heavy and redundant traffic, add and remove members, and keep discussions focused on the work of MJ. Another list reserved for MJ news has approximately 1,200 members. MJ events are also promoted to more than eleven thousand people on the MTR Road Show listserv. The listservs are effective tools for soliciting funds, recruiting volunteers, and raising bail money for anti-MTR actions. Organizations like CRMW use the listserv to encourage timely comments on message boards and public news sites and in letters to the editor.

Occasionally, listserv-based discussion and decision making lead to difficulty as activists attempt to balance the nonhierarchical structure and consensus decision making with the expression of various political, economic, cultural, and philosophical differences. The problems that ensue can consume enormous time and energy; their resolution is complicated by the accessibility of the listserv and participants' ability to comment on and challenge each other's statements in a medium that lacks the nuance of tone, emotion, and social norms that facilitate respect in face-to-face communication. Another limitation is the transparent nature of the listserv; many members do not post sensitive information regarding campaigns or actions, at times creating tension between those who desire open communication and those concerned about "security culture."[10]

Social networking sites like Facebook and MySpace have also become important tools for MJ. These platforms allow users to become "friends" with one another, fund-raise, and post links to news, photographs, blogs, and videos. Additionally, Flickr, Picasa, Google Video, and You Tube allow free, rapid dissemination of photographs, video, and other media accounts of MJ actions. These media can be used (with permission) for press releases, news articles, and documentaries. MJ organizers coordinate media sharing and publicity within hours of actions to ensure timely and widespread distribution of photos and video related to events. For example, following the TVA coal ash disaster in Tennessee, MJ members posted films of the disaster.

Tensions over Tactics, Strategy, Responsibility, and Authority

Since its inception, MJ and allied informal groups have struggled to work effectively with some of the more formal, institutionalized, nonprofit organizations and scholar-activists working on Appalachian coalfield issues. MJ activists experienced significant hurdles working effectively with organizations that have different ideological approaches to community organizing. In the beginning, MJ activists repeatedly reached out to several long-standing organizations in the coalfields in the hopes of developing partnerships and alliances, but were confronted with harsh criticism of the MJ movement. Many established organizations were wary of MJ's ties to EarthFirst!, with that group's anarcho-environmental ideology, decentralized structure, and motto of "no compromise in the defense of mother earth." Some perceived MJ to threaten the long-term efforts of grassroots organizations to build large constituencies and maintain political credibility in the culturally conservative coalfields. Some condemned MJ as an "outsider" organization, even though many MJ activists are native to Appalachia and some are from families that date back generations in the region.

MJ's willingness to engage in civil disobedience and nonviolent direct action has at times been a source of tension with other organizations. These tactics do not have the same repercussions for MJ as for traditionally structured, legally recognized organizations resisting MTR. MJ does not actively approach foundations for funding, maintain a 501(c)3 status, or pay staff. Thus, MJ does not have the same concerns for the potential impacts of civil disobedience or direct action on the financial liability or even viability of the organization. There are additional considerations. Because MJ activists are often from outside the specific coalfield community where an action is planned, and because of the history of violence surrounding strip mining conflicts, there has been justified concern over ensuring local community allies' inclusion in decision making about appropriate tactics so that they do not face unanticipated or unacceptable repercussions.

Mountain Justice and Economic Solidarity

From the beginning of Mountain Justice, activists debated economic issues. Many discussions during listening projects and at actions and other events boiled down to the question, "What about the jobs?" Debunking the false choice of "jobs versus the environment" was a goal of MJ from the start. Historically, opponents to surface mining have pointed out that strip mining employs far fewer miners than deep mining and can damage other sectors of employment.[11] Yet, as communities that have struggled with strip mining for forty years know, the challenges of creating alternative, sustainable, economic opportunities in a region historically characterized by uneven development and dependence on resource extraction are daunting.

Recognizing that economic dependence on coal is a central obstacle to its mission, MJ activists hosted the Beyond Coal Conference at Hindman (Kentucky) Settlement School in April 2006.[12] Approximately one hundred people attended the three-day conference, which focused on tourism, farming, nontimber forest products, small-scale manufacturing, Internet businesses, and renewable energy. Though the event created a sense of possibility and hope, there was little follow-up and it is difficult to measure any long- or short-term results. Between the time-consuming conference planning and the active MJ campaign, many involved were exhausted and stepped back from MJ activities.

But the economic question persisted and the following year there was a new collaborative effort. This time the conference's name, Appalachian Community Economics (ACE), intentionally sidestepped coal and, although the core planners were dedicated MJ activists, organizers from related groups took lead roles for ACE. Held in September 2008 near Abingdon, Virginia, the conference brought together almost two hundred people from across Appalachia to focus on local economic issues. Most attendees were inspired and excited to learn of the diverse, successful organizations, businesses, colleges and universities, and communities that were taking back some control over economic issues at local to regional scales. The High Road Initiative (a partnership between KFTC and the Mountain Association for Community Economic Development) shared its approach to economic transformation in Kentucky, and the Coal River Wind Project described its efforts to save Coal River Mountain from MTR and promote a long-term, clean, job-creating wind farm. The ACE conference attracted more participants than the Beyond Coal Conference, including more women and older adults. However, conference organizers and attendees again struggled to do effective follow-up on the conference proceedings, as the all-volunteer organizers tended to focus on details related to the events themselves rather than effective planning for the long term.

The environmental justice movement's call for Just Transitions—retraining for displaced workers and alternative economic development for communities affected by environmental problems—has been eye-opening as well as challenging for MJ activists working on economic issues in Appalachia. Most activists agree that, along with the call for abolition of MTR, we must address the ramifications for thousands of people employed by the coal industry. However, priorities differ as to how, and how fast, a transition could or should occur. Residents whose human rights of health and safety are being violated demand immediate relief. Some argue that displaced workers could simply be retrained as underground miners. Others assert that, in the face of ecological crises like climate change and the rapacious pressures of global capitalism, we need wholesale reconfiguration of economic production and consumption in local communities. These individuals believe that absentee land ownership by timber, mining, and land companies is at the heart of regional economic problems, and that agrarian and land reform is necessary for a sustainable Appalachia.

MJ activists also debate the wisdom of diverting political energy to the campaign for green jobs. On a national scale, Green For All founder Van Jones has effectively argued for Green Jobs that are Good Jobs—"Green Collar Jobs"—for working-class people and their skills.[13] On numerous occasions, MJ activists have advocated that, in the rapidly evolving new energy economy, green jobs are as important for economic revitalization in rural Appalachia as they are in urban centers, where the Green Jobs push is more advanced. It will be a struggle to ensure that enough of those jobs—however they are defined, which is not always straightforward—end up in Appalachia. Regardless of how one calculates the scale of impacted mine lands, hundreds of thousands of acres throughout Appalachia are in varying stages of "reclamation," and there is potential for thousands of people to achieve good livelihoods and stable jobs restoring fractured forests and severely impaired hydrologic systems. Some MJ activists shy away from this debate altogether, arguing that we must focus our attention on abolishing the root cause of community, mountain, forest, and stream destruction—MTR—and any efforts spent on reclamation allow the coal industry to "green-wash" its destructive habits.

Conclusion

The nature of MJ makes it difficult to generalize as we have done. MJ draws in new recruits to fight MTR from around the country. Radical activists, in the absence of an organized left in the nation or region, may connect the dots but are hard-pressed to decide on practical steps toward revolutionary political change and often struggle to reconcile addressing structural problems while coping with the pragmatic difficulties of survival in coalfield economies.

Since 2004, regional and national awareness of mountaintop removal coal mining has increased. This in part arises from broad concern over climate and energy issues. MTR and strip mining have again become salient issues in presidential and congressional politics, not just local or state matters. Such public awareness owes to the dedicated efforts from many community-based and regional groups. MJ is playing a significant role in the broader consciousness around MTR by training thousands of volunteers, hosting dozens of events, protests, and direct actions, and participating in hundreds of civil disobedience actions not only in the four central Appalachian states, but also in Charleston, South Carolina; Atlanta; Washington, D.C.; New York City; and as far away as Oregon and California. Mountain Justice contributes to this politically complex and wide-ranging movement as it continues the struggle for radical social change in Appalachia and beyond.

Notes

This article is dedicated to the lost communities, cemeteries, homeplaces, habitat, forests, streams, and memories of Appalachia, as well as to Sue Daniels, Jamie McGuinn, Michael Edge, Ann Porter, John Cleveland, and Judy Bonds, who fought for the mountains and have passed on.

1. For a more in-depth discussion of the formation of MJ, see Tricia Shapiro, *Mountain Justice: Homegrown Resistance to Mountaintop Removal, for the Future of Us All* (Oakland, Calif.: AK Press, 2010).

2. A more complete history of MJ actions can be found on its Web site, http://www.mountainjustice.org/actions/index.php.

3. The campaign for a safe school for the students has been led by Ed Wiley and is the subject of the film *On Coal River*. More info is available at www.penniesofpromise.org.

4. Among others, "Here's To the Long Haul," a string band created by MJ activists, has encapsulated many stories and memories from the movement into its music and performances.

5. The development and evolution of the Alliance for Appalachia is an interesting story that deserves more in-depth research. See www.theallianceforappalachia.org/.

6. www.ran.org/campaigns/global_finance.

7. Ronald D. Eller, *Uneven Ground: Appalachia since 1945* (Lexington: University Press of Kentucky, 2008), 258–59. This action followed the Southeast Convergence for Climate Action. Asheville Rising Tide organized both the action and the convergence, with MJ cosponsoring.

8. www.beehivecollective.org.

9. Ken Ward Jr., "DEP Turns Down Another Massey Silo Permit," *Charleston Gazette*, February 23, 2006.

10. Most MJ activists assume that their activities may be monitored by various government agencies and the coal industry. Accordingly, details of sensitive activities are often not discussed on telephones, listservs, the Internet, or other digital media. For more on "security culture," visit: http://www.animalliberationfront.com/ALFront/ELF/sec-handbook.pdf.

11. Chad Montrie, *To Save the Land and People: A History of Opposition to Surface Coal Mining in Appalachia* (Chapel Hill: University of North Carolina Press, 2003).

12. The Beyond Coal Conference drew inspiration from a similar conference hosted by the Oak Ridge Environmental Peace Alliance (see chapter 1 in this volume).

13. www.greenforall.org.

CHAPTER 16

Who Knows? Who Tells?

Creating a Knowledge Commons

Anita Puckett, Elizabeth Fine, Mary Hufford,
Ann Kingsolver, and Betsy Taylor

With a land mass the size of Rhode Island denuded by mountaintop removal coal mining, the southern Appalachian coalfields have become a national sacrifice zone. Confined to less populated areas, beyond the view of travelers on major highways, this growing social and ecological disaster has been invisible for decades to nearly everyone, including environmental activists, in the United States. A long history of viewing Appalachia as outside mainstream national concerns has contributed to this invisibility. Cyber-activism is changing this neglect by making images of mountaintop removal (MTR) and its impacts accessible to Internet users. But the astonishing invisibility of MTR continues, due in part to the institutionalized privileging of professional expertise over local, experientially based knowledge regarding the consequences of MTR. Moreover, the targeted delivery of "expertise" vetted by the coal industry produces friction between local miners and residents, who square off as either "friends of coal," or those who "love mountains." The result is a complex struggle between different constructions of expert and experiential knowledge over territory that is paradoxically both "home" and the commodity known as the "coalfields."

Many academics, including the authors of this chapter, have been drawn into these highly politicized contexts through our involvement with the remarkable grassroots movement against mountaintop removal that has grown in the region since the mid-1990s. Dozens of local and regional organizations, often containing academics and other "experts" of various sorts, have allied in creative ways with each other, with national and international community organizations, and with artists, filmmakers, journalists, creative writers, coalfield citizens, and other individuals. This anti-MTR movement has produced powerful, eloquent films, magazine, newspaper, and e-zine articles, television reports, celebrity interventions, Internet information sites, YouTube videos, political protests, public, professional, and academic conferences, and legislative campaigns, all of which flash with increasing frequency across national mediascapes. As a result, MTR is becoming more prominent in the public consciousness. Nevertheless, it is still marginal to national debates about fossil fuels, climate change, and green job creation.

We therefore ask how grassroots organizations and academics can work together more fully to transform the difficult local, regional, and national political terrains in which these organizations have to operate. By "terrains" we mean the physical and virtual places where those who have *experienced* the real environmental and community impacts of MTR (activists, citizens, civic organizations, policy advocacy groups, and local environmental groups) come in contact with the communications constructed by institutionally validated academics and professionals who assert a more abstract *expertise* and the power that commonly goes with it. We examine not only the structure of these contact arenas but also argue for creating venues where these "experts" *must* engage in *experientially based* dialogues with those whose knowledge derives from practical, pragmatic, and physically real engagements with the outcomes of MTR mining. We call such venues "knowledge commons," for it is here that different ways of thinking and acting on issues must merge experiential knowledge and ways of talking about it with credentialed expertise. Expertise itself is not the villain here, but the ways experts ignore and dismiss those having local experience. If exchanges occur at all, experts treat local knowledge and people as beside the point when, in fact, they are crucial in devising solutions that protect residents and promote democratic participation.

We claim that constructing knowledge commons is critical to anti-MTR movement building and to the development of social justice activism more generally. Speech and its written forms must become objects of strategic focus to change underlying power relations and promote full community and grassroots organizational participation. In this chapter, we provide a brief theoretical and historical context for this argument, followed by individual examples from four of us. Fine rhetorically analyzes how an Internet mode of communication can construct a powerful knowledge commons. Puckett describes ways that activist academics can cross the borders of normally segregated academic terrains. Taylor discusses the often invisible influence of the coal industry over the ability to have public and democratic debates about MTR. Hufford illustrates how to transform the corporate state's expert domains into sites of public dialogue with local experiential knowledge. Finally, Kingsolver contributed to discussions of the overall argument and to the chapter's final form.

Theoretical and Historical Context

Many contemporary social justice movements demand that local efforts link closely to regional, national, and international political terrains. In coal-producing Appalachia, control of resources at the local level, including verbal ones, has always been part of "King Coal's" power and monolithic economic pre-eminence.[1]

But since the 1980s, neoliberal power structures have forced "places" all over the planet to market themselves transregionally and globally, and this has led to a new form of argument and control over regional resources. Situated within larger neoliberal projects, new "place managers" or "place entrepreneurs"[2] broker among local, regional, national, and global contractors to offer incentives such as tax breaks, compliant workers, and local connections to induce mobile capital to relocate. New "growth coalitions," consisting of local-level landowners, politicians, developers, attorneys, bankers, financiers, businesses, and entrepreneurs, market their particular locales for future development in hope of bringing in jobs and investment that directly benefit them. Universities increasingly have taken on roles in these "growth coalitions," often by claiming large economic payoffs at the local level from research and development.[3] Most basically, these coalitions utilize the same verbal resources and rely on strategies sustained, reproduced, and created by their communicative activities to keep opposition out and convince the general public that their views are natural, moral, and inescapable. In very few contexts are there knowledge commons that include contradictory, experientially based evidence or oppositional views.

However, at the grassroots level, an explosion of efforts has created citizen-led visions and projects for alternative development that steward the environment, grow jobs, and decouple various links in the global partnerships of the neoliberals. Anti-MTR struggles have taken place in the thick of this grassroots struggle, and their ways of talking about alternative development have created new ways of communicating that encourage, if not compel, development of knowledge commons that are, in turn, strongly encouraging transformations in the roles of academic "experts."

From the mid-1990s to the present, these struggles have taken two different paths. For Larry Gibson, Judy Bonds, Maria Gunnoe, among many other courageous individuals, there has been the brave and often lonely path of direct confrontation and public speech about the vast destruction of beloved and historic landscapes, homes, health, and the forest commons on which many traditional Appalachian livelihoods depend.[4] By the late 1990s, a number of Appalachian nonprofits (for example, Ohio Valley Environmental Coalition, Appalachian Voices, and a few regional Sierra Club organizations) began to focus on MTR and to work with such individuals' grassroots efforts in political campaigns, public education and awareness, and regional and national networking. These grassroots attacks on the existing neoliberal constructions of political economic power were direct, as they were in earlier coalfield labor disputes, but have not effectively challenged elite control over hegemonic discourse.

The second path has been more indirect, and often did not seem to relate to coal mining at all: the struggle for democratic takeover of local planning structures and creation of multi-issue coalitions with the political strength to imagine and create place-based, sustainable economies. These efforts tapped into powerful legacies of local economies that use the forest commons (ginseng, herbs, hunting, and so forth), local agriculture, crafts and artisanship, and strong traditions of interdependence among neighbors and family,[5] as well as love of community and the land. Some promoted sustainable lifestyles and jobs by implementing green technologies and "going local," which expanded local efforts into regional socioeconomic enterprises.[6]

These two paths are now converging in exciting and potentially transformative ways that can, in turn, compel the construction of local knowledge commons that dismantle the impact and force of the global marketplaces of neoliberalism. The Internet and access to it are critical to developing this third, combined path.

Crossing Communication Boundaries: Traditional and Virtual Efforts

This third path reveals how activist groups have challenged the time-honored ways corporations and governments have constructed their power and authority. In this first example, Fine uses rhetorical analysis to assess how Internet modes of communication advance these new paths of communication. Although subject to filtering and monitoring by Internet service providers, schools, libraries, and other institutions, they are still amazingly open to anyone with Web connectivity and are highly interpersonal yet global in scale. Although various coal companies intimidate potential opponents through direct and indirect means (for example, guarded gates that block direct access to their MTR sites, surveillance of listservs, physical intimidation, and control of K–12 educational content on coal mining), coal company advocates cannot stop flyover or satellite imagery, nor can they restrict the images, photos, and videos of the destruction that appear on Web sites supported in large part by Google Earth. The Web is crucial to dismantling the current communication system that is advancing MTR and environmental destruction more generally.

One new Web site, in particular, has been successful in bringing MTR to the forefront of U.S. environmental debate and countering the hegemony of neoliberal-dominated industry and coal "expert" sites: http://www.iLoveMountains.org. Early in 2006, the grassroots organizations Appalachian Voices, Coal River Mountain Watch, Keepers of the Mountains Foundation, Kentuckians For The Commonwealth, Ohio Valley Environmental Coalition, Save Our Cumberland Mountains, and Southern Appalachian Mountain Stewards began working collaboratively on a Web site to serve as a hub of information and activism on mountaintop removal mining. Launched in September 2006, iLoveMountains.org exemplifies how the Internet can create a communication commons visible to all with online access, regardless of credentials, and, in rendering MTR destruction visible, lead to protection of the Appalachian mountains.

One of the most effective ways that iLoveMountains.org creates a communicative commons is through photographic imagery. Images circumvent the limitations of language and literacy and are immediate and iconic in their psychological and emotional impact. The iLove Mountains.org National Memorial for the Mountains utilizes Google Earth software to show the destructive impact of mountaintop removal. For example, a 2009 page design shows American flags at half-mast superimposed on a map of central Appalachia. Clicking on a flag brings up a separate page for each mountain that has been removed and memorialized. Each page shows high-resolution pictures of before and after mountaintop destruction. In addition, each page is accompanied by articles about the mountains and people affected, short video clips, comments by viewers, and a link to donate to the memorial and to organizations working to stop MTR. Reputable and accurate, this information forms the seedbed for constructing a public and professional knowledge commons. In another application of Google Earth, iLoveMountains.org enables viewers to overlay a map of the largest MTR site, the Hobet Mining Complex near Mud, West Virginia, over thirty-six U.S. cities, allowing them to visualize better the site's sprawling fifteen-square-mile surface.

The memorial to Kayford Mountain page includes a number of links about local activist Larry Gibson and articles about Kayford Mountain, as well as a link to donate to Gibson's organization, Keepers of the Mountain Foundation. The page also features a CNN video clip interview with Gibson, who in 2007 was chosen as a "CNN Hero."

Negative and positive responses to the MTR images appear on the response page, as in this example from the Kayford Mountain memorial: "My god, these people who are coal mining and stripping Kayford Mountain are just plain sick. What is wrong with them? . . . If we do not come together as one and realize we are literally destroying our planet . . . OUR HOME . . . we will be destroying ourselves as well. . . . STOP THE MOUNTAINTOP STRIPPING!" One negative response to the CNN video on Larry Gibson, posted on August 17, 2007, says: "What powers your house? it is coal if you are so serious about what you belive [sic] in call the power company and tell them to cut your power off. Why would you want to use more power shut down the web sites cut off your power and go back to living in the 1940s. You don't tell about all the good things that coal brings. . . . You continue to do what you think is right and so will I blowing off the tops of mountains providing for my kids and suppling [sic] energy for the nation." With Internet access, local people expressing themselves as citizens, whether academically credentialed or not, can voice their opinions with limited fear of reprisal and find a world stage for their voices. Thus, the iLoveMountains Web site fosters communicative exchanges between proponents and opponents of MTR, bringing to the forefront how different groups construct the issue. A rich, multivocal, and democratic knowledge commons is created.

One of the most widely used features of the site[7] is the "What's my connection to mountaintop removal?" link, where viewers can personalize their connection to MTR by typing their zip code into a box and bringing up the name of their power company with a list of the energy plants in their grid that make use of MTR coal. People writing stories about where the energy in their communities comes from frequently contact the Web site for more specific information about the power companies and mines. Journalists writing about MTR begin with a Google search, and as of 2009 iLoveMountains.org is one of the first sources identified; as a result, they frequently contact the organization's staff for more information.

By showing the damage to the Appalachian mountain commons and building a participatory and networked knowledge commons, iLoveMountains.org is effectively leading in constructing Web-based communications that reveal hidden and commonly forbidden paths of neoliberals' power. In so doing, it makes significant inroads into constructing new paths of communication and interpersonal/interorganizational connections. These are both local and global; above all, they constitute human communal places and the ecologies that sustain them as primary over the sterile, deterritorialized spaces of disembodied capital.

Creolizing "Expertise" Inside the Academy: Changing Mining Engineering Ideologies

When academics assume the role of "civic professionals" committed to creating knowledge commons, they necessarily develop personal tugs of war with respect to identity and what kinds of authority should be legitimated. Many of these conflicts arise when working outside academic campuses, but ethical issues also develop within the academy as different faculty and departments construct their professional identities. Well-institutionalized debates among disciplines are reconfigured and further exacerbated by extensive adoption of neoliberal corporate policies in the academy. Rather than generating interdisciplinary knowledge commons, these debates often create balkanized knowledge enclaves. MTR issues can be central to the construction of these enclaves at mining engineering universities such as Virginia Tech, where engineering students are subject to a rigid curriculum that supports the coal industry's economic and technological needs. In return, departments garner support for postgraduate employment, scholarships, and internships for majors, as well as research funding and departmental endowments. As a result, students' value systems and professional ethics are closely linked to those of the coal industry. Nevertheless, Puckett has found opportunities to create knowledge commons within the academy.

One of her duties as director of the Appalachian Studies program at Virginia Tech is to advance regional issues across campus at an institution noteworthy for providing the most mining engineers to the domestic coal industry. In February

2008, she organized a screening of the documentary *Sludge,* followed by a presentation and discussion by Jack Spadaro, an anti-MTR activist, expert witness on environmental and mine health and safety issues, and former federal mining engineer whose courageous whistle-blowing led to concerted harassment by the Bush administration. The event lasted four hours, as mining engineering students stayed to ask questions and demand answers. This campus venue opened possibilities for debates among engineering students and faculty, MTR student activists representing the Mountain Justice organization, community members from the Coal Mining Heritage Association, other Virginia Tech students, and Appalachian Studies faculty. Spadaro countered virtually every critique from engineering students and faculty by relying on engineering ways of talking—emphasizing "facts" and "factual evidence," discussing mining technologies and methods, coal production levels, environmental damage, harm to individuals and communities, and legal considerations. Spadaro's visit, and his ways of talking, served to create possibilities for a knowledge commons that includes future industry employees (students) and could change the ways knowledge is valued at higher levels of the university.

The outcomes of this event have been several: Mountain Justice students have held several mediated sessions with mining engineering students to discuss differences and look for common ground; more joint Appalachian Studies and mining engineering events have been planned and cohosted, and initiatives to merge curricula are underway, thanks to the willingness of mining engineering professors to assist in program development. Puckett's role has been that of an "expert," using her position to nurture the emergence of these creolized communication spaces, not as an autonomous researcher but as a collaborator and coinstructor planning a joint curriculum. Academic borders that previously were nearly impenetrable are being crossed in ways that question and potentially dismantle the corporate marketing of both knowledge and "place."

Academic experts can work to construct knowledge commons and must strive to do so if the anti-MTR movement is to be successful. Academics, professionals, grassroots organizers, students, and individual citizens must be more reflective about the roles we play and how to construct those roles intentionally as we talk and respond to the talk of others. In this sense, discourse is a resource and tool that must be more attentively integrated into not only anti-MTR movements in Appalachia but movement building more generally.

King Coal and the Appropriation of Academic Expertise

This section explores negative contexts that threaten democratizing citizen efforts, such as those described in preceding and following sections. In states containing coalfields, contemporary regional "growth coalitions" emerge from a context in which coal industries have had great power over jobs, land, and resources for more than a century. This history has left widely ramifying webs of profit and influence that are variously called "King Coal,"[8] or "coal interests,"[9] or "Big Coal."[10] These powerful networks between government, industry, and academe are largely hidden from public view but continue to suffuse public life. Most important are the effects on local speech. Local public spaces such as community meetings are crucial in developing effective knowledge commons because they are where local communities should be able to decide democratically whether MTR is what they want in their area and, if not, what alternatives they seek. However, this can be a hard conversation to hold publicly in MTR-affected communities because many people fear to speak openly in any way that might sound "anti-coal." Threats are very real when local coal mining jobs have been reduced from 119,000 to 16,000 while coal production has increased through the use of MTR.[11]

Coal interests also have chilling effects on regional institutions (such as academe). This section explores an episode in which Taylor felt that a veil was lifted from everyday patterns of corporate/academic relations. In the spring of 2005, Taylor organized a public forum on coal waste impoundments, inspired by student enthusiasm in an undergraduate Appalachian Studies course she was teaching at the University of Kentucky (UK). Internet and traditional public relations efforts resulted in a call, within hours, from an administrator in a powerful, statewide, coal industry lobbying organization, who told her that the panel needed to be "balanced" and "based on good science," and should therefore include himself and his list of suggested UK faculty (rather than her invited panelists). He praised Taylor's "enthusiasm" as commendable in someone so "junior." In daily calls, he spoke of the recognition she would get at the university if she spoke before proceeding with more "senior" UK people whose names he mentioned. The covert message behind his words seemed to be that he was well connected with powerful people at UK. Carefully polite, Taylor repeated the same points in each call: the panel was focused on community, not industrial, well-being (environmental, health, risk assessment and disaster management, civic capacity); the panel included experts in those topics or community members directly affected; the lobbyist and the faculty he recommended had expertise in fields other than the panel topics, but that she hoped to work with them in the future as scholarly goals overlapped.

On the night of the panel, the coal lobbying group had a slide show and literature tables set up well before the event. The room quickly filled, including many coalfields residents who had driven for hours. The staff of the coal lobbying group stood in a line that reached across the back wall, including many lawyers taking notes. As Taylor stood to introduce the panel, the coal lobbying group's administrator walked from the back of the room and sat down (uninvited) in her seat with the invited panel members. The invited panel members were superb. They marshaled rich and rigorous data that was calmly assessed and civilly deliberated upon, and ensuing public debates were lively and substantive. The next day, the coal lobbyist called several times after the panel to get the names of students who had spoken out against MTR (which Taylor withheld because she feared negative consequences for them or their families).

One striking feature of this interaction was the extent to which the coal lobbyist used the language of science and academe. First, he argued for scholarly "balance" and "objectivity" by invoking notions of specialized expertise. Second, he argued that coal slurry impoundments were primarily a technical issue, so the panel had to be made up of industry representatives and faculty from one applied sector of the university—not the social sciences or medicine. Third, he objected to the presence and perspectives of any representatives of affected communities as biased "advocates." On the surface, he spoke in the language of disinterested, specialized expertise but invisible threats were implied. This episode suggests the political power of speech—to open up or to close democratic debate and action. How often does the hidden speech of King Coal in the back corridors of power have the effect of chilling or aborting free speech?

Creating Knowledge Commons: The Appalachia Forest Action Project

Our last example considers how the academically based community researcher can facilitate knowledge commons construction. In her work on cultural policy and environmental decision making at the Library of Congress, Hufford saw how the process of environmental assessment used by state and federal governments not only marginalizes but annihilates local perspectives and ways of talking about communities and the land in which they are located. When the land is detached from discourses of experience and reinscribed into discourses of expertise, local resistance to neoliberal marketing of place disappears from the view of larger-than-local publics.[12]

In West Virginia, federally mandated environmental impact assessments for proposed mountaintop removal projects display the specialized language of experts employed by the coal industry. This language constructs a sieve through which locally valued goods such as ginseng, ramp patches, productive headwaters, and family graveyards are strained into the category of "overburden": industry's term for everything covering a seam of coal. The environment is reduced to a short list of amenities checked against existing data in state and federal offices. Local communities are rarely consulted, even in the assessment of cultural resources, for which the coal industry hires archeologists.[13] One strategy for democratizing the process of environmental planning involves cultivating and normalizing a role for communities as clients for academic and technical expertise.[14] Ethnographers in particular are trained to recognize ways in which communities name and measure cultural assets, and to bridge between local terminologies and state terminologies, with special attention to the relevance of protections for air, water, soil, cultural resources, and endangered species for local cultural resources.

The Appalachia Forest Action Project (AFAP), conducted from 1994 to 1997, offers one model for integrating community-based scientific and ethnographic research. AFAP began in 1993, when science writer and forest activist John Flynn took seriously the observations of longtime users of the forested coves and ridges along the Marsh and Clear Forks of the Big Coal River Valley in southern West Virginia. Men and women who had spent many decades hunting, gathering, gardening, and fishing in the area had noticed, and were troubled by, escalating symptoms of forest species decline: oaks and hickories failing to mature, lesions appearing on the trunks of tulip poplars, numerous trees snapping off in midtrunk during heavy winds, premature leaf drops, and more. Flynn invited Orie Loucks, an eminent forest ecologist from Oxford University in Miami, Ohio, to look at what Flynn's neighbors were observing. Loucks looked, listened to the concerns of citizens of the Coal River Valley, and within a year designed, co-organized, and obtained funding for a "citizen-science" monitoring project dependent on the dialogue of local experience with larger-than-local expertise.[15]

The research question, which Loucks distilled from conversations with people on Coal River, was one that neither the U.S. Forest Service nor the West Virginia Department of Natural Resources (DNR) had asked: "Are species mortality rates escalating in Appalachia's Mixed Mesophytic forest?" Monitoring over a three-year period affirmed the observations and experience of community members and correlated the sites of highest species decline (five times higher than historic rates) with the sites of highest wet ozone deposition from sources of fossil fuel combustion upwind of the region.[16]

AFAP's citizen science monitoring proposal sparked a firestorm of criticism from professional foresters with the multinational paper company Westvaco and the West Virginia DNR. Trivializing local ways of talking about the land, the foresters challenged the validity of research initiated in response to "anecdotes" from old-timers. West Virginia DNR had been issuing forest reports soothing to stockholders of Westvaco, claiming the forests were in "robust health." Giving credence to community preferences for mixed aged, biologically diverse forests surviving beyond "readiness for harvest" to achieve the fullness of time signaled by den trees and bee trees, AFAP contradicted the state's claims about forest health and exposed the timber- and coal-dominated politics governing the definition of forest health.

Because the forest covering the central Appalachian plateaus is one of the two oldest temperate-zone hardwood systems worldwide, it is also one of the most biologically diverse. Loucks and Flynn engaged Hufford, then a folklorist with the American Folklife Center, Library of Congress, to develop a community-based ethnographic study to address the question: What does species decline mean for local communities? Hufford explored AFAP's shaping of a discursive space in which different groups of stakeholders were able to make common cause. Here ethnographic research helped shape a new public space by turning discourses of expertise and experience into objects of shared inquiry and reflection. "Tending the Commons," an online presentation of sound recordings and still photographs, was curated by Hufford as part of the American Memory Project at the Library of Congress.[17] The Web site has served as a documentary resource for the Coal River Mountain Watch[18] (which developed out of AFAP) in public hearings challenging mountaintop removal mining permits.

A graphic of the seasonal round of social, cultural, and economic practice supported by this biologically diverse forest system illustrates the potential for community-based ethnography to bridge the discourses of expertise and experience.[19] Developed by Hufford with members of communities along the Coal River, the seasonal round graphic depicts times and spaces named in stories told by residents, and foregrounds local experiential terms and ways of classifying forest resources. Of special interest is the biocultural solution posed by the seasonal round to the scientists' problem of how to define ecological integrity. Customized to reflect subregional variation, the seasonal round could be adapted for ongoing assessment and management of biodiversity. The seasonal round graphic thus offers a tool for cross-disciplinary academic and community research partnerships throughout the mixed mesophytic forest region. Framing a dialogue between experience and expertise, it can facilitate and, indeed, codify, creation of a knowledge commons.

Collaborative research that assesses the ongoing status of forest resources would support the integrity of the mixed mesophytic forest ecosystem while empowering and lending authority to experiential ways of knowing as captured through verbal discourse. The civic labor of such research is indispensable to democratic governance, for it continually articulates the local geographic and cultural commons into a national commons anchored in the same substantive goods.

Conclusion

We have sought to expose select communication paths of the forbidding political landscape of the "coalfields" to understand how academics functioning as "civic professionals" can promote movement building that decouples neoliberal global partnerships and constructs local, citizen-based stewardship over environment and community. We looked at several situations of public discourse where groups that normally are isolated from or dismissive of each other have come together to create (or have been forced to create) new ways of communicating and have thereby made visible the hidden or veiled speech of the powerful. From this discussion come the following recommendations for anti-MTR movement building in Appalachia:

1. We argue for and support the aggressive and active development of innovative ways to incorporate Internet users into forms of communication that compel hidden power structures to be made public and visible, thereby stimulating creation of new, progressive, and global networks of environmentally invested citizens who value democratization, environmental sustainability, and an alternative ethics. Appalachia has always been tied into the global economy, even if images of rurality and isolation have masked that connection. New perspectives on the mountainscape, such as the way iLoveMountains.org uses Google Earth, can be used to urge new vantage points on the region's history and future and its connectedness to global concerns; increasing Internet access across Appalachia is important to these citizenship collaborations.

2. We advocate for the continued development of "civic professionals" in academe[20] so that experiential knowledge is integrated more fully with expert knowledge. Boundaries that separate experiential and expert knowledge are then broken and reconfigured in ways that break down and reconfigure the ivory-towered isolation of academic scholarship.

3. To advance movement building more generally, we need to treat speech as a resource and the discourses it creates as objects that must be considered in strategizing resistance and reconstituting activist approaches to life-threatening issues.

4. We need to develop large-scale, transnational strategies that illuminate and dismantle the ways those in power who support and advance MTR and other environmental exploitations hide and forbid access to their communications and the venues in which these communications occur. Though this may seem an argument for "transparency," we are actually advocating far more: exposure of deeply masked ignorances, dehumanizing and ecologically devastating ideologies, and economically driven immoralities that motivate the massive destruction compounding literally every day. This requires participatory remapping of the coal-producing Appalachian region, along with other endangered regions of the planet, emphasizing local knowledge of resources and, in the case of Appalachia, the region's importance as a biosphere reserve with strategic, immediate significance in the face of, for example, global warming. Putting Appalachian and Amazonian forests in the same frame raises the potential for transnational knowledge commons and related environmental organizing that press toward visionary change.

Notes

1. John Alexander Williams, *Appalachia: A History* (Chapel Hill: University of North Carolina Press, 2002), 259–63.

2. Herbert Reid and Betsy Taylor, *Recovering the Commons: Democracy, Place, and Global Justice* (Urbana: University of Illinois Press, 2010); See also Dorothy Holland et al., *Local Democracy under Siege: Activism, Public Interests, and Private Politics* (New York: New York University Press, 2007), 189.

3. Jennifer Washburn, *University, Inc.: The Corporate Corruption of American Higher Education* (New York: Basic Books, 2005).

4. See Catherine Pancake, dir. *Black Diamond* (Oley, Pa.: Bullfrog Productions, 2006).

5. See, for example, Mary Hufford, "Building the Commons: Folklore, Citizen Science, and the Ecological Imagination," *Indian Folklife* 1 (October 2000): 15–16.

6. See Van Jones with Ariane Conrad, *The Green-collar Economy: How One Solution Can Fix Our Two Biggest Problems* (New York: HarperOne, 2008); and Michael Shuman, *Going Local: Creating Self-reliant Communities in a Global Age* (New York: Routledge, 2000).

7. Benji Burrel, telephone and e-mail interview with Elizabeth Fine, January 17, 2009.

8. Mary Hufford, *Waging Democracy in the Kingdom of Coal: OVEC and the Movement for Environmental and Social Justice* (New York and Philadelphia: New York University School of Public Service and University of Pennsylvania Center for Folklore and Ethnography, 2004), http://www.sas.upenn.edu/folklore/center/waging_democracy2.pdf.

9. Shirley Stewart Burns, *Bringing Down the Mountains: The Impact of Mountaintop Removal on Southern West Virginia Communities* (Morgantown: West Virginia University Press, 2007).

10. Jeff Goodell, *Big Coal: The Dirty Secret behind America's Energy Future* (New York: Houghton Mifflin, 2006).

11. Pancake, *Black Diamond*; Burns, *Bringing Down the Mountains,* 13–14.

12. The term "larger-than-local" comes from Amy Shuman's "Dismantling Local Culture," *Western Folklore* 52 (April–October 1993): 335–64.

13. For background on the coal industry's reliance on archeology for cultural resource documentation, see Thomas F. King, "How the Archeologists Stole Culture: A Gap in American Environmental Impact Assessment Practice and How to Fill It," *Environmental Impact Assessment Review* 18 (March 1998): 117–33.

14. See Samuel R. Cook and Betsy Taylor, eds., "Academics, Activism, and Place-based Education in the Appalachian Coal Belt," special issue of *Practicing Anthropology* 23 (Spring 2001).

15. For more on the Appalachia Forest Action Project, see Harvard Ayres, Jenny Hager, and Charles E. Little, eds., *An Appalachian Tragedy: Air Pollution and Tree Death in the Eastern Forests of North America* (San Francisco: Sierra Books, 1998).

16. See Ken Wills et al., *Patterns of Forest Health: A Report on Citizen Monitoring in the Eastern Mountains, 1994–97* (Birmingham, Ala., Oxford, Ohio, and Washington, D.C: Lucy Braun Association for the Mixed Mesophytic Forest and Trees for the Planet, 1997).

17. http://memory.loc.gov/ammem/collections/tending/index.html.

18. Following the tragic and untimely death of John Flynn in 1996, AFAP volunteer Randy Sprouse, at that time a resident of Sundial, assumed Flynn's duties as AFAP coordinator. In 1997, with continuing support from AFAP cosponsors, the Rock Creek Forest Watch was reorganized as the Coal River Mountain Watch. Randy Sprouse coordinated the organization's efforts until 1999. See http://memory.loc.gov/ammem/collections/tending.

19. http://memory.loc.gov/ammem/collections/tending/season1.html.

20. Herbert Reid and Betsy Taylor, "Appalachia as a Global Region: Toward Critical Regionalism and Civic Professionalism," *Journal of Appalachian Studies* 8 (Spring 2002): 9–32.

CHAPTER 17

North and South

Struggles over Coal in Colombia and Appalachia

Aviva Chomsky and Chad Montrie

This chapter examines links and disjunctures among several different constituencies associated with coal mining struggles in southern Appalachia and Colombia. It focuses particularly on the interactions among labor unions, environmental groups, and social justice campaigns in both places. The orientation and goals of the different organizations have sometimes coincided or been mutually supportive, but in other moments, they have sharply conflicted. The swings between collaboration and tension, solidarity and single-minded defense of self-interest, speak to a complex mix of factors, including varying economic conditions, definitions of "union" issues, and conceptions of environmentalism.

During the first decade of the twenty-first century, coal production in Appalachia reached a record high, while membership in the United Mine Workers of America (UMWA) fell to its lowest point since the 1890s. In this position of weakness, union leaders—even those who claim to care as much about employment and the regional economy as mountains and streams and wildlife—face obstacles to forming new, sustaining alliances with unionized coal miners abroad and environmental activists at home. Some obstacles are of the union's own making, including disinclination to a broader critique of capitalism in general and surface mining in particular, as well as restrained efforts to reach out beyond its own constituency to Appalachian communities and to unions in Colombia, where U.S.-based corporations developed new mining operations during the 1980s. Typically, the UMWA leadership positions itself as a part of the "coal industry," defines its interests as similar if not identical to those of corporations, and chooses to protect dwindling mining jobs in the short term rather than assessing and acting in imaginative ways to shore up broadly defined, long-term concerns of the rank and file.

Labor is not the only organized group that has been limited by a narrow focus. Mainstream environmental organizations in the United States have been slow to acknowledge the class dimensions and global aspects of their goals. During the 1960s and 1970s, leaders from the Sierra Club and Environmental Policy

Center all but ignored Appalachian residents' linking of environmental and economic problems in their arguments against surface coal mining. Likewise, they diverted efforts away from the growing and nearly successful campaign for a ban on stripping so that they could play an instrumental role in winning a weak federal regulatory law, now proven a failure. Although environmental problems inherently raise issues of interconnectedness, environmental activists were too often focused on one piece without examining the larger puzzle.[1]

Mining unions and community groups in Colombia present some contrast to the directions taken by those in the United States. Unions there adhere to a form of leftist nationalism, arguing that foreign companies are raping their country, destroying its land, and displacing its people. This has led them into alliance with environmental and Afro-Colombian and indigenous organizations. To a great extent they have rejected the claim by coal companies and energy conglomerates that there has to be a choice between "jobs" and "environment," and this position has facilitated their relationships with local communities as well as active solidarity with groups opposing stripping in Appalachia.

Our chapter compares the trajectory of popular organizing in Appalachia and Colombia in the context of these different but interrelated histories and investigates how different peoples affected by coal mining have defined local and particular identities and interests. We also look at moments when groups have deepened their political analysis to intersect with each other on both local and global scales. We draw on contemporary examples of solidarity, including a growing relationship between Kentuckians For The Commonwealth (KFTC) and unions and communities in the Colombian coal region. Despite disappointments working with U.S. unions and environmental organizations, some members of Appalachian coal communities are at the epicenter of a growing global solidarity network that ties economic to environmental rights and seeks to create a global challenge to corporate power.

Appalachia

Although the UMWA was established in 1890, it took several decades to bring Appalachian coal miners into the fold. Miners faced efforts by coal operators to divide them along racial and ethnic lines, brutal treatment at the hands of private security agents and National Guard troops, as well as various paternalist schemes. Nevertheless, after a renewed organizing drive, in 1933 union president John L. Lewis signed a collective bargaining agreement that covered nearly all of the Appalachian coalfields and made miners there some of the best-paid blue-collar workers in the country.[2] From the depths of the Great Depression to the end of World War II, the UMWA proceeded to negotiate ever more substantial wage increases and expanded benefits, including a health and retirement fund financed by a royalty on each ton of mined coal. With the advance of mechanization, however, including the advent of surface or strip mining, by the 1950s job losses were significant. Strip mining required far fewer miners per ton of coal than underground methods, and most of the operations were nonunion, diminishing royalties for the UMWA benefit funds.[3] Some district leaders responded with organizing campaigns, yet most failed. Jurisdictional disputes with a rival union of operating engineers, collusion among police, operators, and government officials, high unemployment, as well as discouragement of rank and file activism by International leaders proved formidable obstacles. Once the UMWA presidency passed to Tony Boyle in 1963, rampant corruption further impeded any opposition.

At the local level, mountain residents from various backgrounds began to organize *against* surface mining. Deep miners, keenly aware of the threat stripping posed to their employment, were often at the center of these efforts, many galvanized by participation in the "roving pickets," a dissident movement within the UMWA. Like many of their neighbors, miners were outraged about the devastation surface mining caused to the land and water where they lived. "Overburden" dumped on steep slopes caused massive (sometimes deadly) landslides, bare mountainsides led to rapid runoff during rainstorms and exacerbated flooding, acid mine water killed fish and polluted wells, while blasting cracked foundations and sent flyrock hurtling through the air. In response, miners joined with farmers, teachers, and others to demand control laws and, once those were passed, to secure better enforcement, fighting against industry "capture" of regulatory agencies. Because this approach largely failed to halt or contain the damage caused by surface mining, a growing number of opponents began advocating a complete ban through state legislation.[4]

The abolition movement was especially active in eastern Kentucky, due in part to the way the state's highest court had interpreted "broad form" deeds. When coal and land company agents came through Appalachia in the late nineteenth and early twentieth centuries, they often arranged to buy only the mineral rights from landowners, assuming that deep mining would not significantly disturb farming aboveground. Once coal operators started to use strip methods, however, they claimed that mineral rights took precedence over surface rights and that there was no obligation either to acquire surface owner consent or pay for damages caused by mining. When the Kentucky Court of Appeals ruled in their favor, surface operations spread throughout the hills, mostly to meet increased demand by Tennessee Valley Authority power plants.[5]

In the mid-1960s, militant opponents of stripping in eastern Kentucky joined together as the Appalachian Group to Save the Land and People (AGSLP) which, even in its name, spoke to members' comprehensive concerns. They used a variety of tactics, including petitions, lawsuits, and nonviolent civil disobedience, influenced by the social ferment taking place in other parts of the United States. When the Puritan Coal Company started to clear the land of Pike County farmer Jink Ray in the summer of 1967, for example, his neighbors gathered and stopped the work by putting their bodies in the way, finally convincing the governor with their courage and tenacity to suspend the permit. Some activists also resorted to industrial sabotage, sneaking onto surface mine sites and blowing up mine machinery, very likely using knowledge and skills acquired through the use of explosives as underground miners. Damage to equipment was significant, enough to halt stripping at the targeted operations, yet nobody was ever caught in the act.[6]

While the campaign to ban stripping evolved, the UMWA began to see the rise of a rank and file insurgency. Miners first organized themselves around the issue of occupational lung disease (black lung) and shortly after made a direct challenge to Tony Boyle's hold on leadership, supporting Pennsylvania district leader Jock Yablonski for president in the 1969 elections. Boyle won the contest by a huge margin but the U.S. Department of Labor found widespread irregularities in the balloting and quickly ordered a new election. Before that could happen, UMWA officials close to Boyle had Yablonski and members of his family murdered. At the funeral, insurgents created Miners for Democracy (MFD) and selected a slate of candidates to continue the struggle. For president they chose Arnold Miller, who had not only led West Virginia's Black Lung Association but also participated in rallies and lobbying efforts that galvanized deep miner support for ending strip mining. During the campaign, however, Miller stepped back from a hard-and-fast abolitionist position to shore up votes among a growing surface mine membership, and instead adopted a commitment to good control laws with adequate enforcement. When he and other reform candidates barely won, the stage was set for internal divisions to drive the union back into a collaborative relationship with operators on this and other environmental questions. That then undermined the ability of the union to work with advocates for a ban.

Still other factors made it difficult for the UMWA to combine forces with militant abolitionists despite a reform-minded leadership. These included the so-called "energy crisis" of the 1970s, a spell of uncertainty about the availability of cheap oil that helped usher in rising prices and stagnant economic growth known as "stagflation." This downturn allowed the coal industry, or more exactly the energy conglomerates gobbling up coal companies, to more effectively pit "jobs" against "environment," insisting that Americans had to choose and warning against environmental regulations that would restrict an economic sector showing signs of health. In the face of the campaign to rein in the worst environmental abuses of surface mining, mineworkers tended to embrace the divisive corporate rhetoric wholeheartedly. "If you're going to say that you've got to quit strip mining because you're tearing up the land," asked Virginia stripper Wayne Keith, "what's people going to do?" If the only alternative was welfare, he continued, "why don't they let them go ahead and make a living?"[7]

As demands for abolition moved to the federal level, largely through organization of the Appalachian Coalition Against Strip Mining by AGSLP and other groups in October 1972, environmental militancy in the coalfields was on the wane as well, and mainstream environmental organizations (assisted by the UMWA) helped undermine what remained with an offer of compromise. The Sierra Club and Environmental Policy Center, in particular, subverted mountain residents' call for a ban and also West Virginia Congressman Ken Hechler's bill toward that end by lobbying the House and Senate for regulatory legislation instead. The coal industry and its allies in Congress saw the retreat as an opportunity to back off on control measures they had previously felt compelled to support in a calculated attempt to prevent passage of the abolition bill. Similarly, mounting pressure by strip miners within the UMWA pushed Arnold Miller to step away from support for a federal regulatory bill altogether, allowing the union to come out once again in favor of state control. Thus the Surface Mining Control and Reclamation Act (SMCRA) was enacted and signed in 1977, despite pleas from Appalachian activists to President Carter to use his veto power. Similar to proposals made by coal operators in various hearings, SMCRA essentially legalized the destruction caused by strip mining. It was lacking in many ways (for example, no steep-slope limitations and no requirement for surface owner consent or compensation) and nothing had changed to suggest enforcement would be any better than inadequate state-level efforts in preceding years.[8]

As a result of provisions in SMCRA that allowed "mountaintop removal" (MTR), valley fills, and impoundments for slurry waste, surface mining methods evolved beyond familiar area, contour, and auger operations. During the 1980s, an increasing number of operators in eastern Kentucky, southern West Virginia, and east Tennessee began to get at Appalachia's mostly horizontal coal seams by leveling whole mountains, dumping the soil and rock "overburden" in nearby valleys, and storing wastewater from washing the coal behind huge earthen dams. This proved to be an exceptionally efficient way to mine, but it had serious environmental and economic consequences. The process destroyed mountains and the hardwood forests that grew on ridges, buried miles and miles of streams, and put whole communities in jeopardy from burst dams that could cause disastrous toxic floods. And MTR ate away at the remaining jobs in the region, making for record-high levels of production, record-low levels of employment, as well as continued decline in UMWA membership, though the union leadership continued to see coal operators as more friendly than environmentalists to miners' interests.

Meanwhile, in the wake of SMCRA's passage and implementation, opposition groups either disappeared or devolved into more benign citizen watchdogs. By the 1990s, the few organizations working on the issue had all but ceased using confrontational tactics and demanded little more than improved enforcement of existing regulations. There has since been a rebirth of militancy, however, marked by emphasis on the links between the environmental and economic costs of surface coal mining, the factors that impede even the most well-meant efforts to control it, and the need to use a variety of tactics, including nonviolent civil disobedience. These groups are also looking beyond the coalfields for new allies, both among those working in the larger movement against climate change and those challenging foreign corporations and mining abuses worldwide.

Groups like Coal River Mountain Watch (CRMW), formed by residents of Whitesville, West Virginia, in 1998, are resolutely opposed to mountaintop removal, and they have been steadily organizing local people. In 2004, CRMW was joined by another group of activists, many associated with the global justice movement and Earth First!, loosely affiliated as Mountain Justice (MJ). From organizing houses established throughout Appalachia, the mostly young participants have conducted "listening projects" and outreach, initiated marches and rallies, and planned direct actions such as lockdowns and sit-ins. At the same time, blunt and exceptionally forthright leaders, including Teri Blanton and Maria Gunnoe, who have personal experience with strip mining and are increasingly frustrated with giving coal companies and regulators any benefit of the doubt, have emerged within established organizations like KFTC. They have begun to work with Mountain Justice activists, encouraging them to help seed an uprising in the coalfields, despite discomfort with MJ on the part of many KFTC leaders.

To be sure, some question the new activism, particularly the way it can alienate politicians, regulatory officials, and hesitant or fearful mountain residents. Some mainstream activists continue to insist that SMCRA and other control laws are part of a gradual encroachment on the coal industry's control over political systems, economic development, and the natural environment, affording at least some tools for protecting hills, streams, forests, and wildlife. Equally notable is the chilly relationship between strip mining opponents and UMWA leaders and rank and file. As Cecil Roberts, a past member of Miners for Democracy and now president of the UMWA, put it in 1999, "The environmental extremists do not want to listen to our ideas for compromises, because their goal is simply to shut down the nation's coal industry."[9] More recently, in a 2009 *Charleston Gazette* op-ed, Roberts defended his union's effort to stand apart from environmental and community activists and plainly stated the UMWA leadership's main concern: "To do our best to preserve, defend, and expand the jobs of our members and improve their economic well-being."[10]

Of course, the UMWA does have an obligation to look out for the immediate interests of its membership, and there are some precedents for achieving this through collaboration with the coal industry. Hemmed in by present circumstances—a coal industry now long-dominated by strip mining rank and file with little in the way of a radical social consciousness, a political system that allows inordinate influence by corporations, and an economy wedded to fossil fuel consumption—it might be impossible for the UMWA to do anything else. Yet history suggests that the union has not been well-served by a pragmatic and insular perspective, and its only salvation may lie with the sort of progressive tendency represented by the insurgency that once brought MFD to power. This makes the case of mineworkers' unions in Colombia even more instructive.

Colombia

Coal mining came to Colombia in the late 1970s as part of a major restructuring of the global coal industry. Rising oil prices, stricter environmental regulation, and railroad deregulation all contributed to coal companies' shift from unionized, underground mines in the eastern United States to nonunion strip mines in the West. Exxon participated in this trend but took it further, signing a contract with the Colombian government in 1976 to develop what was to become the world's largest open-pit coal mine, destined almost entirely for export. In the late 1980s, the Birmingham, Alabama–based Drummond company followed suit, beginning its own coal project in Colombia and gradually shutting down its Alabama mines. The UMWA, not surprisingly, responded with dismay to the closure of unionized mines in the United States and, in keeping with the AFL-CIO's growing attention to globalization and capital flight as threats to its stability and accomplishments at home, sought tentatively to reach out to Colombian miners. Colombian mineworkers and communities in the areas affected by mining found their struggles immersed in a global context from the start.

Colombia's coal region, in the Cesar and La Guajira provinces in the north of the country, has a long history of relative isolation. Several indigenous groups maintained their distinctive languages and cultures over centuries of colonial rule. The area also became a haven for slaves who escaped or were freed from bondage and others who sought to escape the hierarchies and restrictions of colonial society. Through the twentieth century, the region was known for lawlessness and independence and received little attention from state authorities. Small subsistence farming, livestock, hunting, and fishing, combined with day labor on local ranches or migration as far as the Venezuelan oil fields, sustained the majority of the population.

The coming of the multinationals changed everything. Village leader José Julio Pérez explained:

> When the mine first came, we all thought that our land would be preserved intact, that the mine wasn't going to cause us problems. What we didn't know was that what they called "progress" was going to mean the destruction of our towns. . . . When [Intercor] first arrived, they were so nice to everyone. They held meetings and invited the heads of the households, they looked around to see who the leaders were in the communities, and they tried to seduce them. They did all kinds of nice things for them, they brought them gifts, and people believed that they were wonderful people. In their meetings they made themselves out to be the best people in the world. They made us think that with them people were going to get everything they needed—gasoline, favors, anything people needed. That they would be there to take care of the communities.[11]

"We thought it was true what they told us, that the mine would bring progress for the world, progress for Colombia, but what it brought was sadness and destruction for Colombia because we were displaced from our villages, from our lands," added Inés Pérez.[12]

One village, Tabaco, was razed by company bulldozers in August 2001. For years, Tabaco had been subject to the effects of blasting, dust, land loss, job loss, and air and water contamination. Residents insisted that their village—founded in the late eighteenth century by Africans who liberated themselves at sea and landed in Colombia as free men and women—should be collectively relocated, its history and culture acknowledged. The company refused, instead offering individuals minimal prices for their property. Some eventually agreed to sell, and those who did not were dragged from their homes one fateful day in August. Half a dozen smaller settlements suffered the same fate; nearby villages and indigenous reservations that remained found their lands and livelihoods destroyed, while the mine refused to acknowledge that its operations were affecting them.

Finding little recourse in Colombia, villagers—working through a local lawyer and the indigenous organization Yanama—sought international support. "We've exhausted all avenues here in La Guajira, in all of Colombia," Emilio Pérez explained. "We've gone to the courts and they've refused to help us. The mine has so much power, wherever we go, we talk to officials one day, and the next day the mine goes and when we return the officials won't meet with us because the mine has paid them off."[13]

During the 1980s and 1990s, solidarity organizations in Europe and the United States had grown to challenge U.S. and multinational interventions in Latin America and to support movements for social change there. Some, like the London-based Partizans (People Against Rio Tinto and its Subsidiaries), focused particularly on the abuses of multinational mining companies. Representatives from the Colombian mining region traveled to address Exxon shareholders in Dallas and, when the mine was sold to a consortium of European-based companies, to their headquarters in England and Switzerland. Coal-burning power plants from Massachusetts to New Brunswick and Nova Scotia acknowledged that they were importing Cerrejón coal, and local organizations in these regions, including environmental groups, unions, and Latin America solidarity groups, began to ask questions about the impact of the Colombian mines.[14] By 2002, these organizations were sponsoring regular tours by Colombian activists and, in 2006, they sponsored the first international delegation to the region in conjunction with Witness for Peace. The international networks had grown out of years of work opposing U.S. military interventions and corporate abuses in Latin America. As Colombia surged to the forefront of U.S. hemispheric involvement in terms of both investment and aid, the coal connection proved a potent organizing focus.

Colombian mining unions also faced adverse conditions at home, with weak labor laws, powerful multinationals, and right-wing paramilitaries with ties both to government and foreign companies. When the army occupied the Cerrejón mine during contract negotiations in the 1990s, or when paramilitaries murdered three union leaders at the Drummond mine in 2001, the Colombian unions sought support from the UMWA, the United Steelworkers of America (USWA), and the AFL-CIO Solidarity Center.

The international campaign grew to include regular speaking tours by Colombian representatives in the United States, Canada, and Europe, protests at shareholders' meetings, letter-writing campaigns, support from politicians, publication of a book about the company's human rights violations, and four international delegations to the Colombian mining region.[15] Unions in the United States, Canada, and Europe, including the USWA and the Public Service Alliance of Canada, played an important role in supporting both Colombian unions *and* the communities fighting the coal companies.

Organized labor in Colombia has played a strikingly different role in the country's late-twentieth-century social struggles than its counterpart in the United States. Colombia's coal unions grew from a tradition of militantly leftist and anti-imperialist unions in the energy sector. The oil workers' union had strong links with Colombia's Communist Party and played a key role in demanding nationalization of the country's oil industry. Today the two main coal mining unions, Sintracarbón and Sintramienergética, share an analysis that combines a strong class orientation and militant critique of capitalism—known in Spanish as *clasista*—with a nationalist anti-imperialism that denounces foreign companies for looting the country's natural resources and opposes U.S. interventionism and its economic agenda for Latin America. This stance naturally leads to some suspicion of the AFL-CIO, which has a history of antileftist activities in both the United States and Colombia. Nevertheless, international solidarity has been very important to these as well as other Colombian unions.

The ideological orientation of the unions in the coal region leads them to see the social and environmental impact of coal mining as part of an unequal global economic system and the exploitation of the Third World poor. Foreign companies loot natural resources, they understand, and the same corporations destroy the livelihoods of the Afro-Colombian and indigenous inhabitants of the region. The unions' national and class interests position them clearly on the side of the communities against the foreign companies—even if their members' own livelihoods depend on the companies.

Despite the unions' theoretical orientation, however, it was not until international solidarity activists contacted the Colombian unions that they made contact with mining communities. The gap between the mine workers and the indigenous and Afro-Colombian communities is vast: union workers are mostly from nearby cities, not the small villages where residents have no access to running water, schools, electricity, or health services. Union leaders visited the communities with an international delegation in the fall of 2006 and, inspired by the experience, began a process of working with community leaders to develop an unprecedented demand for their 2006 collective bargaining proposal: company recognition of and negotiation with the communities. Since then the union has been a strong and vocal advocate of communities' rights, and community members have come out to demonstrate and protest in support of the union during contract negotiations and when union leaders have been threatened by right-wing paramilitaries. International interest in the communities was a factor inspiring the unions to get involved, given the importance of international support for Colombian unions and other social movements faced with domestic repression. As with the Kentucky-Colombia connection, linking with new allies led both groups to deepen their analysis of their place in a global economy.

In December 2008, the campaign won an important victory when Cerrejón signed an agreement with the displaced community of Tabaco promising to purchase land for a new village, compensate those displaced, and build a community center, roads, infrastructure, and sustainable development projects for the relocated population.

Connecting North and South

Unions, environmentalists, and communities in Appalachia are entangled in the same web of global relations and transformations as those in Colombia. Late-twentieth-century global economic restructuring that shifted production and even coal mining to the Global South has profound implications for organizations in both regions. Yet their different positions in the global system mean unions and communities in the two regions have very different histories, goals, and strategies. When they first made contact at the beginning of the twenty-first century, activists in both regions felt that new world-views were opened, and their potential spheres and imaginations for organizing expanded.

Though certain members of coal-affected communities in Appalachia have been disappointed with the role the UMWA has taken in recent years, Colombian communities have found a strong ally in unions prepared to advocate for their demands. The communities, meanwhile, are more limited in their demands: they are seeking relocation. Although community members articulate a substantive critique of coal mining, given the political and economic climate, they do not feel empowered to seek larger-scale change that could affect how—or whether—coal mining occurs at all. In Colombia, it is in fact the union movement that is leading the battle for substantive changes in the economic and environmental structure of the coal industry. And the unions clearly see this as part of a global struggle.

One might imagine that unions in the North would be more militant and take stronger and more daring social positions than in the South. In the North, legal rights and protections for labor are stronger, and companies are more restrained by law and less likely to resort to extralegal attacks on unions. However, often the opposite has occurred. Unions in the North are more timid and prone to concessions, while unions in the South have taken the lead globally in radical thought and action that challenge foreign investors, neoliberalism, and even capitalism itself. In eastern Kentucky, the site of epic battles for labor rights through the 1970s, there are now no unionized coal mines at all.[16] When community organizations there have sought union support in their campaigns, they have often found their goals and tactics undercut as the UMWA urged compromise with the mining industry in the interest of saving jobs. Several Kentuckians commented, after meeting with Colombian unionists, that the Colombians' working conditions and the violence they faced for their union activities reminded them of Kentucky's labor history. "Maybe they can learn from what happened here," one KFTC member suggested, "so that their unions don't suffer the same decline ours has."

Inhabitants of the coal regions of Appalachia and Colombia might not belong to explicitly environmental organizations, and may not even identify themselves as environmentalists. Their struggles to preserve the land, air, water, and ecosystems in the face of open-pit coal mining, however, put them on the forefront of environmental justice movements North and South, even if mainstream environmental groups have been slow to acknowledge their leadership or role. Organizations in the two areas felt the power of this link when they first met in the summer of 2008. Members of KFTC who participated in a Witness for Peace delegation to the Colombian coal region were struck by the devastation around Colombian mines, the similarities to their own situation in Kentucky, the union's open critique of the coal industry and support for mining communities, and began to see their own struggle in a global context.

KFTC member Raúl Urias observed after participating in the delegation: "Here in America, we're worried about our X-Boxes and what color our cell phones are. To witness what's happening in the rest of the world, to feel their words, their sorrow and despair wash over you—*it changed me*. I've already started doing things differently when it comes to what I buy and how I use electricity. I'm not going to do anything that fuels other people's despair and hurt. I've talked to my family and we're definitely going to wean ourselves off of what we don't need."[17] Another delegation participant, Sara Pennington, contributed a section entitled "Eastern Kentucky: Turning Mountain Tops into Mine Waste" to a Greenpeace report on the global impact of coal.[18]

KFTC was eager to participate in a fall 2008 tour in the eastern United States by Colombian coal union leaders. The union leaders spent two weeks in Kentucky and West Virginia, and were overwhelmed with the devastation they saw. "I knew this happened in Colombia," one marveled. "But this is the first world! I can't believe the lack of regulation here. They are doing things in Kentucky that are worse than what they do in Colombia."

In subsequent presentations, the Colombians continually emphasized their shock at viewing firsthand the conditions in Kentucky. KFTC members who accompanied them were also moved at seeing their own struggle through the eyes of Colombian unionists. Audiences were compelled by the stories they heard, but also by the invitation to understand the global nature of the problem. At the Hindman Settlement School, the Colombians spoke to an audience of longtime KFTC members. The question and answer session after their talk turned into a forum for sharing stories and experiences. "One of our members, the widow of a coal miner who died of black lung, who is dealing with strip mining now herself, made a strong connection to what's happening in Colombia to what happened to her husband as a worker, and what is happening to her community. She really wanted to share. Based on the presentation, she, and others, began to comment that the same thing is happening in both places, for the same reasons—for profit for outsiders."

"We are starting to think about our own struggle in different ways," explained one KFTC member. "Our exchanges with the Colombians have encouraged us to think about our situation in terms of human rights. There are organizations we had never thought about working with, who we now see as potential allies."[19]

In the summer of 2009, KFTC worked with Witness for Peace to put together a binational delegation to both the Kentucky and Colombian coalfields. Both

Wayuu indigenous Colombian leader Jairo Fuentes Epiayu speaks of the true cost of coal at a Mountain Justice training, Whitesburg, Kentucky, May 2010. (Photo by Patricia Tarquino)

groups felt that the opportunity to understand the global and systemic nature of the problems their communities faced had a profound effect on their consciousness and organizing. Applications from KFTC members to participate in this second trip skyrocketed.

Meanwhile, coal consumers are also beginning to look beyond the power plants that pollute their own cities and toward the life cycle of coal. Local environmental activists from Nova Scotia to Massachusetts have traveled to Appalachia and Colombia to see where their coal comes from.[20] Campaigns that began with the goal of cleaning up individual plants are now looking more structurally at global inequality and foreign and energy policies. At the March 2009 youth Power Shift demonstrations in Washington, D.C., demanding federal action on climate change, coalfield residents were on the front lines. "We're starting to see that we're attached to the climate movement, and the climate movement sees that they're attached to us, because we're on the extraction end," one participant noted. "And we don't just want to stop coal here so they can mine it somewhere else. Our struggle is connected to coal regions around the world."[21]

Notes

1. See, for example, Tom Athanasiou, *Divided Planet: The Ecology of Rich and Poor* (University of Georgia Press, 1998), for a discussion of the narrow social and geographical focus of mainstream environmental organizations in the United States.

2. Robert H. Zieger, *John L. Lewis: Labor Leader* (Boston: Twayne Publishers, 1988), 60.

3. Ibid., 150.

4. For more on the history of control and prohibition legislation, see Chad Montrie, *To Save the Land and People* (Chapel Hill: University of North Carolina Press, 2003).

5. *Buchanan v. Watson* (290 S.W. 2nd 40), 40–43; David Schneider, "Strip Mining in Kentucky," *Kentucky Law Journal* 59 (1971): 654; Harry Caudill, *My Land is Dying* (New York: E.P. Dutton, 1973), 65, 69; Bruce Daniel Rogers, "Public Policy and Pollution Abatement: TVA and Strip Mining" (Ph.D. diss., Indiana University, 1973), 8–9.

6. *New York Times*, July 30, 1967, 29; Caudill, *My Land is Dying*, 87; *Louisville Courier Journal*, August 10, 1967, 1; T. N. Bethel, "Hot Time Ahead," in *Appalachia in the Sixties: Decade of Reawakening*, eds. David S. Walls and John B. Stephenson (Lexington: University Press of Kentucky, 1972), 116–19.

7. Wayne Keith was a son-in-law to Robert Hamm and was present when Hamm was interviewed, interjecting at times with his own views about coal mining in southwestern Virginia. Robert W. Hamm, interview by Ray Ringley, September 30, 1973, Tapes 186 A & B, Transcript No. 81, 7, Appalachian Oral History Project—Emory & Henry College Oral History Collection.

8. Montrie, *To Save the Land and People*, 177–78.

9. Ken Ward Jr., "Mining the Mountains: Industry, Critics Look for Mountaintop Removal Alternative," *Charleston Gazette*, June 6, 1999.

10. Cecil E. Roberts, "Time for Some Facts about Coal," *Charleston Gazette*, May 3, 2009.

11. José Julio Pérez, "Testimony from the Community of Tabaco," in Aviva Chomsky, Garry Leech, and Steve Striffler, eds., *The People Behind Colombian Coal: Mining, Multinationals and Human Rights* (Bogotá: Casa Editorial Pisando Callos, 2007), 192.

12. Interview with Don McConnell, November 2006. Transcript in possession of Aviva Chomsky.

13. Emilio Pérez, interview with Don McConnell, November 2006. Transcript in possession of Aviva Chomsky.

14. These organizations included, in Canada, the Atlantic Regional Solidarity Network and the Public Service Alliance of Canada; in the United States, the United Steelworkers, HealthLink (in Massachusetts), and Colombia Vive (a Colombia solidarity group); in Great Britain, the Colombia Solidarity Campaign and the Mines and Communities Network; and, in Switzerland, the Switzerland-Colombia Working Group (ASK).

15. Chomsky, Leech, and Striffler, eds., *People Behind Colombian Coal*.

16. See Mary Jo Schafer, "UMWA has no working miners in Eastern Kentucky, but union's heritage remains strong," Institute for Rural Journalism and Community Issues, August 2007, http://www.uky.edu/CommInfoStudies/IRJCI/UMW.htm, and United States Department of Energy, Energy Information Administration, *Coal Industry Annual,* Table 11: Coal Production by State, Mine Type, and Union Type, 2000. http://www.eia.doe.gov/cneaf/coal/cia/html/tbl11p01p1.html.

17. KFTC staff, "KFTC members return from coal tour of Colombia," June 9, 2008. http://www.kftc.org/blog/archive/2008/06/06/colombia1.

18. Sara Pennington, "Turning Mountain Tops into Mine Waste," in *The True Cost of Coal: How People and the Planet Are Paying the Price for the World's Dirtiest Fuel,* 58–61. http://www.greenpeace.org/raw/content/international/press/reports/cost-of-coal.pdf.

19. Both quotes come from a telephone interview by Aviva Chomsky with a KFTC member in April 2009. The interviewee preferred to remain anonymous. Transcript in Chomsky's possession.

20. Chomsky led these delegations in August 2006, November 2006, August 2007, May 2008, and May–June 2009.

21. KFTC member, April 2009 interview.

Transformations in Place

Barbara Ellen Smith and Stephen L. Fisher

"Place" in Appalachia is, for many who call it home, the place of mountains. As the ground on which we stand, this place is at once material and symbolic: tangible residue of geologic time, the mountains are also the home of our memories and the imagined landscape of our future. Invoking mountains as the "place" of Appalachia does not mean, of course, that all residents find this the most personally relevant depiction; nor does it mean that place, more generally, is a physical backdrop or fixed and bounded territory. Although in one sense specific to individual context and biography (birthplace, homeplace, and so forth), place is above all a collective product, experience, and possibility. The feminist geographer Doreen Massey describes it as "a particular constellation of social relations, meeting and weaving together at a particular locus," to which historian Arif Dirlik adds, emphasizing the environmental dimension, "place is the location where the social and the natural meet."[1]

In this era of ruthless deracination called globalization, place attachments and the politics of place have become increasingly salient in collective mobilizations across the spectrum of political life. Whether seeking to defend cherished places and ways of life or inventing new place-based meanings and futures—and the most successful campaigns do both—activists worldwide are mobilizing place-related symbols, metaphors, demands, and affinities as countervailing sources of resistance. Never self-evident, never "given," place is coming alive as a potent force in the hands of those who understand not just its shortcomings but its critical, democratic, and collective potentials and are able to harness its emotive and symbolic powers for progressive political organizing.

This conclusion draws on contemporary theory from several perspectives and disciplines to illuminate lessons from the place-based struggles documented in this book. The first section explores some of the ways that power in Appalachia is exercised through the production and control of space—for example, through the militarization, privatization, marginalization, or outright destruction of specific places. This approach illustrates why place matters in the present political moment and allows us to analyze the potential of place as a "resource for change." The second section focuses on lessons about "bridging divides" and "scaling up" to identify some of the multiple meanings of and strategies for transforming places in Appalachia and beyond.

We turn to theory in this conclusion because we find that it can open our eyes to new ways of seeing that which we might otherwise take for granted or miss altogether. At its best, theory shines a bright light on present social realities, illuminating both underlying sources of injustice and hidden possibilities for alternative futures. The theory that we discuss in the following sections underscores that place is fundamental to the operation of power, the production of inequality, and the mobilization of resistance. In so doing, it also reveals that there is nothing fixed or inevitable about the current production of Appalachia as a place of intensive human and environmental exploitation. Another place is possible if we have the imagination to envision it and the collective political will to create it.

The Politics of Place

The resonance of place with human memory, emotion, and relationships lends it great evocative power but does not necessarily render it political for those in pursuit of social justice. The case for the politics of place, as we argue below, lies elsewhere. In this section, we draw selectively from recent theoretical literature on place-based organizing to explore several propositions that serve to situate the case studies in this volume within more general arguments. These propositions are partial and by no means exhaust the relevant literature, which is vast and growing like kudzu.

We have found the work of critical geographers particularly helpful in thinking through the political meaning and potential of place-based struggles. Concepts of "space" and "place," among many others, are central to geography but not necessarily familiar as theoretical terms to activists and scholars in Appalachia, so a few words of definition are in order.[2] Popular usage of the terms space and place often parallels the opposition between global and local: space is large, abstract, universal, "out there," whereas place is small, tangible, particular, close by. Place is where the embodied person lives; space is the locus of nonhuman systems and forces such as capitalism and neoliberalism that impinge on but so often escape the constraints of (and political demands emanating from) specific places. In the present era of global capitalism, David Harvey, for example, argues that space is the terrain of capital; labor and oppositional citizens' groups have on occasion been able to influence social relations in specific places, but never to command space.[3]

We find this formulation useful insofar as it points to the power-laden reality that those with wealth and position are able to initiate and coordinate social and economic activities, networks, and relationships across the globe; their capacity thereby to influence fundamental aspects of daily life—from the local supply of food to the allocation of national budgets for education—in far-flung places is great, and at present exceeds the countervailing efforts and capacities of transnational activists. Nonetheless, this opposition between global/local and space/place also tends toward a determinist conclusion: global processes always happen elsewhere (in space), and place is the passive victim of forces that are seldom if ever susceptible to local intervention.

An alternative perspective redefines these polar oppositions as deeply embedded, mutual interactions: virtually every place on the globe has long been shaped by and continues to participate in networks of relationships that stretch far beyond its boundaries; at the same time, the global is continuously *produced* through the activities of human beings in specific locales.[4] Processes of globalization, even as they may shape local ways of life, can only "take place" within—and are thereby everywhere dependent on—the contingencies, particularities, and potential resistance of specific locales. Distinctions between the global and the local, as well as between space and place, become more blurry from this perspective, as their coproduction comes into view. In the words of Doreen Massey, every place is a "meeting place," in the sense that it represents a node in wider "networks of social relations and understandings . . . And this in turn allows a sense of place which is extroverted, which includes a consciousness of its links with the wider world, which integrates in a positive way the global and the local."[5]

Within this relational approach, space becomes the ensemble of interconnected social relations, which at their widest stretch across the globe, and every place appears as a unique nexus within these interconnections. Numerous political questions and implications for place-based organizing ensue from these assertions. What specific social groups or processes tend to dominate space at this moment in history, and how can those who believe in democracy and social justice effectively challenge that domination when it threatens those values? What place-based strategies are most effective in gaining traction with wider relations of power? Which places are most crucial for political organizing and intervention?

It is notable that "defense of place"—even though this rhetoric is important in certain struggles examined in this book—does not in any straightforward sense become a primary aim of activism that reaches toward transformation of wider relations of power. This is, above all, because every place, even the beloved homeplace of Appalachia, is marked by and implicated in the exploitation and injustice that are produced beyond, but also within, its boundaries. The privileged and powerful are not only "outsiders" but also in our midst—indeed, in some instances are *us*. Transforming places requires internal transformation; the struggle for democracy and social justice has a home front.

The Place of Appalachia

Returning to the diverse, place-based struggles documented in this book, how does a theoretical perspective help us understand their political significance and potential? First, place matters in the pursuit of social justice because inequality and the power relations that produce it are spatial. Some of the earliest and most influential efforts to theorize Appalachia as a region through a critical lens (as opposed to sentimental or manifestly pejorative approaches) recognized this reality. Rick Simon, for example, employing a Marxist framework, asserted that Appalachia represented a spatialized manifestation of class exploitation.[6] In an era of protracted labor uprisings, particularly in the central Appalachian coalfields, and increased recognition of the relationship between regional poverty and a monoeconomy that produced occupational disability and death as routinely as commodities, this was a compelling formulation. More popular and lasting in influence was an internal colony approach, that is, the assertion that Appalachia was constituted as a region/place through colonization by "outside" interests that ripped off the natural wealth of timber, natural gas, and coal, and justified doing so with a repertoire of vicious stereotypes of Appalachian people. The persistence of corporate domination and offensive hillbilly stereotypes has reinforced this perspective over time, with the unfortunate result that reductive moralisms (insider "good," outsider "bad") too often have tended to substitute for deeper social analysis and political critique.[7]

Neither theory applied the implicit premise, that inequality is spatial, to social relations *within* Appalachia, even though racism, racial segregation, sexual oppression, homophobia, and class exploitation were and are significantly present. It is a measure of the deepening complexity and reach of organizing in Appalachia that, compared with the essays in Stephen L. Fisher's *Fighting Back in Appalachia* (published in 1993), so many chapters in this book document serious efforts to address such social divisions and inequities among organizational constituents and across coalitions.[8] For example, intermediary organizations like the Center for Participatory Change (chapter 9) and the Southern Empowerment Project (chapter 8), the statewide Virginia Organizing (chapter 12), and the regional Appalachian Women's Alliance (chapter 7), although quite different in their strategic approaches, have all foregrounded racial justice as a political priority.

Second, place matters because Goliaths like capitalism, neoliberalism, and globalization are produced in specific places, where the "particular constellation of social relations" conditions the prospects and strategies for effective resistance to these otherwise giant abstractions. Globalization, for example, as it is generated in Appalachia, less frequently involves the frenetic space-time compression epitomized in financial trading, multinational jumble of languages and cultural symbols, or cosmopolitan placelessness described and theorized by observers of global cities.[9] Space-time compression in Appalachia more likely takes form as an exhausted working-class woman: recall the pregnant Latina poultry worker (chapter 11), who was forced to work intensively without bathroom breaks, organized outside of work to contest the company's inhumane treatment, prepared at home for her new baby, and communicated regularly across national borders to maintain family and community ties.

These contrasting examples point more to class distinctions than to any absolute difference between Appalachia and large urban centers, for globalization and neoliberalism generate similarities and linkages between these two spaces. Many of these commonalities, however, tend to be obscured by racial and spatial difference. Abandonment of specific racialized zones of central cities by capital and the state (except in its coercive apparatus of law enforcement) finds parallels across vast portions of rural Appalachia, where deindustrialization and disinvestment are no less severe.[10] The human consequences of social and economic marginalization can also coincide, as revealed in the recognition of similarities between the scourge of OxyContin abuse in rural southwest Virginia and the drug traffic of Harlem (chapter 13). There are related, even more direct, linkages: "development" in rural Appalachian areas has at times taken form as prison complexes, which provide jobs to rural whites who facilitate the containment of incarcerated, disproportionately poor, disproportionately black and Latino men and women from distant urban areas.[11]

Such linkages—and there are far more—caution those who would find meaning in the presumed uniqueness of Appalachia and its many places or, for that matter, who would elevate the achievements and desirability of the urban over all other spaces across the globe.[12] Interdependent and mutually defining economic, social, cultural, and political bonds between the urban and the rural become in many instances thicker and more complex with the accelerated global expansion of capitalism; they illustrate the relational understanding of place articulated above: a specific "place" does not acquire meaning through some bounded, internal history, but through the specificity of its relationships with social processes and histories that stretch far beyond a particular locale.[13]

Third, place matters because the earth and its ensemble of places, including those uninhabited by humans, are in peril. Urban sprawl, "grow or die" philosophies of economic development (chapter 3), consumerist excess, and the disappearance of small farms (chapter 14)—these and other expansionary and destructive elements of global capitalism are at stake in the environmental crisis. Within Appalachia, mountaintop removal coal mining (MTR) is the most egregious, visible, and heartbreaking example. The controversy over MTR, as illustrated in chapters 15–17 of this volume, is in one sense a classic instance of "jobs versus environment." But it also illuminates additional elements of place-based struggles: the "place" that people seek to defend, restore, revitalize, or transform is rarely self-evident in its boundaries or meanings in that the visions of its past and desires for its future are not identical among those who would claim it as home. In the case of MTR, Appalachian residents are deeply divided over whether the mountains where they live represent primarily beloved homeplaces, ancient ecosystems, God's creation, or coalfields through which they and their ancestors have proudly made a living. These varied perspectives and the different knowledge that each entails drive the vision of a "knowledge commons" (chapter 16).

The struggle over MTR is intensely emotional not only because the stakes are so high but also because these competing claims to place collide within the same social groups and geographic locales. For those who view place as constituted through the material and metaphorical homeplace of mountains, practices that systematically level mountain peaks, reducing them to rubble that clogs and acidifies watersheds, are destroying not only the physical environment but the very soul of the place itself. They sometimes call on a past of intergenerational continuity on the land to condemn the destruction of MTR and, similar to and at times in collaboration with activists in Mountain Justice (chapter 15), envision a future of "green jobs" and clean energy production through, for example, wind farms. But for those who view place through a different past, the intergenerational legacies of coal mining and struggles for unionization (chapter 17), a "green" future beyond coal is both unimaginable and undesirable and entails destruction of the very place they claim as home. The result is a battle over place that resembles civil war.[14]

The three propositions discussed above argue for the political importance of place based on the spatial dimensions of social hierarchies and the ways that large social processes are produced in specific places. The remainder of this section argues for the *advantages* of place-based organizing, while recognizing that there are other important approaches to the goal of social justice and that place-based strategies must confront many obstacles to effectiveness and success.

Place as a Resource for Change

Perhaps most obviously, place-based organizing can be advantageous because political governance and electoral processes are organized territorially (via city councils, county commissions, state legislatures, and so forth). The corruption of democracy by intentionally antidemocratic structures (for example, the Electoral College and the two-party, winner-take-all system) and corporate money and influence heightens the importance of political spaces where democratic ideals and practices might still be nurtured and modeled. Local and even state-level political organizing offers a feasible scale to work toward this goal, but the potential for recapturing democracy is uneven and requires extraordinary effort to pursue. As chapter 3 on land-use organizing in Blount County, Tennessee, illustrates, local businesses, political elites, and entrenched discourses about what is possible and desirable can converge to stymie challenges to the status quo and preclude alternative visions of the future. Moreover, the lack of anonymity in rural locations, combined with the increased significance of patronage as industries and jobs disappear, can silence potential opposition. However, as Virginia Organizing demonstrates, state-level action can offer political traction and impact, even in the absence of shared political goals and priorities, through such practices as "borrowing and sharing power" that unify constituents in a common political space (chapter 12).

Although state-based, multi-issue organizational models have become significant in Appalachia (examples include not only Virginia Organizing but also Kentuckians For The Commonwealth and Statewide Organizing for Community eMpowerment in Tennessee), it is important to recognize as well the novel organizational forms that do not define their spatial reach in terms of established political territories. Mountain Justice, for example, partakes of and contributes to a network of environmental activists that spans places, national borders, and social identities, and, utilizing electronic communication through a flat organizational structure, links civil disobedience against mountaintop removal and other actions on the ground to this wider network. For Mountain Justice, "claiming space" is less about developing credibility and influence in established political units and more about intentional, visible trespass into spaces that mountain-destroying corporations produce and presume to control (whether their urban corporate headquarters or the actual sites of mountaintop removal). The organization "jumps scale" in the sense that it does not build incrementally from local chapters toward ever higher levels of political influence (county, state, national), but rather engages in "guerrilla" tactics that, as the authors of chapter 15 acknowledge, can antagonize counterpart organizations accountable to place-based constituencies in specific locations.

Second and far less obviously, place-based organizing can build on the fact that material survival, even in the U.S. capitalist economy, involves noncapitalist economic practices that are central to the social relations of any place. Feminists have long pointed to the enormous amount of unpaid and often unrecognized labor, typically performed by women, that is required for children to be raised, families to be fed, houses to be cleaned.[15] Moreover, in the context of chronically scarce, or at least erratically available, jobs and other sources of income, people in places across Appalachia—like those in low-income, inner-city neighborhoods and other locations of relentless economic adversity—have borrowed, shared, bartered, reciprocated, and in other ways sought to ensure their own and others' survival.[16] Domestic labor and small-scale, face-to-face economic relations will not somehow bring down and replace capitalism. But we do suggest that envisioning a future beyond neoliberal globalization and endless capitalist expansion (and destruction) can best be cultivated from existing seeds of possibility. This requires recognizing the presence of noncapitalist economic relations and, to the extent that they represent socially just alternatives, working to reinvent ourselves and our social relations accordingly in tangible ways. As Julie Graham and Katherine Gibson (whose collaborative pen name is J. K. Gibson-Graham) observe in *The End of Capitalism (As We Knew It)*, feminist (and anti-racist) organizations presume that, despite (indeed because of) the present context, it is possible, in fact urgent, to create alternative feminist living arrangements, workplaces, cultural products, and institutions. But the possibility that class exploitation and capitalist excess might also be overcome in part through similar, admittedly partial, re-envisioned economic arrangements in the present is far more rarely acknowledged or pursued.[17]

Several initiatives described in this book exemplify related possibilities: the Burnsville Land Community, which created a land trust that purchased a mobile home park where many Latino residents of Asheville live, and the worker-owned cooperative, Opportunity Threads, a small, environmentally friendly textile plant, are among the relevant examples (chapter 9). The place-based organizing of the Community Farm Alliance (CFA) also illustrates a step toward economic alternatives (chapter 14). These rural tobacco farmers reinvented themselves as food producers and cooperatively organized a direct distribution system to urban markets (not such a foreign idea in many agricultural settings, but one that had faded with dominance and control by corporate agribusiness). Their capacity to develop a Locally Integrated Food Economy was dependent in part on securing capital investment through the state of Kentucky, where their political influence attested to the wisdom of a long-haul organizing strategy: CFA organizers had spent fifteen years developing leadership skills and county-based chapters among its farmer-members across rural Kentucky, so the organization was in a position to mobilize quickly and effectively when opportunity arose.

Third, the concept of "place" bundles together cultural memories, practices, and beliefs with social relations to generate the potential for powerful, unifying identities. Once again, however, the meaning of place and any associated identity is produced, not received. Guy and Candie Carawan argue, based on decades of experience as cultural organizers at the Highlander Center in east Tennessee, that Appalachian identity and related cultural expressions must be deliberately cultivated and nourished by individuals and institutions that recognize the value of cultural forms, place, and identity to resistance efforts.[18] These points are repeatedly illustrated throughout this book: "place," in every chapter where it figures prominently as a form of identity, is a product of intentional organizing. In some cases, this place-based identity is regional. It is telling in this regard that a primary example of regional identity used effectively as a platform for organizing involves migrants who "become" Appalachian in part through becoming embattled "minorities" in an urban locale, Cincinnati, outside the geographic territory of the region (chapter 4).

In this identity-based organizing among Appalachian migrants in Cincinnati, as well as in similar efforts described in other chapters, cultural repertoires are central to the development of politicized identities. Katie Richards-Schuster and Rebecca O'Doherty's discussion of the innovative Appalachian Media Institute

(AMI), which utilizes photography and video to foster positive regional identity among Appalachian youth so that they might re-envision themselves, their communities, and their role in changing them (chapter 5); Maureen Mullinax's analysis of how community-based arts, oral history, and religious music help build community capacity for democratic practice in Harlan County, Kentucky (chapter 6); and the Appalachian Women's Alliance's use of the arts and women's stories to promote an Appalachian feminist agenda (chapter 7)—all attest to the importance of cultural practices in creating and reinforcing place-based identities. They illustrate how deliberate claiming of identity can be an act of resistance, a way of fighting back against Appalachian stereotypes, which in turn can undergird organizing against exploitation and discrimination in the region.

However, place-based identity is always at risk of becoming place-bound, that is, insular and exclusionary. The tendency for place to be romantically conflated with "community," envisioned as a harmonious (and homogeneous) space of shared interests and values, often informs such insularity.[19] AMI's efforts, for example, reveal that claiming Appalachia can for some youth actually inhibit cross-community collaboration. In seeking to avert this possibility, the organizations mentioned above tend to use loosely defined notions of identity as bridges rather than as insulators, as connections struggled for and created. Their cultural strategies are highly varied and open-ended, for being Appalachian means something different depending on race, sexual identity, and other factors, including where you live in and out of the region. As a consequence of such intentional cultural politics, place-based identity in Appalachia can become critical, relational, and "extroverted," linking rather than insulating individuals and groups. By creating a place-defined people, bonded by oppression as well as resistance, place conveys a sense of who we are and want to become, and helps connect our lives and struggles in a particular place to related life experiences and struggles elsewhere.[20]

Fourth, place-based organizing works within the politically potent reality that place is inherently shared, it is collective; however, it is not necessarily public or democratic in the sense of accessible to and collectively governed by all. The tension between a collective investment in place, a shared sense of identity with place, and the private appropriation and even destruction of place forms a crucible of possibility that is just beginning to be realized. Privatization and securitization of public space are eradicating "the commons," but they are also making the struggle over space, enunciated in specific places, intensely political.[21] The opening chapter on the Oak Ridge Environmental Peace Alliance illustrates how trespassing on militarized space, in this case the blue line around the Y-12 bomb plant, can have transformative effects not only on those who engage in civil disobedience but also those who witness their courage. Similarly, anarcho-environmentalists affiliated with groups like Mountain Justice (chapter 15) intentionally and visibly trespass on the private property of coal companies, disrupting mining operations and refusing to leave, and in so doing question with their very bodies the right

Alissa Walsh participates in nonviolent civil disobedience protesting Dominion Power Company's plans for a new plant in Wise County, Virginia, June 30, 2008. (Photo by Rachel Sarah Blanton)

of corporations to destroy the potentially public space of mountains, watersheds, and wildlife.

The organizing strategy of RAIL Solution (chapter 2) is another excellent example of this conflict between the shared, potentially public character of place and its private appropriation. RAIL Solution was able to turn an anonymous (but publicly financed) stretch of interstate highway into a shared place via, among other actions, the rhetorical strategy, "I-81, it's our Main Street." Calling on this symbol of small-town Americana, RAIL Solution framed the residents of small cities and towns along the I-81 corridor as an egalitarian collectivity and reinforced that solidarity through e-mail and face-to-face meetings. In responding to that appeal, based on an invented but highly strategic definition of shared place, supporters of RAIL Solution worked to defeat the privatization of I-81 in part because, by their own accounts, they were inspired by belief in democracy, the desire to reclaim their political voice, and the possibility that, collectively, they could actually defeat a corporate giant.

The political potential of this fundamental tension between public claims to and private appropriations of place raises tough, unanswered questions for organized labor in the United States. The contrasts between the environmental stance of the

Colombian miners' union and the United Mine Workers of America (UMWA) turn in part on these unions' different relationships to and understandings of the politics of place (chapter 17). To be sure, the Colombian miners' union invoked deep and abiding class antagonisms to inform its response to the destruction of indigenous places. But that is part of the point: members of the Colombian union did not restrict their vision or solidarity to other miners but recognized that the wanton corporate destruction of small, indigenous communities represented a strand in the same web of power relations that they confronted in very different contexts as workers. Although the UMWA has episodically pursued linkages with community- and faith-based organizations, it most often remains uncommitted to place, that is, to the recognition that *the union and its members are implicated in place* and thereby in social relations that spill beyond but profoundly influence the strength of the UMWA and the labor movement more generally.

The brief and fragile strike-related cooperation between faith-based organizations and organized labor in Appalachia argues for, among other changes, labor's deeper engagement with the place-based, class-specific complexities of organized religion, including their own members' intertwined place- and faith-based loyalties (chapter 10). Latino poultry workers' successful, bottom-up organizing drive in east Tennessee (chapter 11) underscores the potent blend of class and racial/ ethnic solidarities that were forged in not only the workplace but also the wider immigrant community of Morristown, then bolstered by the place-based labor support organization, Jobs with Justice of East Tennessee (JwJET). At the end of the successful strike, JwJET found itself with no further role in relation to the fledgling local, while the Nashville-based headquarters of the local union found itself hard-pressed to service a distant group of new, Spanish-speaking members. But this is not the only potential outcome. Imagine the different strategies, commitments, and outcomes if the union had viewed this organizing drive as an occasion not just to build its membership base and enhance its leverage in relation to a corporate employer but as a wedge that could begin to open up notoriously anti-union Morristown as a more public and democratic place claimed by union members, community-based labor supporters, Spanish-speaking immigrants, and other progressive forces. What then? What if the unions that formed brief coalitions with faith-based organizations for the sole purpose of strike support during the Peabody Coal and Appalachian Regional Hospital campaigns had instead viewed these as long-term, strategic alliances that could reach both more deeply into working-class communities in Appalachia and more powerfully into state and national policy-making bodies? What then?

The need for such public spaces—and the political organizing to demand them—has become more intense with the neoliberal onslaught against government programs and regulations designed to promote social well-being and the ethos of collective responsibility that they represent. Aside from churches and other places of worship, there are fewer and fewer physical sites and social contexts in which people in places across Appalachia are able to come together for any collective purpose. De-unionization, consolidation of public schools, closure of regional organizations like the Commission on Religion in Appalachia and the Southern Empowerment Project, and the loss of other social gathering places and political organizations contribute to neoliberalism's valorization of individualism and hostility to the common good. Such a context requires political organizing that intentionally creates spaces in which constituents can gather, share a meal, sing a song or two, hold a meeting (or ten), and build the relationships that are central to contemporary organizing in the region. These gathering spaces may be in part virtual (blogs, listservs, social networking sites, and so forth), but the strong bonds that political organizing seeks to create, as the experiences of RAIL Solution, Mountain Justice, and the Oak Ridge Environmental Peace Alliance demonstrate, also require face-to-face contact.

Creating institutional spaces means not only procuring actual physical sites, such as Mountain Justice's campaign houses, but also "making space" for new people within nominally public institutions and existing social justice organizations by widening their purpose and constituency.[22] So, for example, the community college in Harlan County, Kentucky, has become a public space for bridging fundamental social divisions and building a more inclusive and democratic community through strategies of cultural transformation (chapter 6). In a more episodic and transitory fashion, certain local churches have become institutional spaces for supporting striking union members, distributing critical messages about nuclear weapons production, and creating farmers' markets in inner-city neighborhoods.

Social justice and cultural organizations can themselves model a form of public space.[23] This requires stretching their reach and accessibility so that new constituencies are able to participate and existing ones are able to do so more fully. Appalshop, the community-based media arts and education organization, has used several strategies to make its work more inviting to young people, with the Appalachian Media Institute (AMI) a prime example; many youth who participate in AMI's programs view it as a rare "safe space" for developing and expressing their personal and political identities. The Southern Empowerment Project and the Appalachian Women's Alliance took on homophobia when gay participants reported problems in local communities. Women loosely affiliated with the Urban Appalachian Council formed their own subgroup to address their health-related concerns (chapter 4). The Center for Participatory Change (CPC) extended its grassroots support organizing to emergent Latino groups and leaders and in so doing transformed itself, learning, among other lessons, that "multilingual spaces are not optional."

These institutional spaces resemble but are not precisely the "free spaces" identified by neopopulists and critiqued by Fisher in his "conclusion" to *Fighting Back in Appalachia*. These institutional spaces must be intentionally created; they are not necessarily part of the traditional fabric of social life, in part because they seek to welcome those who do not ordinarily encounter one another as equals in the same social space. These spaces are thus not seamlessly unified or internally homogeneous, they are messy and sometimes fractious. But they are also spaces of crucial encounters across difference and thereby seedbeds for the growth of new collectivities and more democratic practices.

Certain models of political organizing in urban settings also reach in this direction. In New York, Los Angeles, and other major cities, nascent movements are combining an array of local labor unions and community-based organizations in powerful coalitions to demand the "right to the city," a goal that aims far beyond access to an expanded array of public services. In the words of Edward W. Soja, "Seeking the right to the city is a continuous and more radical effort at spatial reappropriation, claiming an active presence in all that takes place in urban life under capitalism."[24] Put somewhat differently by Don Mitchell, the "right to the city" is an effort to *produce* space that is public; it is in demanding the right to the city that public space is created over and against the claims of property, propriety, security, and privatization.[25] In Appalachia, we see stirrings, exemplified by chapters in this book and many more efforts beyond, that move toward similar production of space and that could become far more expansive and intentional. "The coal belongs to the people," disabled coal miner Walter Burton Franklin of southern West Virginia doggedly argued.[26] Perhaps the mountains do as well. By building political power at different scales, implementing cooperative economic arrangements, inventing new places and place-based identities, and creating more open, accessible institutions, organizers are re-visioning places across the region as more public, democratic space.

Transforming Places

There is an inherent though by no means insurmountable contradiction between a localistic, romantic "sense of place," which equates place with home and longings for the deeply familiar, and the critical, outward-looking definition of place articulated here. There are also related tensions between the necessity of wide, extralocal (ultimately global) political reach and the localism of much place-based identity, motivation, and organizational capacity.[27] David Harvey's exploration of both the importance and limitations of "militant particularisms," the solidarities and visionary alternatives forged through continuity in place and local struggles against injustice and exploitation, is relevant here. How, he asks, can we "fight to transform militant particularism into something more substantial on the world stage of capitalism?"[28]

This section focuses on several key lessons from chapters in this book that begin to answer this question. Taken together, they do not constitute a recipe. There is not a dominant model of how social change occurs or a single vision of organizing. Indeed, these lessons and the organizing approaches that give rise to them are diverse and in some instances contradictory. Rather than view this variety as a weakness, we consider it a strength in that it begins to depict the complexity and range of "militant particularisms." Our purpose here is neither to critique these different approaches nor repeat the significant lessons that the authors have articulated in their chapters; rather, it is to lift up their insights about transforming relations within and among places and thereby expanding future possibilities beyond those defined by global capitalism.

Bridging Divides

The place-based organizing documented in this book is first and foremost about creating strong collectivities of people that can alter relations of power within and across specific places. Accomplishing this involves, among other strategies, relational organizing, that is, building strong interpersonal relationships and social bonds, particularly among people who would not otherwise encounter one another and/or recognize their political commonalities. Their solidarity is in some instances based on shared social identity (for example, race or gender), but more commonly on a shared politics that emanates from their common context of place-based struggle and collective knowledge of injustice and exploitation. Intentional relationships create a bridge that can span one's own experience of oppression and the different forms of injustice that others experience. As organizers for the Center for Participatory Change argue in chapter 9, "Relationships seem to be the force that overcomes . . . paralysis [in the face of so many issues and needs]: when someone I care about is affected by injustice, then I feel that injustice myself, and I am moved to speak and to act." By the same token, as the experience of the Southern Empowerment Project in chapter 8 illuminates, the *loss* of key individuals attests to the importance of specific relationships in holding together organizations.

Drawing out, reflecting on, and collectively deepening knowledge among those who directly experience the problems they seek to address are key processes in relational organizing. These may take the form of sharing music and stories across deep social divides in Harlan County, Kentucky, creating, distributing, and discussing videos that view specific, locally manifested issues through a critical lens, or organizing transnational exchange visits between coalfield residents in Kentucky and Colombia. The seemingly simple but, in contexts of oppression, challenging process of *naming* the problem can be an important act of resistance and source of solidarity: for migrants in Cincinnati, identifying discrimination and hostility as collective problems they faced as Appalachians was a crucial step in their political development; similarly, for participants in the Appalachian Women's Alliance, naming domestic violence as a collective problem they would no longer tolerate generated solidarity as well as repercussions that further unified participants.

Collective knowledge production explicitly does *not* mean calling on academic and professional experts to define social problems and identify potential solutions; only in discrete instances where such expertise can serve political organizing goals, as, for example, in the medical and legal knowledge brought to bear on the problem of OxyContin abuse, do organizers call out the "experts." Those who live the problems own the solutions. At the same time, what can be known through immediate experience does not represent the limits of the knowledge required to understand local particularities in relation to wider social systems. Abstract concepts and theoretical knowledge are indispensable in this regard. A knowledge commons seeks to create a "meeting space" where differently situated individuals and groups can learn from one another and make the processes of knowledge production and circulation more widely collective and visible (chapter 16).

This, of course, does not mean that participants' perceptions, experiences, and knowledge seamlessly coincide. Attaining solidarity often involves contestation that is deeply complicated by not only political difference but also related dynamics of class, gender, race, national origin, sexual identity, and other social divides. The Appalachian Women's Alliance, for example, experienced the painful and turbulent consequences of class division among participants, which took a heavy toll on individuals and the organization as a whole.[29] However, in courageously facing class and other divisive differences head-on, the Alliance also became a regional support group for women embattled by sexism, racism, and homophobia in their local settings. Their commitment to internal transformation exemplifies an important insight with wide political relevance for all but the most narrow and homogeneous groups: the inequities we seek to overcome are not just "out there" but in our midst. Recognizing that these inequities can paralyze our capacity to overcome them, render our internal organizational practices antidemocratic and unjust, and undermine our political efforts to pursue social justice, many organizations, including the Alliance, Mountain Justice, and the Center for Participatory Change, have structured themselves according to principles of radical egalitarianism.

Relational organizing, then, may be seen as a strategic response to the observation that every place is a node in wider networks of social relations. This strategy goes beyond the politics of rational self-interest—here is what I and my group need and this is how we are going to get it—to recognize that the web of social relations and the operations of power within and through them implicate us in the lives of many different others. Race, gender, and class are not frozen categories of difference, rigid boxes of identity, but social relationships in which we are all engaged and for which we are all responsible. We do not create these relationships, they precede and shape us; but through relational organizing we seek to reinvent them. The prospect for—indeed, the very meaning of—social justice in any moment hinges on the practices of coalitions, alliances, and internally diverse organizations that can turn these divisive manifestations of oppression and domination into recognition of mutual interdependence and political solidarity.

Pursuing such solidarity means pushing against the combined weight of social custom, emotional self-protection, and entrenched power. It is exhausting. The Appalachian Women's Alliance is again instructive. The hostility that participants encountered in their local communities reinforced their allegiance to and need for the Alliance, but it also pulled the organization in the direction of mutual support and insularity rather than outward expansion and organizing. In these embattled times, when visionary alternatives seem so scarce and unlikely, how do we persist in the hard work of relational organizing and bridging divides? Even further, how do we scale up to achieve political impact across ever-wider stretches of social space?

Scaling Up

Globalization is reconfiguring the scale of political organizing. The proliferation of transnational organizations focused on issues ranging from climate change to sex trafficking derives in part from the seemingly self-evident reality that global problems require intervention at a global scale. Though we do not ultimately disagree with this premise, we do reject the corollary that is sometimes implied if not explicit: place-based organizing, particularly in rural areas, is "merely" local, necessarily place-bound, and therefore largely irrelevant or at least ineffective with regard to the global political challenges of the day. By contrast, we argue that globalization is produced in specific places in ways that reconfigure social relations within and among places and offer new opportunities for place-based organizing. Moreover, the political efforts documented in this book indicate that place-based organizing in Appalachia is increasingly "scaling up" in ways that include but are not limited to strategies directed toward attaining a wider geographic reach.

In the first instance, scaling up involves recognizing wider social processes and relationships that are already present in specific places. When Latino immigrants arrive in Morristown, Tennessee, to find jobs in the local poultry processing plant, global processes are at work. When truck traffic along the I-81 corridor in Virginia increases due in part to the North American Free Trade Agreement (and the desire of transnational shippers to bypass relatively powerful labor unions on the West Coast), global processes are at work. The point is not only (to recall Doreen Massey's words) that every place is a "meeting place" but also that globalization is rendering certain places more porous and the relations among such places more visible. This means that, in specific places across Appalachia, the effects of wider social processes are becoming more transparent and palpable, and the interconnections among diverse places, political issues, and social groups are becoming more dense.

A crucial question for place-based organizers then becomes: of all the interconnected issues and constituencies with which we might deliberately intensify our relationships, which are the most strategic to pursue? For activists in Jobs with Justice of East Tennessee, involvement in immigrant rights organizing was a logical but strategic outgrowth of their support for a unionization drive among Latino workers. Members of the Oak Ridge Environmental Peace Alliance, recognizing connections among nuclear weapons production, militarism, institutionalized racism, and an array of unmet social needs, intentionally created an alliance spanning diverse faith-based groups, students, and other social justice organizations, including anti-racist groups. When the Community Farm Alliance sought urban markets for its farmers' food products, the organization created relationships with African American churches and organized distribution in low-income, African American neighborhoods as well as contacting "foodie" groups in Louisville. "Scaling up," then, also means "scaling across" social and geographic space, intentionally creating strategic lateral relationships among peoples, places, and ideas that transcend social, spatial, and ideological barricades (such as between immigrants and labor, peace, environmental, and anti-racist activists, rural and urban, white and black).

This does not mean that such strategic choices are self-evident or easy to make. For example, the failure or refusal of key organizations in Appalachia to take on the devastation of families and communities across the region by OxyContin abuse at a visible statewide or regional level remains contested. At the same time, stretching an organization toward new constituencies, as the Southern Empowerment Project's leaders did in launching direct organizing among Latino immigrants, can have problematic political and organizational consequences. How such strategic decisions are made—not only by whom and in what contexts, but also according to what criteria—is a crucial political question that demands more attention from activists and organizations throughout the region.

Another choice involves the scale—local, state, regional, national, global—at which strategic relationships should be cultivated and distinct political issues most effectively addressed. For example, Virginia Organizing leaders argue forcefully for the advantages of state-level organizing, while also acknowledging that certain issues require them to reach beyond the state toward wider alliances. The inescapable need for political influence at the federal level, most commonly around national coal-related policies, has at times led to the formation of region-wide alliances, such as the current Alliance for Appalachia, which is focused on mountaintop removal.[30]

For organizations that seek to reach across geographic distance, whether to invent a new place-based collectivity along the I-81 corridor or garner international allies to oppose nuclear weapons production in Oak Ridge, developing strategic relationships means creating communication linkages among far-flung constituencies. Use of e-mail, social networking sites, and other forms of electronic technology has become critical to such efforts. These decentralized modes of communication nonetheless make enormous demands on organizers' time and budgets and, as our authors emphasize, cannot substitute for face-to-face relationships.

Electronic communication technologies also have a more subtle but powerful potential to expose and politicize social relations and interconnections across geographic and social space. Innovative Web sites such as iLoveMountains.org make visible the production, circulation, and consumption of commodities—in this instance, coal from mountaintop removal operations that is used in coal-fired utilities—and call individuals to account for participation in economic relations that they may not recognize or may take for granted. The possibilities for similar sites to expose the operations of global capitalism, lay bare the economic relationships in which differently situated people are implicated, and call on viewers to join in political response are only beginning to be realized. Insofar as unjust power relations endure in part because those who benefit from them are able to naturalize and obscure the operations of power, the subversive potential of such uses of the Internet is enormous. This is a fundamental insight behind the call for a knowledge commons: we need to create diverse venues in which different forms of knowledge and potentially subversive information may be systematically shared and utilized to challenge dominant definitions of what is true and what is possible.

Scaling up, of course, has practical requirements such as building capacity, developing leaders, and raising funds, which vary significantly with organizational structure and strategy. This volume documents diverse approaches to each of these vital tasks. For example, the Southern Empowerment Project and the Center for Participatory Change illustrate widely divergent models of leadership development, yet their common goal is democratic practice, that is, active participation in the decision-making processes that fundamentally shape collective life and the prospects for social justice. CPC also offers seed grants, as does the Appalachian Community Fund; a number of smaller groups have been able to supplement small grants with volunteer resources in order to survive. However, regardless of an organization's size, purpose, and need, securing financial resources has become more challenging with the loss of regional funding groups like the Council of the Southern Mountains and the Commission on Religion in Appalachia, the shift of foundation focus from Appalachia to other areas and issues, and the current economic crisis. For organizations that have paid staff or seek this capacity, such constraints on fund raising are particularly challenging. We underscore the importance of the many practical challenges of scaling up and urge readers to take account of the variety and ingenuity of approaches to meeting them recorded in these chapters.

By scaling up in Appalachia, we do not mean unifying the diverse instances of place-based organizing discussed in this book around one focus or creating a single regional movement. Throughout the last century there have been various attempts to build an Appalachian social movement, but all have failed for reasons that are instructive: insufficient resources, class conflicts, turf wars, top-down approaches, lack of support by the UMWA, and confusion and divisions over strategy, structure, and vision. But in the end, the primary reason was that region provides neither an adequate political and economic focus nor a sufficiently unifying social identity for building a movement.

There are no significant levers of political power configured at the regional level, nor do most corporations operate within a regional framework. The crucial decisions that affect people's lives are made at other sites and scales. This is undoubtedly one of the major reasons why the most successful citizen organizations in Appalachia are organized at the state level. Moreover, there exists no overarching connection among Appalachians (except perhaps that created by noxious stereotypes of hillbillies, which is a thin cultural bond), and people's life experiences are vastly different depending upon their race, gender, class, sexual identity, national origin, and geographical location. Thus, it should not be surprising that the great majority of people in the Appalachian region either consciously reject the label "Appalachian" or have no sense of being connected to other "Appalachians."

But the failure to create a self-consciously Appalachian social movement does not mean that change efforts in the region have occurred in isolation. Though many struggles have been local and concerned with a single issue, those involved have often been assisted by and associated with other groups and individuals within a loose alliance or network of Appalachian organizations. Two examples of this network at its best—the Appalachian Land Ownership Task Force and the labor/community partnerships that occurred during the 1989–1990 UMWA strike against the Pittston Coal Company—are discussed in the introduction. Organizations and activists come and go and financial support is rarely stable; but this loose, informal network persists and, indeed, may be the form that an Appalachian movement has taken.[31]

There are similarities between obstacles to the creation of an Appalachian movement and those confronting activists who seek to build movements at a global scale: lack of meaningful political representation and the absence of unifying social identities, among others. There are also similarities between the loose networks, alliances, and coalitions that characterize the Appalachian "movement" and the efforts that fall under the wide umbrella of "globalization from below."[32] The final example of place-based organizing contained in this book analyzes just such a transnational effort, in this instance to create direct personal and political linkages between struggles in the Appalachian coalfields and those in Colombia. We intentionally position it at the end of the book in part to underscore the importance of such interconnections and the global political consciousness that they both reflect and can create. But we are also aware that the majority of us cannot participate in transnational exchanges and that, fortunately, scaling up does not require them. What we can do is transform relations within and among places by exposing, critiquing, politicizing, and working to change the wider web of power relations as they are produced in specific locales.

Imagining New Places

It is profoundly difficult to envision a world beyond capitalism. Why this is true is far beyond the scope of this conclusion, but the fact that such a world is relatively unimaginable, at least in practical terms, makes the cultivation of visionary alternatives profoundly important. In the wake of the financial collapse of 2008 and beyond, questions about the viability of capitalism—certainly in its unregulated, neoliberal version—are proliferating, creating political opportunities that call out for imaginative responses. In the absence of such responses, efforts to resurrect and defend familiar economic arrangements and social policies inevitably prevail.

For working-class people on the ground in Appalachia, "economic crisis" does not consist of lost investments in unstable, newfangled financial instruments; it means doing without and barely getting by. The political consequences of economic adversity are by no means straightforward, however; openness to drastic change and radical alternatives does not necessarily follow. Indeed, the anxiety produced by embattlement on so many fronts—fractured families, hollowed-out communities, low to no paychecks, fears about national security and all manner of borders—also leads to bitter, even violent, defense of tradition. Coal miners' enthusiasm for industry-sponsored groups like Friends of Coal, bankrolled in part by infamously anti-union coal companies, is paradigmatic in this regard.[33] Threats to some established ways of life—cherished for familiarity despite their destructive and exploitative elements—work to deepen many Appalachians' investment in current economic and social relations. Right-wing demagoguery that conflates the nation or "homeland" with whiteness, heterosexuality, Christianity, and free enterprise, and demonizes its presumed enemies as terrorists, "illegals," heathens, and "feminazis" can resonate all too well in such a context.

This renders countervailing processes by which we re-envision and remake our social relations, economic arrangements, and collective political agency all the more urgent. These do not necessarily need to challenge capitalism directly to be effective in the present political economy. Privatization of public resources and the erosion of democratic life create openings for single-issue campaigns like that of RAIL Solution, which not only opposes privatization of I-81 but also, very importantly, advocates an environmentally sustainable alternative to interstate highways. The absence of an alternative vision, as the various land-use groups in Blount County, Tennessee, experienced, can also contribute to the defeat of place-based organizing. It was not sufficient to oppose the dominant economic philosophy of "grow or die"; they needed to create a unifying vision of alternative futures that could compel support from diverse constituencies across the county.

We are well aware that small-scale cooperatives, land trusts, and other egalitarian, collectivist economic institutions, along with isolated political victories that avert further privatization of public resources, though important, are insufficient. Scaling across social and geographic space in the promulgation and implementation of visionary alternatives, as the Community Farm Alliance was able to do, is imperative. A heartening development in this respect is the eroding distinction between social justice activists, with their critical perspectives and (in some cases) relatively wide organizing base, and community economic development practitioners, who possess practical skills in leveraging capital to organize community-oriented economic institutions.[34] Another promising initiative is the solidarity economy, which offers a values-based alternative to the dominant model of economic growth while working to create sustainable communities worldwide (chapter 3).[35]

A major obstacle to envisioning and pursuing such alternatives is that empire has become a way of life in the United States. As William Appleman Williams, Cynthia Enloe, and others have demonstrated, the militarization of our economy and the costs of U.S. foreign policy in pursuit of empire rob us of both the resources and imagination necessary to transform a grim landscape of privation and violence. Empire as a way of life sidelines movements for progressive change and substitutes paranoid togetherness for community. By distorting our knowledge of the rest of the world, empire prevents us from discovering how we are linked with others through common oppressions, goals, struggles, and dreams and from learning from grassroots experiments in land reform, public ownership, and democratic participation that are occurring throughout the world.[36] Pointing up contradictions between the human and financial costs of empire and escalating needs for meaningful work, health care, education, child care, environmental restoration, and other social goods is fundamental to the cultivation of alternative futures.

Equally critical to the success of visionary alternatives are vernacular cultural practices that imagine, valorize, and thereby help to produce those alternatives. Storytelling about sharing a mountain commons and living in sustainable relationship with the land in the past, however accurate, communicates values that implicitly critique social inequality, privatization, and environmental exploitation, and points toward alternatives. Songs that make visible the back-breaking, socially necessary, care-giving labors of women (as the Appalachian Women's Alliance has done in its performance art) convey fundamental precepts of a feminist political economy. Religious rituals and texts that affirm a radical egalitarianism and ethos of care—"We are all children of God," and "Do unto others . . ."—provide an ethical framework for not only how human beings should treat one another, but also how we might organize our social and economic lives. Values regarding "what should be" are the wellspring of visionary alternatives that we seek to create. They beckon, sustain, inspire, and guide. They allow us to "sing across dark spaces" in these violent and demoralizing times.[37] Their expression in myth, song, oral history, religious ritual, and other place-specific cultural forms continually reminds us that present circumstances do not constitute the whole of what is possible.

Every place is in this sense an ensemble of social relations, cultural practices, and "unmapped possibilities that are present in every situation—if only we are ready to encounter them."[38] We cannot create what we cannot imagine.[39] To transform places, we are required to discern latent opportunities that are ordinarily obscured by an overwhelming number of social problems—violence, exploitation, drug addiction, poverty—as well as our own attachments to what is familiar. In the words of J. K. Gibson-Graham: "Combating capitalism means refusing a long-standing sense of self and mode of being in the world, while simultaneously cultivating new forms of sociability, visions of happiness, and economic capacities."[40] By contrast, the champions of capitalism and neoliberalism would foreclose more desirable futures by insisting on the inevitability of human exploitation, ecological devastation, and their dismal, contradictory vision of globalization: interconnectedness without collectivity, rabid individualism without social accountability.[41] Place is the grounds of this struggle over how we shall live in relation to one another and to the earth. Our capacity and willingness to imagine, hope, share, risk, and cooperate are critical elements in making possible visionary alternatives. In transforming places, we turn such "alternatives" into present reality and thereby open up the future for us all.

Notes

1. Doreen Massey, *Space, Place, and Gender* (Minneapolis: University of Minnesota Press, 1994), 154; Arif Dirlik, "Place-based Imagination: Globalism and the Politics of Place," in *Places and Politics in an Age of Globalization,* ed. Roxann Prazniak and Arif Dirlik (Lanham, Md.: Rowman & Littlefield, 2001), 18.

2. Use of these terms varies among geographers and depends in part on political and theoretical perspective. Some key texts include David Harvey, *Spaces of Capital: Towards a Critical Geography* (New York: Routledge, 2001); Henri Lefebvre, *The Production of Space,* trans. Donald Nicholson-Smith (Cambridge, Mass.: Blackwell, 1991); and Yi-fu Tuan, *Space and Place: The Perspective of Experience* (Minneapolis: University of Minnesota Press, 1977).

3. David Harvey, *The Condition of Postmodernity: An Enquiry into the Origins of Cultural Change* (Cambridge, Mass.: Blackwell, 1989).

4. Massey, *Space, Place, and Gender*; Saskia Sassen, *The Global City: New York, London, Tokyo* (Princeton, N.J.: Princeton University Press, 2001); J. K. Gibson-Graham, *The End of Capitalism (As We Knew It): A Feminist Critique of Political Economy* (Minneapolis: University of Minnesota Press, 1996).

5. Massey, *Space, Place, and Gender,* 154–55.

6. Richard M. Simon, "Regions and Social Relations: A Research Note," *Appalachian Journal* 11 (Autumn–Winter 1983–1984): 23–31.

7. Helen Matthews Lewis, Linda Johnson, and Donald Askins, eds., *Colonialism in Modern America: The Appalachian Case* (Boone, N.C.: Appalachian Consortium Press, 1978); Dwight B. Billings, "Introduction: Writing Appalachia: Old Ways, New Ways, and WVU Ways," in *Culture, Class and Politics in Modern Appalachia: Essays in Honor of Ronald L. Lewis,* ed. Jennifer Egolf, Ken-Fones Wolf, and Louis C. Martin (Morgantown: West Virginia University Press, 2009), 1–28.

8. Stephen L. Fisher, ed., *Fighting Back in Appalachia: Traditions of Resistance and Change* (Philadelphia: Temple University Press, 1993). Indeed, Don Manning-Miller in his essay in that volume accuses progressive citizen organizations and organizers of failing to address racism in the region in any systematic and effective manner. See Don Manning-Miller, "Racism and Organizing in Appalachia," in Fisher, *Fighting Back,* 57–68.

9. Sassen, *The Global City*; see the discussion in Massey, *Space, Place, and Gender,* 162–72; Mary K. Anglin, "Moving Forward: Gender and Globalization in/of Appalachian Studies," *Appalachian Journal* 37 (Spring–Summer 2010): 286–300.

10. Ronald D. Eller, *Uneven Ground: Appalachia since 1945* (Lexington: University Press of Kentucky, 2008).

11. Appalshop, located in Whitesburg, Kentucky, has creatively used its community radio station, film-making, and theater troupe to explore how poor, rural Appalachians and poor, inner-city African Americans have been pitted against each other. See Rend Smith, "Survival and Resistance: Appalshop's First 40 Years," *National Alliance for Media + Culture,* December 19, 2008. http://www.namac.org/mode/6630/.

12. Much of the theoretical work on place and space arises from urban geography, which tends to follow Marx in condemning the "idiocy" of rural life. As Don Mitchell explains in *The Right to the City: Social Justice and the Fight for Public Space* (New York: Guilford Press, 2003): "Idiocy in this sense does not refer to the intelligence of the inhabitants, or even the nature of their customs, but to the essential *privacy*—and therefore isolation and homogeneity—of rural life" (p. 18). We believe that the chapters in this book indicate otherwise.

13. Doreen Massey repeatedly and powerfully makes this point. See *Space, Place, and Gender.*

14. Rebecca R. Scott, *Removing Mountains: Extracting Nature and Identity in the Appalachian Coalfields* (Minneapolis: University of Minnesota Press, 2010); Shannon Elizabeth Bell and Richard York, "Community Economic Identity: The Coal Industry and Ideology Construction in West Virginia," *Rural Sociology* 75, no. 1 (2010): 111–43.

15. For an astute summary of the theoretical issues surrounding domestic labor, see Lise Vogel, *Marxism and the Oppression of Women: Toward a Unitary Theory* (Piscataway, N.J.: Rutgers University Press, 1987).

16. Rhoda H. Halperin, *The Livelihood of Kin: Making Ends Meet "The Kentucky Way"* (Austin: University of Texas Press, 1990); Carol B. Stack, *All Our Kin: Strategies for Survival in a Black Community* (New York: Harper & Row), 1974.

17. Gibson-Graham, *The End of Capitalism.*

18. Guy and Candie Carawan, "Sowing on the Mountain: Nurturing Cultural Roots and Creativity for Community Change," in *Fighting Back In Appalachia,* ed. Fisher, 245–61.

19. James DeFilippis, Robert Fisher, and Eric Shragge, *Contesting Community: The Limits and Potential of Local Organizing* (Piscataway, N.J.: Rutgers University Press, 2010).

20. See the specific examples offered by Guy and Candie Carawan ("Sowing on the Mountain") and case studies such as Stephen William Foster, *The Past Is Another Country: Representation, Historical Consciousness, and Resistance in the Blue Ridge* (Berkeley: University of California Press, 1985); Mary Ann Hinsdale, Helen M. Lewis, and S. Maxine Waller, *It Comes from the People: Community Development and Local Theology* (Philadelphia: Temple University Press, 1995); and Sherry Cable, "From Fussin' to Organizing: Individual and Collective Resistance at Yellow Creek," in *Fighting Back in Appalachia,* ed. Fisher, 69–83.

21. Herbert Reid and Betsy Taylor, *Recovering the Commons: Democracy, Place, and Global Justice* (Urbana: University of Illinois Press, 2010).

22. Sonia E. Alvarez, "Afterword: The Politics of Place, The Place of Politics: Some Forward-looking Reflections," in *Women and the Politics of Place,* ed. Wendy Harcourt and Arturo Escobar (Bloomfield, Conn.: Kumarian Press, 2005), 256.

23. Richard A. Couto with Catherine S. Guthrie, *Making Democracy Work Better: Mediating Structures, Social Capital, and the Democratic Prospect* (Chapel Hill: University of North Carolina Press, 1999).

24. Edward W. Soja, *Seeking Spatial Justice* (Minneapolis: University of Minnesota Press, 2010), 96.

25. Mitchell, *The Right to the City.*

26. Smith worked with Walter Burton Franklin, now deceased from the disabling effects of working as an underground coal miner, in the context of the black lung movement during 1974–1976 in McDowell County, West Virginia. This was one of his favorite sayings.

27. See DeFilippis, Fisher, and Shragge, *Contesting Community.*

28. The phrase originates in the work of Raymond Williams. See Harvey, *Spaces of Capital,* 175.

29. Our mention of class is not meant to suggest that this dimension of social inequality is necessarily the most determinant or politically significant, as some have argued in the context of Appalachia. Moreover, as Mike Yarrow argues, class solidarity and conflict in the Appalachian coalfields have been powerfully intensified by masculinity. See his "The Gender-Specific Class Consciousness of Appalachian Coal Miners: Structure and Change," in *Bringing Class Back In: Contemporary and Historical Perspectives,* ed. Scott G. McNall, Rhonda F. Levine, and Rick Fantasia (Boulder, Colo.: Westview, 1991), 285–310. See also Rebecca R. Scott, "Dependent Masculinity and Political Culture in Pro-Mountaintop Removal Discourse: Or, How I Learned to Stop Worrying and Love the Dragline," *Feminist Studies* 33 (Fall 2007): 484–509.

30. See www.theallianceforappalachia.org/.

31. Bill Horton, review of John Glen's *Highlander: No Ordinary School, 1932–1962* (Lexington: University Press of Kentucky, 1988) in the *Appalachian Journal* 16 (Summer 1989): 370.

32. Donatella delia Porta et al., *Globalization from Below: Transnational Activists and Protest Networks* (Minneapolis: University of Minnesota Press, 2006); Jeremy Brecher, Tim Costello, and Brendan Smith, *Globalization from Below: The Power of Solidarity* (Cambridge, Mass.: South End Press, 2000).

33. Bell and York, "Community Economic Identity."

34. See, for example, the collaboration between Kentuckians For The Commonwealth and the Mountain Association for Community Economic Development: www.appalachiantransition.net; "Special Issue: The Future of Appalachia," *The Solutions Journal,* www.thesolutionsjournal.com.

35. Emily Kawano, Thomas Neal Masterson, and Jonathan Teller-Elsberg, *Solidarity Economy I: Building Alternatives for People and Planet* (Amherst, Mass.: Center for Popular Economics, 2010).

36. William Appleman Williams, *Empire as a Way of Life: An Essay on the Causes and Character of America's Present Predicament, along with a Few Thoughts about an Alternative* (New York: Oxford University Press, 1980); Cynthia Enloe, *Globalization and Militarism: Feminists Make the Link* (Lanham, Md.: Rowman & Littlefield, 2007); Chalmers

A. Johnson, *Dismantling the Empire: America's Last Best Hope* (New York: Metropolitan Books, 2010). For an analysis of the costs of empire in Appalachia, see Steve Fisher, "The Nicaraguan Revolution and the U.S. Response: Lessons for Appalachia," *Appalachian Journal* 14 (Fall 1986): 22–37.

37. Jim Sessions and Fran Ansley, "Singing across Dark Spaces: The Union/Community Takeover of Pittston's Moss 3 Plant," in *Fighting Back in Appalachia,* ed. Fisher, 195–223.

38. J. K. Gibson-Graham, *A Postcapitalist Politics* (Minneapolis: University of Minnesota Press, 2006), xxxvii.

39. Lawrence Goodwyn, "Organizing Democracy: The Limits of Theory and Practice," *Democracy* 1 (January 1981): 43.

40. Gibson-Graham, *A Postcapitalist Politics,* xxxv.

41. See Doreen Massey, *For Space* (London: Sage Publications, 2005) for a theoretical discussion of the relationship between the concept of space as fixed and, among other problematic implications, the inevitability of capitalist globalization; she argues instead for opening up space conceptually and politically and thereby opening up the future.

CONTRIBUTORS

FRAN ANSLEY is Distinguished Professor of Law Emeritus at the University of Tennessee College of Law. She has been engaged with issues of social and economic justice in east Tennessee for many years and currently focuses on low-wage immigrant workers and the terms of their encounter with local economies, communities, and movements.

YAIRA ANDREA ARIAS SOTO, a native of Colombia, South America, is a staff member at the Center for Participatory Change. Experienced in immigrants' rights issues and multilingual work, she is a founding member of a Latino center in Brevard, North Carolina, and of a western North Carolina coalition of Latino grassroots groups.

DWIGHT B. BILLINGS is professor of sociology at the University of Kentucky. He studies Appalachia and the American South and recently completed a National Science Foundation–funded project with Jenrose Fitzgerald titled "The Messy Politics of 'Clean Coal': Contested Energy Alternatives in the Appalachian Coalfields."

M. KATHRYN BROWN is an environmental epidemiologist, formerly at the University of Cincinnati College of Medicine. She is a founder of the Frank Foster Library on Appalachian Migrants and a founding member of the Lower Price Hill Women's Wellness Group.

JEANNETTE BUTTERWORTH is a former staff member at the Center for Participatory Change. She served for two years with the Peace Corps in Paraguay and is a grassroots community leader and organizer of immigrant rights advocacy in Henderson County, North Carolina.

PAUL CASTELLOE is one of the founding members of the Center for Participatory Change. He is currently involved in elementary school education and remains active in grassroots social justice research and advocacy in western North Carolina.

AVIVA CHOMSKY is professor of history and coordinator of Latin American studies at Salem State University in Massachusetts. Her books include *Linked Labor Histories: New England, Colombia, and the Making of a Global Working*

Class (Duke, 2008) and *The People Behind Colombian Coal: Mines, Multinationals, and Human Rights*. She works in solidarity with Colombian communities affected by coal mining and organizes annual delegations to the Colombian and Kentucky coalfields.

DAVE COOPER is an environmental activist in Lexington, Kentucky. Since 2003, he has been a traveling volunteer speaker on the Mountaintop Removal Road Show (www.mountainroadshow.com).

WALTER DAVIS is executive director of the National Organizers Alliance in Washington, D.C. He has been an organizer and community-based trainer since the mid-1960s and served as the organizing training coordinator of the Southern Empowerment Project from 1988 and as its director from 2004 to 2007.

MEREDITH DEAN has led the Appalachian Women's Alliance's journey to unite anti-racist education with creative feminist action in mountain communities since 1992. She also writes, parents, and teaches for social justice in Floyd County, Virginia, near her family's homeplace of eight generations.

ELIZABETH FINE is professor and director of the humanities program in the Department of Religion and Culture at Virginia Tech. She is the author of *Soulstepping: African American Step Shows* (Illinois, 2003, 2007) and *The Folklore Text: From Performance to Print* (Indiana, 1984, 1994).

STEPHEN L. FISHER is Professor Emeritus at Emory & Henry College. He is the editor of *Fighting Back in Appalachia: Traditions of Resistance and Change* (Temple, 1993). He has been active in a number of Appalachian resistance efforts and has worked to build links between the academic community and activists in the region.

JENROSE FITZGERALD is a research associate at the University of Kentucky's Appalachian Center. Her current work focuses on how environmental and social justice groups help shape energy debates in the Appalachian region. She recently completed a postdoctoral fellowship from the National Science Foundation titled "The Messy Politics of 'Clean Coal': Contested Energy Alternatives in the Appalachian Coalfields," in collaboration with Dwight Billings.

DOUG GAMBLE lives on a small farm in Blount County, Tennessee, and has been active in numerous community organizations. He has been a university history professor and a staff member for the Highlander Research and Education Center, the Tennessee Committee on Occupational Safety and Health, and the Union of Needletrades, Industrial, and Textile Employees.

NINA GREGG consults with community-based and nonprofit organizations on governance, planning, program development, and evaluation. She is a founding board member of Citizens Against the Pellissippi Parkway Extension, Inc., coordinator of the Ethics & Responsibility in Organizing project, and was volunteer cofacilitator of the Blount County (Tennessee) Anti-Racism Task Force.

EDNA GULLEY has been a staff person for the Appalachian Women's Alliance for sixteen years and a leader in her community for more than thirty. Born and raised in the coal camp of Clinchco, Virginia, she serves as a powerful advocate for the economic and human rights of people of color, poor people, and women and children in mountain communities.

MOLLY HEMSTREET is a staff member at the Center for Participatory Change (CPC). She has also worked as an English as a Second Language teacher in Burke County, North Carolina, and helped organize and support several immigrants' and women's grassroots groups.

MARY HUFFORD is on the graduate faculty of the program in folklore and folklife at the University of Pennsylvania. A founding member of the Coal River Mountain Watch, she is, with the support of a J.S. Guggenheim fellowship, writing a book about the cultural ecology of the mixed mesophytic community forest of southern West Virginia.

RALPH HUTCHISON has served as coordinator for the Oak Ridge Environmental Peace Alliance since 1990. An ordained minister, he has served as pastor of Bethel Presbyterian Church in Dandridge, Tennessee, and is active in a broad range of progressive organizations in the Knoxville area.

DONNA JONES is an outreach worker with the Urban Appalachian Council. She is a past president of the Lower Price Hill (LPH) Community Council and a founding member of the LPH Women's Wellness Group.

ANN KINGSOLVER is professor of anthropology and director of the Appalachian Center and Appalachian Studies program at the University of Kentucky. Her latest book is *Tobacco Town Futures: Global Encounters in Rural Kentucky* (Waveland Press, 2011), based on twenty-five years of individual and collaborative documentation in her hometown.

SUE ELLA KOBAK is an attorney and activist/organizer with a lifelong commitment to civil rights issues within the central Appalachian region. She was raised in east Kentucky by parents who always supported work involving labor and poverty issues.

JILL KRIESKY is on staff with the West Virginia Center on Budget and Policy and the National Center of Excellence in Women's Health at West Virginia University. She has served as executive director of the Clifford M. Lewis, S.J., Appalachian Institute at Wheeling Jesuit University and worked as a university-based labor educator in Alabama, Oregon, and West Virginia.

MICHAEL E. MALONEY is an Appalachian organizer who was the first executive director of the Urban Appalachian Council in Cincinnati and has taught Appalachian Studies for twenty-five years. His publications include *The Social Areas of Cincinnati: A Study of Social Needs* (Cincinnati School of Planning, 2006), with Stephen Auffrey; and *Appalachia: Social Context Past and Present* (Kendall/ Hunt, 2006), coedited with Phillip Obermiller.

LISA MARKOWITZ is associate professor and chair of the Anthropology Department at the University of Louisville and an active member of the Louisville chapter of the Community Farm Alliance. Since the 1980s, she has worked in peasant communities in Andean South America studying producer organizations and food security.

LINDA MCKINNEY, a cofounder of the Appalachian Women's Alliance, is a social worker and longtime board member of S.A.F.E., a model domestic violence shelter in southern West Virginia. A genuine voice for the poor, abused, and disabled, she comes from a Summers County holler where two creeks flow into one, and from stubborn, hardheaded women who speak up when they see wrong being done to the children and to the land.

LADELLE MCWHORTER holds the James Thomas Chair in Philosophy and is also professor of women, gender, and sexualities studies at the University of Richmond. She is the author of *Racism and Sexual Oppression in Anglo-America: A Genealogy* (Indiana, 2009) and other books. She has served on the State Governing Board of Virginia Organizing since 2006.

MARTA MARIA MIRANDA is CEO and president of the Center for Women and Families in Louisville, Kentucky. She is an educator, activist, advocate, community organizer, and licensed clinical social worker whose career focus has been the eradication of violence at the individual, institutional, and societal levels.

CHAD MONTRIE is professor of history at the University of Massachusetts Lowell. His publications include *To Save the Land and People: A History of Opposition to Surface Coal Mining in Appalachia* (2003) and *Making a Living: Work and Environment in the United States* (2008), both from the University of North Carolina Press.

MAUREEN MULLINAX is assistant professor of sociology at Xavier University. She worked for ten years with youth and teachers as a media trainer at Appalshop and has conducted research on the civic engagement strategies of a Harlan County, Kentucky, community-based arts project.

PHILLIP J. OBERMILLER is a senior visiting scholar in the School of Planning at the University of Cincinnati and has been active in the Urban Appalachian Council and the Lower Price Hill Community School for more than thirty years. He is a past president of the Appalachian Studies Association.

REBECCA O'DOHERTY is director of the Appalachian Media Institute, Appalshop's youth media and leadership training program, where she works to change the way emerging leaders think about and act in their central Appalachian communities.

CASSIE ROBINSON PFLEGER is a native of western North Carolina and a graduate of the Appalachian Studies program at Appalachian State University. She has volunteered in the Mountain Justice movement since 2006 and is committed to preserving and promoting Appalachian cultural traditions and folkways. After a three year stint in eastern Kentucky, she returned to the Blue Ridge to start a farm with her husband, Randal Pfleger.

RANDAL PFLEGER has volunteered with Mountain Justice since 2006 and worked at the Pine Mountain Settlement School in Harlan County, Kentucky. A graduate of the Appalachian Studies program at Appalachian State University, he has worked and studied in Appalachia and Central and South America on issues related to sustainability.

ANITA PUCKETT is associate professor in the Department of Religion and Culture at Virginia Tech, where she directs the Appalachian Studies program. A linguistic anthropologist, she is the author of *Seldom Ask, Never Tell: Labor and Discourse in Appalachia* (Oxford, 2000) and numerous other publications.

KATIE RICHARDS-SCHUSTER is an assistant research scientist with the Michigan Youth and Community program at the University of Michigan School of Social Work. Her research focuses on youth organizing and community-based participatory evaluation in low-income and racially segregated communities. She recently collaborated with the Appalachian Media Institute to prepare young leaders to use their media to create community change.

JUNE ROSTAN works as a community organizer for the AFL-CIO. She served as coordinator and director of the Southern Empowerment Project for more than seventeen years and has done education, research, and organizing with textile and furniture workers, women coal miners, and numerous community groups.

REES SHEARER is founder and chair of RAIL Solution. He has been a co-op manager, artist, school dropout prevention coordinator, and elementary school counselor, and served as executive director of the Coalition of American Electric Consumers.

BARBARA ELLEN SMITH is professor of women's and gender studies at Virginia Tech and for more than thirty-five years has been an activist-scholar in Appalachia and the U.S. South. Among her publications are *Digging Our Own Graves: Coal Miners and the Struggle over Black Lung Disease* (Temple, 1987) and *Neither Separate Nor Equal: Women, Race and Class in the South* (Temple, 1999).

DANIEL SWAN is a West Virginia native and a graduate of Wheeling Jesuit University. He works to develop community gardens and sustainable food systems in Wheeling, West Virginia.

JOE SZAKOS has been executive director of Virginia Organizing since 1994 and served as coordinator of Kentuckians For The Commonwealth from 1981 to 1993.

He has also worked as a community organizer in Chicago and Hungary. He and his wife, Kristin, are coauthors of *We Make Change: Community Organizers Talk About What They Do—and Why* (Vanderbilt, 2007) and *Lessons from the Field: Organizing in Rural Communities* (American Institute for Social Justice, 2008).

BETSY TAYLOR is a cultural anthropologist who works for community-driven development and participatory research in central Appalachia and India in such areas as health, agriculture, forestry, culture, and environmental stewardship. She is coauthor with Herbert Reid of *Recovering the Commons: Democracy, Place, and Global Justice* (Illinois, 2010).

THOMAS E. WAGNER is University Professor Emeritus of planning and urban studies at the University of Cincinnati and a founding board member of the Urban Appalachian Council in Cincinnati. He has coauthored or edited three books, including *African American Miners and Migrants: The Eastern Kentucky Social Club* (Illinois, 2004) and *Appalachian Odyssey: Historical Perspectives on the Great Migration* (Praeger, 2000).

CRAIG WHITE is a staff member at the Center for Participatory Change. With a background in social work, he has worked with organizations in rural areas throughout North Carolina and Appalachia.

RYAN WISHART is completing a doctorate in sociology at the University of Oregon. He is an east Tennessee native and became engaged in the region's energy and social justice issues as a student at the University of Tennessee.

INDEX